Second Language Acquisition

Based on classic and cutting-edge research, this textbook shows how grammatical phenomena can best be taught to second language and bilingual learners. Bringing together second language research, linguistics, pedagogical grammar, and language teaching, it demonstrates how linguistic theory and second language acquisition findings optimize classroom intervention research. The book assumes a generative approach but covers intervention studies from a variety of theoretical perspectives. Each chapter describes relevant linguistic structures, discusses core challenges, summarizes research findings, and concludes with classroom and lab-based intervention studies. The authors provide tools to help to design linguistically informed intervention studies, including discussion questions, application questions, case studies, and sample interventions. Online resources feature lecture slides and intervention materials, with data analysis exercises, ensuring the content is clear and ready to use. Requiring no more than a basic course in linguistics, the material serves advanced undergraduates and first-year graduate students studying applied linguistics, education, or language teaching.

Tania Ionin is Professor of Linguistics and Director of Graduate Studies in Linguistics at the University of Illinois at Urbana-Champaign. Her research expertise is in second language acquisition of semantics and in experimental semantics more generally. She has taught courses in second language acquisition, psycholinguistics, research design and methodology for linguists, and pedagogical English grammar, among other subjects.

Silvina Montrul is Professor of Spanish and Linguistics at the University of Illinois at Urbana-Champaign and directs the Second Language Acquisition and Bilingualism Lab. Her research focuses on linguistic and psycholinguistic approaches to second language acquisition and bilingualism – in particular, syntax, semantics, and morphology – and on language acquisition in heritage speakers. She regularly teaches courses in second language acquisition, bilingualism, and the structure of Spanish.

Second Language Acquisition
Introducing Intervention Research

Tania Ionin
University of Illinois at Urbana-Champaign

Silvina Montrul
University of Illinois at Urbana-Champaign

CAMBRIDGE
UNIVERSITY PRESS

Shaftesbury Road, Cambridge CB2 8EA, United Kingdom

One Liberty Plaza, 20th Floor, New York, NY 10006, USA

477 Williamstown Road, Port Melbourne, VIC 3207, Australia

314–321, 3rd Floor, Plot 3, Splendor Forum, Jasola District Centre,
New Delhi – 110025, India

103 Penang Road, #05-06/07, Visioncrest Commercial, Singapore 238467

Cambridge University Press is part of Cambridge University Press & Assessment, a department of the University of Cambridge.

We share the University's mission to contribute to society through the pursuit of education, learning and research at the highest international levels of excellence.

www.cambridge.org
Information on this title: www.cambridge.org/highereducation/isbn/9781316515983

DOI: 10.1017/9781009031585

© Tania Ionin and Silvina Montrul 2023

This publication is in copyright. Subject to statutory exception and to the provisions of relevant collective licensing agreements, no reproduction of any part may take place without the written permission of Cambridge University Press & Assessment.

First published 2023

A catalogue record for this publication is available from the British Library

Library of Congress Cataloging-in-Publication Data
Names: Ionin, Tania, author. | Montrul, Silvina, author.
Title: Second language acquisition : introducing intervention research / Tania Ionin, University
   of Illinois at Urbana-Champaign ; Silvina Montrul, University of Illinois at Urbana-Champaign.
Description: Cambridge ; New York, NY : Cambridge University Press, 2022. | Includes
   bibliographical references and index.
Identifiers: LCCN 2022040816 (print) | LCCN 2022040817 (ebook) | ISBN 9781316515983 (hardback)
   | ISBN 9781009013567 (paperback) | ISBN 9781009031585 (epub)
Subjects: LCSH: Second language acquisition. | English language–Grammar–Study and teaching–
   Foreign speakers. | Spanish language–Grammar–Study and teaching–Foreign speakers.
Classification: LCC P118.2 .I59 2022 (print) | LCC P118.2 (ebook) | DDC 418.0071–dc23/eng/20220826
LC record available at https://lccn.loc.gov/2022040816
LC ebook record available at https://lccn.loc.gov/2022040817

ISBN 978-1-316-51598-3 Hardback
ISBN 978-1-009-01356-7 Paperback

Additional resources for this publication at www.cambridge.org/ionin-montrul.

Cambridge University Press & Assessment has no responsibility for the persistence or accuracy of URLs for external or third-party internet websites referred to in this publication and does not guarantee that any content on such websites is, or will remain, accurate or appropriate.

We dedicate this textbook to our respective families and to all our students: past, present, and future.

Brief Contents

List of Figures	*page* xv
List of Tables	xviii
List of Boxes	xx
Preface	xxi
Acknowledgements	xxvi
List of Abbreviations	xxvii
1 Theoretical Foundations	1
2 Intervention Research and Grammar Teaching	30
3 Articles	57
4 Verb Placement and Question Formation	83
5 Inflectional Morphology	119
6 Subjunctive Mood	153
7 Argument Structure	194
8 Direct and Indirect Objects	232
9 Word Order and Related Syntactic Phenomena	269
10 Where to Go Next	301
Glossary	325
References	342
Index	380

Contents

List of Figures	*page* xv
List of Tables	xviii
List of Boxes	xx
Preface	xxi
Acknowledgements	xxvi
List of Abbreviations	xxvii

1 Theoretical Foundations   1
- 1.1 Linguistics and Second Language Acquisition   2
  - 1.1.1 What Is Linguistics?   2
  - 1.1.2 Second Language Acquisition: Timing and Context   5
  - 1.1.3 Heritage Speakers: In between First and Second Language Acquisition   6
  - 1.1.4 Biological Foundations of Language   9
  - 1.1.5 The Role of Input in Language Acquisition   10
  - 1.1.6 Differences among First Language Learners, Second Language Learners, and Heritage Speakers   12
- 1.2 The Explicit vs. Implicit Distinction   15
  - 1.2.1 Implicit vs. Explicit Knowledge and Learning   16
  - 1.2.2 Characteristics of Implicit vs. Explicit Knowledge   17
  - 1.2.3 How do Implicit and Explicit Knowledge Interact?   19
  - 1.2.4 Implicit vs. Explicit Instruction and Feedback   20
  - 1.2.5 Measuring Implicit vs. Explicit Knowledge and Learning   22
  - 1.2.6 The Explicit vs. Implicit Distinction in Intervention Research   27
- 1.3 What's Next?   27
- 1.4 Discussion Questions   28
- 1.5 Further Reading   28

2 Intervention Research and Grammar Teaching   30
- 2.1 Introduction to Classroom and Lab-Based Intervention Research   30
  - 2.1.1 Where to Start: Pedagogical vs. Theoretical Starting Points   31
  - 2.1.2 The Learning Environment: Foreign Language vs. Immersive   33

      2.1.3 Components of Intervention Research Studies   35
      2.1.4 Control Group vs. Comparison Group Design   37
      2.1.5 (Quasi-)Experimental Design   38
      2.1.6 Timeline of Intervention Research Studies   41
      2.1.7 Summary: The Logic of Intervention Research   43
  2.2 Approaches to Grammar Teaching   45
      2.2.1 Naturalistic vs. Instructed Second Language Acquisition   45
      2.2.2 Choices in Second Language Grammar Instruction   46
      2.2.3 Content-Based Language Teaching   47
      2.2.4 Traditional Focus on FormS Instruction   48
      2.2.5 Communicative Language Teaching   49
      2.2.6 Focus on Form Approaches   49
      2.2.7 Processing Instruction   51
      2.2.8 Summary: Approaches to Second Language Instruction and Sample Application   52
  2.3 A Preview of the Next Eight Chapters   53
  2.4 Discussion Questions   54
  2.5 Further Reading   55

3 Articles   57
  3.1 Terminology   57
      3.1.1 Count vs. Mass Nouns, and Article Omission   59
      3.1.2 Definiteness   59
      3.1.3 Specificity   61
      3.1.4 Genericity   62
      3.1.5 Kind Reference   64
      3.1.6 Summary: Articles in Second Language Acquisition   65
  3.2 Intervention Studies on Articles in English as a Second Language   65
      3.2.1 Intervention Studies with a Focus on Particular Instructional Techniques   67
      3.2.2 Intervention Studies with a Focus on Particular Theoretical Approaches to Articles   72
  3.3 Summary and Implications   77
  3.4 Discussion Questions   79
  3.5 Applications Questions   79
  3.6 Further Reading   81

4 Verb Placement and Question Formation   83
  4.1 Terminology   84
      4.1.1 Functional Categories and Features   84

	4.1.2 The Verb Movement Parameter	85
	4.1.3 Verb Second	87
	4.1.4 Wh-movement: Question Formation	88
4.2	Adverb Placement in Second Language Acquisition	90
	4.2.1 The Verb Movement Parameter in Second Language Acquisition	90
	4.2.2 Classroom Intervention Studies on Adverb-Verb Placement in English	92
	4.2.3 Intervention Studies on Negative Adverb Placement in English as a Second Language	99
	4.2.4 Intervention Studies on Verb Placement in Spanish as a Second Language	100
	4.2.5 Summary: Intervention Studies with Adverbs	102
4.3	Question Formation in Second Language Acquisition	105
	4.3.1 Question Formation: Findings from Second Language Acquisition Research	105
	4.3.2 Intervention Studies on Question Formation	106
4.4	Summary and Implications	114
4.5	Discussion Questions	117
4.6	Applications Questions	117
4.7	Further Reading	118

5 Inflectional Morphology 119

5.1	Terminology	119
5.2	Inflectional Morphology in Second Language Acquisition: Experimental Findings and Theoretical Implications	122
	5.2.1 Errors with Inflectional Morphology as a Representation vs. Processing Problem	123
	5.2.2 Psycholinguistic Studies on Inflectional Morphology in Second Language Acquisition	125
5.3	Intervention Research Studies on Inflectional Morphology	126
	5.3.1 Processing Instruction Studies on Tense Marking	126
	5.3.2 Explicit vs. Implicit Knowledge and Instruction in the Domain of Verbal Morphology	135
	5.3.3 Differential Effects of Corrective Feedback Types on Grammatical Gender	141
5.4	Summary and Implications	149
5.5	Discussion Questions	150
5.6	Applications Questions	151
5.7	Further Reading	152

6 Subjunctive Mood — 153
- 6.1 Terminology — 154
  - 6.1.1 Indicative vs. Subjunctive Mood — 154
  - 6.1.2 The Subjunctive in Spanish — 156
  - 6.1.3 The Subjunctive Mood in Linguistic Theory — 160
- 6.2 First and Second Language Acquisition Studies on the Subjunctive — 161
  - 6.2.1 The Subjunctive in First Language Acquisition — 161
  - 6.2.2 The Subjunctive in Second Language Acquisition — 162
- 6.3 Second Language Intervention Research Studies on the Subjunctive — 168
  - 6.3.1 Processing Instruction Studies with the Subjunctive — 168
  - 6.3.2 Instruction with the Subjunctive in Adverbial Clauses — 176
  - 6.3.3 The Use of Psycholinguistic Methods in Intervention Studies with the Subjunctive — 177
- 6.4 Studies of the Subjunctive with Heritage Speakers of Romance Languages — 183
  - 6.4.1 Experimental Studies on Knowledge of the Subjunctive in Heritage Speakers — 183
  - 6.4.2 Intervention Studies on the Subjunctive with Heritage Spanish Speakers — 185
- 6.5 Summary and Implications — 190
- 6.6 Discussion Questions — 190
- 6.7 Applications Questions — 191
- 6.8 Further Reading — 192

7 Argument Structure — 194
- 7.1 Terminology and Linguistic Background — 194
  - 7.1.1 Transitivity — 195
  - 7.1.2 The Passive — 197
  - 7.1.3 Intransitive Verbs and the Unaccusative Hypothesis — 201
- 7.2 The Acquisition of Passives — 204
  - 7.2.1 Passives in Second Language Acquisition — 205
  - 7.2.2 Classroom Intervention Studies on the Passive — 205
- 7.3 The Acquisition of Unaccusativity — 214
  - 7.3.1 Unaccusatives and Overpassivization — 215
  - 7.3.2 The Unaccusativity Hierarchy — 217
  - 7.3.3 Intervention Studies with English Unaccusatives — 218
  - 7.3.4 Acquisition of Spanish Unaccusatives — 220
- 7.4 Summary and Implications — 229

7.5	Discussion Questions	229
7.6	Application Questions	229
7.7	Further Reading	231

8 Direct and Indirect Objects 232

8.1 Terminology 232
8.2 The English Double Object Construction in Second
  Language Acquisition 233
  8.2.1 Background on Double Objects: Theory and First
    Language Acquisition 234
  8.2.2 Second Language Acquisition Experimental Research on
    English Double Object Constructions 236
  8.2.3 Intervention Studies with English Double
    Object Constructions 238
  8.2.4 Summary and Implications: English Double
    Object Constructions 246
8.3 The Expression of Objects in the Second Language Acquisition
  of Spanish 246
  8.3.1 Background: Object Expression in Spanish 248
  8.3.2 Studies on Object Expression in Spanish as a
    Second Language 252
  8.3.3 Intervention Studies of Spanish Object Expression 253
  8.3.4 Summary and Implications: Object Expression in Spanish 266
8.4 Discussion Questions 266
8.5 Applications Questions 267
8.6 Further Reading 268

9 Word Order and Related Syntactic Phenomena 269

9.1 Sentence-Level Word Order 269
  9.1.1 Noncanonical Word Orders Cross-Linguistically and in
    Second Language Acquisition 273
  9.1.2 Processing Instruction Studies on the Comprehension of
    Non-Canonical Word Orders 275
9.2 Adjective Ordering 281
  9.2.1 Adjective Ordering in Linguistic Theory and in Second
    Language Acquisition 282
  9.2.2 Intervention Studies with Adjective Ordering 283
9.3 Relative Clauses 284
  9.3.1 Relative Clauses in Linguistics and in Second
    Language Acquisition 285

9.3.2 Intervention Studies on Relative Clauses and the Noun Phrase Accessibility Hierarchy in English as a Second Language	286
9.3.3 Intervention Studies on English Relative Clauses, and the Role of Learner Output	288
9.3.4 Intervention Studies with Japanese Relative Clauses	291
9.4 Quantifier Scope	292
9.4.1 Quantifier Scope: Linguistic Background and Terminology	293
9.4.2 Second Language Acquisition and Intervention Studies with Quantifier Scope	294
9.5 Summary and Implications	298
9.6 Discussion Questions	299
9.7 Applications Questions	299
9.8 Further Reading	300

10 Where to Go Next — 301

10.1 Efficacy of Different Instructional Approaches	302
10.1.1 Efficacy of Explicit Output-Based Instruction	303
10.1.2 Efficacy of Implicit Instruction	305
10.1.3 Efficacy of Structured Input and Input Processing Instruction	306
10.1.4 Efficacy of Different Feedback Types	308
10.1.5 Summary	308
10.2 Intervention Research and Linguistic Representations	309
10.2.1 The Role of the First Language	309
10.2.2 Linguistic Theory and Intervention Research	312
10.3 Suggestions for Future Research	318
10.3.1 Issues of Scope, Generalizability, and Study Length	318
10.3.2 Nature of Intervention Activities	320
10.3.3 New Technologies	321
10.4 Conclusion	323
10.5 Further Reading	324
Glossary	325
References	342
Index	380

Figures

1.1	L1 acquisition from initial state to mature steady state (based on L. White, 2003b, p. 3)	*page* 4
1.2	A representation of the Full Transfer/Full Access Model of Universal Grammar in L2 acquisition (Schwartz & Sprouse, 1996) with a role for instruction (adapted from L. White, 2003b).	5
1.3	Heritage language acquisition	7
1.4	Simultaneous bilingual acquisition	8
2.1	Components of intervention research	35
2.2	Focus on Form (FonF)	50
3.1	Direct-only group: Mean percentage accuracy in speeded dictation, writing, and error correction (based on data from Sheen, 2007)	70
3.2	Direct-metalinguistic group: Mean percentage accuracy in speeded dictation, writing, and error correction (based on data from Sheen, 2007)	70
3.3	Control group: Mean percentage accuracy in speeded dictation, writing and error correction (based on data from Sheen, 2007)	71
3.4	Instructed learner group: Mean acceptability ratings for NP-level generics (based on data from Umeda et al., 2019)	75
3.5	Control learner group: Mean acceptability ratings for NP-level generics (based on data from Umeda et al., 2019)	76
3.6	Instructed learner group: Mean acceptability ratings for sentence-level generics (based on data from Umeda et al., 2019)	76
3.7	Control learner group: Mean acceptability ratings for sentence-level generics (based on data from Umeda et al., 2019)	77
4.1	Structure of a clause in generative syntax	85
4.2	Verb movement (V-to-I movement)	86
4.3	Verb second in German (V-to-I-to-C movement)	88
4.4	Embedded clause structure in German	88
4.5	Example of wh-movement in English	89
4.6	Grammaticality judgments, mean *SVAO score: All groups (based on data from L. White 1991; Trahey & White 1993; Trahey 1996)	96

4.7	Mackey (1999, p. 573, Figure 3): Increase in questions at Stages 4 and 5 produced by each group in the posttests	112
5.1	Mean accuracy on the production task by group and instructional treatment (based on data from Benati, 2005)	131
5.2	Mean accuracy on the interpretation task by group and instructional treatment (based on data from Benati, 2005)	132
5.3	Mean percentage accuracy on the written binary-choice test by instructional group (based on data from Lyster, 2004a)	145
5.4	Mean percentage accuracy on the written text-completion task by instructional group (based on data from Lyster, 2004a)	146
5.5	Mean percentage accuracy on the oral object-identification test by instructional group (based on data from Lyster, 2004a)	146
5.6	Mean percentage accuracy on the oral picture-description task by instructional group (based on data from Lyster, 2004a)	147
6.1	Eye tracking during reading and/or listening to linguistic stimuli (picture from Tobii AB: www.tobii.com/group/about/this-is-eyetracking/)	178
6.2	Mean accuracy on subjunctive in temporal sentences with *cuando* with adverbs in the cloze (production) task (based on data from Fernández Cuenca, 2019)	181
6.3	Mean accuracy on subjunctive in temporal sentences with *cuando* without adverbs in the cloze (production) task (based on data from Fernández Cuenca, 2019)	181
6.4	Mean accuracy on subjunctive in temporal sentences with *cuando* with adverbs in the event-selection (comprehension) task (based on data from Fernández Cuenca, 2019)	182
6.5	Mean accuracy on subjunctive in temporal sentences with *cuando* without adverbs in the event-selection (comprehension) task (based on data from Fernández Cuenca, 2019)	182
6.6	Improvement over time by measure and by group (effect size) (based on data from Potowski, Jegerski, & Morgan-Short, 2009)	187
7.1	Mean accuracy judgments on the English verbal passive by instructional group (based on data from Jung, 2019)	214
7.2	The Unaccusativity Hierarchy (based on Sorace, 2000)	217
7.3	Acceptance of ungrammatical passives in the past tense with unaccusative and unergative verbs, instruction group (based on data from Hirakawa, 2013)	222
7.4	Acceptance of ungrammatical passives in the past tense with unaccusative and unergative verbs, no-instruction learner group (based on data from Hirakawa, 2013)	223

7.5	Mean acceptability ratings on alternator intransitive verbs with *se* (*se secó* 'dried out') and ungrammatical versions without *se* (**secó* 'dried out') (based on data from Toth & Guijarro Fuentes, 2013)	228
8.1	Initial feedback session: Percentage accuracy by group for feedback and guessing items (based on data from Carroll & Swain, 1993)	240
8.2	First recall session: Percentage accuracy by group for feedback and guessing items (based on data from Carroll & Swain, 1993)	241
8.3	Second recall session: Percentage accuracy by group for feedback and guessing items (based on data from Carroll & Swain, 1993)	241
8.4	Mean raw scores (out of 10) on the interpretation and production tests (based on data from VanPatten & Cadierno, 1993)	257
8.5	Mean acceptability ratings (from 1-unacceptable to 5-acceptable) on ungrammatical sentences without DOM (based on data from Montrul & Bowles, 2010)	262
8.6	Sample picture stimuli for the oral elicitation task (with priming) (from Hurtado & Montrul, 2021b)	264
9.1	Mean trials-to-criterion by instructional group for the four studies in VanPatten et al. (2013)	277
9.2	+EI groups' mean accuracy (out of 10 trials) (based on data from VanPatten et al., 2013)	277
9.3	−EI groups' mean accuracy (out of 10 trials) (based on data from VanPatten et al., 2013)	278
9.4	Picture matching the inverse-scope configuration of (119a), from Wu and Ionin (2022a)	295
9.5	Picture matching the inverse-scope configuration of (119b), from Wu and Ionin (2022a)	295
9.6	Mean acceptability ratings on the double-quantifier configuration by group (based on data from Wu & Ionin, 2022a)	297
9.7	Mean acceptability ratings on the quantifier-negation configuration by group (based on data from Wu & Ionin, 2022a)	297
10.1	A representation of the Full Transfer/Full Access Model of Universal Grammar	302

Tables

1.1	Input differences between monolingual child L1 learners, heritage language L1 learners, and L2 learners	*page* 7
1.2	The implicit/explicit distinction	15
1.3	Some characteristics of implicit vs. explicit knowledge of L2 grammar (based on R. Ellis, 2005)	18
1.4	Differences between implicit and explicit form-focused instruction (adapted from Housen & Pierrard, 2005, p. 10)	21
1.5	Design features of four different test instruments (adapted from R. Ellis, 2005, p. 157)	24
2.1	Components of an intervention study	44
3.1	Examples of English article uses	58
3.2	Summary of intervention studies on articles	66
4.1	Word order differences between English and French (based on L. White, 1990, 1991)	86
4.2	Verb placement in English and German	87
4.3	Intake scores on negative adverb placement (based on data from Reinders & Ellis, 2009)	100
4.4	Summary of intervention studies on the position of verbs and adverbs	103
4.5	Developmental stages of question formation in ESL (based on Mackey, 1999)	105
4.6	Question formation in English and French	107
4.7	Design of the McDonough and Mackey (2008) study	114
4.8	Summary of intervention studies on question formation in English	115
5.1	Summary of intervention studies targeting inflectional morphology using processing instruction	127
5.2	Summary of intervention studies targeting inflectional morphology using a variety of explicit vs. implicit instructional techniques and feedback types	136
6.1	Indicative and subjunctive verbal forms in Spanish	156
6.2	Summary of intervention studies on the subjunctive	169
7.1	Summary of intervention studies on passives and unaccusative and unergative verbs	206

8.1	Distribution of materials in the McDonough (2006) priming study	244
8.2	Summary of intervention studies on double object constructions in English	247
8.3	Alternation between ditransitive and prepositional constructions in Spanish	251
8.4	Summary of intervention studies on object expression in Spanish	254
9.1	Summary of intervention studies targeting word order and relative clauses	270

Boxes

3.1	Sheen (2007)	*page* 69
3.2	Umeda et al. (2019)	74
4.1	L. White (1991), follow-up studies: Trahey and White (1993), Trahey (1996)	94
4.2	Mackey (1999)	111
5.1	Benati (2005)	130
5.2	Lyster (2004a)	144
6.1	Fernández Cuenca (2019)	179
6.2	Potowski, Jegerski, and Morgan Short (2009)	185
7.1	Hirakawa (2013)	221
7.2	Toth and Guijarro Fuentes (2013)	227
8.1	Carroll and Swain (1993)	239
8.2	VanPatten and Cadierno (1993)	256
9.1	VanPatten et al. (2013)	276
9.2	Wu and Ionin (2022a)	296

Preface

As globalization continues and the world becomes more and more multilingual, the need for trained language teachers will only continue to grow. Teaching second or foreign languages requires foundational knowledge of the process of second language acquisition (SLA) and the factors that affect it, as well as the understanding that research findings from SLA have implications for the classroom. There are many books that introduce students to second language acquisition, on the one hand, and books that focus on approaches to grammar teaching, on the other. At the same time, until now, no book on the market has informed both students of SLA and current and future language teachers about how particular grammatical phenomena can best be taught to students of a second or foreign language. Therefore, we felt a need to fill this gap and wrote this book to bring together linguistics, findings in second language acquisition, and studies on classroom intervention research.

Who Is the Reader?

The intended audience of this book are upper-level undergraduate students and master's students in a variety of fields, such as linguistics, applied linguistics, and education (specifically, language teaching); the book assumes some basic knowledge of linguistics, so readers who have taken an introduction to linguistics course or equivalent should have little difficulty following along. The book does not assume any prior familiarity with SLA or with classroom intervention research.

What Does This Book Do?

This book aims to bring together the fields of linguistics, second language acquisition, and experimental intervention research in the lab and in the classroom. The objectives of this book are:

1. to familiarize current, future, and potential language teachers with existing research findings that bear on how specific grammatical phenomena can best be taught;
2. to strengthen the link between linguistics, SLA, and classroom intervention research, by providing specific information about how linguistic theory and SLA findings have informed classroom intervention research;
3. to inform pedagogical practice with evidence from research about the direct effects of language teaching on specific aspects of language learning; and
4. to provide beginning researchers with information and tools that can help them design their own linguistically informed classroom intervention research studies.

Inside This Book

The book mainly focuses on English and Spanish as the target second languages, both because these are the languages on which by far the most classroom intervention research has been done and because this choice makes our book particularly relevant for courses that prepare future English as a Second or Foreign Language (ESL/EFL) teachers or future Spanish teachers. Despite this focus, we mention several studies with other target languages (Japanese, Italian, French, Russian, etc.), and the studies in the book discuss a great variety of typologically distinct native languages, in order to address the kinds of challenges faced by learners as a result of cross-linguistic influence. In the discussion questions and application activities we have included references to other languages as well.

In terms of populations, we discuss studies of child and adult second language learners and of adult heritage speakers. Heritage speakers are early bilinguals whose first or home language is a minority language. As adults, many of these students seek to relearn their heritage language in the classroom, and very often they are placed in classes with second language learners. In the last two decades, teacher education programs and foreign-language programs have recognized heritage speakers as a bilingual population with specific linguistic needs. Many countries in Europe have policies of mother tongue instruction for heritage speakers, and while this situation does not generalize to other contexts, the education of heritage speakers is a global concern. The last few years have seen significant growth in language classes and programs at the post-secondary level to address the linguistic needs of speakers who do not fully develop their heritage language in childhood. Understanding their specific linguistic development and how they react to instruction about specific forms in the classroom is a topic of significant relevance at the moment. Intervention studies with heritage speakers are very scarce currently, and the few mentioned in this book were carried out in the United States.

Why Did We Choose These Topics?

This book is written in an accessible manner, with all linguistic terms clearly defined and provided in a glossary. The focus of the book is on the findings of classroom and lab-based intervention research studies in several specific areas of the grammar (articles, inflectional morphology, question formation, adverb placement, the subjunctive in Romance languages, argument structure, object expression, and phenomena related to word order). We chose these topics because the studies discussed represent both classic and most recent research in these areas. Each content chapter (as opposed to the introductory and concluding chapters) briefly explains the relevant linguistic structure, discusses the challenges that this structure presents to second language learners, summarizes major findings from experimental SLA research concerning acquisition of the structure, and then discusses existing intervention studies on the topic. Each chapter also provides ideas and discussion points for further research.

As the reader has undoubtedly surmised by this point, the focus of this book is on language structure (morphology, syntax) and meaning (semantics), in both SLA and intervention studies. There are many other topics that this book does not cover, including phonology, pragmatics, and sociolinguistics. These are all worthy topics in their own right, but due to scope and length limitations, we made the choice to limit our topics to intervention studies on syntactic, morphological, and semantic phenomena. This choice is driven both by our own expertise and by the large body of intervention studies done on these topics.

We furthermore largely restrict our focus to intervention studies in which researchers actively manipulate instruction and/or input to learners in the lab or in the classroom. We consider a variety of instructional contexts, ranging from instructed learners in a foreign-language classroom to learners in immersion and study abroad programs to immigrants learning a new language in their host country. However, with very few exceptions, the studies we selected do not examine the effect of the instructional setting itself (e.g., comparing how students might learn via study abroad vs. in a foreign-language classroom). The main reason for our choice is that research on the effects of instructional setting typically focuses on overall language development rather than on specific grammatical areas. There are exceptions: in Chapters 6 and 9, we briefly discuss studies that examined the effects of study abroad on learners' performance with specific grammatical topics (subjunctive mood and adjective ordering); in Chapter 5, we consider how verb conjugations are acquired by children in different types of foreign-language settings. These aside, however, nearly all studies highlighted in this book are intervention studies with researcher-controlled manipulations to the instructional setting.

How to Use This Book

The first two chapters of this book set the theoretical foundations that students need in order to understand the studies on specific grammatical properties described in Chapters 3 to 9. We recommend spending as much time as needed covering this foundational knowledge. After establishing the foundations, instructors can choose to follow the book linearly, from Chapter 3 to Chapter 10, or they can choose to focus on just some chapters or parts of some chapters. For example, those interested only in English as a second language can skip all the sections and studies that focus on Spanish. Conversely, if the focus of a class is on Spanish, then focusing on Chapter 6, the second part of Chapter 7, and the second part of Chapter 8 would be of greatest interest. If the instructor wishes to discuss intervention studies across a variety of target languages (not limited to English and Spanish), then Chapter 9 is the best place to start. If syntactic terminology is beyond the level of understanding of a particular group, the more technical sections of Chapters 4 and 6 could be skipped, without endangering comprehension of the main studies discussed.

For a course that focuses on education, we recommend starting with Chapters 1 and 2 in order to ensure students have the necessary foundational knowledge, and subsequently focusing on those chapters whose topics are most closely related to the course. For example, a course in a Teaching English to Speakers of Other Languages (TESOL) program, or any other program that prepares ESL/EFL teachers, should focus on Chapter 3 (articles) and Chapter 4 (verb placement and questions), the first half of Chapter 5 (verbal morphology), the first half of Chapter 7 (passives), the first half of Chapter 8 (double objects), and parts of Chapter 9 (adjectives and relative clauses). The topics presented in those chapters and sections are especially relevant for the kinds of challenges faced by ESL/EFL learners. Chapter 10 provides a conclusion and further ideas that are relevant for any course. We recommend that instructors of education-focused courses briefly cover the main linguistic phenomena at the start of each chapter or section, and spend more time on sample intervention studies on the topic, as well as on the discussion and applications questions.

Key Features

Each chapter includes suggestions for further reading as well as discussion questions, which invite students to think critically about the topics covered in the corresponding chapter. Chapters 3 through 9, which cover intervention studies on specific areas of the grammar, include applications questions in addition to discussion questions. The applications questions ask students to apply what they have learned, for example, by outlining a new intervention study or by applying a particular instructional technique to a different language, a different phenomenon, or a different population of learners. For Chapters 1 through 9, the discussion and applications questions are in numbered subsections at the very end of the chapter. Chapter 10 (the concluding chapter) is structured differently, in that the discussion questions are scattered throughout the chapter, after individual subsections.

The discussion and applications questions are open-ended, rather than requiring specific answers, which we thought is most appropriate to generate critical thinking and discussion in upper-level courses. Instructors can supplement the information presented in each chapter with additional linguistic explanations or exercises, or by assigning other related reading material that complements the information presented in each chapter. The book comes with an online companion site that contains supplementary resources, including lecture slides for the main studies presented in Chapters 3–9 and sample instructed intervention materials.

Acknowledgements

We would like to thank Emily Watton and Rebecca Taylor from Cambridge University Press for their enthusiasm, support, and engagement with our project. We also thank Kilmeny MacBride for her outstanding job with the copy editing. Our colleagues Melissa Bowles (University of Illinois at Urbana-Champaign) and Roumyana Slabakova (University of Southampton), as well as our graduate student Amy Atiles (University of Illinois at Urbana-Champaign), generously read preliminary versions of several chapters. Their feedback at earlier stages of this project was invaluable for shaping this book. We are also very grateful to the fourteen reviewers for CUP, and to Lydia White (McGill University), who provided substantial feedback on several chapters of this book. We have done our best to address all the issues raised in the reviews but remain responsible for any errors and omissions that may remain.

Abbreviations

1:	first person
3:	third person
ACC:	accusative case
CAUS:	causative particle
DAT:	dative case
DEC:	declarative mood
DOM:	differential object marking
FEM:	feminine gender
FUT:	future tense
IMPERF:	imperfect tense
IND:	indicative mood
INF:	infinitive
INST:	instrumental case
MASC:	masculine gender
NEG:	negation
NEUT:	neuter gender
NOM:	nominative case
PART:	partitive clitic
PASS:	passive particle
PAST:	past tense
PL:	plural number
PRES:	present tense
PRET:	preterit tense
REFL:	reflexive clitic
SG:	singular number
SUBJ:	subjunctive mood

1 Theoretical Foundations

Second language acquisition (SLA) is the acquisition of a language after the grammatical foundations of the native language are in place, typically after four years of age. It is very common around the world to learn a second language in a classroom or institutional setting. Our goal in this textbook is to discuss how the linguistic knowledge that second language learners develop can be guided and positively affected by instruction. To achieve this goal, in this textbook we focus on **intervention** research. We begin with an overview of major topics in linguistics and in second language acquisition that are particularly relevant to research with instructed second language learners. The focus of this textbook is on experimental studies of second language acquisition in the classroom or in a lab environment, where aspects of the **input** are manipulated to enhance the acquisition of specific grammatical forms. Depending on the study, this may be achieved through, for example, explicit explanations about grammatical forms, use of different instructional methods, or exposing learners to specific grammatical forms. These types of experimental studies are called **intervention studies** because linguistic knowledge is measured before and after the input manipulation (the intervention), to see whether there was a change (an effect) as a result of the intervention.

Our primary objectives in this book are three:

1. to inform current and future language teachers about findings from second language acquisition (variously termed **L2 acquisition** or SLA) and classroom intervention research that are relevant to language teaching;
2. to inform students and researchers working in the field of classroom intervention research about SLA findings that can potentially lead to classroom intervention research studies; and
3. to give students and researchers of SLA the foundational knowledge and tools they need to carry out intervention research studies.

We envisioned this book as a resource both for students of SLA who are interested in learning more about classroom intervention research and for current and future language teachers who are interested in learning about theoretically informed classroom intervention research beyond the basics. For a more introductory coverage of these topics, see Henshaw & Hawkins (2022).

Before we get to the specifics of how intervention studies work (see Chapter 2), we lay out the underlying assumptions and the central concepts of formal approaches to second language acquisition that we adopt in this book.

1.1 Linguistics and Second Language Acquisition

What is a language? How does one learn a language? Does **first language acquisition** proceed in the same way as second language acquisition, or are the two processes different? Do children learn the same way as adults? Does learning two languages simultaneously differ from learning first one language and then another? Does your knowledge of one language influence how you learn a new language, and if so, how? These are just some of the questions that researchers who work in linguistics and language acquisition often ask. In this section, we review some of the key terms and findings about language and language acquisition, to set the stage for studies about instructed SLA, the focus of this book.

1.1.1 What Is Linguistics?

Linguistics is a science that studies the nature of human language: its form (grammar) and function, its representation in the brain, and its use in society. In this textbook we are concerned with the knowledge of language represented in the mind of both first language (L1) speakers and learners of a second language (L2). In particular, we focus on how grammatical knowledge is acquired in the first place, how it develops further over time by itself and with the help of instruction, and how it is represented and used for production and comprehension during this process. We are concerned with grammar as an abstract cognitive system that develops in the minds of speakers. Before we proceed, there are other interpretations of grammar that we need to clarify. The term **prescriptive grammar** refers to a set of norms or rules governing how a language should or should not be used rather than describing the ways in which a language is actually used by speakers. It is also called **normative grammar** because it tries to impose the "norms" of the language. **Pedagogical grammar** is a grammar which is intended to teach second language learners; it is informed by scientific descriptions of language and theories of second language acquisition (Newby, 2000).

Although there are many branches of linguistics, in this textbook we will be mostly concerned with aspects of **morphology** (the structure of words), **syntax** (the structure of phrases and sentences), and **semantics** (the meaning of words and sentences) that are challenging in SLA. The vast majority of instructed SLA research has focused on grammar (morphology and syntax), and most of the literature on theoretical aspects of SLA focuses on formal aspects of syntax and morphology. This book focuses primarily on intervention studies of syntax, morphology, and sentence-level semantics. Intervention studies of phonology, vocabulary (words in isolation) and pragmatics fall beyond the scope of this book.

The approach to linguistics we favor in this book is the Chomskyan model of language that sees aspects of language as universal, common to all human languages, and part of inborn grammatical knowledge represented in the mind (Chomsky, 1965, 1986). **Universal Grammar** (UG) is a cognitive construct that is assumed to constrain the form of all languages. UG limits the hypotheses that child L1 learners entertain as they acquire the language spoken (or signed) in their environment on the basis of input. UG includes **principles** or general rules, such as constraints on the referents of pronouns (like *she/her, he/his, they/them*) and reflexive anaphors (*herself, himself, themselves*). UG also includes **parameters**, which capture crosslinguistic variation. An example of a parameter, the verb-movement parameter (Pollock, 1989), determines where verbs are placed in the sentence (before or after adverbs, before or after the subject in a question, etc.). This parameter is discussed in Chapter 4. UG also accounts for other universal properties of language. Chapter 7, for example, discusses a syntactic distinction between different types of **intransitive verbs**. This distinction is universal but shows different syntactic and morphological reflexes in different languages.

Figure 1.1 illustrates how the construct of UG guides the L1 acquisition process from initial state, throughout development to the final, steady state: mature native speaker competence. The input consists of naturalistic samples of speech (or sign) in the first years of life.

We favor the generative Chomskyan perspective because the **generative linguistic framework** (Chomsky, 1965) considers grammar as a complex abstract system. This approach provides a rich research base on the syntax, semantics, and morphology of many languages around the world, and on the second language acquisition of many of these languages (L. White, 2003b), including English, Spanish, Japanese, Russian, among many others. This approach has always asked how human language is learned by children acquiring their L1 and what form the **linguistic competence** (underlying knowledge) of both child and adult speakers of a language takes (Chomsky, 1986). Therefore, language acquisition is at the center of the generative

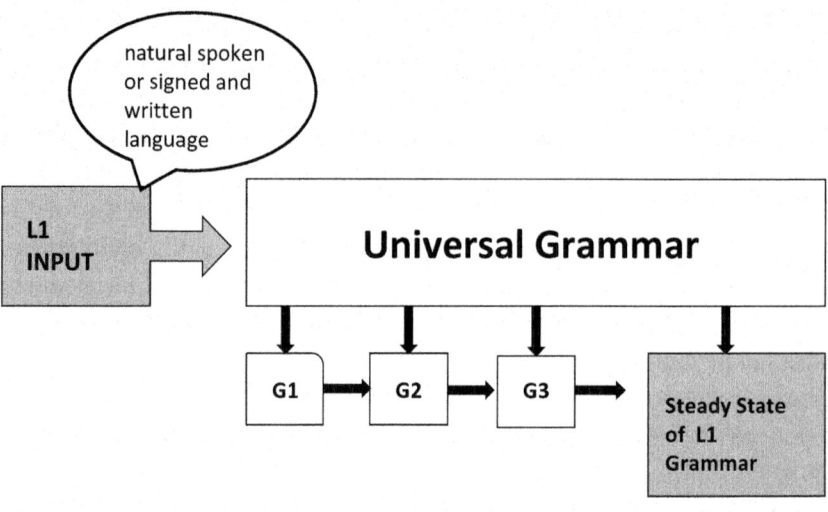

Figure 1.1 L1 acquisition from initial state to mature steady state (based on L. White, 2003b, p. 3)

theory of grammar. Finally, the learnability questions raised by how children acquire or discover the rules of the grammar of their L1 from exposure to input are also relevant in L2 acquisition and in bilingual acquisition by heritage speakers.

Since the mid 1980s, the generative approach to L2 acquisition has generated a vast body of work on the acquisition of various grammatical aspects of diverse languages. Some of these studies include instructed interventions in the classroom, such as the famous study on adverb placement in English conducted by L. White (1991), which we discuss in Chapter 4. Furthermore, guided by questions about the role of age of acquisition, several studies of heritage language speakers in linguistics and applied linguistics have been conducted since the early 2000s. Since heritage speakers are an increasingly visible and important population in many foreign/second language classrooms, some of the incipient research in this area has compared what heritage language speakers and L2 learners have in common when it comes to learning the target language, and whether formal instruction affects their grammatical development differentially. Some of these studies include instructed interventions, such as studies by Potowski, Jegerski, and Morgan-Short (2009) on the subjunctive discussed in Chapter 6 and by Montrul and Bowles (2010) on object marking covered in Chapter 8. Although not all the studies examined in this book assume the generative framework, they all deal with grammatical properties of English, Spanish, and other languages that have had a long research tradition in generative linguistics.

1.1.2 Second Language Acquisition: Timing and Context

As mentioned in the opening of this chapter, second language acquisition is the acquisition of an additional language after the structural foundations (i.e., basic grammar) of the L1 are in place. The term *second* implies a sequence: first one language, then the other. Therefore, L2 acquisition (or SLA) can happen early in childhood (after age three), later in childhood (elementary school), at or around puberty (secondary school), or at any age in adulthood. There are several differences between L1 acquisition by children and L2 acquisition by children and adults. One major difference is the learner's age: by definition, an L2 learner who has already had time to acquire one language is older than an L1 learner who is just beginning the language acquisition process. Another major difference is the **initial state** of the acquisition process. For the L1 child, the initial cognitive state at the onset of L1 acquisition is UG (see Figure 1.1) or, on non-generative views, general cognition. In contrast, L2 learners already start with the linguistic knowledge of their L1 and may or may not, depending on the theory, have access to aspects of UG as well. Figure 1.2 illustrates our representation of the Full Transfer/Full Access model of L2 acquisition (Schwartz & Sprouse, 1996); we include a role for instruction. In this model, the initial state of L2 acquisition is the mature L1 knowledge already developed through UG, as in Figure 1.1. UG remains available from initial state to the final state of the interlanguage development. The endstate of L2 acquisition can be near-native or nonnative in different aspects of grammar.

L2 acquisition can happen naturalistically, as in L1 acquisition, or in a formal, instructed environment (the classroom). Thus, Figure 1.2 shows that the input to L2 learners may potentially include naturalistic speech and written language, as well as classroom instruction, which includes grammar

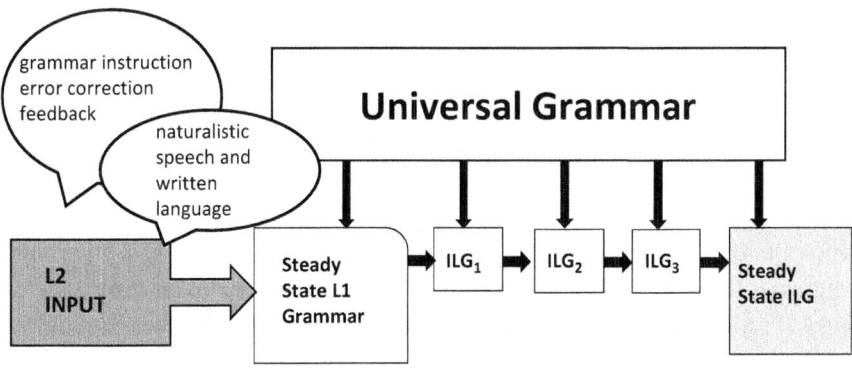

Figure 1.2 A representation of the Full Transfer/Full Access Model of Universal Grammar in L2 acquisition (Schwartz & Sprouse, 1996) with a role for instruction (adapted from L. White, 2003b).

explanations, error correction, and other forms of feedback. The context of acquisition depends on the age of the L2 learner and their sociolinguistic circumstances. Many L2 children are children of immigrants (heritage speakers of their native language) who come to a new country where a different language is spoken and who must learn the L2 naturalistically in the society and at school through academic instruction in the L2. Both adult and child immigrants often take formal classes in which they are instructed about the structure of the L2. Children and young adults who are not immigrants typically have foreign-language instruction at school (in cases where the school offers L2 instruction) or in after-school programs. Exactly when such foreign-language instruction begins at school depends on the country. For example, in the United States, most L2 learners start acquiring their L2 at around puberty, since foreign-language education typically begins in middle school or high school, or in young adulthood, at university. In contrast, in many other countries all over the globe, foreign-language instruction begins as early as elementary school.

In most cases, L2 learners continue to be exposed to their L1 while receiving exposure to their L2; this means that the amount of input that the L2 learner is exposed to is significantly less than the amount of input that an L1 acquiring child in a monolingual setting receives daily. In some instructed settings, exposure to the L2 may be two to five hours a week, as in a foreign-language environment. On the other hand, for a learner who lives in the country where the L2 is spoken (e.g., a learner of English in the United States), exposure to the L2 can be several hours a day. In some cases, L2 exposure may even occur 100 percent of the time (if the learner has no interaction in their L1).

1.1.3 Heritage Speakers: In between First and Second Language Acquisition

Many L2 learners living in a second language environment all over the world are also heritage speakers of their L1. As we will see, some recent intervention studies have included heritage speakers. This is because the L1 or heritage language of these speakers does not develop fully by the time these children become adults. On the surface, many grammatical areas that are difficult for L2 learners to master are also not fully mastered by heritage language learners. Intervention studies with heritage speakers may seek to answer theoretical questions about the nature of linguistic knowledge and/or to identify how heritage speakers learn or which strategies help them relearn their native language in a classroom environment. Figure 1.3 captures the fact that heritage speakers share some situational and some linguistic features with both L1 and L2 acquisition (see also Table 1.1).

1.1 Linguistics and Second Language Acquisition

Table 1.1 Input differences between monolingual child L1 learners, heritage language L1 learners, and L2 learners

Input	Monolingual child L1 learners	Heritage language L1 learners	L2 learners
Timing	birth	birth	early (age 4–10), late (around and after puberty)
Setting (in the early stages)	naturalistic (home)	naturalistic (home)	instructed (classroom)/ naturalistic (study abroad, immigration)
Mode	aural (birth–age 4) written (after ~age 4–5)	predominantly aural (literacy in some cases)	aural and written (literacy)

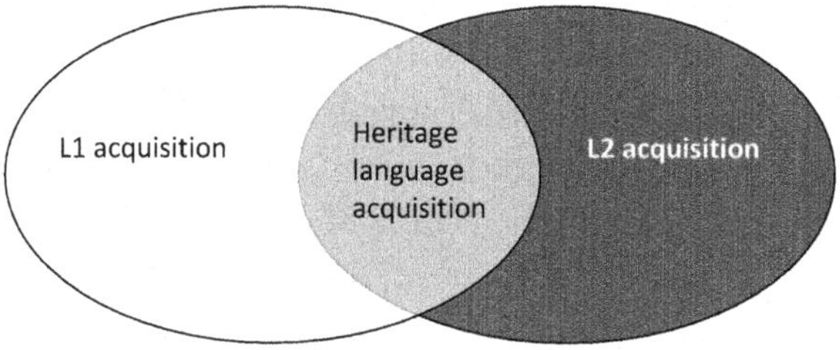

Figure 1.3 Heritage language acquisition

Most heritage speakers are early bilinguals whose L1 is a sociopolitically minority language in the society (Polinsky, 2018). Some heritage speakers are born to immigrant parents or immigrate to an L2 environment in childhood. Others grow up in bilingual or multilingual societies where their home language is one historically spoken in the community (Basque, Frisian, Balochi) or an indigenous language (Quechua, Sami). Some heritage speakers are **simultaneous bilinguals** who are exposed to the heritage language and the society language from early childhood, thus having two L1s. Other heritage speakers are **sequential bilinguals** who have experienced some years of monolingualism in the heritage language (the L1) prior to immersion in the society language (the L2). Figure 1.4 depicts the linguistic development of simultaneous bilinguals, exposed to two languages (A and B) since birth, also guided by UG.

While many heritage speakers become native-like in the majority language of the society as they assimilate to the society, their **heritage language acquisition** is often interrupted. This leads to the heritage language not reaching the same level of development as in monolinguals or the same level as the majority language. The result is what has been termed delayed, partial,

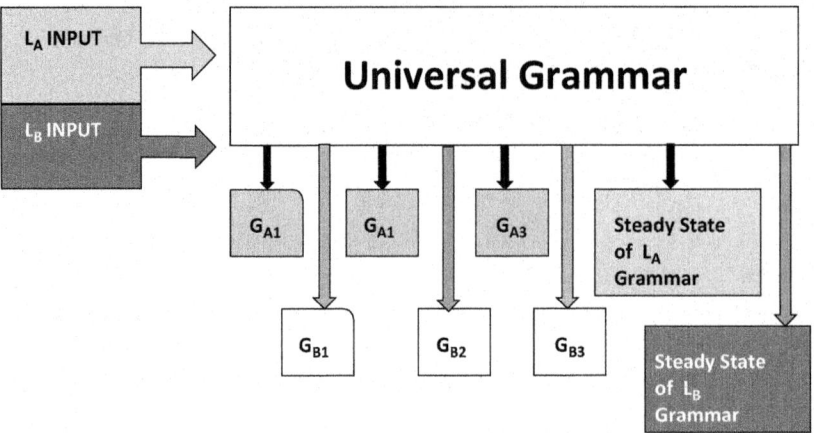

Figure 1.4 Simultaneous bilingual acquisition

or incomplete acquisition of the heritage language (Montrul, 2008, 2016a, O'Grady et al., 2011, Polinsky, 2007, Silva-Corvalán, 2018). Although heritage speakers are native speakers of their home language, many of them do not use the language outside the home after age five, when schooling in the majority language typically starts. Significant reduction of input and decreased use of the language between the ages of five and eighteen years often profoundly hampers the lexical and structural development of the heritage language. Table 1.1. compares monolingual child L1 learners, heritage language L1 learners, and L2 learners with respect to timing and nature of input received.

Many child heritage speakers fall behind in the linguistic development of their L1 (their heritage language) compared to monolingual children of the same age (Daskalaki et al., 2020; Montrul & Sánchez-Walker, 2013). They may even fall behind relative to younger monolingual children (Armon-Lotem, Rose, & Altman, 2021; Coşkun Kunduz & Montrul, 2022). Heritage speakers are native speakers of the heritage language because they were exposed to the language naturalistically at home from birth, like monolingual L1 learners. Yet, in later childhood and adulthood they show many of the nonnative features typical of second language learners. These are observed in the areas of morphology (Montrul, 2008; Polinsky, 2018), some aspects of syntax (Lohdal, 2021) and some aspects of semantics (Ionin, 2021). In general, heritage speakers pattern more closely, yet not always identically, to monolinguals in phonology (C. Chang, 2021). As adults, many heritage speakers seek to learn or relearn the heritage language in the classroom. While some institutions offer classes and language programs specifically tailored to the linguistic and communicative needs of heritage speakers, most others place heritage speakers in the same classroom as L2 or foreign-language learners. In the last few years, classroom-based research on heritage language learners has become critical to understanding how different types of learners react to or benefit from explicit instruction to help them advance in their linguistic development (Bowles & Torres, 2021; Montrul & Bowles, 2017).

1.1.4 Biological Foundations of Language

Although language is a system of human communication that takes place in a sociocultural environment and expresses different meanings, in this textbook we are concerned with the form of language – its grammar – as instantiated in the minds of speakers, including language learners. How is language, in our case, grammatical knowledge, acquired? Following the Chomskyan approach to language, we assume that language is in the mind, and that without cognition and the biological foundation of language, there is no language. In essence, all human beings are biologically endowed with a cognitive capacity that allows them to develop language. Therefore, the biological component is essential: Human beings develop an abstract, symbolic, generative system of rules that creates new sentences from a finite set of elements (words) to communicate meaning. In contrast, other biological organisms do not develop a complex and abstract language system capable of communicating knowledge and expressing meanings about past, future, or hypothetical events.

But in order to acquire language, a learner must be exposed to samples of language in the environment, in a social context through interaction with other speakers. This is very similar to what happens in the botanical world: Plants are born from a seed (a biological program), but in order to grow to their full potential they need optimal amounts of water and sunlight (environmental triggers). Turning to the animal world, many birds, such as zebra finches, acquire their singing ability between twenty-three and sixty-five days after hatching, by imitating a member of their species (Gobes, Jennings, & Maeda, 2019). Introduction of a second bird "tutor" after Day 65 results in limited song learning. In a similar manner, input in the form of exposure to language through spoken (or signed) and written language samples is a critical component for language development.

Like the zebra finch, if a child is not exposed to language input (oral in case of spoken languages and signed in the case of sign languages) during the **critical period** for language, the morphology, syntax, and semantics of the native language are not acquired (Curtiss, 2014). This is just as true for hearing children deprived of spoken language as for deaf children deprived of sign language (Mayberry, 2012). Mayberry and Kluender (2018) argue that there is a critical period for L1 acquisition because language acquisition and development of the brain language system appear to reciprocally affect one another. However, this takes place only when the onset of language experience is synchronous with the onset of postnatal brain development. **Age effects** are not as critical in L2 acquisition as they are in L1 acquisition, because it is possible to learn a second language after puberty and communicate in it successfully, even though full mastery of the phonology, morphology, and other aspects of the language at native levels are not guaranteed. In L2 acquisition by older children and adults, brain development and L1 acquisition are more advanced when the acquisition of the L2 starts (Montrul, 2022).

Similarly, incomplete acquisition due to age effects (but not a critical period) arises in heritage language acquisition as well, when the input to the heritage language is suboptimal. Heritage speakers are exposed to their heritage language during the critical period for learning. However, in both L2 acquisition and heritage language acquisition, full mastery of all aspects of the language are not guaranteed. The timing of input, the type of input, and the amount of exposure to the L1 (heritage language) or the L2 all play a significant role in the speed, complexity, and accuracy of acquisition of the L2 or the heritage language (Montrul, 2008). We turn to this next.

1.1.5 The Role of Input in Language Acquisition

In L1 acquisition, a child who is born into a monolingual environment is exposed to the native, ambient language during much of the time when they are awake. Exposure to input happens in a naturalistic setting (the home) through spoken (or signed) interactions with caregivers and other interlocutors (see Figure 1.1). The child hears language (or sees it, in the case of signed languages) and observes the matching reality; through this exposure and interactions with other interlocutors, the child builds a grammatical representation of their native language. This is called **positive evidence**, as opposed to negative evidence. Positive evidence informs the child about the words and structures that are possible in the language, and from this input the child must extract rules and generalizations about the structure of language, inductively.

In contrast, negative evidence is information about what rules or structures are *not* part of the language, and has been argued by Chomsky to be unavailable to the child. One might imagine that such negative evidence comes from parents correcting their children's grammatical errors. However, there is in fact much evidence that parents do not engage in regular or consistent error correction. While parents do provide some **recasts** (rephrasing their children's ungrammatical utterances using corresponding grammatical forms), research suggests that parents do not do this regularly or consistently, and that this is unlikely to play a role in the acquisition of grammar (see Marcus, 1993; Yang, 2015 for more discussion).

To understand how children learn from positive evidence, consider the following example. Children learning English learn through exposure to their language that the regular past tense in English is formed by adding the morpheme -ed to a root: *play–played, talk–talked, jump–jumped*. Children receive positive evidence (the appearance of both *played* and *jumped* in the input). We know children extract this rule inductively from exposure to input and without instruction because (i) once they learn the past tense rule, they apply it productively to new verbs, and (ii) in applying this rule they make overgeneralization errors. That is, they overapply the -ed past tense rule to irregular verbs that do not take -ed, producing errors such as: **I swimmed in the pool, *I runned, *Daddy comed*, etc. (Brown, 1973; Pinker, 1994). The very existence of such overgeneralization errors indicates that children are not simply repeating what they hear but instead formulate and apply a rule. Eventually, young children overcome these errors and learn, without explicit teaching and through exposure to positive evidence, that the -ed rule applies to many verbs but not all of them. How children discover the rules of their language and eventually come to know what are rules and what are exceptions to a rule has been a topic of important debate in the language acquisition field (Yang, 2016).

Furthermore, children are able to acquire rules for which they do not ever receive direct evidence: As discussed by Crain (1991), children acquire constraints on which structures and interpretations are possible vs. impossible in the language, without ever being explicitly taught. As an example, consider (1): In (1a), *she* can refer to Alice (i.e., Alice was falling down the rabbit hole), but in (1b), *she* must refer to a different person, not Alice. This is the case even though *she* precedes *Alice* in both sentences; the difference between (1a–b) is structural. It is unlikely that any parents would explain the difference between (1a–b) to their young children, especially considering that unless the parents are linguists, they are unlikely to be consciously aware of this difference themselves. Yet experimental work has shown that children respect the rule, allowing *she* to refer to the name that follows (Alice) in examples like (1a) but not (1b).

(1)   a. While she was falling down the rabbit hole, Alice found a marmalade jar.
        b. She was falling down the rabbit hole while Alice found a marmalade jar.

For young, preliterate children (both monolingual speakers and bilingual heritage speakers) positive evidence consists of language samples in their exposure to spoken (or signed) language. Older literate children receive positive evidence through written language exposure as well, when they start reading and writing at school. Older, instructed L2 learners are exposed to positive evidence in the classroom, through samples of spoken and written language in context. Additionally, unlike young children, older L2 learners may also receive negative evidence, in the form of explicit classroom instruction and/or error correction.

Although the L2 and the heritage language learner may be exposed to less input than a monolingual L1 learner, all learners (monolingual and bilingual, L1 and L2) face the same problem of learning the language rules and the exceptions to the rules based on available evidence. Like monolingual children, bilingual heritage speakers and L2 learners must build an abstract grammatical representation from positive evidence, based on naturally occurring language in the input. They must also determine which rules are productive and what data are exceptions in the **target language** (the L2 in L2 learners and the L1 in heritage speakers). However, there are important differences between monolingual and bilingual/L2 acquisition, as we will see next.

1.1.6 Differences among First Language Learners, Second Language Learners, and Heritage Speakers

The different populations of monolingual, bilingual, and L2 learners differ along many dimensions, as shown in Table 1.1. Differences among these populations include the learners' age, knowledge of another language, the quantity and quality of the input, and the learning environment.

One difference is that the L2 learner (child or adult) is more cognitively and linguistically mature than the child L1 learner and the heritage language learner when acquisition starts. As shown in Table 1.1, both monolingual and bilingual (heritage-language speaking) children start acquisition of the target language at birth; child and adult L2 learners do so later, after age four or even in adulthood. When trying to derive meaning from the L2 input, older learners may engage in cognitive strategies, such as analogy, not yet available to L1-acquiring children (Bley-Vroman, 1989, 1990), leading to different types of analyses of the input data, different hypotheses, and different developmental trajectories.

The second difference is previous or other linguistic knowledge. The L2 learner already knows another language, while the heritage language learner is either an L1 speaker or an early simultaneous bilingual speaker with two L1s. The linguistic representation of the L1 in L2 learners or of the dominant language in heritage speakers is another powerful source of information, one not available to monolingual L1 learners. This is especially the case at lower levels of development or proficiency. It is during early development that the L1 (in L2 learners) or the dominant language (in heritage speakers) is most likely be a default hypothesis for input processing and assigning a linguistic representation to the L2 (Schwartz & Sprouse, 1996) or the heritage language. With sufficient and sustained exposure to the target language and with increased proficiency, many L2 learners are able to eventually overcome L1 influence and converge on the grammar of the L2, at least in some specific domains.

Heritage speakers who are dominant in the L2 can also exhibit transfer from the L2 to the L1. Studies with heritage speakers typically compare them to a control group of speakers. These may be monolingually raised native speakers in the homeland or, alternatively, the parents of the heritage speakers, who live in the same L2 environment as the heritage speakers. Thus, for example, heritage Mandarin speakers in the United States might be compared to monolingual Mandarin speakers in China or Taiwan or, alternatively, to their own Mandarin-speaking parents in the United States.

The nature of heritage language knowledge is a burgeoning area of research (Benmamoun, Montrul, & Polinsky, 2013; Montrul & Polinsky, 2021; Scontras, Fuchs, & Polinsky, 2015). Heritage speakers show many signatures of monolingual L1 acquisition and complete ultimate attainment in phonetics and phonology and in aspects of syntax, semantics, and morphology. At the same time, they often display reduced vocabularies in the heritage language, gaps in morphology, overregularization and simplification errors in syntax and morphology, and crosslinguistic influence in some areas of semantics. In some cases, but not always, the dominant language is a source of transfer in heritage language acquisition (Montrul, 2010a, Montrul & Ionin, 2012).

Monolingual child L1 learners eventually overcome developmental or overgeneralization errors they may make during the course of language development (recall the discussion of how children acquire past-tense marking in section 1.1.5). In contrast, many L2 learners and heritage language learners do not overcome many of their errors. One obvious reason is that, compared to monolingual child L1 learners, heritage language and L2 learners receive quantitatively less exposure to input, and the input is restricted to specific environments. Another reason is that the cognitive, linguistic structure of the other language plays a significant, but not exclusive, role in L2 and bilingual development. Many of the nontarget hypotheses entertained by heritage speakers and L2 learners may stem from influence of the other language. In order to overcome these errors, L2 and heritage language speakers may benefit from instruction and information about what is grammatical and what is not grammatical in the target language, including explicit correction.

This brings us to the final difference between L1 and L2 learners: the nature of the available evidence (compare input in Figure 1.1 and Figure 1.2). Young monolingual L1 acquiring children are not instructed about their native language (by the time they are taught prescriptive or normative grammar in elementary school and beyond, their L1 is already fully formed). In contrast adult (and even child) L2 learners typically do receive instruction, from teachers and textbooks, as do some (child and adult) heritage language learners.

Explicit instruction in the language provides negative evidence: evidence about what is impossible or ungrammatical in the language. Negative evidence can also be provided implicitly, for example, through recasts of learners' ungrammatical utterances. While negative evidence does not seem to play a role in the acquisition of an L1 in childhood (Marcus, 1993), it may be beneficial in heritage language acquisition in an instructed context (Bowles & Torres, 2021), as we will see in this textbook. Sometimes, explicit instruction can also cause errors in second language learners that arise from erroneous generalizations triggered by the instruction (Rothman, 2008; Selinker, 1972).

It is important to clarify that linguistic theory seeks to describe and explain the implicit grammatical system that native speakers have of their native language, regardless of whether what speakers produce or accept is correct in prescriptive or normative grammar terms. Prescriptive and normative grammars are socially guided by what is perceived as correct or standard from a more sociolinguistic perspective. Now, pedagogical grammars are grammars that may be related to some extent to abstract linguistic grammars, but very often the rules of pedagogical grammars are simplistic at best and incomplete. For example, to say that the **copula** (linking) verb *ser* 'be' in Spanish is used with adjectives that express permanent attributes whereas *estar* is used with temporary attributes or states, as many grammar books explain the rules and distribution of these two verbs in Spanish, does not fully capture the linguistic knowledge and internalized rules that native speakers of Spanish have. Many pedagogical rules are not actual rules of linguistic knowledge. For example, a study on knowledge of the coreference restrictions of the subjunctive in temporal clauses mentioned in Chapter 6 (Bruhn de Garavito, 1997) found that the implicit knowledge that advanced L2 learners develop surpasses or goes beyond the misleading and incomplete rules that L2 learners are exposed to in the classroom. Now, to the extent that pedagogical grammar accurately captures the implicit rules and constraints of our mental grammars, then it may be of value to second language teaching. Linguistic theory and analysis could in fact enhance intervention research, as we discuss next.

In the rest of this book, we will discuss the effects of different types of instruction on second language development. First, however, we need to discuss the fact that knowledge, learning, and instruction can all be explicit as well as implicit.

1.2 The Explicit vs. Implicit Distinction

So far we have used the terms *acquisition* and *learning* interchangeably, but for some researchers, notably Krashen (1981, 1982), there is a key theoretical distinction between these two terms. Krashen made an epistemological difference between "acquired" vs. "learned" linguistic knowledge. **Acquisition** takes place incidentally, occurs through processing language during comprehension for meaning, and results in implicit knowledge of language. By contrast, "learned" linguistic knowledge occurs when L2 learners learn explicit grammatical rules in the classroom: They may learn "about" the language, but may not be able to really use the language. Over the years there has been refinement and confirmation of these original ideas (for example, in Schwartz, 1993; M. Paradis, 2009), which today are embodied in the distinction between **implicit** and **explicit knowledge, and learning.**

The implicit/explicit distinction in the domain of language has been made with regard to knowledge, memory, learning, instruction, and experimental tasks (Schmidt, 1994; Hulstijn, 2005; N. C. Ellis, 2008; Godfroid et al., 2015). Table 1.2 summarizes some of the major characteristics of the implicit/explicit distinction as applied to those areas; these characteristics are elaborated on in the following subsections.

Table 1.2 The implicit/explicit distinction

	Implicit	Explicit
Knowledge	unconscious, automatic	conscious, verbalizable
Learning	without awareness	with awareness
Instruction	does not attract attention to the form	attracts attention to the target form
Feedback	indirect (e.g., recast)	direct (e.g., overt correction)
Experimental tasks[a]	focus on meaning, involve time pressure	focus on form, do not involve time pressure

[a] Tasks are not, strictly speaking, "implicit" or "explicit": rather, they are designed to tap into implicit vs. explicit knowledge.

1.2.1 Implicit vs. Explicit Knowledge and Learning

The difference between knowing something implicitly as opposed to explicitly is much discussed in cognitive psychology and is by no means specific to language. It can be described as the difference between *knowing how* and *knowing that*. Examples of implicit knowledge (knowing how) include knowing how to read and knowing how to ride a bike. Examples of explicit knowledge (knowing that) include knowing that Paris is the capital of France or knowing that yesterday one ate an apple pie for dessert. There is evidence from psychology and neuroscience that the two types of knowledge are stored in different memory systems: declarative memory for explicit knowledge vs. nondeclarative/procedural memory for implicit knowledge (Schachter & Tulving, 1994; Squire, Knowlton, & Musen, 1993).

Every native speaker or signer of a language also has both implicit and explicit knowledge of that language. An example of implicit knowledge is that even someone who has never studied phonology knows which sound sequences are licit in their native language (e.g., that an English word can start with *sn* but not with *ns*). In contrast, many aspects of vocabulary knowledge (for example, being able to define *cat* as an animal that is furry, meows, and purrs) are explicit. With regard to grammar, all native speakers or signers of a language have implicit knowledge of how grammar works; some but not all also have explicit knowledge, to varying degrees. To come back to the example in section 1.1.5, a typically developing three-year-old English-acquiring child already knows implicitly that the English past tense is formed by the addition of a 'd' or 't' sound at the end. Not only does this child produce forms like *played* or *walked*, but she may well overgeneralize and also produce *goed* or *sitted*. Yet this three-year-old does not have explicit knowledge of how the English past tense works: She probably does not know what "past tense" means and would not be able to explain *why* she turns *go* into *goed* when talking about something that happened yesterday. While adults generally have some degree of explicit knowledge of their native language, especially if they studied grammar at school, it is still quite limited: An adult native Spanish speaker who is not a linguist or a language teacher probably cannot explain why the subjunctive works the way it does, yet he still uses the subjunctive correctly.

For adult L2 learners, the situation is reversed: At least in the case of classroom learners, explicit knowledge appears to develop before implicit knowledge. A typical instructed L2 English learner probably *can* explain the explicit rule for past-tense formation (add an *-ed* suffix to the verb) and knows the terms for "past tense" vs. "present tense." At the same time, this learner is still likely to omit past tense marking and produce utterances such as *I walk to the store yesterday* in spontaneous speech (see Lardiere, 1998a for examples). This suggests that the rule for past-tense formation is not fully a part of the learner's implicit knowledge of English grammar, or, alternatively, not part of their integrated knowledge (Jiang, 2007). Research on heritage language acquisition has uncovered that heritage speakers, unlike L2 learners, often have enhanced implicit knowledge of the heritage language but underdeveloped explicit knowledge (Montrul, Foote, & Perpiñán, 2008; Bowles, 2011; Zyzik, 2016).

According to Schmidt (1994) implicit vs. explicit learning is related to implicit vs. explicit knowledge but is a distinct concept. Explicit learning involves awareness of the fact that one is learning, while implicit learning happens without such awareness. In principle, learners could learn a structure explicitly (by memorizing and practicing a rule), yet eventually internalize this structure and know it at an implicit level, or at least have automatized knowledge of the structure (DeKeyser, 2003). SLA literature has been concerned with the distinction between implicit and explicit knowledge and learning for close to four decades, going back at least to the Monitor Model of Krashen (1981) discussed above, on which the distinction was framed as being between acquired (implicit) and learned (explicit) knowledge.

1.2.2 Characteristics of Implicit vs. Explicit Knowledge

What exactly qualifies as explicit vs. implicit knowledge? R. Ellis (2005) building on prior literature, lays out seven different criteria that distinguish the two types of knowledge from each other; these are summarized in Table 1.3. While implicit knowledge is automatic and intuitive, explicit knowledge requires effort and involves awareness. Explicit knowledge is verbalizable on demand, but implicit knowledge is accessed more quickly and automatically. Implicit knowledge is generally believed to be more systematic and to involve greater certainty than explicit knowledge. Most controversially, some researchers (e.g., Bialystok, 1994) argue that implicit knowledge, unlike explicit, is acquirable only early in life, during a critical or sensitive period. However, this is subject to much debate (for overviews of the debate about critical periods in SLA; see, for example Birdsong, 1999; Herschensohn, 2007).

Under the Declarative/Procedural Model (Ullman, 2001), the two types of knowledge are served by different memory systems. On this model, native speakers utilize both memory systems (declarative for vocabulary, procedural for grammar), whereas adult L2 learners rely primarily on declarative memory for learning grammar. However, the idea that adult L2 learners cannot rely on procedural memory has been subject to debate, and there is

Table 1.3 Some characteristics of implicit vs. explicit knowledge of L2 grammar (based on R. Ellis, 2005)

	Implicit knowledge	Explicit knowledge
Awareness	intuitive	conscious
Type of knowledge	procedural (knowing how)	declarative (knowing that)
Systematicity and certainty	greater systematicity and certainty	less systematicity (more variability) and less certainty
Accessibility of knowledge	automatic	controlled
Use of L2 knowledge	used in tasks that require automaticity	used in tasks that demand analysis and control
Self-report	not verbalizable	potentially verbalizable
Learnability	is only learnable early in life (but this is highly controversial)	can be learned at any age

evidence that procedural memory is involved at least for higher-proficiency learners (e.g., Morgan-Short et al., 2014).

As discussed by R. Ellis (2005) the existence of implicit linguistic knowledge can be captured under very different theoretical frameworks. For generative approaches to language and language acquisition (Chomsky, 1986), implicit knowledge corresponds to our linguistic competence: For example, we have the competence to judge a sentence in our native language as either grammatical or ungrammatical, even if we have never heard this sentence before, and even if we have no metalinguistic knowledge (such as knowledge of grammatical terminology). On the generative view, all humans are born with implicit knowledge of UG, a set of basic grammatical categories and rules that are common to all human languages. In contrast, on connectionist and statistical learning approaches (MacWhinney, 1997; Rebuschat, 2015; Rebuschat & Williams, 2012b; Rumelhart & McClelland, 1986), implicit knowledge is a result of pattern association and develops gradually in learners, driven primarily by input. While these two approaches are very different, they both aim to explain the nature of implicit knowledge. Both generative accounts of SLA (e.g., Gregg, 1989; Schwartz, 1993, Zobl, 1995) and connectionist ones (e.g., N. C. Ellis, 1996) distinguish between explicit and implicit knowledge and the learning of an L2.

At the same time, until relatively recently, generative SLA research did not typically address or control for this distinction in experimental studies. For instance, it was quite common in SLA studies of the 1980s and 1990s to use untimed grammaticality judgment tasks to tap into learners' underlying linguistic competence (=implicit knowledge) (Ionin, 2012a). As we will see in section 1.2.5, this type of test instrument is argued to tap primarily into explicit knowledge, depending on how it is set up and administered. In more recent generative research, it has become increasingly common to use a variety of psycholinguistic methodologies which rely on reaction times rather than on grammaticality judgments in order to tap into what learners know at an implicit level (Marinis, 2003, 2010).

1.2.3 How Do Implicit and Explicit Knowledge Interact?

The fact that (most) adult L2 learners possess (some) explicit knowledge of their L2 grammar is uncontroversial; it is also uncontroversial that L2 learners are able to develop (some) implicit knowledge of the L2 grammar as well, at least at higher proficiency levels. A major source of debate in SLA is whether the two types of knowledge are interrelated, and whether explicit knowledge can ever become implicit knowledge. The literature on L2 learning traditionally distinguishes between three positions on the question of how implicit and explicit knowledge interface (R. Ellis, 2005; Williams, 2016): the strong interface position, the weak interface position, and the no interface (or noninterface) position. See Sharwood Smith and Truscott (2014) and Truscott and Sharwood Smith (2011) for attempts at modeling these distinctions.

On the **strong interface position** (DeKeyser, 1998; Sharwood Smith, 1981), explicit and implicit knowledge do interface: Explicit knowledge can become implicit, and vice-versa. For example, learners may at first learn a rule explicitly and subsequently internalize the rule at a more implicit level through practice. Different variants of the **weak interface position** (N. C. Ellis, 1994; R. Ellis, 1993; Pienemann, 1989) posit constraints on when explicit knowledge can become implicit, in terms of developmental readiness, and/or specify a particular role for explicit knowledge. Crucially, both strong and weak interface positions allow for explicit knowledge to become implicit (perhaps with some limitations, or under certain conditions). This in turn has clear implications for instruction: If explicit knowledge can become implicit, then it is reasonable for teachers to teach grammar explicitly and expect that the explicit knowledge that learners develop through instruction will eventually become implicit.

This is very different from what is expected under the **no interface position** (Krashen, 1981; Hulstijn, 2002), on which explicit knowledge does not turn into implicit knowledge, because the mechanisms underlying the two types of knowledge are distinct. On this view, the two types of knowledge are acquired or learned through different processes and are served by different regions of the brain (M. Paradis, 1994; Ullman, 2001). The no interface position is clearly articulated from the generative perspective in Schwartz (1993), who uses the terms "linguistic competence" for implicit knowledge, and "learned linguistic knowledge" for explicit knowledge. As discussed in section 1.1.5, on the generative approach to language acquisition, young children acquire their native language fully despite receiving no negative evidence: no information about what is ungrammatical in their native language. In contrast, as Schwartz (1993) notes, adult classroom learners get such negative evidence all the time, through explicit instruction about what is grammatical vs. ungrammatical in their L2, as well as through error correction. Yet unlike L1 acquiring children, adult L2 learners often fail to achieve full mastery of the L2. Schwartz argues that negative evidence can only influence learned, explicit knowledge, and cannot cause changes to learners' underlying linguistic competence, and that this is why explicit instruction and negative evidence do not result in L2 learners becoming fully target-like. Schwartz's argument is based in part on the findings from White's study on adverb placement (L. White, 1990, 1991), discussed in Chapter 4.

Ultimately, the question of whether explicit knowledge can become implicit is an empirical one. In order to definitively answer this question, research needs to look at whether learners who are taught explicitly develop only explicit knowledge, or implicit knowledge as well. In order to address this point, we first need to know both what constitutes explicit vs. implicit instruction and how to measure what learners know at more explicit vs. more implicit levels.

1.2.4 Implicit vs. Explicit Instruction and Feedback

There is a great variety of instructional approaches to grammar in the L2 (Savage, with Bitterlin, & Price, 2010; Loewen & Sato, 2017). On the extremes, we have purely communicative instruction that incorporates no grammar instruction whatsoever, vs. traditional grammar-focused instruction that involves explicit rule presentations and memorization drills. But there are also many in-between approaches which involve **focus on form** (Long, 1988), in which a grammatical focus is incorporated into communicative activities. As we will discuss in Chapter 2, this approach is distinct from traditional **focus on formS**, in that it ties form-based instruction with meaning-based activities, rather than focusing on forms in isolation. Some types of focus-on-form instruction involve **input enhancement** and **consciousness raising** (Rutherford, 1987; Sharwood Smith, 1991), in which learners' attention is directed towards particular grammatical properties. Another influential approach is **processing instruction** (VanPatten & Cadierno, 1993, and much subsequent work by

VanPatten and coauthors), in which learners complete structured input activities. We will discuss these and other types of grammar instruction in more depth in Chapter 2.

How do we determine whether a given instructional approach is explicit or implicit? According to R. Ellis (2008), in the case of implicit instruction, learners should not be consciously aware that they are being taught a particular grammatical structure: for example, their attention is focused on meaning instead of a specific grammatical form. On the other hand, explicit instruction does involve conscious awareness; indeed, the development of such awareness may be one of the goals of the instruction. Housen and Pierrard (2005) concentrate specifically on form-focused instruction, that is, instruction about grammatical forms, and lay out six criteria according to which explicit and implicit form-focused instruction differ. Table 1.4 is adapted from a table in Housen & Pierrard (2005).

It should be quite clear that not every instructional method will fall neatly into either the lefthand or the righthand column of this table. As we discuss specific intervention studies throughout this book, we will consider the extent to which the intervention is implicit vs. explicit. Meta-analyses (that is, studies that bring together and review multiple prior studies on the topic) generally show that explicit instruction is more effective than implicit instruction (Spada & Tomita, 2010; Goo et al., 2015). However, a critique that has been leveled at this type of finding is that the measures of learners' knowledge in many studies favor explicit knowledge (Andringa, de Glopper, & Hacquebord, 2011; Andringa, 2020). Thus, it is quite possible that explicit instruction is more effective than implicit instruction in helping learners gain explicit knowledge, but that does not necessarily mean that they gain implicit knowledge as well. Another important point is that implicit knowledge may take longer to develop than explicit knowledge (Hulstijn, 2015). Thus,

Table 1.4 Differences between implicit and explicit form-focused instruction (FFI) (adapted from Housen & Pierrard, 2005, p. 10)

Implicit form-focused instruction	Explicit form-focused instruction
Attention attracted to the target form	Attention directed to the target form
Spontaneous instructional delivery	Planned instructional delivery
Does not interrupt (or minimally interrupts) communication	Does interrupt communication
Forms presented in context	Forms presented in isolation
No metalanguage	Use of metalanguage
Free use of target form is encouraged	Target form is subject to controlled practice

an intervention that spans only days or weeks may not be long enough to lead to gains in implicit knowledge.

In addition to providing learners with input about the target language, teachers also react to learners' output; such reactions often take the form of **corrective feedback**. The implicit/explicit distinction is relevant here as well. Implicit corrective feedback, unlike its explicit counterpart, does not directly inform the learner that they have made an error. Perhaps the most common (or at least most commonly studied) form of implicit feedback is recasts, which involves the instructor repeating the learner's utterance, but changing the nontarget form to the target one (Long, 2017). In contrast, explicit feedback directly informs the learner that an error has been made and may provide a correction and/or explain the rule; in the latter case, we are dealing with metalinguistic feedback (Lyster & Ranta, 1997).

For example, suppose that a learner produces a sentence such as *My dog like grapes*, omitting the third person singular -s on the verb. Implicit feedback in the form of a recast could be, *Isn't that interesting? Your dog likes grapes!* Explicit feedback in the form of error correction could be, *No, it should be "likes", not "like"*. Explicit metalinguistic feedback could be, *You need to put an '-s' suffix on "like" because you have a third person singular subject.* Explicit feedback clearly provides negative evidence (information about what is ungrammatical in the language). Implicit feedback, in contrast, may provide only positive evidence (information about what is grammatical: the recast is itself part of the positive evidence, or input, that the learner receives). Whether a recast also provides negative evidence depends on whether the learner recognizes that she is being corrected (Nicholas, Lightbown, & Spada, 2001).

As we will see throughout this book, many intervention studies compare different types of feedback and their effectiveness as an instructional tool.

1.2.5 Measuring Implicit vs. Explicit Knowledge and Learning

One of the questions that we will address throughout this book is the degree to which interventions lead to learners gaining explicit or implicit knowledge. We should not simply assume that learners who are taught with an explicit instructional method will gain explicit knowledge, and that learners who are taught with an implicit instructional method will gain implicit knowledge. It has been noted across several studies that adults who are taught an artificial language implicitly nevertheless gain some explicit knowledge, such as awareness of the rules that they were not explicitly taught (DeKeyser, 1995; Morgan-Short, 2007; Lichtman, 2016).

1.2.5.1 Operationalization of Explicit vs. Implicit Knowledge

In order to test the different interface positions discussed in section 1.2.3, as well as to establish the efficacy of different instructional methods, we need to know what kind of knowledge, if any, learners gained as a result of an intervention. This brings us to the final aspect of the explicit/implicit distinction: how to measure explicit vs. implicit knowledge.

Implicit and explicit knowledge are abstract concepts; before they can be measured, they need to be operationalized: **Operationalization** refers to turning abstract concepts into measurable constructs. For example, one could operationalize explicit knowledge in terms of an ability to explain an error using **metalanguage** (that is, language about language). If a learner is able to judge sentences like *I saw two cats* as grammatical but *I saw two cat* as ungrammatical, and furthermore, to explain *why* the latter is ungrammatical, the learner has explicit knowledge of English plural marking. And one might operationalize implicit knowledge in terms of naturalistic production. If a learner correctly supplies plural *-s* when referring to multiple entities in a conversation, the learner has implicit knowledge of English plural marking.

The influential study by R. Ellis (2005) set out to examine which tasks are more likely to target explicit vs. implicit knowledge. Ellis operationalized the two types of knowledge as involving seven different characteristics, six of which can be manipulated by means of different experimental manipulations. These were degree of awareness, time available, focus of attention, systematicity, certainty, and metalinguistic knowledge (the seventh characteristic had to do with learners' age, and is not relevant for our purposes). Systematicity and certainty can be investigated by looking at learners' responses: the degree to which the responses are systematic, and learners' indications about how confident they are in their responses. The other four characteristics can instead be investigated by constructing a variety of tasks. According to Ellis's criteria, tasks that target explicit knowledge make the learners aware of the grammatical form (so that learners respond based on rules) and do not place learners under time pressure. Such tasks furthermore direct learners' attention to grammatical form, and involve the use of metalanguage. On the other hand, tasks that target implicit knowledge do not make learners aware of the grammatical form (so that learners respond by feel) and do not involve the use of metalanguage; they do place learners under time pressure and focus attention on meaning.

R. Ellis (2005) tested L2 English learners from a variety of L1s using five different tasks: oral imitation, oral narrative, timed and untimed **grammaticality judgment tasks** (GJTs), and a metalinguistic knowledge task. All five

Table 1.5 Design features of four different test instruments (adapted from R. Ellis, 2005, p. 157)

	Imitation task	Oral narration task	Timed GJT	Untimed GJT	Metalanguage test
Awareness	Feel	Feel	Feel	Rule	Rule
Time pressure	Yes	Yes	Yes	No	No
Attention focused on	Meaning	Meaning	Form	Form	Form
Involvement of metalinguistic knowledge	No	No	No	Yes	Yes

tasks tested the same syntactic and morphological phenomena. Table 1.5, adapted from R. Ellis (2005), shows how each task behaves on the four relevant characteristics. The two oral tasks meet all the criteria for tasks that target implicit knowledge; the untimed GJT and the metalinguistic task meet all the criteria for tasks that target explicit knowledge; the timed GJT falls in between.

The learners' performance in Ellis's study largely supported the division in Table 1.5. A statistical technique known as principal component factor analysis provided evidence that the five tests tested two different constructs. The two oral tasks and the timed GJT largely loaded (or clustered together) on one factor, while the untimed GJT and the metalinguistic knowledge task loaded (or clustered together) on the other. Ellis interpreted these results as indicating that the first three tasks targeted primarily implicit knowledge, and the last two targeted primarily explicit knowledge. The oral imitation task and the metalinguistic knowledge test were found to be the best measures of implicit and explicit knowledge, respectively.

1.2.5.2 More on Measuring Implicit vs. Explicit Knowledge

Ellis's study set the stage for continued investigations into which tasks target primarily implicit vs. primarily explicit knowledge. Ellis's findings were largely replicated with different populations by Bowles (2011) and Zhang (2015). Godfroid et al. (2015) replicated Ellis's findings concerning timed vs. untimed GJTs. This study provided further evidence, using **eye-tracking** methodology, that timed and untimed GJTs tap into different constructs, which may correspond to implicit and explicit knowledge, respectively. Spada, Shiu, and Tomita (2015) confirmed that elicited imitation targets implicit knowledge, as proposed by R. Ellis (2005).

Other research studies, however, have made more fine-grained distinctions in the types of knowledge that experimental tasks may be testing. Suzuki and DeKeyser (2015) made a distinction between truly implicit knowledge, truly explicit knowledge, and automatic explicit knowledge. This last type is very similar to implicit knowledge in function yet does not draw on the same mechanisms as implicit knowledge. Suzuki and DeKeyser (2015) argued that elicited oral imitation, which according to R. Ellis (2005) taps into implicit knowledge, in fact taps into automatized explicit knowledge. Their findings with L2 Japanese learners showed that performance on elicited imitation correlated with metalinguistic knowledge. In contrast, performance on a word-monitoring task (a task in which participants have to press a button every time they hear a particular word) instead correlated (among advanced learners only) with a nonlinguistic task designed to measure aptitude for implicit learning. Suzuki and DeKeyser (2015) concluded that while word monitoring taps into truly implicit knowledge, elicited imitation taps into automatized explicit knowledge instead.

Other work by Suzuki and colleagues challenged Ellis's conclusion that timed GJTs tap into implicit knowledge. Suzuki (2017) used six different grammar tasks with a large sample of L1 Chinese L2 Japanese learners. These included three time-pressured judgment tasks (both visual and auditory timed GJTs, and a timed fill-in-the-blanks test) and three online, psycholinguistic tasks (**self-paced reading**, word monitoring, and a visual-world task with eye tracking). In word monitoring, participants keep track of a particular word while listening to a mixture of grammatical and ungrammatical sentences. If learners are able to detect ungrammaticality, this should be reflected in a slowdown in their word monitoring response. This task is considered implicit because learners are not asked to detect ungrammaticality but instead have their attention focused on word monitoring and comprehension. The self-paced reading task follows a similar logic: Learners read sentences word by word and answer comprehension questions about them. Some of these sentences are ungrammatical, and if learners are able to detect the ungrammaticality, they slow down (see also Jegerski, 2014). Finally, in the visual world paradigm, learners listen to sentences and look at pictures while a camera tracks their eye movements to determine whether they look at the correct picture (e.g., the picture of the agent).

Suzuki (2017) found that the three online tasks tested a different construct than the three time-pressured judgment tasks, and concluded that the online tasks targeted implicit knowledge, while the timed judgment tasks targeted automatized explicit knowledge. The same conclusion was reached by Vafaee, Suzuki, and Kachisnke (2017). However, R. Ellis and Roever (2021) point out that performance on the three online tasks correlated only weakly in Suzuki (2017), which undermines the conclusion that all three tasks target implicit knowledge. R. Ellis & Roever (2021) further argue that such psycholinguistic tasks include quite artificial procedures and thus may not be valid tests of language knowledge.

In sum, there is still quite a bit of debate about which tasks most successfully tap into implicit knowledge, and whether it is possible to separate out implicit knowledge from automatized explicit knowledge. As discussed by R. Ellis and Roever (2021), any test of language comprehension or production will potentially tap into both types of knowledge, but certain task characteristics increase the likelihood that implicit knowledge is being targeted. These include use of the aural modality, time pressure, and focus on production or comprehension instead of judgments. Fully distinguishing between implicit and automatized explicit knowledge may not ultimately prove possible.

1.2.5.3 Measuring Implicit vs. Explicit Learning

While there are many studies that focus on measuring explicit vs. implicit knowledge, rather less is known about the process by which such knowledge is attained. One approach to examining explicit vs. implicit learning employs subjective measures of awareness, that is, of whether learners are aware of the grammatical rules (see Rebuschat, 2013, Maie & DeKeyser, 2020 for overviews).

In a recent study on the relationship between awareness and learning, Andringa (2020) taught participants a miniature language based on Esperanto, in which (following Williams, 2005) nouns were preceded by determiners that encoded both animacy and distance. In the test phase, participants' eye movements were recorded as they looked at pictures, in order to examine whether they could use the determiner to predict an upcoming noun. For example, consider the following two conditions: In one condition, participants see pictures of a nearby pig and a faraway cat; in another condition, both the pig and the cat are near. If participants hear a determiner that marks near objects, it is predictive in the first condition (informing participants that they should look at the nearby pig), but not in the latter (where both objects are near). The participants in Andringa's study were not instructed about the meaning of determiners, and learning was therefore **incidental**, arising through exposure to multiple examples.

Andringa (2020) examined the relationship between learning and awareness by asking participants after the experiment whether they had tried to predict the picture and, if so, how. About a third of the participants in the study developed awareness of the meaning of the determiner. The aware learners but not the unaware ones showed some evidence of learning, as measured by eye movements towards the target object on the basis of the determiner. Thus, in this study, no implicit learning (learning without awareness) seemed to have taken place.

As another example, consider Lichtman (2016), a study which taught children and adults about gender marking in an artificial mini-language. Half of the participants were taught implicitly (through presentation of sentences in the context of animations), while half were explicitly taught grammatical rules. All participants completed a **debriefing questionnaire** that allowed Lichtman to determine whether they noticed and/or understood the target structure. Not surprisingly, all the adults and most of the children who were explicitly taught the rules showed understanding of the rules. Interestingly, about a third of the adults who were taught implicitly still showed evidence of understanding the rules, and the rest at least noticed the rules. In contrast, none of the children who were taught implicitly showed evidence of understanding, and only about a third showed evidence of noticing. This study thus found that adults may learn explicit rules even when taught implicitly, which is not the case for children.

1.2.6 The Explicit vs. Implicit Distinction in Intervention Research

Throughout this book, we will discuss intervention studies that target a variety of grammatical phenomena. When we discuss the nature of the intervention, we will address the question of whether it involves primarily explicit or primarily implicit instruction and/or feedback. When we discuss the tests (pretests and posttests) that are used to measure what learners know before and after the intervention, we will note whether the tests are designed to target primarily implicit or primarily explicit knowledge. We will see that some studies manipulate the nature of the instruction as explicit vs. implicit, while others manipulate the tests in order to get measures of both explicit and implicit knowledge. Lichtman (2016), discussed above, is an example of a study that did both. Many other intervention studies do not set out to manipulate or test the explicit/implicit distinction but are instead concerned with the efficacy of a particular pedagogical method or with applying linguistic theory to classroom research. Nevertheless, even for studies that do not focus on the explicit/implicit divide, it is important to consider whether the knowledge that the learners gain is primarily explicit or implicit, and whether this knowledge resulted from largely explicit or largely implicit instruction.

1.3 What's Next?

In this chapter, we have discussed the ingredients of language acquisition, different types of learner populations, and different types of knowledge, learning, and instruction. The rest of this book goes over specific examples of classroom and lab-based intervention research studies across different grammatical phenomena. But before we do so, in the next chapter, we will cover different instructional approaches, as well as lay out the components of a typical intervention study.

1.4 DISCUSSION QUESTIONS

1. Compare and contrast the acquisition of the native language by children and the acquisition of a second language by adults with respect to access to positive evidence, access to negative evidence, and the role of age (critical period vs. age effects).
2. How does the dominant language affect the acquisition of the L2 in L2 learners and of the heritage language in heritage language learners? Do you think that both groups would benefit from instruction in the classroom? Think of a language pair that you are familiar with and specify which one is the dominant language and which one is the target language to be learned; assuming that the learners' target language is influenced by properties of their dominant language, consider which properties of target language it would be particularly beneficial to address in instruction.
3. Consider the following three adult populations: adult monolingual native speakers of a language; adult heritage speakers of the same language; and adult second language learners of the same language. For each population, do you expect the individuals to possess primarily explicit knowledge of the language, primarily implicit knowledge of the language, or both to about the same extent? What are your expectations based on? What else might it be helpful to know about these populations that would allow you to give a more definitive answer?
4. Choose three task properties that make a task more likely to target implicit rather than explicit knowledge. For each one, discuss *why* you think it makes a task more likely to tap into implicit knowledge.

1.5 FURTHER READING

- Ellis, R., & Roever, C. (2021). The measurement of implicit and explicit knowledge. *The Language Learning Journal, 49*(2), 160–175.
  This paper defines the criteria for explicit vs. implicit knowledge, and reviews research on the measurement of the two types of knowledge through a variety of task types.

- Montrul, S. (2016a). *The acquisition of heritage languages.* Cambridge, UK: Cambridge University Press.

  This book provides an overview of heritage languages around the world and how they are acquired. Particularly recommended are chapter 2, which defines and illustrates the concept of "heritage language" and "heritage speaker"; chapter 3, which discusses the typical properties of heritage speakers' linguistic skills; and chapter 8, which compares heritage speakers and second language learners.

- Paradis, M. (2009). *Declarative and procedural determinants of second languages.* Amsterdam: John Benjamins.

  This book discusses the contributions of declarative and procedural memory to the representation and processing of a second language. Particularly recommended is chapter 1, which sets out the key concepts within the neurolinguistic theory of bilingualism.

- Polinsky, M. (2018). *Heritage languages and their speakers.* Cambridge, UK: Cambridge University Press.

  This book provides an overview of heritage languages across all linguistic domains. Particularly recommended are chapter 1, which provides an introduction to heritage speakers and their linguistic knowledge, and chapter 3, on methodological approaches to studying heritage languages.

2 Intervention Research and Grammar Teaching

In the previous chapter we discussed the different contexts in which a second language or a heritage language is acquired, and we addressed the question of the kinds of knowledge (explicit vs. implicit) that learners might acquire. We now move on to the relationship between **second language acquisition (SLA)** and classroom instruction. We will first go over components of an intervention study, while in the second part we will provide a brief overview of approaches to grammar teaching. After studying this chapter, students with no prior experience in intervention research should be ready to evaluate the specific intervention research studies discussed later in the book.

2.1 Introduction to Classroom and Lab-Based Intervention Research

Classroom research on language learning comes in a great variety of forms (Loewen & Philp, 2012). These include **observational studies**, in which researchers observe what is happening in a classroom, and do not intervene or manipulate the instruction in any way; **noninterventionist studies**, in which researchers measure the performance of students in a particular type of instructional setting but without manipulating the nature of the instruction; **intervention studies**, in which researchers do manipulate the nature of instruction, input, and/or feedback; and **action research**, in which the teachers themselves are the researchers and conduct the study in order to address a specific question or issue in their classroom (see, for example, Redmond, 2013). Unlike the other types of classroom research, action research does not have as its goal the formulation of generalizations.

Of all these methods, we focus exclusively on **intervention** research studies in this textbook. In such studies, some aspects of the instructional/learning context are manipulated, and students' performance is (typically) measured both before and after the intervention, as discussed in more detail below. Furthermore, as discussed in Chapter 1, we focus specifically on intervention studies that address morphosyntactic and semantic knowledge and learning. Thus, we leave aside intervention studies on phenomena such as vocabulary, discourse, and interaction. See Loewen and Sato (2017) for in-depth discussion on all of these areas in instructed second language acquisition.

Intervention studies are important because they directly test the efficacy of particular pedagogical approaches and provide evidence about what approaches are more rather than less likely to lead to successful outcomes. Teachers who wonder about how to improve their students' knowledge of such grammatical phenomena as English articles, Spanish gender marking, or word order in Russian (to take just a few examples) can turn to intervention studies, including the ones discussed in this book, to find out what techniques have proved most effective. In the rest of this section, we lay out the logic and the methodology of intervention studies.

2.1.1   Where to Start: Pedagogical vs. Theoretical Starting Points

A common starting point of intervention studies about grammar is a particular pedagogical approach. Researchers may be interested in finding out whether students learn better under a more implicit or explicit approach to grammar instruction (see also Chapter 1), whether a particular instructional framework is more effective than a different one (see section 2.2 for an overview of approaches to grammar teaching), whether some feedback types are more effective than others, and so on.

For example, the classic study of VanPatten and Cadierno (1993) (discussed in more detail in Chapter 8) takes as its starting point the question of whether **processing instruction** (PI; discussed in section 2.2.7) is more effective than **output-based instruction**. VanPatten and Cadierno examined a particular grammatical structure, the placement of object pronouns in Spanish. This structure was chosen because it is one in which overreliance on default word-order strategies results in incorrect interpretation, and the goal of PI is specifically to help learners override such default strategies. Thus, in this case, the choice of instructional approach drives the choice of linguistic structure, rather than the other way around. This is confirmed by the fact that the research questions posed in VanPatten and Cadierno (1993, p. 229) all make reference to the nature of learners' input processing and the efficacy of this particular instructional approach. The research questions do not mention the linguistic structure under consideration.

Another example of a pedagogical starting point in an intervention study is McDonough (2005), a study of question formation in English as a second language (ESL), discussed in more detail in Chapter 4. McDonough's research question (p. 83) is about whether negative feedback to the learners and modified output that results from this feedback both predict the development of question formation in ESL learners. Question formation was chosen because it is a linguistic phenomenon with well-defined developmental stages (based on prior studies). However, the focus of McDonough's study is on the relative contributions of negative feedback and modified output, rather than on a linguistic analysis of question formation.

While it is very common for intervention studies to start from pedagogically oriented research questions, other studies start from a theoretically oriented question instead. Perhaps the most often-cited example is White's research on verb–adverb placement (L. White, 1990, 1991), discussed in detail in Chapter 4. White's starting point was a particular linguistic analysis (Pollock, 1989) of verb–adverb ordering in English and French, framed in terms of different parameter settings in these two languages. Adopting this theoretical framework, White asked whether French-speaking pre-adolescent L2 learners of English would be able to successfully reset the parameter from the French to the English setting. Furthermore, she asked whether learners instructed on one linguistic construction (question formation) would gain knowledge of a different construction (adverb placement). The link between question formation and adverb placement is not something that would be obvious to a language teacher but follows naturally from the theoretical framework adopted in White's study (see Chapter 4 for more discussion). In this case, the choice of linguistic structure is primary: The focus of the study is specifically on the learnability of this structure. Other examples of studies that begin with a linguistic framework rather than a pedagogical approach are several recent studies on articles in L2 English (e.g., Lopez, 2019; Umeda et al., 2019). These studies set out to teach learners about the meaning of English articles using theoretically informed definitions of such concepts as specificity and genericity (see Chapter 3 for the details). For more discussion of the relationship between linguistic theory, generative SLA research, and classroom instruction, see Whong, Gil, and Marsden (2013) and the special issue of *Language Teaching Research*, 23(2), 2019.

Finally, some studies take both theoretical and pedagogical considerations as their starting point. Examples of this are Carroll and Swain (1993), a study on the English double object construction, discussed in more detail in Chapter 8, and the studies on the subjunctive discussed in Chapter 6. On the pedagogical side, Carroll and Swain were interested in which type of feedback (implicit vs. explicit vs. metalinguistic – see Chapter 1) was most effective for learning. On the theoretical side, Carroll and Swain asked whether L2-English learners could successfully learn the constraints on the English double object alternations. Thus, the study was informed by syntactic theories of morphological and semantic constraints on this construction. J. F. Lee and Benati (2007), discussed in Chapter 6, investigated the acquisition of the subjunctive in Italian and in French. Their main goal was to compare the effects of PI and modified output instruction in improving accuracy with the interpretation and production of the subjunctive.

All the above approaches are equally valid. Any given intervention study about grammar may set out to test the efficacy of a particular instructional approach, to ask learnability questions based on linguistic theory, to develop an instructional approach based on theoretical considerations, or to do some mixture of the above. In this book, we cover both more pedagogically oriented and more theoretically oriented intervention studies, as long as they focus on particular grammatical constructions.

2.1.2 The Learning Environment: Foreign Language vs. Immersive

A distinction that is very important for instruction, but sometimes glossed over in research studies, is that between learners in a foreign language setting vs. learners who are residing in the country where the **target language** (TL) is widely spoken. Traditionally, this distinction is often referred to as one between "foreign language" and "second language" learners. We find this distinction to be imprecise; after all, a foreign language being learned in one's country of origin is also often the learners' second language. We prefer to distinguish between **foreign-language settings** and what we term **immersive settings**, to emphasize the nature of the TL exposure. In a foreign language setting, there is uniformity of exposure to the TL, which is likely to be largely limited to the classroom (although learners may also receive exposure to the TL through the media or through interactions with speakers of the TL). Additionally, the foreign language environment, such as students in Korea learning English in the classroom, is generally characterized by greater uniformity. The learners are not only all learning the same TL (e.g., English) but also are likely to share the same native language (e.g., Korean). This means that the students are likely to communicate among themselves in their native language, rather than in the TL. This said, in multilingual societies, the learners may not all share the same native language. For example, learners in a college Russian classroom in the United States may certainly include many native English speakers but also speakers of other languages with varying levels of English proficiency, as well as speakers fully bilingual in English and another language.

In an immersive setting, there is much variability in both the native languages and the exposure situations of learners. Learners may be immersed in the TL through a variety of experiences, including the following: They may be immigrants to a country where the L2 is widely spoken. They may be classroom learners who are experiencing study abroad. Or they may be early bilingual heritage speakers (see Chapter 1) who are exposed to the TL primarily at home through their family. Most intervention studies, by virtue of testing classroom learners, include only those immersed learners who are also studying the TL in the classroom. Given the heterogeneity of the immersed speakers' L1 backgrounds, the students in such an environment (e.g., an ESL classroom in the United States) are more likely to interact with each other in the TL. As a result, such students provide an additional source of TL input for each other.

Another potential source of difference between a foreign-language and an immersive context has to do with native-speaker status of the teacher. In a foreign-language context, the classroom teachers providing the input to learners may be nonnative speakers of the TL themselves. In an immersive context, where the TL is the language of the society, the teachers are more likely to be native speakers of the TL. Of course, there are exceptions in both directions. For example, in the United States, there are many nonnative English speakers working as ESL instructors. Conversely, some countries (Japan and Korea, most notably) often require English as a Foreign Language (EFL) teachers to be native English speakers. While ideologically there has long been a native-speaker bias with regard to language teachers, research does not support there being a need for language teachers to be native speakers. In fact, being proficient in the TL is quite sufficient (see Calafato, 2019). Nevertheless, sometimes researchers consider it to be important to control for the status of teachers as native or nonnative speakers. As an example, consider L. White (1991), a study of adverb placement in the L2 English of French speakers discussed in Chapter 4. All teachers taking part in the study were native speakers of English, because, according to L. White (1991, p. 141), ESL teachers who are native speakers of French could potentially make errors with English adverb placement themselves, thus providing misleading input to the learners.

The many sources of variability among learners lie beyond the scope of this book (for more information, see section V on individual differences in instructed SLA in Loewen and Sato, 2017). What matters for our purposes are specific differences among intervention studies conducted in a foreign-language vs. an immersive setting. Studies conducted in a foreign-language setting, where learners typically share the same L1, often provide the instruction and teaching materials in the learners' native language to facilitate understanding. For example, VanPatten, Collopy, and Qualin (2012), a study with English-speaking L2 learners of Russian at a US university, presented the instructional materials in English. Similarly, Umeda et al. (2019), a study with Japanese learners of English in Japan, presented the instruction in Japanese. In contrast, intervention studies conducted in the country of the TL typically use the TL (e.g., English in the United States) for the intervention.

There is another important consideration that is particularly relevant for studies conducted with immersed learners, and especially studies that take more than a few days. The consideration is that the study participants are receiving exposure to the TL, and quite possibly to the target structure, outside of the classroom. This is why it is particularly important for such studies to have a control group in order to tease apart the effects of overall exposure from those of instruction (see section 2.1.4).

2.1.3 Components of Intervention Research Studies

A typical intervention study has the following components: a **pretest**, the **intervention** itself, and one or more **posttests**, as illustrated in Figure 2.1.

The pretest examines the state of the learners' grammatical knowledge prior to the intervention, also known as **baseline knowledge**. The posttests measure learners' knowledge after the intervention, to examine whether the intervention has been effective compared to the baseline. In studies with more than one posttest, the immediate posttest, administered shortly after the end of the intervention, examines what knowledge was gained during the intervention, again, compared to the baseline. A delayed posttest or posttests may be administered days, weeks, months, or in some cases, even one or two years after the intervention, to examine whether the knowledge has been retained. Some researchers (e.g., Schwartz & Gubala-Ryzak, 1992, in a critique of the study by L. White, 1990, 1991) argue that the knowledge demonstrated immediately after the intervention (in the immediate posttest) is "explicitly acquired knowledge," which has not necessarily been internalized. In contrast, knowledge still retained months or years later is much more likely to be internalized, implicit knowledge (see Chapter 1 for more discussion of the implicit vs. explicit knowledge divide).

The pretests and posttests are linguistic tasks that can take a variety of forms. Depending on the study, the tests can involve oral or written picture descriptions, **grammaticality judgment tasks** (GJTs), fill-in-the-blank tests,

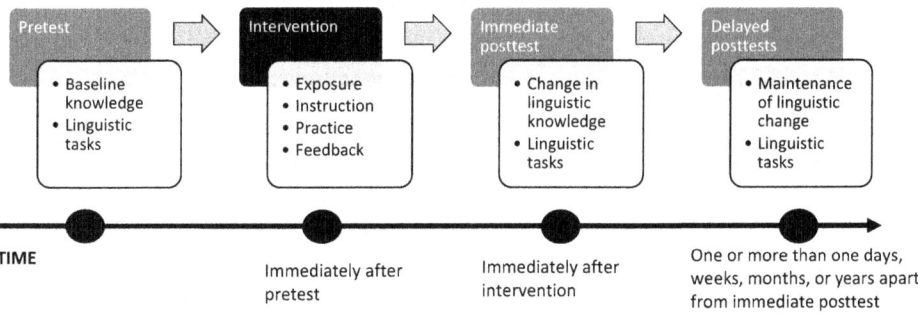

Figure 2.1 Components of intervention research

eye-tracking tasks, and much else. The pretest serves at least two purposes. One is to provide a baseline to the posttest, in order to establish whether improvement from pretest to posttest did take place. The second is to provide a comparison across the multiple groups tested in the study, to ensure that they begin with the same level of knowledge. As discussed in Mackey (2017), some studies dispense with the pretest and use a posttest-only design. For example, this might be done when it is crucial to keep participants from knowing anything about the nature of the study. Mackey notes that in such situations, comparability across multiple groups can be established by some other means, such as a background questionnaire. Plonsky (2013), an assessment study of quantitative studies in SLA published between 1990 and 2010 in two major journals (*Studies in Second Language Acquisition* and *Language Learning*), found that out of 172 **(quasi-)experimental** studies, only 67 percent included a pretest. The question remains, however, how one can measure improvement as a result of the intervention in the absence of a pretest. For example, if participants score 70% correct on a posttest, we do not know whether they improved from 0% correct, or from 30% correct, or showed no improvement at all.

One situation in which having a posttest but no pretest is fully acceptable is when the participants have no knowledge of the TL, or at least of the relevant linguistic structure, prior to the intervention. This is the case, for example, for instruction on artificial mini-languages (see section 2.1.5). Interaction studies (e.g., Egi, 2007) also typically do not include pretests, since researchers do not know in advance which linguistic properties will arise during the interactions. We largely leave interaction studies aside in this book.

Finally, another component that some intervention studies include is a **debriefing questionnaire**, administered at the very end of the study. These questionnaires, while not very commonly used, can be very helpful to the researchers in establishing what knowledge participants gained during the study. Such questionnaires can also inform researchers as to whether participants used any outside sources when completing the study tasks (which can potentially undermine the validity of the study). Debriefing questionnaires are often used in studies that examine whether learners have gained explicit or implicit knowledge (e.g., Rebuschat & Williams, 2012a; Lichtman, 2016; Issa & Morgan-Short, 2019; see the discussion of explicit vs. implicit knowledge in Chapter 1). By asking learners whether they found any regularities, discovered rules, and so on, the researchers can more definitively establish whether learners gained explicit knowledge. For example, as discussed in Chapter 1, Lichtman (2016), an artificial-language study, taught both child and adult participants under either explicit or implicit instructional conditions. The debriefing questionnaire results indicated that some adults gained explicit knowledge (i.e., discovered grammar rules) even when taught implicitly, whereas children only discovered rules when taught explicitly.

2.1.4 Control-Group vs. Comparison-Group Design

Intervention studies can adopt either a **control-group** or a **comparison-group** design (see Mackey & Gass, 2022, section 6.5.2). The assessment study by Plonsky (2013), mentioned earlier, found that the vast majority (87 percent) of all studies reviewed had at least one control or comparison group. In a control-group design, one group (the **instructed group**, also known as the experimental group or the intervention group) receives the intervention while the other (the control group) does not, but both groups take the pretests and posttests. This design ensures that any improvement from pretest to posttest in the instructed group is indeed due to the intervention. If the control group improves as much as the experimental group, then the improvement is likely due to factors not related to the intervention itself, such as an effect of taking similar tests multiple times or a general learning effect over time. The latter is especially likely if the study spans weeks or months and participants are exposed to the TL outside of the intervention. In a sample study with a control group design, Toth and Guijarro-Fuentes (2013), described in more detail in Chapter 7, the instructed group received communicative explicit instruction on the Spanish clitic *se*. The control group received no such instruction, but both groups completed the pre/posttests.

An alternative to the control-group design is a comparison-group design, in which different groups receive different interventions. For example, the study by VanPatten, Collopy, and Qualin (2012) on Russian word order had two groups receiving two different kinds of interventions. Both groups received PI (see section 2.2.7), but one of the groups additionally received explicit information about Russian word order. This allowed the researchers to assess whether adding explicit information to PI affected the outcome (see Chapter 9 for more discussion).

It is quite common for studies that include three or more groups to combine the control-group and comparison-group designs. On the one hand, two (or three or four, etc.) groups receive different kinds of interventions, serving as comparison groups to one another. On the other hand, there is also a third (or fourth or fifth, etc.) group that receives no intervention, serving as the control group. For example, the study of English double objects by Carroll and Swain (1993) (discussed in Chapter 8) included five different groups of learners: While four of the groups received four different kinds of feedback, the fifth group was the control group which received no feedback or other intervention.

One decision that must be made with any design that includes a control group is what the control group should be doing while the instructed group or groups receive the intervention. In some studies, the control group simply does nothing. For example, if the study takes place in the lab and members of the instructed group come into the lab to complete the intervention (see also the next subsection), then members of the control group simply do not come in. In such a design, it is important to ensure that the time that elapses between the pretest and the immediate posttest (as well as between the immediate and any delayed posttests) is the same in the control group as in the instructed group. This ensures that any improvement in the instructed group was not simply a function of the time elapsed. For example, Wu and Ionin (2022a), a study of quantifier scope discussed in Chapter 9, contained two instructed groups as well as a control group. All three groups completed the pretest and then, a week later, the instructed groups completed the intervention followed by the immediate posttest, while the control group completed the posttest only. All three groups completed the delayed posttest one month after the immediate posttest. Thus, the timeline was the same for all three groups, and the control group simply didn't take part in the intervention.

However, when the study is done in the classroom (see the next subsection), it is not feasible to have the control group simply "doing nothing." The class period or periods that are taken up by the intervention for the instructed group or groups must somehow be occupied for the control group. A common solution in such cases is to have the control group complete language study that does not include any focus on the grammatical structure of the intervention. This is also termed the "placebo treatment" by Long, Inagaki, and Ortega (1998). For example, Toth and Guijarro-Fuentes (2013), a study of Spanish *se* mentioned earlier, incorporated their intervention into high school students' Spanish classes. While the instructed group received instruction about *se* over three 90-minute lessons, the control group spent the same time period completing pen-pal writing activities with no grammatical focus. Thus, exposure to Spanish was kept constant across the two groups, but only one group was specifically instructed about the structure in question.

2.1.5 (Quasi-)Experimental Design

In intervention studies, as in experimental studies more generally, researchers manipulate some aspects of the experiment, known as **independent variables**. Such manipulations may affect assignment to groups (e.g., instructed vs. control groups, as discussed above), the types of measures (e.g., pretest vs. posttest), or specific categories of items within a test (e.g., grammatical vs. ungrammatical sentences that participants rate with regard to their grammatical acceptability). The researchers measure participants' performance in the study, and the measures correspond to the **dependent variables**: They are so called because, according to the research hypothesis, the measures *depend* on the experimental manipulation. For example, researchers might measure learners' accuracy in responding to the pretest vs. the posttest and examine whether accuracy improves as a result of the intervention. The independent variable in this case is the test (pretest vs. posttest) while accuracy is the dependent variable. For more discussion of **experimental design** and variable types, see, among others, Rasinger (2014) and Mackey and Gass (2022).

As introduced in the previous subsection, intervention studies can potentially take place in the lab or in the classroom. The two settings seem to be about equally common. The meta-analysis of Spada and Tomita (2010) reports on eighteen studies conducted in the classroom and sixteen in the lab; Plonsky (2013) reports on 55 percent of the 172 experimental studies assessed being in the lab and 45 percent in the classroom.

2.1.5.1 Study Design and Study Setting

The decision to conduct the study in a lab as opposed to in a classroom is also related to the distinction between experimental and quasi-experimental intervention studies (see also Mackey & Gass, 2022, section 6.5.2). In a lab-based experimental design, participants are tested individually or in small groups, coming into the lab to complete the study. This allows researchers to randomly assign participants to the different groups: For example, the first participant who comes in gets assigned to the instructed group, the second to the control group, and so on. An example of a study that practiced such **random assignment** is Long, Inagaki, and Ortega (1998) (see also Mackey & Gass, 2022, chapter 4, for more on random assignment). The group assignment may also be pseudo-random so that the researchers ensure that the two (or more) groups are fully comparable with regard to such factors as learners' age, gender, L1, status as a heritage vs. nonheritage speaker, and so on. This still corresponds to a fully experimental design. Plonsky (2013) found that about half (48 percent) of ninety-four studies placed in the lab used random assignment of individual participants.

Not surprisingly, random assignment of individuals to groups is much less common in studies placed in the classroom. Plonsky (2013) reports that only 23 percent of seventy-eight classroom-based studies had random assignment of participants. An alternative approach is to work with **intact classes**, as in the study by Toth and Guijarro-Fuentes (2013) discussed in the previous subsection. Rather than bringing participants into the lab and randomly assigning them to groups, researchers take advantage of natural groupings in the form of existing classes, with each class assigned to one of the experimental conditions (instructed group vs. control group, different comparison groups, etc.). In this design, random assignment is not possible, since students participate in whatever experimental condition their class was assigned to; this design is therefore known as quasi-experimental. It is still possible to randomly assign entire groups (classrooms) to particular experimental conditions (e.g., one class corresponds to the instructed group, another to the control group), as was done by Potowski, Jegerski, and Morgan-Short (2009), discussed in Chapter 6, but this is not common. Plonsky (2013) found that only 17 percent of classroom-based studies used random assignments of groups.

2.1.5.2 The Lab or the Classroom? (Dis)advantages of Different Study Settings

Both experimental and quasi-experimental designs have their advantages and disadvantages. Due to its lack of random assignment, the use of intact classrooms runs the risk of having unbalanced groups (e.g., a class of twenty compared to a class of thirty-five, or different combinations of ages, L1s, etc. in the classes). Such a design also runs the risk of **confounding variables,** that is, variables that are not being manipulated by the researchers but that may influence the results and make the results look right for the wrong reason. For example, students in different classes may differ in proficiency, or in L1 background. Or, students in an 8 a.m. class may be sleepier than those in a 10 a.m. class and therefore complete the pre/posttests with lower accuracy, thus skewing the results. If the classes are taught by different teachers, they may also have very different learning experiences that are independent of the nature of the intervention. To the extent possible, researchers should strive to avoid such confounding factors by selecting classes that are similar in size and student make-up, are taught by the same teacher, meet at the same or very similar times of day, etc. However, full researcher control over these variables is often simply not possible, especially in the case of a less commonly taught language or a particularly advanced class level, such that very few intact classes are available for the study.

Despite the potential confounds listed above, the intact-classroom design also has many advantages. Students are completing the tests and the intervention in a familiar classroom setting and may feel considerably more comfortable as well as motivated to perform well than students in a more artificial lab setting. If the research study is naturally integrated into the classroom, this is also likely to diminish the **Hawthorne Effect,** which refers to the effect of participants changing their behaviour due to being observed by the researchers (see Mackey, 2017 on the Hawthorne Effect in classroom research). On the practical side, it is often much easier for the researchers to recruit large numbers of participants by using intact classes than by depending on individual learners' willingness to come into the lab.

Researchers typically use the lab option if it is not feasible for practical reasons to conduct the study in a classroom, as well as to ensure random assignment. Another reason to run a study in the lab is if the intervention and/or the pre/posttests use psycholinguistic methods such as eye tracking, which can only be administered in a lab. Finally, intervention studies that, by definition, cannot use intact classrooms are artificial-language studies. In such studies (for examples, see Hudson Kam & Newport, 2005; Lichtman, 2016; Morgan-Short et al., 2015), participants are brought into the lab and taught a mini-language. The mini-language is either created from scratch by researchers or corresponds to a highly simplified version of a real language unfamiliar to the participants, such as Latin. Such studies typically aim to examine how participants learn under different kinds of conditions (explicit vs. implicit, with consistent vs. inconsistent input, etc.). An artificial mini-language gives the experimenters full control over learners' exposure to the language, and allows for direct and fast manipulation of the learning conditions. Since the focus of this textbook is on how learners acquire grammatical properties of real languages, we leave artificial mini-language studies aside. We do, however, review studies with real languages that manipulate the learning conditions in the lab, including priming studies of language production, such as Hurtado and Montrul (2021b), discussed in Chapter 8.

Finally, we note that studies that are classified as being in the "lab" as opposed to in the classroom may actually occur in another setting, such as the researcher's office. Some studies also place at least some components of the intervention online. During the global covid-19 pandemic, the remote testing format has been the only one available for many researchers. For example, Wu and Ionin (2022a), mentioned earlier, began the data collection in the lab but had to move it online as the pandemic hit, with the result that some of the data were collected remotely.

2.1.6 Timeline of Intervention Research Studies

Intervention studies vary greatly in length. The Spada and Tomita (2010) meta-analysis, appendix B, reports intervention lengths ranging from as little 0.17 hours to as long as eight hours (the latter presumably spread over several days or weeks). The mean intervention length is a little under or a little over three hours, depending on whether the study used explicit or implicit instruction, and targeted simple or complex structures.

An example of an extremely short intervention is the study of quantifier scope in Wu and Ionin (2022a), where learners completed a single 30-minute intervention with explicit instruction prior to taking the immediate posttest. Studies that use PI (see section 2.2.7) also tend to have fairly short interventions; for example, in the experiments reported in VanPatten et al. (2013), each experiment, including the intervention, took an hour or less.

Many studies take a day or a few days for the intervention: e.g., Loewen, Erlam, and Ellis (2009) provided instruction about the third person -*s* in English over two days, one hour per day. Some studies spend longer on the intervention: e.g., the studies on adverb placement by L. White (1990, 1991) had the intervention span a two-week period. Interventions longer than two weeks exist but are fairly uncommon. An example of a particularly long intervention is found in the Umeda et al. (2019) study on articles in L2 English. The intervention spanned a full eight weeks, but was divided into several discrete periods (three weeks for instruction on one property of English articles, three weeks on another, and two weeks of review - see Chapter 3 for more discussion).

The length of the intervention is often determined by practical considerations. Lab-based interventions which span weeks or months require participants to come in multiple times, and may therefore be subject to participant attrition. In studies with intact classrooms, it is rare for teachers to be able to allot more than one or two class periods for study participation, given the other material that needs to be covered. However, longer interventions are possible if the intervention tasks are assigned as homework. While students have to be in class regardless of whether they are participating in a study, attrition still occurs with intact classrooms. If students miss a class on which the pretest, posttest, or a component of the intervention takes place, this often results in their exclusion from the participant sample.

As pointed out by Mackey and Gass (2022), p. 201, if a long time elapses between the pretest and the posttest, participants may be gaining knowledge of the TL through daily exposure, making it difficult to measure the effects due specifically to the intervention. This is more of a concern in immersion than in foreign-language contexts (see section 2.1.2).

When there is clear evidence of learning even after a short intervention (with the instructed group or groups improving significantly more than the control group), this provides evidence that even a very short intervention can be effective. (A separate question is whether it leads to gains only in explicit knowledge, or also to changes in the underlying grammar - more on this below). However, a null result - the lack of significant improvement for the instructed group - is difficult to interpret. It could be due to the instructional method being ineffective in general, or to the study not having sufficient participants or observations to yield a statistically significant result, or to the intervention not lasting long enough for the method to have had an effect. In particular, as discussed in Chapter 1, implicit knowledge takes longer to develop than explicit knowledge (Hulstijn, 2015), so a short intervention may not succeed in helping learners gain implicit knowledge.

In addition to the length of the intervention, researchers also need to determine the timing of the posttests. An immediate posttest is a must in any intervention study, since without one, it is impossible to know whether the intervention had any effect. Most studies administer the immediate posttest shortly after the end of the intervention, either on the same day as the intervention, or within one to three days afterwards. (See Spada & Tomita, 2010, appendix B, for the specifics.) Delayed posttests, designed to test whether knowledge has been retained, are less common, for practical reasons (it can be difficult to bring participants back for testing weeks or months after the end of the study.) Spada and Tomita (2010, table 4) report on only seventeen studies out of the forty-one in their sample having a delayed posttest, and only four of them having a second delayed posttest. Plonsky (2013) reports on a delayed posttest being present in 38 percent of the 172 studies surveyed.

The time elapsing before the delayed posttest is commonly measured in weeks. It is an open question whether knowledge retained two or three weeks after the intervention will be retained long term, after additional months or years, and very few studies have addressed this question. A rare exception is L. White (1991), a study of adverb placement, which followed up the original intervention group a year after the intervention. Another example is the study by Trahey (1996) which followed up on Trahey and White (1993) by testing the participants from the original study a year later (both studies examined adverb placement in L2 English). See Chapter 4 for more details on both of these sets of studies.

While delayed posttests are relatively infrequent for logistical reasons, they are of great importance to the field of SLA, more so than immediate posttests since, ultimately, we need to know whether instruction can result in long-term effects.

2.1.7 Summary: The Logic of Intervention Research

In this section, we have laid out the typical components, timelines, and settings of intervention studies in language learning. Table 2.1 specifies which of those components are obligatory, optional, or desirable. While an ideal study will have every single component (including multiple posttests as well as control and/or comparison groups), the feasibility of including all of these components is subject to the resources and participants available to the

Table 2.1 Components of an intervention study

Component	Obligatory or optional?	When should it be used?
Pretest	Nearly always obligatory	In most intervention studies, with some exceptions (such as artificial-language studies and interaction research)
Immediate posttest	Obligatory	In any intervention study
First delayed posttest	Optional, but desirable	In any study interested in examining whether knowledge is retained over time
Second delayed posttest	Optional	In any study interested in looking at long-term effects
The intervention	Obligatory	By definition, in any intervention study
Instructed group	Obligatory	By definition, in any intervention study
Control group	Obligatory in a control group design; optional but desirable in a comparison group design	In any intervention study that needs to establish baseline knowledge in the absence of the intervention; recommended even for a comparison group design
Comparison groups	Optional	In any intervention study that compares two or more instructional approaches
Debriefing questionnaire	Optional	Can help establish validity of any intervention study, and especially important in studies that examine whether learners gain explicit or implicit knowledge

researchers. At a minimum, an intervention study should have two groups (the instructed and the control groups), a pretest, and an immediate posttest, as well as, naturally, the intervention itself.

Not every study discussed in this book contains every component in Table 2.1, but familiarity with what is meant by terms such as pretest, posttest, intact classrooms, and so on, is crucial for understanding information presented in the rest of the book. For studies that are discussed in some depth in the following chapters, we will always specify the nature of the pretests and posttests, the setting and length of the intervention, and the study timeline.

The rest of this chapter focuses on major approaches to grammar teaching, whose efficacy is tested the intervention studies described in later chapters.

2.2 Approaches to Grammar Teaching

Some intervention studies on grammar adopt a specific pedagogical approach and are designed to isolate the effects of a particular component of instruction; other studies test the efficacy of one instructional approach over another. In order to understand intervention studies that are conducted within a specific pedagogical approach, it is important to first present what the major approaches to L2 instruction are. In this section, we provide a brief overview of the major approaches to L2 classroom instruction. We do not provide in-depth coverage of the many different approaches to classroom instruction; the interested reader is referred to Loewen and Sato (2017) and the references cited therein. Rather, we focus first and foremost on those approaches that are adopted in some of the intervention studies discussed later in this book.

2.2.1 Naturalistic vs. Instructed Second Language Acquisition

Learners acquire their L2 in a great variety of circumstances. As already discussed in Chapter 1, learners may acquire the L2 naturalistically, in an instructed setting, or a mixture of both. Heritage speakers acquire their heritage language (which is also their L1, or one of their L1s) naturalistically at home, from family members. They may receive formal instruction in their heritage language later on, for example, through community schools, bilingual immersion programs (e.g., for Spanish in the United States) or mother-tongue instruction (in many European countries), or through high school or college foreign-language classes. Child L2 learners who are either children of immigrants or child immigrants themselves often acquire the L2 naturalistically from peers and through content instruction in the L2 at school. Depending on the child's age and situation, they may also receive targeted L2 instruction at school. Adult L2 learners in an immigrant setting commonly receive at least some formal instruction in the L2, prior to immigrating and/or after immigration. And both child and adult learners exposed to the L2 in a foreign-language context typically receive formal instruction in the L2.

Intervention studies are nearly always conducted with learners who are either learning the L2 in a classroom setting at the time of the study or who have received formal instruction prior to taking part in the study. Similarly, intervention studies with heritage speakers are typically done with heritage speakers who are enrolled in formal language classes (see Montrul & Bowles, 2010 for a sample study discussed in Chapter 8). In light of these considerations, we focus only on instructed learners in this book (see also Loewen & Sato, 2017 for more on instructed SLA). We acknowledge that generalizations based on studies with instructed learners may not necessarily generalize to naturalistic learners.

The great majority of intervention studies are conducted with adult rather than with child learners. To the extent that intervention studies examine child L2 learners, they are most typically adolescents of high school age; a few intervention studies look at preadolescents (e.g., L. White, 1990, 1991; Doughty & Varela, 1998). Inclusion of younger, elementary-school-age children in intervention studies is very uncommon. This is most likely due to foreign-language education in elementary school being less common than in secondary schools or universities, at least in some countries (but see Shintani & Ellis, 2010 for a study of young Japanese children learning English). Young children are, however, sometimes participants in artificial mini-language studies that are specifically designed to address how children vs. adults learn (Hudson Kam & Newport, 2005; Lichtman, 2016).

In the rest of this section, we examine grammar instruction methods typically used with adult learners, noting that some of those methods have also been used with adolescents.

2.2.2 Choices in Second Language Grammar Instruction

In a seminal article about choices in grammar teaching from an SLA perspective, R. Ellis (2006) makes the case that grammar does need to be taught. Contrary to Krashen (1981), who argued that grammar instruction makes no difference to acquisition, Ellis argues that grammar instruction does lead to acquisition (of implicit knowledge) as well as to learning (of explicit knowledge; see Chapter 1 for more discussion). Ellis also points out that teachers need to make many choices in grammar teaching, including which aspects of the grammar to teach, whether to teach grammar at the very beginning (to learners just starting to learn an L2) or to wait until learners reach higher proficiency, whether grammar instruction should be concentrated into a few lessons or spread over the entire semester or academic year of instruction, whether instruction should focus on a single grammatical property at a time or cover multiple properties or structures in one lesson, and whether grammar should be integrated with more communicative activities or taught separately from such activities. The answers to these questions depend on many factors, including the goals of the students and the teachers, as well as the time and resources at the teacher's disposal. Curricular choices made at the level of the program or otherwise outside the teacher's purview may impact the nature of the instruction as well.

Researchers in SLA generally agree that the ultimate goal of the acquisition process is for learners to gain implicit knowledge, or linguistic competence, in the TL. R. Ellis (2006) addresses the question of whether there is any value in teaching explicit grammatical knowledge. As discussed in Chapter 1, there are different positions in the field of SLA about the extent to which explicit knowledge can become implicit. On the **weak interface** and **strong interface positions**, there is value in teaching explicit knowledge in such a way that the explicit knowledge becomes internalized, and/ or leads learners to attend to particular grammatical features (see R. Ellis, 2006 for more discussion). We note additionally that there are situations when explicit knowledge is precisely what learners need to gain, independently of whether they also need to gain implicit knowledge. For example, if learners are preparing to take a standardized test in the L2, explicit and metalinguistic knowledge can be just as necessary as implicit knowledge. This said, however, the common approaches to L2 instruction discussed in this section ultimately aim to have learners gain implicit grammatical knowledge. To the extent that explicit instruction takes place, it is with the goal of the explicit knowledge gained by learners eventually being converted into implicit knowledge.

2.2.3 Content-Based Language Teaching

Lyster (2017) discusses **Content-based language teaching** (CBLT), which occurs when learners in an immersion program are taught content classes, such as science, in the TL. For example, the French-speaking learners of English in L. White (1990, 1991) were part of such an immersion program for English. In Europe, similar programs are known as **Content and language integrated learning** (CLIL) program (see, e.g., García Mayo & Lázaro Ibarrola, 2015). CBLT/CLIL generally does not involve actual grammar teaching (since the focus is on teaching content material rather than on teaching grammar). As discussed in Lyster (2017), CBLT programs often unintentionally result in learners receiving restricted input, for example, verbs primarily in the present tense or the imperative, to the exclusion of other tenses and moods.

One way in which content-based instruction can teach learners about grammar is through feedback, both explicit correction and recasts. (See Chapter 1 on more about different types of feedback.) However, studies have found that teachers in CBLT also provide feedback (such as repetitions and recasts) not intended to correct grammar (e.g., Lyster, 1998), so it is not clear how beneficial feedback is for grammar learning.

Lyster (2017), building on Lyster (2007), proposed a proactive approach to CBLT, in which content-based activities lead students to notice linguistic features, through such approaches as **input flooding** and **input enhancement**, discussed in later subsections. Lyster (2017, p. 99) notes that seven quasi-experimental intervention studies that incorporated form-focused activities into French-immersion classrooms led to improvements in students' proficiency.

2.2.4 Traditional Focus on FormS Instruction

Throughout history, many approaches to grammar teaching have focused on grammatical forms, with the teaching of grammatical rules and language forms largely divorced from communication. These approaches are sometimes grouped under the heading **focus on formS**, (with a capital -S), to distinguish them from the **focus on form** approach (Long, 1988), which addresses grammatical forms in the context of communication (see section 2.2.6).

Here, we briefly review some well-known focus on formS approaches. (For more discussion, see the papers in Richards & Rodgers, 2001.) The grammar-translation method, which goes back at least to the nineteenth century, teaches grammar rules explicitly, relies on translations between the learners' L1 and their L2, and focuses on reading. This method is still commonly used today in many East Asian countries, where the focus is on preparation for English exams (Butler, 2017). The audiolingual method, popular in the 1950s and beyond, used drills and rote rule learning, while under the cognitive approach of the 1970s, learners were taught about grammar rules. While these methods are vastly different, what they have in common is that grammatical forms are taught largely in isolation, through such techniques as translation, mechanical drills, and repetition for memorization. In such approaches, the focus is primarily on accuracy rather than fluency. Research has suggested that teaching forms in isolation is not as effective as integrating grammatical forms with meaning and communication. (See Nassaji, 2017 for a recent overview.)

2.2.5 Communicative Language Teaching

Communicative language teaching (CLT) arose in the 1970s (see, e.g., Brumfilt, 1984). Unlike traditional approaches to language teaching in vogue at the time, CLT placed the focus of the instruction primarily on communicating for meaning. Since the term first came into being, a large variety of approaches all grouped under the heading of CLT have emerged, as discussed by Spada (2007) and R. Ellis (2017). While early versions of CLT focused quite heavily on fluency, later variants used communicative tasks in order for learners to practice particular linguistic structures, under the presentation-practice-production (PPP) approach.

There is evidence that purely communicative instruction without any focus on grammatical forms is not very effective for improving learners' grammatical accuracy. For example, Harley et al., (1990) found that immersion education that focuses entirely on meaning does not lead to grammatical accuracy. More recently, Lyster (2004b) found that integrating form-focused instruction into immersion programs in Canada led to improvement with regard to grammatical accuracy. Given that all the intervention studies discussed in this book include at least some degree of form-focused instruction, as opposed to purely communicative instruction, we do not discuss the CLT approach any further.

In the remainder of this chapter, we consider several approaches to integrating grammatical form with meaning-based instruction. Some of these approaches focus on changing learners' output, while others manipulate the input to the learners; some use more explicit and others more implicit instructional techniques. While there are a variety of different grammar instruction approaches in use today, we focus on those that are used most commonly in the studies reviewed in this book.

2.2.6 Focus on Form Approaches

There are many different approaches to grammar teaching which focus on grammatical form, as opposed to only meaning and communication. Traditional focus on formS instruction focused on form to the exclusion of meaning or communication, with explicit presentation of rules followed by practice drills (see section 2.2.4). In contrast, modern-day approaches, starting in the 1980s and 1990s, strive to incorporate focus on form into communicative lessons, as illustrated in Figure 2.2 (see Loewen, 2014, chapter 4, and Doughty & Williams, 1998 for overviews).

Many of these approaches focus on output, that is, the linguistic productions of the learners (e.g., Swain's Output Hypothesis, Swain, 1985). Many point to the importance of interaction through conversation (e.g., the Interaction Hypothesis, Long, 1981; the Noticing Hypothesis, Schmidt,

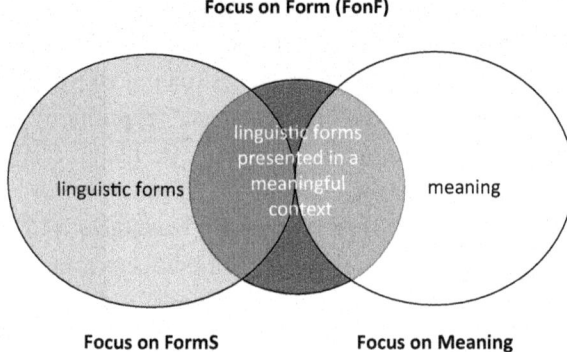

Figure 2.2 Focus on form (FonF)

1993). For an overview, see Y. Kim (2017). The various output-based instructional approaches include both instruction and corrective feedback; the feedback can be either written or oral, and more explicit or more implicit, as discussed in Chapter 1.

An influential approach that addresses forms in the context of communication is the **focus on form** (FonF) approach first put forward by Long (1988) (see R. Ellis, 2016 for a recent critical review). FonF instruction directs students' attention to linguistic forms, but unlike traditional instruction that focused on form to the exclusion of meaning, FonF addresses forms as the need arises, in otherwise meaning-focused lessons. The FonF approach involves interaction, and can be incorporated with **task-based learning** (see Long & Crookes, 1992).

Many of the intervention studies discussed in this book employ FonF output-based approaches with regard to instruction and/or feedback. For example, Sheen (2007), a study of articles in L2 English discussed in Chapter 3, examines the effect of written corrective feedback, with or without metalinguistic information. McDonough (2005), a study of question formation (see Chapter 4) examines the effects of both feedback and modified output.

Focus on form can also involve input-based rather than output-based techniques. The input flooding method is based in part on Schmidt's Noticing Hypothesis (Schmidt, 1990, 1993, 1994). On this hypothesis, learning requires noticing of the required structure in the input. The input flooding method encourages noticing by artificially increasing the quantity of the relevant structures in the input (e.g., by providing learners with texts in which the relevant structure is particularly prevalent). The input-enhancement method (also known as **input enrichment**) (Sharwood Smith, 1991, 1993) is more explicit, as it involves enhancing the relevant forms in the text (e.g., through underlining or highlighting). For example, Reinders and Ellis (2009) examined whether input enrichment or input enhancement led learners to develop explicit knowledge and implicit knowledge of negative adverbs in English. Trahey and White (1993) discuss the efficacy of input flooding in an intervention about English adverb placement. See Chapter 4 for more on both studies.

Input enhancement is often associated with **consciousness raising,** by which learners' attention is directed to the enhanced forms, and learners complete various activities that focus their attention on the forms (e.g., Fotos, 1993).

2.2.7 Processing Instruction

Another approach to grammar instruction that focuses on input rather than output is processing instruction, put forth by VanPatten and colleagues (see VanPatten, 2002, 2004; VanPatten & Cadierno, 1993). Several studies reviewed in the later chapters in this book were conducted in the PI framework, so we provide more information about this approach relative to the others. We note that PI, like other FonF approaches, integrates instruction about grammar into meaning-based activities.

In PI, learners are often first presented with explicit information about the target structure. For example, in VanPatten and Cadierno (1993), L2-Spanish learners were presented with information about subjects and objects, and about the position of Spanish object pronouns (see Chapter 8 for more details). In many PI studies, the explicit information is followed by a warning about the kinds of difficulties that learners often have in processing the input. For example, Benati (2005) used PI for instructing learners about the English past tense (see Chapter 5). Explicit presentation about use of the English past tense *-ed* ending was followed by a warning against relying on temporal adverbs, and instructions to pay attention to the tense ending.

One of the first principles of PI is that learners start out processing the input for meaning and not paying sufficient attention to grammatical form. In processing the input for meaning, learners tend to use strategies that will sometimes, but crucially not always, lead them to the correct interpretation. One strategy much discussed in PI research is learners' overreliance on word order for interpretation, using the default strategy of treating the first **noun phrase** (NP) as the agent. While this works for canonical word order sentences (with subject-verb-object order), this strategy leads to misinterpretation of noncanonical word orders (such as object-verb-subject). Examples where this strategy does not work include the position of object pronouns (**clitics**) in Spanish (VanPatten & Borst, 2012b; VanPatten & Cadierno, 1993 see Chapter 6) and word order changes in Russian and other free-word-order languages (VanPatten et al., 2013; VanPatten Collopy, & Qualin, 2012; see Chapter 9). Another default strategy is learners' overreliance on lexical items instead of functional ones for semantic information. For example, learners rely on temporal adverbs like 'yesterday' instead of on past-tense marking in English in order to establish past-tense reference, which leads to difficulties with past-tense morphology (see, e.g., Benati, 2005, chapter 5). Similar problems arise with subjunctive morphology (see Farley, 2004, discussed in Chapter 6). PI has the goal of moving learners away from such default strategies through activities that require learners to fully process the input. For example, PI may be used to lead learners to rely on case marking rather than word order for interpretation, or to attend to tense marking in the absence of temporal adverbs. This means that the input provided in PI studies is not naturalistic but is modified in order to require learners to move away from default strategies. For example, such modified input might include past-tense sentences without temporal adverbs or sentences with noncanonical word orders. After the input is provided, the learners engage in meaning-based activities, where the form is practiced in meaningful interactions (e.g., answering questions about themselves or stating whether something is true or false in the real world).

Early studies on PI often tested the efficacy of PI against traditional output-based or modified output instruction. In the pre/posttests, learners are tested on both output-based and input-based activities, in order to determine whether input-based instruction can still have an effect on the output (e.g., VanPatten & Cadierno, 1993). Later studies have aimed to isolate the effects of specific components of PI, for example, the role of explicit rule presentation (e.g., VanPatten et al., 2013).

2.2.8 Summary: Approaches to Second Language Instruction and Sample Application

The brief overview provided above shows that there are many different approaches to grammar teaching, depending on whether the primary focus is on form or meaning, input or output, the development of explicit vs. implicit knowledge, and so on. Explicit instruction is generally found to be more successful with regard to grammatical improvement at least in the short-term, in meta-analyses (Spada & Tomita, 2010; Goo et al., 2015). As discussed in Chapter 1, this could be because explicit instruction typically leads to explicit knowledge, which is what most studies test, and also because implicit knowledge takes longer to develop.

To illustrate some of the major approaches to grammar teaching, let us consider how they might apply to a specific structure: English articles. A purely communicative-based approach would not include any instruction about articles but assumes that learners would somehow "pick them up" on their own. This is notably not the case; see Chapter 3 for the challenges L2-English learners face with articles. At the other end of the spectrum, a traditional grammar-drills approach might have learners complete activities with no meaning component, such as filling in the blanks with the right articles or correcting article errors in a text. In contrast, FonF instruction would integrate instruction about articles with meaning and communication. Exactly how this would be done would depend on the particular instructional approach. For example, output-based FonF instruction might engage learners in a communicative task (ordering items from a menu, talking about their daily routine, etc.) but with teachers providing recasts every time there is an error of article omission or article misuse. An input-flooding approach would provide learners with texts in which articles are especially frequent, while an input-enhancement approach would additionally have each article highlighted or underlined. Adding in a consciousness-raising activity might mean having learners classify article uses into definite vs. indefinite, used with plural as opposed to singular vs. mass nouns, referring to specific vs. non-specific entities, and so on. Finally, under PI, the goal would be to get learners away from a tendency to disregard and omit articles by having them interpret sentences where article presence vs. absence is crucial. For example, learners might be asked to determine whether a sentence such as *She bought a water* matches a context where she bought a bottle of water or one where she bought several gallons of water (the context might be represented by a short story or a picture). The learners would then be asked to do the same for *She bought water*. Such an exercise would attract learners' attention to the role that *a* plays in the sentence.

Researchers in the instructed SLA community have generally agreed that an integration of grammar instruction into meaning-based and communication-based lessons via FonF techniques is superior to traditional focus on formS as well as purely communicative approaches (see, e.g., Spada, 1997; Loewen, 2014). Still, there is not a consensus about exactly which types of FonF techniques (output-based FonF instruction, PI, input enhancement, etc.) are most effective for grammar teaching. It is also far from settled whether some approaches work best for the development of implicit as opposed to explicit knowledge. Throughout this textbook, we will review intervention studies that take a variety of instructional approaches and try to draw limited generalizations about which approaches are particularly effective, depending on the structure targeted and the type of knowledge that learners ultimately develop.

2.3 A Preview of the Next Eight Chapters

This chapter and the previous one have set the stage for the rest of the book: We have discussed the nature of SLA, the types of knowledge that learners have in their TL, the different instructional approaches commonly used for grammar teaching, and the logic and time course of intervention studies. The next seven chapters build on those concepts and examine intervention studies within seven specific grammatical areas. The choice of the seven grammatical areas covered in this book was determined by the difficulty they cause learners and the attention they have received in the extant research. We focus first and foremost on those grammatical phenomena on which multiple intervention studies have been done in the literature. The seven grammatical areas addressed in this book are: articles (Chapter 3); verb placement relative to adverbs and in question formation (Chapter 4); inflectional morphology, both on the verb (tense/agreement) and in the nominal domain (grammatical gender) (Chapter 5); the subjunctive mood (Chapter 6); sentence structure with passive and intransitive verbs (Chapter 7); the expression of objects (Chapter 8); and a variety of phenomena related to word order, including noncanonical sentence-level word order in free-word-order languages, adjective ordering, relative-clause formation and quantifier scope (Chapter 9). The final chapter, Chapter 10, brings the findings of the earlier chapters together and discusses the themes that emerge.

2.4 DISCUSSION QUESTIONS

1. Consider the components of an intervention study listed in Table 2.1. What makes some components obligatory and others optional? For those components that are optional, under what conditions should researchers be advised to include the component, and under what conditions might it be dispensed with?
2. Discuss at least two advantages of conducting an intervention study in the classroom; at least two advantages of placing it in the lab; and at least two advantages of implementing the study online, using web-based tools. Which of these advantages do you consider to be particularly important (critical), and why?
3. Suppose that you would like to teach L2 English learners about the use of plural marking with count nouns (*two tables* vs. **two table*) and its impossibility with mass nouns (**two furnitures*, **two mustards*). Discuss how you might approach this question using each of the following approaches: output-based focus on form, input enhancement, and PI. For assistance, see section 2.2.8 for a hypothetical application of these approaches to a different linguistic structure (articles).
4. Take a look at the study of Benati and Angelovska (2015), which uses PI to teach learners about the English past tense. Identify elements of the

intervention that are specific to PI: What is the explicit instruction component? What is the warning? What is the nature of the structured input activities?

2.5 FURTHER READING

- Doughty, C., & Williams, J. N. (Eds.) (1998). *Focus on form in classroom second language acquisition.* Cambridge, UK: Cambridge University Press.
  This edited volume examines FonF instruction and its implementation in L2 classrooms. Particularly recommended are the introductory and concluding chapters by the editors: chapter 1, which introduces FonF, and chapter 10, which discusses pedagogical choices in FonF.
- Ellis, R. (2006). Current issues in the teaching of grammar: An SLA perspective. *TESOL Quarterly, 40*(1), 83–107.
  This paper links SLA findings and grammar teaching, addressing eight questions about whether, when, and how to teach grammar to L2 learners.
- Ellis, R. (2016). Focus on form: A critical review. *Language Teaching Research, 20*(3), 405–428.
  This paper provides a review of research on FonF instruction and includes a classification of different types of FonF activities.
- Loewen, S., & Sato, M. (2017). *The Routledge handbook of instructed second language acquisition.* New York: Routledge.
  This handbook covers a number of topics in instructed L2 acquisition. Particularly recommended are chapter 1, by the editors, which provides an overview of instructed SLA, and chapters 6 through 11, which introduce the reader to a variety of language teaching approaches.
- Mackey, A., & Gass, S. (2022). *Second language research: Methodology and design* (3rd ed.). New York: Routledge.
  This volume serves as a guide to research design and methodology in second language research. Particularly recommended are chapter 1, which introduces the readers to research in SLA, and chapter 3, which provides an overview of different data collection measures.
- VanPatten, B. (2002). Processing instruction: An update. *Language Learning, 52*(4), 755–803.
- VanPatten, B. (Ed.) (2004). *Processing instruction: Theory, research, and commentary.* Mahwah, NJ: Erlbaum (in particular chapter 1, pp. 5–31).
  These two works set out the major tenets of processing instruction (PI), an input-based approach to grammar teaching used in many intervention studies discussed in this textbook.
- Whong, M., Gil, K.-H., & Marsden, H. (2013). *Universal Grammar and the second language classroom.* Dordrecht: Springer.

This book makes connections between linguistic theory, theoretically oriented SLA, classroom research, and classroom instruction. Chapter 1, by the editors, introduces the link between generative SLA and language teaching. Chapters that are particularly relevant for the topics covered in this textbook include chapter 4 (Rankin) on verb movement, chapter 5 (Stringer) on modifiers, chapter 7 (Hirakawa) on argument structure, chapter 8 (Gil, Marsden, & Whong) on quantifiers, and chapter 9 (Snape & Yusa) on articles.

3 Articles

Now that you have learned about the key issues and theoretical models of second language acquisition and about the characteristics of instructional models and intervention research, the rest of the chapters (including this one) will delve into how specific linguistic properties are acquired and have been investigated through interventions.

Articles, the topic of this chapter, are used to introduce **noun phrases** (NPs) and are notorious for the difficulty that they present to L2 learners of languages such as English and Spanish. The difficulty that learners face is largely about acquiring the mapping between linguistic form (e.g., *the* or *a* in English) and linguistic meaning (e.g., the meaning of **definiteness** vs. **indefiniteness** – more on this below). In languages including Spanish or Italian, articles take different forms depending on the gender and number of the noun. This creates an additional challenge of learning which form corresponds to which gender/number combination, and of using the right forms with the right nouns. See Chapter 5 for more on gender and number morphology.

In this chapter, we address the learning task of assigning articles in the L2 to the right meaning. This learning task is particularly challenging for learners whose native languages do not have articles, such as Mandarin Chinese, Korean, or Russian, to name a few. In these languages, there is no single word or morpheme that expresses the precise meaning expressed by *the* or *a* in English. The challenge, therefore, is in learning the precise meaning that articles in the L2 encode. When both the L1 and the L2 of the learners do have articles (for example, in the case of English speakers learning Spanish), the challenges are largely limited to those contexts where the two languages differ.

3.1 Terminology

This chapter focuses on English, the target language in most article studies in SLA. As shown in Table 3.1, we use the terms **definite article** and **indefinite article**, respectively, for *the* and *a* in English. The indefinite article has an

Table 3.1 Examples of English article uses

Term	Form	Can be used with	Example of correct use	Example of incorrect use
Definite article	*the*	count and mass nouns	*The sun is shining brightly. The milk in the fridge is sour.*	#*I want to visit the famous city.* In a context where no city has been previously mentioned. [target: *a*]
Indefinite article	*a (an)*	singular count nouns	*I have a cat. They need to buy a new car.*	#*A moon is out.* [target: *the*]
No article	–	mass and plural count nouns	*Cats like milk.*	**I ate sandwich.* [target: *a*]

Note: The * means the sentence or phrase is incorrect or ungrammatical. The # means that it is grammatical but unacceptable in a given context.

allomorph, *an*; the choice of *a* vs. *an* is phonologically conditioned (e.g., *an apple* vs. *a banana*) and has no bearing on linguistic meaning. Throughout this chapter, we use *a* as a stand-in for *a/an*. Finally, we use the term "no article" when describing NPs in which no article or other determiner is present. Both research papers and instructional materials variously use the terms "no article," "zero article," "null article," "bare noun," and "bare NP." In English, the "no article" option is grammatical with plural and **mass (non-count) nouns** but ungrammatical with singular **count nouns** (more on this distinction in section 3.1.1).

As Table 3.1 shows, there are potentially three types of errors that L2 learners can make with articles (see the column labeled "example of incorrect use"). They might misuse *the*, they might misuse *a*, or they might drop an article when one is required (which is the same as saying that they misuse the "no article" option). The literature on L2 acquisition of articles (see, among many others, Goad & White, 2009; Huebner, 1983; Ionin, Ko, & Wexler, 2004; Master, 1987; Robertson, 2000; Thomas, 1989; and the contributions in García-Mayo & Hawkins, 2009) finds two major types of L2 article errors. These are article omission (that is, misuse of the "no article" option when *a* or *the* is required) and misuse of *the* (that is, use of *the* when either *a* or no article is the grammatical option). Misuse of *a* is also attested but seems to be less common and has received rather less attention in the literature.

Textbooks provide many different rules and explanations for how articles are used (see, e.g., Larsen-Freeman & Celce-Murcia, 2015, chapter 15 for an overview of English articles), but these rules ultimately oversimplify how language works. This is the case not only for articles but for just about any linguistic phenomenon where the mapping between form and meaning is nonobvious. Ultimately, no one rule or set of rules can successfully capture every single type or instance of article use. This is because articles fall at the interface between **morphosyntax** (article form), **semantics** (article meaning), and **discourse** (the context of article use).

3.1.1 Count vs. Mass Nouns, and Article Omission

A central distinction related to article use is that between count nouns such as *book(s)*, *chair(s)*, *girl(s)*, etc. and mass nouns such as *milk, water, gold*, etc. Count nouns typically name entities that can be counted and individuated, while mass nouns do not. There are exceptions, though, for example, nouns such as *furniture*, which are mass even though pieces of furniture can be counted and individuated; see Choi, Ionin, and Zhu, 2018 for more discussion and relevance to L2 acquisition. As shown in Table 3.1, both count and mass nouns can occur with *the*. While both mass and count nouns can occur with no article, count nouns must be plural rather than singular for this happen. Furthermore, only count nouns can combine with *a*, although some mass nouns can take *a* if they are forced (i.e., coerced) into a count interpretation, as in *I bought a water* to mean 'a bottle of water'.

Omission of both *a* and *the* in contexts where they are required has been attested with L2-English learners, but there is also much variability. A given learner might use articles correctly in some utterances but drop them in others (see Robertson, 2000 for more discussion). Studies of article omission suggest that, despite this variability, learners do not drop articles randomly: There is more omission in some types of contexts than in others. For example, Trenkic (2009) gives an overview of studies on article omission with learners from different article-less L1s. Such studies show that article drop in L2 English is more common when the noun is more salient in the discourse context, for example, referring to a previously mentioned entity or referring to a discourse topic.

With regard to the count/mass divide, some studies (Wakabayashi, 1998; Hiki, 1991) have found that learners are more successful on the definite article with singular count nouns than with mass nouns. Snape (2008b) found that the Japanese speakers (whose L1 lacks articles) made many errors of article omission with both plural and mass nouns while being more accurate with singular count nouns.

3.1.2 Definiteness

In both English and Spanish (as well as other Germanic and Romance languages), a major distinction marked by articles is that of (in)definiteness. While one article or set of articles (e.g., *the* in English; *el/la/los/las* in

Spanish) marks definiteness, another (e.g., *a* and *an* in English; *uno/una/ unos/unas* in Spanish) marks indefiniteness. There are many definitions of (in)definiteness in the semantic literature: While some emphasize the importance of speaker vs. hearer knowledge, others focus on the importance of uniqueness (see Abbott, 2003 for an overview). Here, we adopt the informal definition of definiteness from Ionin, Ko, and Wexler (2004), which has been adopted in much SLA literature on articles. While Ionin, Ko, and Wexler (2004) use the terms *speaker* and *hearer*, we add the terms *reader* and *writer*, to indicate that the rule applies to the written as well as the spoken modality. As indicated in (2), definiteness involves a **presupposition** (shared background information).

(2) Definiteness: informal definition (based on Ionin, Ko, and Wexler, 2004)
If an article + NP sequence is [+definite], then the speaker (or writer) and hearer (or reader) presuppose the existence of a unique individual in the set denoted by the NP.

As an illustration, consider the examples in (3). In (3a), when a broomstick, a spider, and a cat are mentioned, the writer has no expectation that the reader is familiar with them. The writer uses *a* in all three cases because there is no shared knowledge with the reader concerning which broomstick, spider, or cat are under discussion. In the second sentence in (3a), however, there *is* such shared knowledge: The cat under discussion is the one that was mentioned in the first sentence. The writer and the reader now share knowledge of a unique cat, the conditions in (2) are satisfied, and the definite article is used.

(3) a. Renata (a witch) had a broomstick, a spider and a cat. *The cat* was very old.
b. Renata's cottage was quite old. *The roof* had been patched many times.

As shown in (3a), previous mention is one way of establishing definiteness. However, it is not the only way. As shown in (3b), it is also quite possible to use *the* with no previous mention, as long as the speaker/reader and hearer/ writer share knowledge of the entity in question. For example, in (3b), the uniqueness of *the roof* is established in relation to previous mention of *Renata's cottage*, since a cottage normally has only one roof. There are many other ways of establishing definiteness and licensing the use of *the* (J. Hawkins, 1978).

For L2-English learners whose native languages lack articles, the challenges are at least two-fold. They need to acquire the meaning of definiteness given in (2), and they also need to recognize that the properties of definiteness – uniqueness and hearer/reader knowledge – can be established in a variety of ways, as shown in (3). With regard to the latter point, a number of

SLA studies have examined different types of definites in L2 English (Chrabaszcz & Jiang, 2014; Liu & Gleason, 2002; Wakabayashi, 1998; among others) and have found that learners do not behave uniformly across all types of definite contexts. For example, learning to use *the* for previous mention tends to be easier than learning when it is used with proper nouns (such as *the Amazon*).

3.1.3 Specificity

Many SLA studies of articles in L2 English, going back to at least Huebner (1983), have found that at least some learner errors with article choice can be traced back to **specificity** (sometimes called "specific reference"). The definitions of what exactly specificity means vary in the literature. (See Bickerton, 1981 on specific reference, and Ionin, 2010 for an overview of different approaches to specificity.) Here, we adopt the informal definition of specificity used in Ionin, Ko, and Wexler (2004), which has been adopted and tested in many experimental SLA studies, as well as several intervention studies:

(4) Specificity: informal definition (based on Ionin, Ko, and Wexler, 2004)
If an article + NP sequence is [+specific], then the speaker (or writer) intends to refer to a unique individual in the set denoted by the NP, and considers this individual to possess some noteworthy property.

The crucial difference between the definition of specificity in (4) and the definition of definiteness in (2) is that specificity only makes reference to the state of knowledge of the speaker/writer. In contrast, definiteness also takes into account what the hearer/reader knows. Consider the examples in (5), which are based on learner data and test items in Ionin, Ko, and Wexler (2004).

(5) a. My friends gave me *a small Siamese kitten*.
b. I would like to sell you *a beautiful silver necklace*: it has been in my family for one hundred years.

In (5a), the writer has a very specific kitten in mind, who is important to her and whom she intends to refer to. The noteworthy property of this kitten (per (4)) could be that it is small and Siamese, or it could be something not mentioned here, such as the fact that the writer loved this kitten. In (5b), the speaker intends to refer to a very specific necklace that is important to him and whose noteworthy property might be the fact of it having been in the speaker's family for one hundred years. Notably, the italicized phrases in (5a–b) are both indefinite, so that *a* rather than *the* is the target form: The particular kitten or necklace is not part of the shared discourse between the speaker/writer and the hearer/reader.

Ionin, Ko, and Wexler (2004) found that L2-English learners from two typologically distinct article-less L1s (Russian and Korean) often misused *the* in place of *a* in the kind of contexts exemplified in (5). For example, an L1-Russian L2-English learner produced the phrase *the small Siamese kitten* in a sentence similar to (5a) in a narrative, with no prior mention of a kitten. Example (5b) was part of an experimental item in a forced-choice task, and learners often selected *the* rather than *a* in front of *beautiful silver necklace*, unlike native English speakers, who selected *a*. Importantly, the learners were quite target-like in other context types, correctly using *a* with indefinites that did not meet the conditions on specificity, as well as correctly using *the* with previous-mention definites. Ionin, Ko, and Wexler (2004) proposed that L2-English learners from article-less L1s have access to the semantic universals of definiteness and specificity through **Universal Grammar** but do not know which of these semantic universals is encoded by articles in English. As a result, learners fluctuate between the two meanings and make specificity-based errors. Ionin, Ko, and Wexler (2004) found specificity-based errors with L1-Russian and L1-Korean learners; in later work, Ionin, Zubizarreta, and Bautista Maldonado (2008) showed that such errors are not made by learners whose L1 (Spanish) has articles that encode definiteness. Other studies have replicated the basic finding of specificity-based errors with learners from other article-less L1s, including Japanese (R. Hawkins et al., 2006; Snape, 2008a) and Mandarin Chinese (Trenkic, 2008; but see Tryzna, 2009). At the same time, there has been disagreement about the explanation of these errors (Trenkic, 2008; Tryzna, 2009). For example, Trenkic (2008) argues that specificity-based errors are traceable to strategies adopted by the learners, rather than the role of a semantic universal (see also Butler, 2002 on strategies that underlie article choice).

Whatever the explanation of article errors, the recurrent finding that L2-English learners tend to overuse *the* with indefinites when referring to a specific entity is quite robust. As a result, a number of intervention studies have addressed this issue. These studies have attempted to explicitly teach learners about the concepts of definiteness and specificity, as well as the fact that only the former is relevant for English, with the goal of helping learners acquire the semantic distribution of articles in a more target-like manner. We will come back to this in section 3.2.2.

3.1.4 Genericity

Genericity is another much-studied topic in SLA of articles. All languages can make generic statements about what the world is generally like. For example, (6a) states that cats in general sleep a lot. In English, if one wants to make a statement about cats (or any other entities) in general, one can use a bare, article-less plural NP, as in (6a). If a definite plural is used instead, as in (6b), we have a statement about what particular cats do. For example, if I am describing the behavior of my two pet cats, I might utter (6b) in order to describe my cats' habits. In contrast, in Spanish (as well as other Romance languages), the equivalent of (6a), with a bare plural subject (*Gatos duermen mucho), is not grammatical. The Spanish equivalent of (6b) (Los gatos duermen mucho), with a definite plural subject, has a generic interpretation (cats in general sleep a lot) as well as a regular definite one (some particular cats sleep a lot).

(6)   a. Cats sleep a lot.   [generic]
        b. The cats sleep a lot.   [nongeneric]

In a series of studies, Ionin and Montrul (2010) and Ionin, Montrul, and Crivos (2013) capitalized on this cross-linguistic difference in order to examine whether the meaning of articles is transferred from English to Spanish and vice-versa. In one of the experiments, participants would read a story and see a picture about unusual representatives of a species: e.g., tigers who like carrots instead of meat, birds who live in caves instead of nests. The participants would then have to make a **truth-value judgment** (Crain & Thornton, 1998; Gordon, 1996), judging a sentence such as *Tigers like carrots* or *The tigers like carrots* as either true or false. In English, *Tigers like carrots* is false, because tigers in general do not like carrots, but *The tigers like carrots* is true in the context of a story about unusual vegetarian tigers, because those particular tigers like carrots. In the Spanish version of the task, the equivalent of *The tigers like carrots* was usually judged as false by native Spanish speakers, suggesting that at least in this task, the generic interpretation was primary, with Spanish speakers interpreting this as a statement about tigers in general, not about the particular tigers in the story.

Ionin and Montrul (2010) and Ionin, Montrul, and Krivos (2013) found evidence of cross-linguistic influence in both directions. English-speaking learners of Spanish judged the Spanish equivalent of *The tigers like carrots* as true (indicating reference to the particular vegetarian tigers in the story) more often than native Spanish speakers did. Conversely, Spanish-speaking learners of English often judged *The tigers like carrots* in English as false, unlike native English speakers, an indication that they treated *the tigers* as generic. Thus, even though Spanish and English both have articles, which are similar in many respects, learners do make errors (in this case, errors of misinterpretation) in those linguistic environments where English and

Spanish articles differ. For other studies that find evidence of transfer with definite plurals in generic contexts, see Cuza et al. (2012); Kupisch (2012).

3.1.5 Kind Reference

Another aspect of genericity has to do with **kind reference**. In English, if one wants to refer to an entire kind or species, such as werewolves, it is possible to use a bare plural (7a) or a definite singular form (7b). (We should add that we cannot make any definitive claims about the current werewolf population).

(7) a. Werewolves are becoming extinct. [kind reference]
    b. The werewolf is becoming extinct. [kind reference]
    c. #A werewolf is becoming extinct. [no kind reference available]
    d. A werewolf hunts when there is a full moon. [generic sentence]

Interestingly, such kind reference is not possible for an indefinite singular form (7c), even though indefinite singular NPs are fine as subjects of generic sentences (7d). Note that the difference here is quite subtle. Generic sentences like (7d) and (6a) talk about what the situation is *usually* like: usually, if something is a werewolf, it hunts during a full moon; usually, if something is a cat, it sleeps a lot. Both bare plurals and indefinite singulars can be used in this way. In contrast, the sentences in (7a–b) are *not* generic: they don't mean that usually, werewolves are becoming extinct. Rather, such sentences talk about the property of all members of a particular kind or species. The members of the species *werewolf* are undergoing extinction. In such instances of kind reference, English can use a bare plural (7a) or a definite singular (7b), but not an indefinite singular (7c) (see Krifka et al., 1995 for theoretical discussion).

Ionin et al. (2011) examined whether L1-Russian and L1-Korean L2-English learners can acquire the subtle distinctions exemplified in (7). Russian and Korean lack articles and use only bare, article-less NPs in generic sentences as well as with kind reference. Ionin et al. (2011) found that the learners were quite target-like with indefinite singular NPs, accepting sentences such as (7d) (or rather, their non-werewolf versions) in a generic context, but rejecting sentences such as (7c). Thus, the learners correctly disallowed kind reference for indefinite singular NPs. However, the learners failed to recognize that definite singular NPs have kind-reference: they rejected sentences such as (7b) and accepted only (7a) (the variant with a plural subject) for kind-reference. Ionin et al. (2011) proposed that the learners had not acquired the English-specific properties of definite singular generics, which are also quite rare in the input. Snape, García Mayo, and Gürel (2013) found similar difficulties with definite singular generics for Turkish-speaking and Japanese-speaking learners of English. In contrast,

L2-English learners with Spanish as their native language were quite target-like in this study, which is consistent with transfer from Spanish which, like English, has definite singular generics.

3.1.6 Summary: Articles in Second Language Acquisition

To summarize, prior research on articles in SLA has found the following patterns of difficulties:

- article omission (of *a* with singular count nouns; of *the* with all noun types, but especially mass and plural nouns)
- misuse of *the* in place of *a* (particularly prevalent in specific indefinite contexts, when the speaker refers to a specific entity)
- difficulties with articles in generic contexts (misinterpretation of the definite article as generic in English or nongeneric in Spanish, based on L1 transfer; lack of knowledge of singular definite generics).

The next section addresses intervention studies that have been conducted on articles in L2 English.

3.2 Intervention Studies on Articles in English as a Second Language

Intervention studies on articles can be roughly divided into two types, depending on whether the starting point is an instructional technique or a theoretical analysis. One type corresponds to studies that are primarily focused on testing the efficacy of a particular classroom instructional technique, such as corrective feedback (Sheen, 2007) or output-based instruction (Erlam, Loewen, & Philp, 2009). Articles are chosen as the linguistic structure under instruction, largely because articles are known to be problematic for learners, but no particular linguistic analysis of articles or article errors is adopted. The study objective in such a case is to determine whether a given instructional method can successfully improve learners' performance with English articles. A different approach is taken by a recent set of studies that take particular linguistic analyses of articles as their starting point (Snape & Yusa, 2013; Umeda et al., 2019; Lopez, 2019). These studies adopt the proposals about definiteness and specificity in Ionin, Ko, and Wexler (2004) and about different types of generics in Ionin et al. (2011) and develop interventions that involve explicitly teaching learners about specificity or genericity, respectively. This section provides an overview of both types of studies, while Table 3.2 provides an overview of the major components and findings of each study.

Table 3.2 Summary of intervention studies on articles

Publication	Structures/phenomena under instruction	Participants' linguistic background	Nature of the intervention	Length of intervention	Major findings
Master (1994)	Use of *the*, *a* and 'no article' in discourse	47 ESL learners in the USA, from a variety of L1s, mainly East Asian; Replication with 54 ESL learners, same linguistic profile	Explicit presentation of rules for article usage	9 weeks, in the classroom; 14 weeks for the replication study	Experimental group improved relative to control group
Sheen (2007)	Use of *a* for first-mention and use of *the* for previous-mention	91 ESL learners in the USA, from a variety of L1s, mainly Korean, Spanish and Polish	Correction with vs. without metalinguistic feedback	1 week, in the classroom	Both experimental groups improved relative to control group, but the group that received metalinguistic feedback improved the most
Erlam, Loewen, & Philp (2009)	Use of *a* in generic sentences	51 ESL learners in New Zealand, from a variety of L1s, mainly East Asian	Output-based instruction (OI) vs. processing input-based instruction (InI)	2 days, in the classroom	Relative to control group, OI group improved on both elicited imitation and grammaticality judgments; InI only on the latter
Snape & Yusa (2013)	Definiteness vs. specificity, genericity, perception of articles	14 L1-Japanese EFL learners in Japan	Explicit instruction about definiteness, specificity, genericity and perception of articles	3 weeks, in the lab	No improvement for experimental group, except on perception
Lopez (2019)	Definiteness and specificity	50 L1-Chinese ESL learners in the UK	Explicit instruction about specificity vs. standard (traditional) instruction on articles	4 weeks, in the classroom	Some improvement for the standard instruction group, but none for the specificity instruction group
Umeda et al. (2019)	Genericity: generic sentences vs. kind-reference	37 L1-Japanese EFL learners in Japan	Explicit instruction about genericity	3 weeks, in the lab	Experimental group improved on immediate posttest, especially on accepting definite singulars with kind-reference, though the improvement was later lost

3.2.1 Intervention Studies with a Focus on Particular Instructional Techniques

The studies of Master (1994), Sheen (2007), and Erlam, Loewen, & Philp (2009) all focused on improving L2-English learners' accuracy with English article use. (Master, 1994 is one of a series of pedagogical studies on articles conducted by this author; see also Master, 1990, 1997, 2002). All three studies tested learners from a variety of L1s; while the studies did not control for whether the learners' L1 had articles, the majority of learners in each study came from article-less L1s, such as Chinese, Korean, and Polish. Thus, all aspects of English article choice might be expected to be challenging for the learners tested. Each study used a different instructional approach.

3.2.1.1 Teaching Articles via Explicit Rule Presentation

Master (1994) used explicit rule presentation, focusing on the central distinctions that underlie English articles, such as the countable/noncountable, singular/plural, definite/indefinite, and specific/generic distinctions. The participants were learners attending ESL classes at an American University. The learners in Master's study completed a fill-in-the-blanks test prior to the intervention, and again during the tenth week of the intervention. During the intervention, the experimental group received systematic instruction about the properties of English articles, while the control group went on with their regular writing instruction and no particular focus on articles. Compared to the control group, the experimental group improved significantly from the pretest to the posttest, even though the improvement was numerically small. The experiment was subsequently replicated with ESL learners at a different university, with a slightly different timeline and with smaller experimental and control groups. Despite the differences, the findings showed the same pattern as in the original study, with significant improvement only by the experimental group.

In the Erlam, Loewen, and Philp (2009) study, the learners were also presented with explicit rules; however, the rules focused only on the use of the indefinite article to make generalizations (as in *A cheetah runs fast*). Erlam, Loewen, and Philp (2009) furthermore contrasted the effectiveness of output-based instruction to that of input-based instruction based on VanPatten's processing instruction (see Chapter 2 for more discussion of this approach). The intervention lasted only two days, and both groups received explicit instruction at the beginning of each day. Day-1 instruction was about the use of *a* to mean 'one' and to make a generalization, and Day-2 instruction was about expressing generalization with noncount nouns. The input-based instruction group was also explicitly taught that the common strategy of using the indefinite article to refer to one entity is not effective, since it does not extend to generic statements: for example, *A cheetah runs fast* is not a statement about one particular cheetah but rather about cheetahs in general.

The output-based and input-based instruction groups completed, respectively, eight output-based or eight input-based activities; all activities were meaning-based, with a communicative goal. An example of an output-based activity involved students naming animals in an animal quiz (e.g., "a lion" in response to the description "This animal is a very dangerous animal."). In the corresponding input-based activity, students were shown two pictures, e.g., one of a lion sleeping and another of three lions advancing on a frightened man. The students had to choose which picture was a better match for the sentence "A lion is a very dangerous animal." Note that this activity forces students to go against the common strategy of "*a* means *one*," which would lead them to select the picture of a single lion sleeping. Rather, the correct response would be to pick the picture which had three lions but that was a better match for the description of a lion as dangerous. The two instructed groups and the control group completed both oral elicited imitation tests and written grammaticality judgment tests for the pretest and two posttests. Both experimental groups outperformed the control group on the oral elicited imitation posttests, but only the output-based instruction group outperformed the control group on the grammaticality judgment posttests. At the same time, the two instructed groups did not differ from each other on any of the posttests. Overall, both instructional treatments were effective, but with greater improvement in the case of learners receiving output-based instruction.

3.2.1.2 Teaching Articles while Varying the Type of Feedback

Whereas both Master (1994) and Erlam, Loewen, and Philp (2009) presented information about articles to learners using particular instructional techniques, the study of Sheen (2007) instead examined the role of feedback. In this study, learners first wrote narratives and then received written corrective feedback to all article errors in their narratives: While the direct-only correction group received only error correction, the direct metalinguistic group received both error correction and metalinguistic information about the error (see Box 3.1 for more details). The control group did not take part in the intervention at all. All three groups completed a pretest, an immediate posttest, and a delayed posttest administered three to four weeks after the intervention. During all three pre/posttest sessions, three separate tests were administered. One was a speeded dictation test, in which participants had to write down sentences read by the researcher, under time pressure; the sentences included a variety of article uses. The second test was a writing

BOX 3.1 Sheen (2007)

Publication Title: The effect of focused written corrective feedback and language aptitude on ESL learners' acquisition of articles

Research Questions:

1. Does focused written corrective feedback have an effect on intermediate ESL learners' acquisition of English articles?
2. Is there any difference in the effect of direct correction with and without metalinguistic feedback on ESL learners' acquisition of English articles?
3. To what extent does the learners' language analytic ability mediate the effectiveness of corrective feedback?

Participants: 91 intermediate-level ESL learners in the United States, from a variety of L1 backgrounds (mainly Korean, Spanish, and Polish) and their 5 ESL teachers, native speakers of American English

Groups: 6 intact classrooms, formed into 3 groups: direct-only correction group (n = 31), direct metalinguistic group (n = 32), control group (n = 28)

Study Timeline:

- Two weeks prior to instruction: language analytic ability test (all groups)
- One week prior to instruction: pretests (all groups)
- Two instructional sessions, one week apart (the two instructed groups)
- Posttest 1 after the sessions (all groups)
- Posttest 2 (delayed posttest) 3 to 4 weeks later (all groups)

Pre/Posttests: Three different tests administered each time

- A speeded dictation test: Each item contained one or two definite and/or indefinite article uses; the test was scored for correct suppliance in obligatory context as well as incorrect suppliance in nonobligatory contexts.
- A narrative writing test: Students wrote a story based on four sequential pictures; the test was scored in largely the same way as the dictation test.
- An error-correction test: Each item consisted of two related statements, one of which contained an error that the learners had to correct.
- All three tests focused on two basic aspects of article use: *a* on first mention and *the* on second mention.

The Intervention:

- During each of the two testing sessions, participants read a story, the teacher discussed it with the class and read the story out loud, and then the students rewrote the story from memory.

BOX 3.1 (cont.)

- The researcher corrected the narratives, with a focus on article errors.
- In the direct-only correction group, each error was indicated and a correction was provided.
- In the direct metalinguistic correction group, in addition to the correction, notes indicated what was wrong, using metalinguistic information.

Results: Both feedback groups improved relative to the control group, across all tests. The direct-metalinguistic group showed the most improvement, especially in the second posttest.

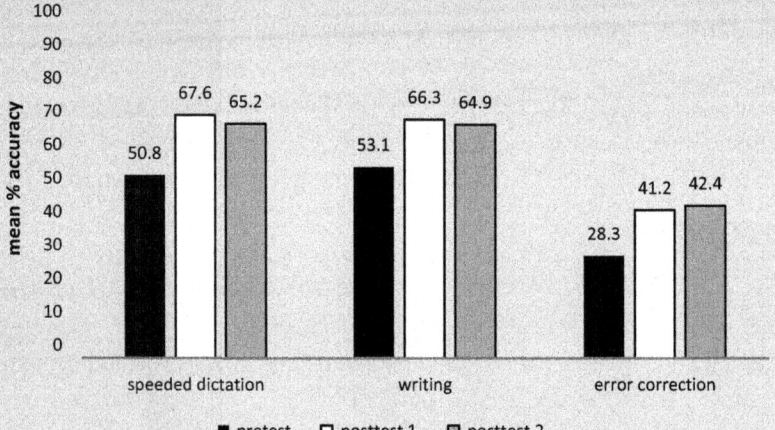

Figure 3.1 Direct-only group: Mean percentage accuracy in speeded dictation, writing, and error correction (based on data from Sheen, 2007)

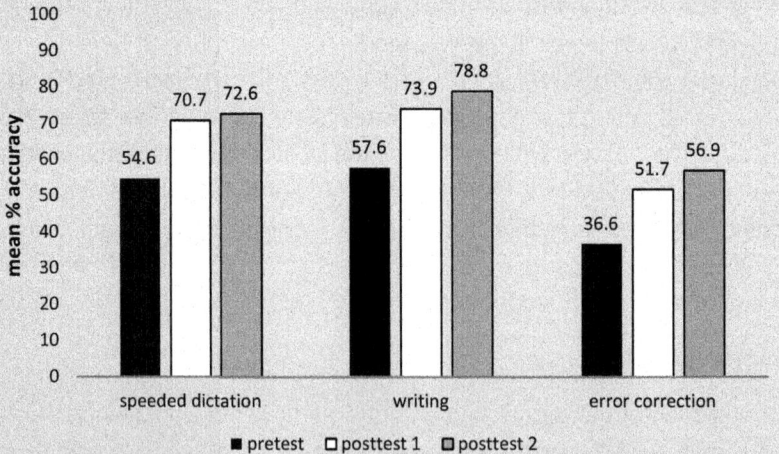

Figure 3.2 Direct-metalinguistic group: Mean percentage accuracy in speeded dictation, writing and error correction (based on data from Sheen, 2007)

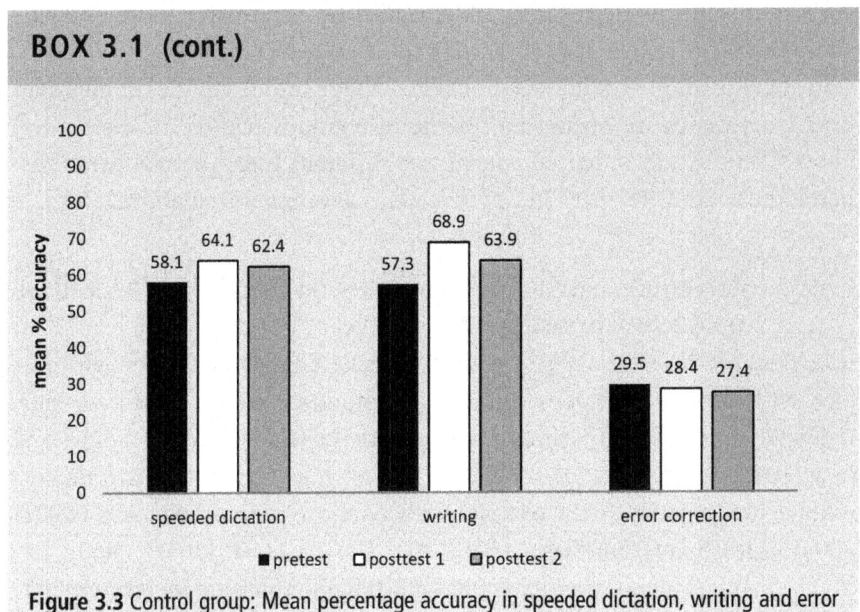

Figure 3.3 Control group: Mean percentage accuracy in speeded dictation, writing and error correction (based on data from Sheen, 2007).

task, in which participants wrote a coherent story based on a sequence of four pictures. And the third test was an error-correction test, in which participants read sentence pairs and had to find and correct the error in one of the sentences.

The results are summarized in Box 3.1. In the speeded dictation test, all three groups improved from pretest to posttest 1, with no between-group differences. At posttest 2, the direct metalinguistic-feedback group outperformed the control group. In the writing test, all three groups, including the control group, improved from pretest to posttest 1, with no between-group differences. At posttest 2, the direct metalinguistic-feedback group outperformed the other two groups. Finally, in the error-correction test, both instructed groups improved relative to the control group, but the direct metalinguistic group improved the most. At both posttest 1 and posttest 2, both instructed groups outperformed the control group; at posttest 2, the metalinguistic group also outperformed the direct-only group. In sum, there was a clear advantage for the metalinguistic group: Metalinguistic feedback with error correction was found to be more helpful and to lead to greater improvement than error correction on its own. This advantage was especially pronounced in the delayed posttest, which suggests that knowledge of article use might be retained better (at least over three/four weeks) following metalinguistic feedback. Since the study focused only on very basic uses of *a* and *the* (first mention vs. second mention), an interesting question is whether metalinguistic feedback would also be helpful for more complex environments of article use.

To sum up, all three studies summarized above found significant improvement from pretest to posttest(s) for the test groups relative to the control groups. Those studies that compared two different types of treatments furthermore found differences in improvement, as summarized above.

3.2.2 Intervention Studies with a Focus on Particular Theoretical Approaches to Articles

Several recent studies have addressed whether L2-English learners' performance with articles improves following instruction that is based on such linguistic concepts as specificity and genericity. The studies of Snape and Yusa (2013) and Lopez (2019) taught L2-English learners about definiteness and specificity, basing their test materials on those of Ionin, Ko, and Wexler (2004). Both Snape and Yusa (2013) and Umeda et al. (2019) taught L2-English learners about genericity and kind-reference, basing their test materials on those of Ionin et al. (2011). The participants in both Snape and Yusa (2013) and Umeda et al. (2019) were EFL students in Japan, of high intermediate and/or advanced proficiency. The participants in Lopez (2019) were Chinese speakers of elementary or lower intermediate English proficiency, enrolled in an intensive English course in the UK.

The instruction about definiteness and specificity in Snape and Yusa (2013) and Lopez (2019) provided learners with definitions and explanations of definiteness, indefiniteness, and specificity based on prior theoretical literature. For example, in Lopez (2019, p. 10) the group that received specificity-based instruction was taught the definitions in (8), which are simplified from the definitions in Ionin, Ko, and Wexler (2004) (see sections 3.1.2 and 3.1.3 above). In teaching the study participants about definiteness, the interventions emphasized the role of uniqueness (in Snape & Yusa, 2013) and hearer knowledge (in Lopez, 2019).

(8) Definiteness and specificity: pedagogical definitions
If a noun phrase is ...
a. [definite], then *both* the speaker *and* the listener can identify the noun, and answer the question "Which one?"
b. [specific], then the speaker is referring to one particular individual.

In a similar vein, both Snape and Yusa (2013) and Umeda et al. (2019) used linguistically informed definitions of genericity and kind reference in order to teach learners about article use in generic environments (see sections 3.1.4 and 3.1.5). For example, the instruction group in Umeda et al. (2019) was taught about genericity at the level of the NP, which is available to definite singulars and bare plurals. They were also taught about genericity at the level of the sentence, which is compatible with indefinite singulars and bare plurals. The instruction involved introducing learners to such concepts as **natural kinds** (9), **kind predicates** (10), and **non-kind predicates** (11) (from Umeda et al., 2019, p. 9).

(9)   Natural kind:
       a. The lion lives in Africa.
       b. Lions live in Africa.

(10)   Kind predicate:
       a. The cell phone was invented in 1973 by Martin Cooper.
       b. Cell phones were invented in 1973 by Martin Cooper.

(11)   Non-kind-predicates:
       a. A cell phone is expensive in Japan.
       b. Cell phones are expensive in Japan.

All three studies used explicit rule presentation to examine whether explicitly familiarizing learners with such concepts as definiteness, specificity, genericity, and kind reference would lead to improved performance with article use. The results were rather mixed. Snape and Yusa (2013), a pilot study with a small sample of participants, found no improvement with respect to either definiteness/specificity or genericity. However, the learners in this study did improve in their perception of articles after perceptual training. Lopez (2019) similarly found no improvement in the group that received specificity-based instruction, relative to the control group and the group that received standard instruction. The control group in Lopez's study had significantly higher proficiency than the two instructed groups. The control group placed at B1 level in the CEFR, the Common European Framework of Reference for Languages (which corresponds to intermediate high/advanced low proficiency in ACTFL, the American Council for the Teaching of Foreign Languages). In contrast, the two instructed groups placed at A2 level (intermediate mid proficiency in ACTFL). This difference in proficiency makes it difficult to compare the groups' performance.

In contrast, Umeda et al. (2019), a study with L1-Japanese L2-English learners, did find an effect of teaching learners about kind reference and genericity. In this study, the experimental group was explicitly taught about different types of genericity over the course of three weeks. They reviewed the material again during the final two weeks of the intervention. The full intervention lasted nine weeks and included instruction on definiteness and specificity, not reported in the paper; see Box 3.2 for details. The pretest and posttests used acceptability judgment tasks modeled on those in Ionin et al. (2011). While five different NP types were tested (see Box 3.2), the paper only

BOX 3.2 Umeda et al. (2019)

Publication Title: The long-term effect of explicit instruction on learners' knowledge on English articles

Research Questions:

1. Can the instruction group gain knowledge of NP-level generics through instruction and practice of the definite singular and bare plural?
2. Does the instruction group exhibit target-like knowledge of the indefinite singular and bare plural for sentence-level generics before instruction begins? If not, can instruction and practice of the indefinite singular and bare plural foster this knowledge?
3. Is the effect (if any) of the instruction durable?

Participants: 37 adult L1-Japanese L2-English learners in an EFL setting in Japan, university students; 9 control participants, native speakers of British English. (The native controls were only tested once and took no part in the intervention.)

Groups: Instruction group (n = 21) and control group (n = 16); participants randomly assigned to groups

Study Timeline:

- Week 1: pretest, for both groups
- Weeks 1–3: instruction about generics (instruction group only), 60 minutes per week
- Week 3: posttest 1, for both groups
- Weeks 4–7: instruction on definiteness and specificity, not reported in the paper
- Weeks 8–9: review of genericity, definiteness, and specificity
- Week 10: posttest 2, for both groups
- 12 weeks later: posttest 3
- One year later: posttest 4

Pre/Posttests: Acceptability Judgment Task (AJT) with a 1-to-4 scale, relevant items based on Ionin et al. (2011). NP-level generics allow only definite singulars and bare plurals, while sentence-level generics allow only indefinite singulars and bare plurals.

(12) [Test condition: NP-level generic (a and b are acceptable responses)]
I know that you like birds. Well, if you ever visit California, you'll see different kinds of birds there. For example, I found out ...

BOX 3.2 (cont.)

  a. the pelican lives on the California coast.
  b. pelicans live on the California coast.
  c. a pelican lives on the California coast.
  d. the pelicans live on the California coast.
  e. pelican lives on the California coast.

(13) [Test condition: Sentence-level generic (a and b are acceptable responses)]
I want to go skiing in December. I heard Northern Japan is popular. Of course, it is very cold. Everyone knows, for instance, ...
  a. a coat is necessary in winter.
  b. coats are necessary in winter.
  c. coat is necessary in winter.
  d. the coat is necessary in winter.
  e. the coats are necessary in winter.

The Intervention:

- Instruction group: explicit instruction, in Japanese, about NP-level vs. sentence-level genericity, and the NP types used for each one, with practice activities
- Control group: no instruction

Results: The instructed group improved in both categories, while the control group did not. However, the improvement of the instructed group was largely lost by the fourth posttest.

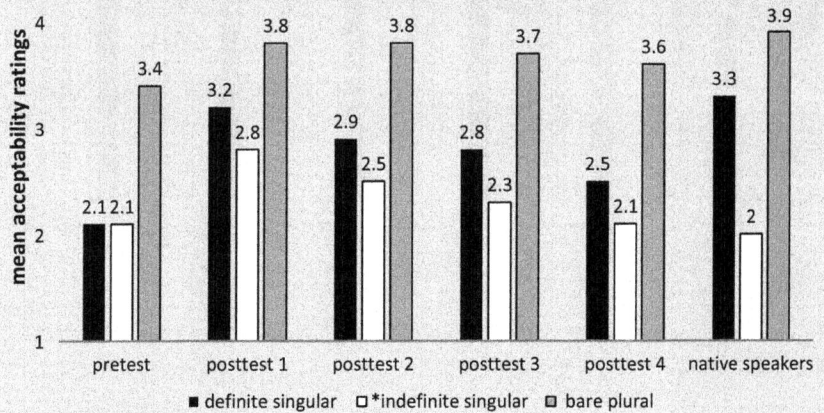

Figure 3.4 Instructed learner group: Mean acceptability ratings for NP-level generics (based on data from Umeda et al., 2019)

BOX 3.2 (cont.)

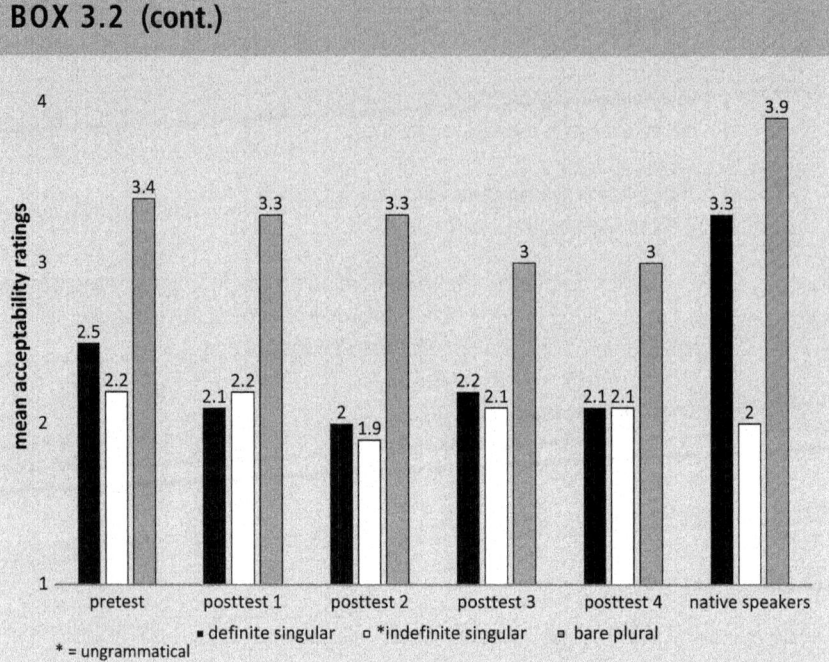

Figure 3.5 Control learner group: Mean acceptability ratings for NP-level generics (based on data from Umeda et al., 2019)

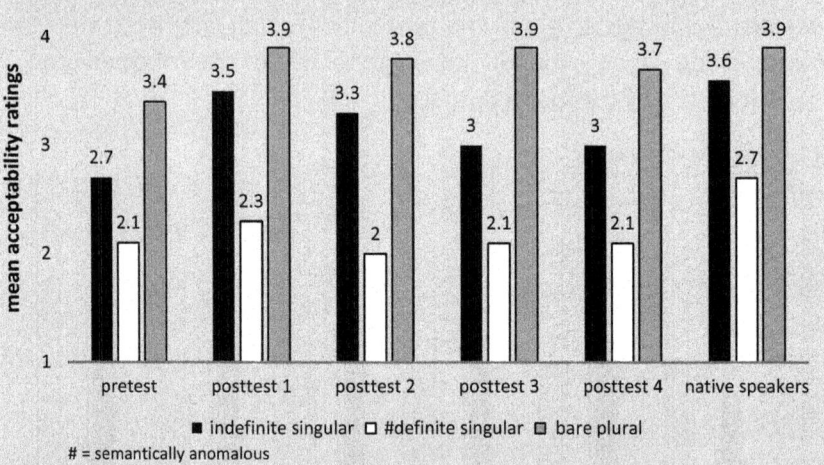

Figure 3.6 Instructed learner group: Mean acceptability ratings for sentence-level generics (based on data from Umeda et al., 2019)

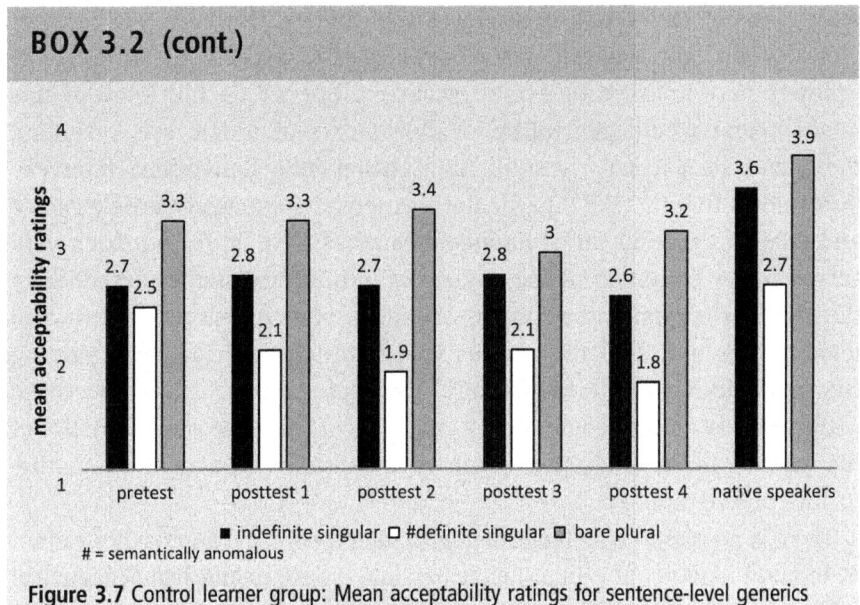

Figure 3.7 Control learner group: Mean acceptability ratings for sentence-level generics (based on data from Umeda et al., 2019)

reports on learners' performance with definite singular, indefinite singular, and bare plural generics. The instruction group showed improvement, in the form of increased ratings of definite singulars in the NP-generic context, indefinite singulars in the sentence-generic contexts, and bare plurals in both contexts. However, the improvement only held through the second or third posttest, and performance on posttest 4 was no different from that on the pretest. The control (no instruction) group showed no improvement. This study showed that linguistically informed instruction on genericity can improve performance, at least on explicit measures; however, the improvement is not retained over time.

To sum up, the (few) studies that have used linguistically informed instruction about articles did not find strong evidence of improvement. Possible reasons for this lack of improvement include small sample sizes and groups not fully balanced for proficiency. Additionally, teaching learners directly about complex linguistic concepts such as specificity or genericity may have resulted in materials that were too complex for learners.

3.3 Summary and Implications

As discussed in the previous sections, pedagogically oriented intervention studies with articles have found improvement, with more improvement for some types of instruction or feedback than others. However, such studies typically do not address particular linguistic aspects of article use: Learners may improve in overall accuracy, but we do not know if this improvement would generalize to all contexts of article use, including those that are particularly subtle and challenging. Conversely, intervention studies that do take a particular theoretical approach to article choice and focus on a small set of linguistic contexts have so far not been very successful. A limitation of the linguistically informed studies described in the previous section is that they used highly explicit instruction. It is also important to note that the various studies tested participants of varying L1s and varying proficiency levels. The fact that one study succeeded while another did not could have as much to do with the characteristics of the learners in the study (e.g., more vs. less proficient) as with the nature of the intervention.

There is no reason why the pedagogical and theoretical approaches cannot be brought together. It is in principle possible to take established pedagogical approaches that have been found to lead to improvement (e.g., consistent feedback; **input processing instruction**; etc.) and to apply them to specific linguistic contexts that are known to present learners with difficulty (such as specific indefinites or definite singular generics). There are also many specific linguistic properties of articles that have not so far been addressed in linguistically informed intervention studies, such as article use with different types of count and mass nouns, and article use with plural generics in English vs. Spanish.

Another direction in which intervention research with articles could be expanded is the adoption of psycholinguistic methods. As discussed in Chapter 1, a major question in the field of SLA is whether explicit instruction can lead to implicit, internalized knowledge or only to explicit knowledge. To address this question, it is necessary to test learners' knowledge on the pretests and posttests using tasks that are more likely to tap into explicit knowledge as well as those that are more likely to tap into implicit knowledge. In the domain of articles, recent years have seen a rise of studies that use online, psycholinguistic techniques (e.g., **eye tracking** and **self-paced reading**) that are arguably more likely to tap into learners' internalized knowledge (see Trenkic, Mirkovic, & Altmann, 2013; Ionin, Choi, & Liu, 2021). Such methods could easily be used in an intervention study in which participants come into the lab for testing; tasks such as self-paced reading could even be implemented in fully classroom-based studies, provided that students had access to computers in the classroom.

3.4 DISCUSSION QUESTIONS

1. As discussed in this chapter, some intervention studies take a particular pedagogical approach as their starting point, while others take a theoretical account of article semantics as their starting point. What do you think are the pros and cons of each approach?
2. Examine Table 3.2 with regard to the length of the interventions. Why do you think some intervention studies take only a day or two while others take several weeks? Is intervention length related to the type of instruction? Do you think the length of the intervention affects learning and retention?
3. As discussed in section 3.1.5, L2-English learners have been found to have difficulty with definite singular generics, for example, *The dodo bird is extinct.* Definite singular generics are relatively infrequent in English, so one might argue that there is no need to teach learners about this type of article use and that intervention studies should focus on more common and frequent article uses. Do you agree or disagree with this? Explain your answer.
4. Some intervention studies of L2 English article choice carefully control for the L1 of the learners in the study, while others test all the learners present in a given classroom, regardless of their L1. What do you think are the pros and cons of each approach? Do you think it is (a) not important to control for the L1 at all; (b) important to control for whether the L1 has articles or not, but fine to group multiple article-less L1s together; or (c) important to control for the specific L1? Explain your answer.

3.5 APPLICATIONS QUESTIONS

1. Consider a hypothetical intervention study on English articles conducted with eighteen L1-Korean L2-English learners in a college English classroom at a Korean university. The class takes a pretest on their knowledge of English articles, then takes part in a five-week intervention study, and subsequently takes a posttest. The improvement from pretest to posttest is quite large and statistically significant, so the researchers conclude that the intervention worked. What is wrong with this conclusion, and why? Hint: Think of what element is missing from this study, and why it is important.
2. Consider the input processing instruction approach discussed in Chapter 2. Discuss how you would apply this approach to teaching L1-Spanish

L2-English learners about the difference between the two languages with regard to plural generics. As discussed in section 3.1.4, a statement such as *The tigers like carrots* can only be a statement about a specific group of tigers in English but can be a statement about tigers in general in Spanish. Your goal is to make learners aware of this difference so that they stop allowing *the tigers* to refer to tigers in general in English. (Similarly, you can think about the opposite study: teaching L1-English L2-Spanish learners that nouns with no articles, such as *tigres* 'tigers', are ungrammatical in Spanish in generic contexts). Remember that in input processing instruction, the focus is on manipulating the input that the learners receive, as well as on getting learners to change their strategies. In this case, you want to change learners' strategy of using "*the* + plural noun" to talk about tigers (or any other entities) in general. How would you manipulate the input in order to address this?

3. As discussed in section 3.1.3, L2-English learners from article-less L1s often mistakenly use *the* when talking/writing about entities that are well-known to the speaker/writer without attending to what the hearer/reader knows (for more discussion of these concepts, see Ionin, Ko, & Wexler, 2004; Snape & Yusa, 2013). Suppose that we want to design a corrective feedback intervention study to address this issue. During the intervention, the learners complete a pair activity designed to elicit many instances of specificity without definiteness: that is, contexts where the learner herself (the speaker) has a particular individual or entity in mind that the learner's partner (the hearer) does not know about. The learners are divided into three groups: Group A is given no feedback at all on any errors of article use; in Group B, the instructor corrects every incorrect use of *the* in place of *a*; in Group C, the instructor corrects every incorrect use of *the* in place of *a*, and furthermore explains the nature of the error, with particular attention paid to speaker vs. hearer knowledge. Answer the following questions about this study:

   a) What form should the pair activity take? Remember that the goal is to get each learner to talk about some entity that her partner does not have knowledge of. How would you set this up?

   b) What form could the pretest and posttest in this study take? Would you use aural or written modality for the tasks, or both? Why?

   c) Given what you have learned in this chapter, which of the three groups do you expect to improve the most from pretest to posttest, and why?

4. The experimental study of Ionin, Choi, and Liu (2021) examined whether L1-Chinese L2-English learners are sensitive to errors of article omission at both more explicit and more implicit levels. In this study, the learners

completed both a grammaticality judgment task (GJT) that targeted more explicit knowledge and a self-paced reading task (SPRT) that targeted more implicit knowledge. In both tasks, participants read sentence pairs such as (14a), where there is an indefinite article in front of *cat*, and its variant in (14b), where this article is missing (there was no underlining in the actual test). In the GJT, participants had to state whether the sentence was grammatical or not; in the SPRT, they read each sentence word by word, and the researchers measured reading times on the word *cat* when it followed an article (as in (14a)) vs. when it followed the verb directly (as in 14b)).

(14) a. Mary felt lonely last week. So she finally got a cat from a shelter.
    b. Mary felt lonely last week. So she finally got cat from a shelter.

Suppose that we want to conduct an intervention study that uses the GJT and SPRT described above as the pretests and posttests. Answer the following questions about this hypothetical study:

a) If learners exhibit at least partial knowledge of English articles in the GJT, what would the results for sentences like (14a) vs. (14b) look like? Specifically, which of these two sentence types would be accepted as grammatical more often?

b) If learners exhibit at least some sensitivity to English articles in the SPRT, what would the results for sentences like (14a) vs. (14b) look like? Specifically, in which sentence type would the word *cat* be read faster?

c) Suppose that we divide learners into two groups: Group A is explicitly taught about the requirement that singular count nouns in English cannot occur without an article; Group B is taught via **input enhancement**: they are provided with a passage in which every instance of an article in front of a singular count noun is highlighted. Which of the two groups do you expect to improve more on the GJT, and which of the two groups do you expect to improve more on the SPRT? Motivate your answer based on what you have learned about explicit and implicit instruction and learning in Chapter 1.

3.6 FURTHER READING

- Ionin, T., Ko, H., & Wexler, K. (2004). Article semantics in L2 acquisition: The role of specificity. *Language Acquisition, 12*(1), 3–69.
  This paper proposes that L2-English learners from article-less native languages fluctuate between using English articles to encode definiteness vs. specificity, and provides experimental evidence for this claim.

- Master, P. (1997). The English article system: Acquisition, function, and pedagogy. *System, 23*(2), 215–232.

  This paper provides an overview of the functions and acquisition of English articles and gives a framework for teaching articles to L2-English learners at different levels of proficiency.

- Snape, N., & Yusa, N. (2013). Explicit article instruction in definiteness, specificity, genericity and perception. In M. Whong, K.-H. Gil, & H. Marsden (Eds.), *Universal Grammar and the second language classroom* (pp. 161-186). Dordrecht: Springer.

  This paper provides a link between theoretically oriented work on articles in L2 English and classroom instruction on English articles.

4 Verb Placement and Question Formation

This chapter turns to syntax (word order) and its interaction with verbal morphology. It is concerned with the position of the verb with respect to other elements in the sentence and, most importantly, the position of the verb in main and embedded clauses and in the formation of questions.

Languages across the world vary with respect to the position of the subject, the verb, and the object in basic sentences; the ordering of these elements is called the basic or underlying word order of a language. English is a subject–verb–(direct-)object **(SVO) language**, as in the sentence *Mary likes ice cream*; that is, the basic sentence structure of English starts with the subject of the sentence, followed by the verb, and then the direct object. In contrast, Turkish, Japanese, Korean, and Hindi are subject–(direct-)object–verb **(SOV) languages**, with the verb at the end of the sentence (e.g. *Mary ice cream likes*). However, this is not a simple two-column list for all languages in regard to verb placement. SVO languages (English, German, Spanish, and French) differ among themselves with respect to the position of the verb in relation to other **constituents** (phrases) that are not the subject and object, and these differences have to do with the strength or richness of the verbal morphology.

Many Germanic languages (German, Swedish, Dutch, Icelandic) exhibit the **verb second** (V2) phenomenon, and in these languages the **finite verb** (marked with tense and agreement) must appear in the second position of the sentence, after another phrase. There is also a well-known difference between English and French regarding the position of frequency and manner adverbs in the sentence, with respect to the finite verb. This difference is subsumed under the **verb-movement** parameter, which has been the subject of influential linguistic and classroom-based studies on the role of negative evidence in resetting parameters of **Universal Grammar** (UG).

In this chapter we discuss studies on the acquisition of verb placement with respect to adverbs and negation as well as in questions, in English and other languages. **Intervention** research on these topics has been motivated by linguistic theory and learnability considerations. The acquisition of subject–verb inversion in question formation in English has been one of the most studied phenomena in classroom-based research. Because most studies on the L2 acquisition of verb placement in French and Spanish, and in English and other Germanic languages, have been conducted within the generative framework, we begin with the specific terminology related to these issues. The research on question formation in English, by contrast, has followed the theory of language development in Pienemann (1984, 1998), **Processability Theory**, which identifies developmental stages and has pedagogical implications (discussed in section 4.3.1).

4.1 Terminology

Before discussing the studies related to verb-movement and question formation, we must review some important concepts in linguistics and in the version of syntax assumed in the studies discussed.

4.1.1 Functional Categories and Features

In generative syntax (Freidin, 1992), verbs and nouns are lexical categories that head the **verb phrase** (VP) and the **noun phrase** (NP), respectively. **Inflectional morphemes** related to subject–verb agreement, tense, complementizers (words such as *that*, which introduce an embedded clause, as in *I know that they are here*), and determiners (such as articles) are represented as functional categories in a syntactic tree above the VP (see also Chapter 5 for more on **inflectional morphology**). VP and NP are **lexical categories**, because they are headed by lexical items that are verbs or nouns. Then, we have **functional categories**, such as the complementizer phrase (CP), the inflectional phrase (IP), and the determiner phrase (DP). The IP has also been split into two phrases, the agreement phrase (AgrP) and the tense phrase (TP) (Pollock, 1989), as shown in Figure 4.1. Each functional phrase has a head (C, Agr, T, D) and a specifier position, which is where the noun phrases that stand for participants in the event described by the verb are generated (e.g., subjects are in the specifier of VP); specifiers also serve as a landing site for movement of other constituents, as we will see.

Features are abstract morphosyntactic properties of lexical items (Chomsky, 1965) and are part of the universal lexicon. For example, nouns have the features [+ N, −V] and verbs [−N, +V]; the category Tense has the features [± past] and Aspect has the features [± perfective], Number has the features [± plural], and so on. Chomsky (1993), following Borer (1984), proposed that bundles of features define the content of functional categories. Each language makes a selection of features from the inventory available from Universal Grammar, and the different combinations of features are at

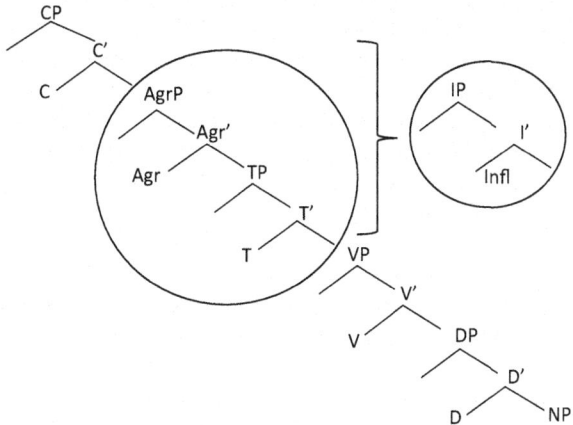

Figure 4.1 Structure of a clause in generative syntax

the heart of the description of language variation. Abstract features also play a key role in syntactic operations such as **Merge, Agree,** and **Move.** The **Move operation** brings elements into a local relationship by displacing them from their base position. For example, in English and similar languages, interrogative words bear a wh-feature, which forces them to move to the front of the sentence into the specifier of the CP in Figure 4.1. The head of the CP, the complementizer in C, bears a wh-feature, and the feature is checked or valued under the operation Agree. In this way the feature is syntactically active and plays a role in syntactic operations.

In the version of syntactic theory in Chomsky (1995), features differ as to their **feature strength,** and differences in feature strength have syntactic consequences for word order that give rise to **parametric** (or crosslinguistic) **variation.** The strength of features plays a role in the movement operations. Strong features need to be checked in a functional projection, and to do so they drive the movement of phrases in the syntax. For example, finite verbs have tense and subject agreement features which have to be checked against or valued with corresponding V-features in Infl, or Agr and T in Figure 4.1. When the V features in Infl are strong (i.e., strong I), the finite verb raises, moving from the VP to Infl (or T, or Agr) to check its features. If the V features are weak (weak I), movement does not take place and the verb stays in the VP.

4.1.2 The Verb-Movement Parameter

A parameter that depends on feature strength is the **verb movement** or the verb-raising parameter, formulated by Pollock (1989) (see also Emonds, 1978), to account for well-known differences in word order between English and French. The two languages are SVO in simple declarative sentences, but they differ in the placement of adverbs and negation, as well as in the placement of the subject with respect to the verb in questions, as shown in Table 4.1.

Under the standard syntactic analysis of French, the particle *pas* is considered to be in the syntactic position for negation, while *ne* is (optionally) attached to the verb. According to Pollock, the difference between the two languages has to do with feature strength of I (inflection or Infl). English has [weak I] features while French has [strong I] features. In French, strong features of Infl drive movement of the verb from the VP to the IP, past adverbs and negation.

The tree in Figure 4.2 illustrates the verb-movement parameter, which ties together all these constructions. Basically, English and French have the same underlying structure for simple sentences, with adverbs and negation adjoined and projected above the verb (V).

Table 4.1 Word order differences between English and French (based on L. White, 1990, 1991)

	English	French
Simple sentences	SVO	SVO
	Mary watches TV.	Marie regarde la télévision.
Negation	Neg-V	V-neg
	Mary **does not** watch TV.	Marie ne regarde **pas** la télévision.
Adverb placement	SAVO	SVAO
	Mary **often** watches TV.	Marie regarde **souvent** la télévision.
Questions	SV	VS
	Does she watch TV?	Regarde-t-elle la télévision?
Feature strength	Weak Infl (V stays in VP)	Strong Infl (V raises to IP)

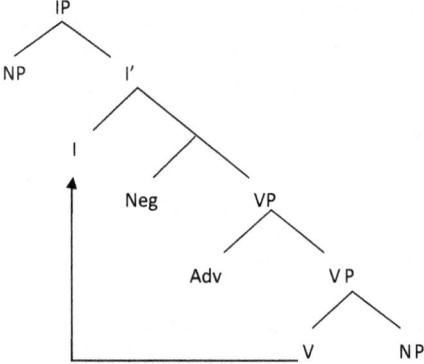

Figure 4.2 Verb movement (V-to-I movement)

Because I is strong in French, the verb moves to I (this is called V-to-I movement). Now the negative element *pas* and the adverb *souvent* (often) appear after the verb, as shown in Table 4.1. Because the verb does not move overtly in English (it has weak I features), the order is Neg-V and Adv-V.

4.1.3 Verb Second

English differs from its sisters (German, Dutch) in the position of the verb in the VP, which is VP initial in English but VP final in German and Dutch. Another main difference is that in German (and, with some variations, other non-English Germanic languages), the verb must appear in the second position in main clauses when a constituent, such as a subject, an adverb, or an object, is fronted (this is known as verb second or V2). The lexical verb appears in final position (known as "verb final") in main clauses containing modals or auxiliaries and in embedded clauses. These differences are illustrated in Table 4.2 with German. (Following the convention in linguistics, an asterisk before a sentence indicates that the sentence is ungrammatical).

According to Platzack (1986) and Schwartz and Vikner (1996), VP and IP in German are verb final, as in Figure 4.3, while in English IP and VP are head initial, as in Figure 4.2. Finite verbs in German undergo two movements, from V-to-I and from I-to-C (see Figure 4.3), driven by strong features on C. The subject also raises to the specifier of CP, and this is how the verb comes to occupy the second position in main declarative clauses and in clauses with constituent fronting. In embedded clauses, C is occupied by

Table 4.2 Verb placement in English and German

	English	German
Main declaratives without modals	SVO Mary **drinks** coffee.	SVO Maria **trinkt** Kaffe. *Maria Kaffe trinkt.
with modals	SVO Mary wants to **drink** coffee.	SOV Maria möchte Kaffe **trinken**. *Maria möchte trinken Kaffe.
Embedded clauses	SVO Mary says that she will **drink** coffee.	SOV Maria sagt, dass sie Kaffe trinken will.
Object fronting	OSV Coffee, Mary **drinks**.	OVS (V2) Kaffe **trinkt** Maria. *Kaffe Maria trinkt.
Adverb fronting	ASVO Often Mary **drinks** coffee.	AVSO (V2) Oft **trinkt** Maria Kaffee. *Oft Maria **trinkt** Kaffee.

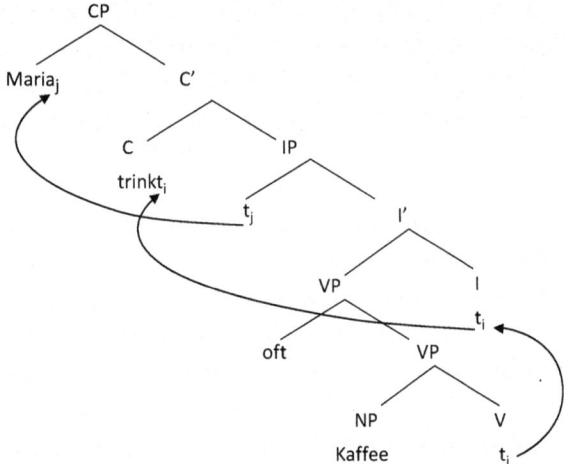

Figure 4.3 Verb second in German (V-to-I-to-C-movement)

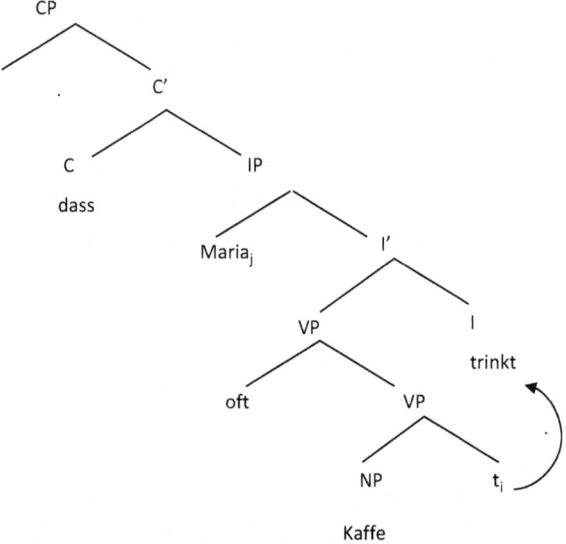

Figure 4.4 Embedded clause structure in German

the complementizer *dass* 'that': for that reason, the subject is in the specifier of IP and the verb only raises to I, as in Figure 4.4.

4.1.4 Wh-movement: Question Formation

In all languages there is a syntactic relationship between sentences that encode a statement, such as *Maria often drinks coffee*, and corresponding question sentences, such as *Who drinks coffee?*, *What is Maria doing?*, or

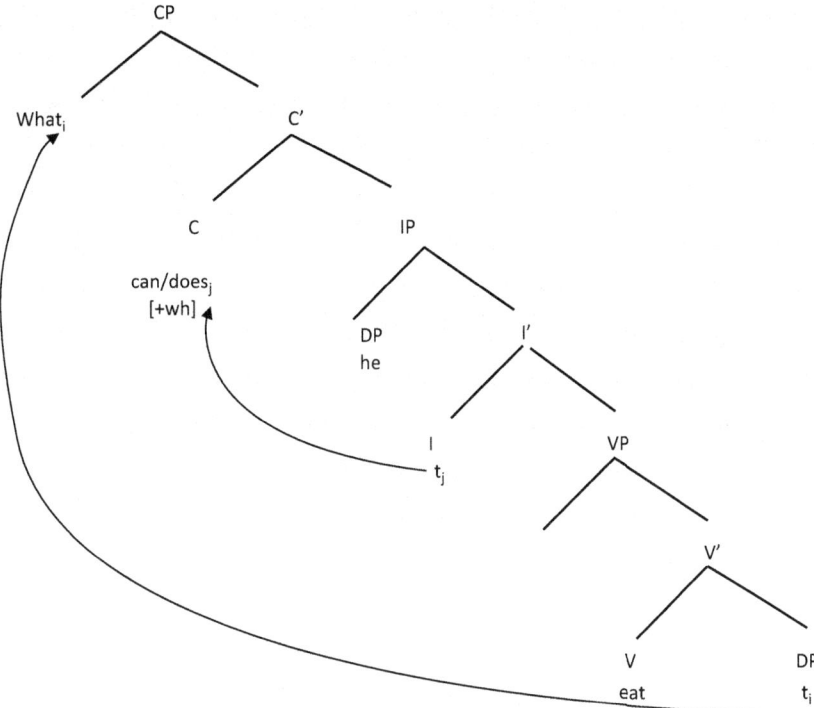

Figure 4.5 Example of wh-movement in English

What is she drinking? Asking questions in English, as in many languages, involves changing the order of words in the sentence, adding some elements, and using different intonation. More specifically, to ask wh-questions in English, we use an interrogative pronoun (wh-word) at the front of the clause. In the tree in Figure 4.5, the object of the verb *eat* is replaced by the interrogative pronoun *what* to create an object question.

In generative grammar this is called **wh-movement,** an operation that is also involved in the structure of **relative clauses.** In addition, because the lexical verb does not move in English, in simple tenses such as the present and the past, there is insertion of the auxiliary verb *do/does/did*, called do-support. Auxiliaries and modals have [+wh] features and move from I-to-C past the subject to yield subject–auxiliary inversion, as in Figure 4.5. In languages including French, German, Spanish, and Italian, the verb moves from V-to-I, then from I-to-C, and carries the feature [+wh] to C (Guasti, 2017).

To ask yes/no questions in English, as in *Can he eat pizza?* Or *Does she eat soup?*, there is also movement of the auxiliary past the subject to C to yield subject–auxiliary inversion.

4.2 Adverb Placement in Second Language Acquisition

In this section we discuss linguistically oriented studies of adverb placement in English and other languages. They show that the position of adverbs with respect to the verb is very challenging to learn. These findings have motivated foundational intervention studies, as we see next.

4.2.1 The Verb-Movement Parameter in Second Language Acquisition

In the 1990s, advances in syntactic theory and comparative syntax within the Principles and Parameters framework of Universal Grammar (Chomsky, 1981, 1986) offered an exciting new perspective on long established findings in second language acquisition. The acquisition of verb placement and word order, subsequently captured by the verb-raising parameter and the V2 parameter described above, were the subject of intense investigation in the context of the lively debate on the availability of UG in second language acquisition (Clahsen & Muysken, 1986; L. White, 1989b). Because child learners of German successfully acquire the correct verb placement in main and embedded clauses whereas L2 learners assume SVO order, Clahsen and Muysken (1986) claimed that this was evidence that UG was not available in L2 acquisition. Another explanation is that L2 learners start with SVO order in German, often guided by their L1 or by what is structurally simpler or most common, but eventually learn the underlying SOV word order.

L. White (1989a) investigated knowledge of adverb placement, specifically the fact that a frequency adverb cannot appear between a transitive verb and a direct object in English, as in *Mary does slowly her homework*, with adult intermediate-level French-speaking L2 learners of English. The learners and a control group of native speakers of English completed a **grammaticality judgment task** (GJT), a multiple-choice task, and a preference task. All tasks presented sentences with different adverb positions. The results consistently showed that the L2 learners accepted and judged as grammatical utterances with sentence-initial or sentence-final frequency adverbs (*Slowly, Ellen drank the hot chocolate/Ellen drank the hot chocolate slowly*) with high accuracy. However, they were very inaccurate with sentences containing adverbs between the verb and the object (**Ellen drank slowly the hot chocolate*), which are grammatical in French but not in English.

This study suggested that French speakers learning English transferred the word order from French. It raised several questions about the role of initial L1 **transfer** in early stages, the possibility of parameter resetting at intermediate and advanced levels, and the nature of **input** in second language acquisition.

In the early 1990s, White launched a major research project to investigate these theoretical issues in the classroom, which produced a set of groundbreaking studies.

White's influential studies on the verb-movement parameter also motivated crosslinguistic investigation of this phenomenon, not necessarily in the classroom. These linguistic studies addressed foundational questions in learnability: for example, in cases when the L2 learners start off with the grammatical representation of the L1, what type of evidence from the L2 input guides grammatical restructuring and acquisition of the L2? Hulk (1991) investigated knowledge of word order and verb placement in L2 acquisition of French by Dutch high school students at different levels of school instruction in French. Like German, discussed above, Dutch is a SOV, V2 language. Results of a written GJT revealed that the learners accepted many French sentences with Dutch word order (SOV), especially those learners at lower levels of proficiency. By college level, the Dutch adolescents knew that the word order of French is SVO in main and embedded clauses. Accuracy with objects and other phrases in sentence-initial position was lower, and some incorrect acceptance of Dutch-type sentences lingered for the university students. Hulk concluded that while the learners had acquired V-to-I movement, they had not acquired I-to-C movement.

Also assuming the parameter resetting model of L2 acquisition and Pollock's proposal of the verb-movement parameter, R. Hawkins, Towell, and Bazergui (1993) and Ayoun (1999) conducted studies with adult L1-English learners of L2 French at intermediate and advanced proficiency. They tested the learners' knowledge of the verb placement possibilities of French with respect to negation, adverbs, and quantifiers. The Ayoun (1999) study also included items testing the position of negation with nonfinite verbs, which is similar in English and French. Both studies found relative success by English-speaking learners of L2 French with adverb placement compared to the French-speaking learners of L2 English studied by L. White (1989a), but the L2 learners were far from nativelike. In both the Hawkins et al. and the Ayoun studies, the L2-French learners' performance did not improve with higher proficiency. Like White, Ayoun concluded that parameter resetting did not occur.

Other studies further concluded that parameter resetting was unsuccessful. Beck (1998) tested English-speaking L2 learners of German and found that the most advanced learners also accepted both grammatical and ungrammatical sentences with adverbs in German, as if they had not reset the V2 parameter in this language. Hamann (2000) conducted a study with high school German students learning L2 English and found that they did not reset the parameter to the negative value of English either.

However, other studies did find evidence of parameter resetting. In three related studies, Conradie (2005) examined the resetting of the two verb-movement parameters (the verb-raising V-to-I parameter and the V2 parameter). The first study was with English-speaking children learning Afrikaans, the second with adult English-speaking and German-speaking learners of L2 Afrikaans, and the third one with Afrikaans-speaking learners of L2 French (Afrikaans, like German, has V2). Conradie found evidence of L1 transfer at initial levels of acquisition and eventual acquisition of the V2 and verb-raising parameters in the three studies.

Finally, Chinese does not have strong I features, and verbs do not raise. Yuan (2001) found that English- and French-speaking learners of Chinese, regardless of proficiency level, recognized the impossibility of verb raising: They did not produce or accept incorrect word orders. Yuan suggested that these learners demonstrated full access to UG without going through a stage of L1 transfer.

As these studies show, the issue of whether the verb-movement parameters (which govern verb raising in French/English, and V2 in non-English Germanic languages) can be reset in L2 acquisition remains inconclusive: Some studies (Yuan, 2001) show it is possible, while others show it is not (L. White, 1989a).

4.2.2 Classroom Intervention Studies on Adverb-Verb Placement in English

The starting point for the studies of L. White (1990, 1991) was whether manipulating input in the classroom helps parameter resetting. As shown in Table 4.1, the verb-movement parameter ties together a number of seemingly unrelated properties regarding the position of the verb in French and in English. The parameter-setting model in vogue at the time theorized that learning one of the syntactic properties of a given parameter through positive evidence would trigger almost simultaneous acquisition of the other structures associated with the parameter (Roeper & Williams, 1987). This was called the clustering effect. For example, a French-speaking child will encounter sentences with postverbal negation (*pas*), and this will trigger the acquisition of [strong I] features which drive verb movement. Then the child will know where to place adverbs. Similarly, *do*-support and auxiliary-subject inversion in English questions would be evidence for the English-speaking child that verbs do not move to I in English because English has a [weak I] feature.

L. White (1989a) found that French-speaking learners assumed verb raising past adverbs in English, suggesting that there is transfer of the parameter settings from the L1 onto the L2. White's (1990, 1991) classroom intervention research subsequently asked the following questions: Is parameter resetting possible in second language acquisition? Does exposing learners to one of the constructions associated with a parameter bring simultaneous or near simultaneous acquisition of the other constructions associated with the parameter, producing a clustering effect?

L. White (1990, 1991) conducted a classroom-based study on acquisition of word order in English by French-speaking, school-age children in Montreal to test whether parameter resetting is possible in second language acquisition. Trahey and White (1993) and Trahey (1996) are follow-ups to these original studies.

4.2.2.1 White's Original Intervention Studies on Verb Movement

The hypotheses tested in the original studies were the following (L. White, 1991):

1. The French-speaking learners of English will be constrained by the parameter setting of their L1 (+verb movement) and assume that the *SVAO (subject–transitive verb–adverb–object) is acceptable in English and SAV (subject–adverb–verb) is not.
2. Specific teaching, which also includes negative evidence, will be effective in helping learners reset the parameter to the English value, and the learners will learn to accept SAV and reject *SVAO sentences in English.
3. Those learners who reset the parameter will show evidence of clustering, adopting the English value (SAV, *SVAO) and rejecting the French value (*SAV, SVAO).

Five intact English as a second language (ESL) classes of twenty-five to thirty French-speaking children (two Grade 5 and three Grade 6 classes) participated in the study. These were beginner classes which had received five months of English instruction when the study was conducted. After three months of regular instruction, all the children were tested on adverb placement in English, together with a group of English-speaking children in Grades 5 and 6 who were the control group (n = 26). Before the study started, the children had not received any instruction on adverbs in their regular program.

The experimental classes were divided into two groups: the adverb group (three classes) and the question group (two classes). The idea was that the children receiving instruction on questions would generalize knowledge of verb movement to the position of adverbs. Immediately after the pretest, the teachers of the adverb group delivered form-focused instruction and learning activities on adverbs for two weeks. During the same period, the question group received instruction and practice on how to form questions in English (see also L. White et al., 1991). After the two-week teaching intervention, the two experimental groups were tested on adverb placement again.

The teaching intervention consisted of a set of materials especially designed for this study. All teachers taught according to what they were instructed by the researchers and were audio recorded. During the first week of the intervention, the children received five hours of teaching and practice on adverbs (the adverb group) or question formation (the question group). In the second week, the experimental classes had two hours of practice with adverb activities (adverb group) or question activities (question group). The adverb intervention included form-focused instruction on the position of manner and frequency adverbs, with information about the possible word orders in English (ASVO, SAVO, SVOA) as well as negative evidence regarding the ungrammaticality of the *SVAO order, which is grammatical in French.

The children completed three written tasks as the pre/posttests (see Box 4.1). The results of the three tasks found the following: First, confirming

---

BOX 4.1 L. White (1991), follow-up studies: Trahey and White (1993), Trahey (1996)

Publication Titles: Adverb placement in second language acquisition: Some effects of positive and negative evidence in the classroom; Positive evidence and preemption in the second language classroom; Positive evidence in second language acquisition: Some long-term effects

Research Questions (White 1991):

1. Is parameter resetting possible in L2 acquisition?
2. Is specific teaching (negative evidence) on English adverb placement effective in helping French learners of English learn that English allows SAV order and disallows SVAO order?
3. Will learners show evidence of a clustering of properties of the verb-movement parameter?

Participants: 220 eleven- and twelve-year old French-speaking children in a English immersion program in Montreal, Canada, plus twenty-six control native-English-speaking children of the same age.

Groups:

L. White (1991): adverb group (n = 82), question group (n = 56).
Trahey & White (1993): input-flood group (n = 56), no-instruction group (n = 26).

BOX 4.1 (cont.)

Study Timeline:

- Day 1: pretest on adverbs (the three instruction groups)
- Two weeks of intervention (the three instruction groups)
- Day 15: posttest 1 (the three instruction groups)
- Day 50: posttest 2 (the three instruction groups)
- One year later: follow-up test (the adverb, input-flood, and no-instruction groups)

Pre/Posttests:

In L. White (1991): a GJT, a preference task, and a manipulation task. The GJT was presented in the context of a cartoon story. There were four types of target sentences, with different adverb positions:

(15) a. Always, Linda takes the metro. (ASVO)
      b. Linda always takes the metro. (SAVO)
      c. *Linda takes always the metro. (*SVAO)
      d. Linda takes the metro always. (SVOA)

In the preference task, each test item was a sentence pair with two response options:

(16) a. Linda always takes the metro.
      b. Linda takes always the metro.
      1. only a is right 2. only b is right 3. both right 4. both wrong 5. don't know

The sentence-manipulation task was a card game. The children were tested individually and were asked to form a sentence with a set of three cards using a given adverb, including both frequency and manner adverbs. Then they were asked to think about other possible sentences with the same cards.

In Trahey and White (1993): the three tasks described above, as well as an oral production in which the children were asked to describe cartoon pictures using adverbs of manner and of frequency.

The Intervention:

- Adverb group: instructional activities with adverbs; positive and negative evidence during the intervention (including correction)
- Question group: instructional activities with questions; positive and negative evidence during the intervention (including correction)
- Input-flood group: activities with many instances of adverbs, but no explicit correction
- No-instruction group: no instruction

BOX 4.1 (cont.)

Results:

The adverb group and to some extent the input-flood group improved after the intervention compared to the question group and the uninstructed group. However, the changes did not survive a year later.

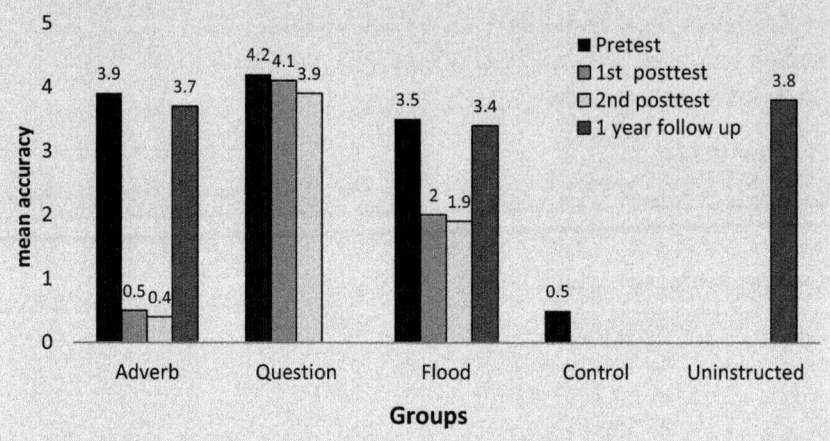

Figure 4.6 Grammaticality judgments, mean *SVAO score: All groups (from L. White 1991; Trahey & White 1993; Trahey 1996)
Note: the control group were English native speakers; the uninstructed group were L2-English learning children in the same classes who received no instructional treatment.

the first hypothesis, French-speaking learners of English start with the setting of the verb-movement parameter for French. In the pretest, the children in the adverb group and in the question group rejected SAV (adverb in between subject and verb) but judged as acceptable *SVAO word order (adverb between the transitive verb and the object) in the GJT and in the preference task, and produced *SVAO word order in the sentence-manipulation task. The English-speaking controls rejected the *SVAO order categorically.

After the instruction intervention, only the group instructed on adverbs came to know that *SVAO is ungrammatical in English, while the question group continued to accept and produce the French-based word order. At the first and second posttests, there were significant differences between the adverb and the question groups on their acceptance and production of *SVAO. Instruction on questions and sustained exposure to English was not effective in triggering parameter resetting for the children in the question group.

So, hypothesis 2 was apparently supported because the children receiving positive and negative evidence on adverb placement appear to have reset the parameter: They correctly rejected *SVAO. (Figure 4.6 in Box 4.1 shows the results of the GJT, which exhibited the same pattern found in the other two tasks.) However, hypothesis 3 was not entirely supported because the children who rejected the *SVAO order after the intervention never actually accepted that SAV word order is a possible order in English. That is, they rejected *SVAO and SAV.

4.2.2.2 Follow-Up Intervention Studies on Verb Movement

The follow-up study conducted a year later and reported in Trahey (1996) (see below) found that whatever knowledge of verb placement was acquired and retained after the intervention was not long-lasting. It seems that the instruction did not alter the children's implicit grammatical knowledge of lack of verb movement in English. What apparently happened was learning in the sense of Krashen (1981) (i.e., explicit learning in today's terms, see Chapter 1) but not acquisition via Universal Grammar (i.e., implicit learning). Furthermore, the children in the adverb group learned that the SVAO order is ungrammatical in English but also considered other grammatical orders ungrammatical, such as SVAPP with intransitive verbs (*John walked quickly to the store*). This suggests that they had overgeneralized the rule about not putting an adverb between a verb and another phrase. Finally, the fact that the children allowed the grammatical SAV order in English alongside the ungrammatical SVAO order made it seem as though they were entertaining the two versions of the parameter (strong/weak I) for English at the same time. Since parameters at that time were considered categorical, entertaining two settings of a parameter was problematic for the learnability theory assumed at the time (Schwartz & Gubala-Ryzak, 1992). A simpler interpretation is that the children were applying an explicit rule of not allowing an adverb after the verb.

If verb movement and question formation were part of the same parameter, as proposed by Pollock (1989), L. White (1990) reasoned that true acquisition of the parameter would involve generalization from questions to adverbs. For example, *do*-support and auxiliary–subject inversion in English questions would be evidence for the French-speaking learners that verbs do not move to I in English and that the SVAO order is ungrammatical. However, this did not happen: Instruction about question formation did not lead to success with adverbs, in contrast to the idea of parametric clustering.

Although it was originally thought that the question group would be exposed to positive evidence with adverbs in the naturally occurring classroom input, this turned out not to be the case. Inspection of the audio recordings from the two weeks of the instruction intervention revealed that the children were not really exposed to adverbs. So, the adverb group received both positive and negative evidence on adverbs during the intervention, while the question group received neither.

Did the explicit learning of the adverb group occur due to the positive evidence on adverb placement, the negative evidence on the impossibility of *SVAO, or both? If naturalistic positive evidence were provided to the learners, would it be sufficient to trigger parameter resetting? If **preemption** (which occurs when learning one form expunges another which is incompatible) is operative in L2 acquisition, then evidence for the grammaticality of SAV in English (a word order ungrammatical in French) should be sufficient to cause the English parameter value [weak I] to preempt the parameter value of the L1 [strong I]. These questions were addressed by Trahey and White (1993) and Trahey (1996) in follow-up studies.

4.2.2.3 Input-Flooding Intervention Studies on Verb Movement

Trahey and White (1993) exposed a group of fifty-six children (from the same ESL program, same age, same grades as in White's studies) to many instances of manner and frequency adverbs, such as *slowly* or *always*, in the context of stories, games, and exercises. Special teaching materials were created so that the lessons included many examples of adverbs in possible word orders in English. This was called the input-flood group: Children were flooded with adverbs. The teachers were instructed not to correct errors if children produced adverbs in the wrong position in English. In addition to the same three tasks used by L. White (1990, 1991), these children completed an oral production task in the pre-/posttests; a new group of twenty-six children in Grade 5 and Grade 6 were tested as an uninstructed control group.

The results of the same three tasks (GJT, preference task, and sentence-manipulation task) revealed that the input-flood group learned that adverbs between the subject and verb (SAV) is a possible word order in English, but they did not strongly reject ungrammatical sentences with an adverb between a transitive verb and the object (SVAO) compared to the adverb group (See Figure 4.1 in Box 4.1). The results suggest that both the SAV and the SVAO orders were permitted in the interlanguage grammars of the children in the input-flood group. Only two of the fifty-four children did not use SVAO in the two posttests, suggesting they had reset the parameter. Overall, the input-flood group improved compared to the question group after the intervention but made less improvement than the adverb group in the original study. A year later, the input-flood group behaved more like the question group, suggesting that the changes observed after the intervention did not survive long term.

Trahey and White (1993) considered that the intervention was not long enough to lead to the resetting of the verb-movement parameter in English.

Trahey (1996) retested the children in the input-flood group a year later and found that their knowledge of adverb placement had not changed: They still used both grammatical and ungrammatical positions for adverbs in English. Trahey concluded that positive or negative evidence alone is insufficient and that some combination of the two, such as positive evidence with **focus on form** (FonF), could be most effective.

4.2.3 Intervention Studies on Negative Adverb Placement in English as a Second Language

In another study, Reinders and Ellis (2009) investigated the effects of enhanced vs. enriched input on the intake and acquisition of negative adverb placement in English, which is like the V2 phenomenon, in that the auxiliary verb occupies the second position of the sentence, as in (17b).

(17)   a. The old wizards had seldom seen such a talented young witch.
         b. Seldom had the old wizards seen such a talented young witch.

Students from a Chinese background learning English in New Zealand (upper intermediate level) were divided into an enriched-input group and an enhanced-input group. The enriched-input group completed tasks with a focus on meaning, with several examples of negative adverbs. The tasks were a dictation, retelling and recalling a text, and collaborative reconstruction of a text in pairs. The enhanced-input group completed the same tasks, but they were also instructed to pay attention to the position of the auxiliary and the subject–auxiliary inversion. Measures of intake were computed from the accuracy on the tasks while acquisition was measured with a timed and an untimed GJT. The untimed GJT is assumed to measure explicit knowledge, while the timed GJT is more indicative of implicit knowledge (see Chapter 1 for more discussion). There was no control group in this study. The groups were compared instead on performance on target and distractor items that were part of the design of the GJTs. The study included a pretest in Week 1 with all participants, followed by three weeks of treatments and the immediate posttest at the end of Week 4, then by a delayed posttest at the end of Week 5.

During the three weeks of treatment, the two groups improved in their recollection and production of sentences with negative adverbs, which was taken as a measure of intake, and the enhanced-input group scored higher than the enriched-input group, just from performing the activities over time, as shown in Table 4.3.

The instruction had no effect on the scores of the timed GJT, which supposedly tested implicit knowledge. However, there was improvement over time with greater acceptance of grammatical sentences with sentence-initial negative adverbs than of ungrammatical sentences with no subject–auxiliary inversion.

Table 4.3 Intake scores on negative adverb placement (Reinders & Ellis, 2009)

Group	n	Week 2	Week 3	Week 4
Enriched input	17	15.5%	32.8%	44.1%
Enhanced input	11	12.6%	45.4%	60.6%

In the long term, the enhanced-input group outperformed the enriched-input group. There was no improvement with grammatical or ungrammatical sentences over time in any of the groups in the untimed GJT. The conclusion was that enriched input facilitated intake and implicit knowledge.

4.2.4 Intervention Studies on Verb Placement in Spanish as a Second Language

The role and usability of negative feedback has been long disputed in L1 acquisition (Bohannon & Stanowicz, 1988) and in L2 acquisition (Schwartz & Gubala-Ryzak, 1992); White's studies (L. White, 1990, 1991; Trahey & White, 1993), which included teaching about the impossibility of certain word orders explicitly, laid bare the fact that whatever learning occurred, it did not persist a year later. It seems that negative evidence in the form of information about what is possible and what is not possible in the language contributes to explicit language learning and perhaps metalinguistic knowledge but not to actual restructuring at the implicit, unconscious level.

Corrective **recasts** are also a form of negative evidence. Children have been shown to imitate all or parts of corrective recasts in child-directed speech (Farrar, 1992), and L2 adults also imitate speech directed at them (Long, 2017). If children and adults can imitate corrective recasts, perhaps this type of negative feedback aids second language acquisition.

Long, Inagaki, and Ortega (1998) conducted a classroom intervention study on adverb placement in Spanish as a second language. With respect to verb movement, Spanish patterns with French and allows several positions for adverbs. Unlike English, Spanish allows SVAO order, as shown in (18).

(18)   a. Todos los días, Juan bebe café. [ASVO]
all the days Juan drinks coffee
'Every day, Juan drinks coffee.'
b. Juan bebe café todos los días. [SVOA]
Juan drinks coffee all the days
'Juan drinks coffee every day.'
c. Juan bebe todos los días café. [SVAO]
Juan drinks all the days coffee
'Juan drinks every day coffee.' (*Note: This word order is not grammatical in English, but it is in Spanish.*)

4.2 Adverb Placement in Second Language Acquisition

Their goal was to investigate the relative contribution of **models** (providing the target form to a learner, as in (19)) and recasts (responding to a learner error with the target form, as in (20)), as types of feedback for grammatical restructuring.

(19) Model
Prompt: Elena   toma   a veces   café.
        Elena   drinks   sometimes   coffee
        'Elena drinks coffee sometimes.'
Learners: Elena toma   a veces   café.
            Elena drinks   sometimes   coffee
            'Elena drinks coffee sometimes.'
Researcher: *Nods* [nonverbal response]

(20) Recast
Prompt: *A veces*
         sometimes
Learners: Elena   toma   a veces   café.
            Elena   drinks   sometimes   coffee
            'Elena drinks coffee sometimes.'
Researcher: Elena   toma   a veces   café,   si?
            Elena   drinks   sometimes   coffee, yes?
            'Elena drinks coffee sometimes, right?'

Three main hypotheses guided this study:

1. Learners who hear models of target L2 structures will show greater ability to produce those structures than learners not exposed to the structures.
2. Learners who hear recasts of target L2 structures will show greater ability to produce those structures than learners not exposed to those structures.
3. Learners who hear recasts of target L2 structures will show greater ability to produce those structures than learners who hear models of those structures.

The study design included a pretest, intervention, and a posttest. There were two experimental groups (n = 12 each) and a control group (called "placebo treatment") with six participants. Because in addition to adverb placement the study also tested other structures, each group received recasts in one structure and models in the other, fully counterbalanced. After completing the pretest, the participants in group 1 received object topicalization recasts, followed by adverb placement models. Group 2 received the opposite: adverb placement recasts and topicalization models. Between pretest and posttest, the control group received the placebo treatment (a semi-structured interview). Alternate test forms (A and B) were used as pretest and posttest. The whole procedure lasted only an hour.

Two communicative tasks were created to deliver the models and recasts with the two structures. Participants and the researcher sat in front of each other separated by a screen and they communicated about objects, actions, and events by manipulating cardboard cutouts on felt boards. Prompts and recasts were prerecorded and delivered via headphones.

The pretest and posttest (forms A and B) consisted of an oral picture-description task and a GJT. No participant exhibited knowledge of these constructions at the pretest. Posttest results showed no learning of adverb placement or object topicalization by the control participants, and no learning of object topicalization at the posttest by any of the groups. The two experimental groups had higher scores on adverb placement at the posttest compared to the group receiving the placebo treatment, and those students who received recasts with SVAO sentences scored higher at the posttest than those receiving models. The results provide weak evidence that implicit negative feedback plays a facilitative role in L2 acquisition, at least with some structures. At the same time, it seems that it is not difficult to learn adverb placement in Spanish, compared to English and French.

Mandell (1996) investigated the acquisition of verb movement in L2 Spanish by adult English-speaking learners of different proficiency levels, including adverb placement with frequency and manner adverbs (*a veces* 'sometimes', *rápidamente* 'quickly'). He found evidence of parameter resetting to the Spanish value (+V movement or strong I), which is the same as in French. Acquisition occurred gradually, since more native-like knowledge was observed with higher levels of proficiency. Other subsequent studies claiming resetting of the verb-movement parameter in Spanish are Bruhn de Garavito (2003) and Guijarro-Fuentes and Larrañaga (2011). Both studies suggest that with increased exposure (and without intervention) learners are able to reset the parameter, probably because Spanish is a more morphologically rich language than French and English, and overt morphology is linked to the strength of the Agr features that drive the movement of the verb in the syntax. So, it is likely that the intervention with models and recasts implemented by Long, Inagaki, and Ortega (1998) may not be solely responsible for success in learning the position of adverbs in L2 Spanish, although it is also noteworthy that the control group who did not receive the treatment did not show the same improvement.

4.2.5 Summary: Intervention Studies with Adverbs

Table 4.4 summarizes the intervention studies on verb movement and adverbs discussed above.

Overall, linguistically oriented studies and classroom intervention studies have shown that learning adverb placement in English, especially the

Table 4.4 Summary of intervention studies on the position of verbs and adverbs

Paper	Structures/phenomena under instruction	Participants' linguistic background	Nature of the intervention	Length of intervention	Major findings
L. White (1990, 1991)	Position of frequency adverbs with respect to the verb (ungrammaticality of SVAO order)	French-speaking grade 5 and grade 6 ESL learners in Montreal, Canada	Explicit presentation of rules of adverb placement and 8 hours of practice activities	2 weeks, in the classroom	Improvement of the adverb group after the treatment, compared to the question formation group (who received no instruction on adverbs) in immediate posttests and delayed posttest; improvement did not last a year later
Trahey & White (1993)	Position of frequency adverbs with respect to the verb (ungrammaticality of SVAO order and grammaticality of SAV)	French-speaking grade 5 ESL learners in Montreal, Canada.	Input flood with adverbs and 8 hours of practice activities	2 weeks, in the classroom	The input-flood group learned that the SAV order is grammatical in English but did not learn that SVAO is ungrammatical
Trahey (1996) (follow-up of Trahey & White, 1993)	Position of frequency adverbs with respect to the verb (ungrammaticality of SVAO order and grammaticality of SAV)	French-speaking grade 6 ESL learners in Montreal, Canada (same children as in Trahey & White, 1993 tested a year later)	Input flood with adverbs and 8 hours of practice activities (a year earlier)	2 weeks, in the classroom (a year earlier)	The children's knowledge of adverb placement did not change from the year before

Table 4.4 (cont.)

Paper	Structures/phenomena under instruction	Participants' linguistic background	Nature of the intervention	Length of intervention	Major findings
Long, Inagaki, and Ortega (1998)	Adverb placement in Spanish (grammaticality of SVAO)	30 university level L2 learners of Spanish	In two communicative activities, learners interacted with native speakers during oral production; they received feedback with models and recasts with adverb placement	1 hour outside the classroom	Learners who heard models and learners who heard recasts of adverb placement in Spanish outperformed the control group who did not receive the treatment; the group receiving recasts scored higher on the target structure than those receiving models
Reinders & Ellis (2009)	Placement of negative adverbs in English (with subject–verb inversion)	28 ESL students in New Zealand (upper intermediate level)	Oral and written activities with input enhancement and input enrichment	3 weeks	Intake scores taken during the three weeks of treatment showed improvement; timed and untimed GJTs scores showed no effects of instruction on explicit and implicit knowledge of adverb placement in English

impossibility of placing adverbs between a transitive verb and an object, is quite difficult for L2 learners. Studies of French as an L2 also provide mixed results. However, learning adverb placement in Spanish is easier, perhaps because Spanish allows many more positions for adverbs than English and French and because it has richer overt verb morphology compared to French.

4.3 Question Formation in Second Language Acquisition

We now turn to studies of question formation in English, which have been the focus of many intervention studies because L2 learners go through specific developmental stages in their acquisition. It takes them a while to learn and eventually master wh-movement, *do*-support, and subject–auxiliary inversion.

4.3.1 Question Formation: Findings from Second Language Acquisition Research

Most of the studies of question formation in L2 English and word order in L2 German and other languages have followed the Processability Theory of language development (Pienemann, 1984, 1998), which identifies developmental stages derived from spoken language in naturalistic SLA. It is well known that during the learning process, language learners go through developmental stages, and interlanguage grammars pass through these stages (see Figure 1.1 in Chapter 1 for intermediate stages of interlanguage development). Each stage represents a set of grammatical rules with processing routines. For question formation in English, the sequence in Table 4.5 has been proposed.

Learners who are at Stage 3 or lower attempting to produce target questions with auxiliary–subject inversion have been found to produce

Table 4.5 Developmental stages of question formation in ESL (based on Mackey, 1999)

Stage	Structure	Example
Stage 1	Fragments	A spot on the dog?
Stage 2	SVO question	*He live here?
Stage 3	Wh + SVO	*Where he is?
Stage 4	Copula inversion	Where is he?
Stage 5	Auxiliary–subject inversion	Where has he been?
Stage 6	Negative question/tag	Haven't you seen a dog? It's on the wall, isn't it?

interlanguage variants which are ungrammatical in the target language, such as *Where he been? *Where has been? *Where he has been? *He has been where? Although these stages have been identified in naturalistic acquisition, if they are universal, they should be observed in classroom learners as well. Studies by R. Ellis (1984, 1989), Lightbown (1983), and Weinert (1987), among many others, have found that ESL classroom learners with different native languages go through similar developmental stages. The instructional implications are that learners need to be developmentally ready in order to learn the target structure, and that it is not possible to move learners directly from Stage 1 or 2 to Stage 4 successfully; they must first pass through Stage 3. Some structures are best learned if the instruction coincides with the learners' next stage in the developmental continuum.

Unlike the verb-raising studies carried out by L. White (1990, 1991) and collaborators discussed in section 4.2.2, the intervention studies on question formation do not assume a linguistic analysis of question formation, as in Figure 4.5. Instead, they have been carried out to test the tenets of Pienemann's Processability Theory and the **Teachability Hypothesis**. Processability Theory (Pienemann, 1998, 2005) focuses on how language is processed and used. Conceived as theory of L2 development guided by Lexical Functional Grammar (Bresnan, 2001), Processability Theory relies on the architecture of the human language processor and states that at any stage of language development the learner can only comprehend and produce the linguistic forms that their language processor can handle. Pienemann (1998) proposed that there is an implicationally ordered processability hierarchy that constrains the language acquisition process but that this implicational hierarchy is language specific. A corollary of Processability Theory is the Teachability Hypothesis. Pienemann (1998) claimed that while some structures can benefit from instruction at just about any time in the learners' development, other structures are best learned if the focused instruction is planned to coincide with the learners' next stage along a developmental continuum.

4.3.2 Intervention Studies on Question Formation

In this section we will examine several intervention studies of question formation in English. Some of these studies were conducted as part of the adverb-placement studies mentioned earlier.

4.3.2.1 Form-Focused Instruction with English Question Formation

A major classroom intervention research project led by Lightbown and Spada examined the role of instruction in the acquisition of English question

Table 4.6 Question formation in English and French

English	French
Is John/he playing tennis?	Est-ce que Jean/Est-ce qu'il joue au tennis?
Does he play tennis?	–
*Plays he tennis?	Joue-t-il au tennis?
He plays tennis?	Il joue au tennis?
*Plays John tennis?	*Joue-Jean au tennis?
Where does Mary/she live?	Où est-ce que Marie/est-ce qu'elle habite?
Mary lives where?	Marie habite où?
*Where lives she?	Où habite-t-elle?
*Where lives Mary?	*Où habite Marie?

formation (Spada & Lightbown, 1993, 1999; L. White et al., 1991) in French-speaking children attending a communicative language program in Montreal. Table 4.6 shows the difference between how questions are formed in English and how they are formed in French.

L. White et al. (1991) investigated the extent to which form-focused instruction and input enhancement through corrective feedback contribute to learners' accuracy in English question formation. The participants were some of the children who participated in the L. White (1990, 1991) adverb-placement studies, as part of the question group, discussed earlier in this chapter. There are differences between questions in English and French related to verb movement, as discussed earlier and shown in Table 4.6. Subject–verb inversion is optional with subject pronouns (such as *he, she, they*) in French but ungrammatical with subject noun phrases (such as *Mary* or *the dog*). When inversion occurs, main verbs can invert (or raise), and wh-in-situ is permitted.

Because of how questions are formed in French, L1-French L2-English learners may say *What John/he wants?* However, there is sufficient positive evidence from the input from questions like *What does John/he want?* to eventually make them realize that there is subject–auxiliary inversion in English.

Phase 1 of the teaching and testing of questions in this study was the control condition in L. White's (1991) adverb-placement study. Recall that two classes received form-focused instruction on question formation, and three classes on adverb placement (the research design is in Box 4.1). After the two-week teaching intervention, the children completed a correction task with written questions with incorrect word order or without subject–auxiliary inversion.

The group instructed on question formation performed significantly better (mean 8.4 out of 10) than the group instructed on adverbs (mean 3.58 out of

10). Ungrammatical questions without inversion accounted for 58 percent of the responses from the adverb group, compared to 34 percent in the question group. These results show that the instruction had a positive effect on children's accuracy.

The main focus of the second phase was the effect of instruction on the development of yes/no and wh-questions. More participants were added to the question and adverb groups, together with a control group in this second phase. After the teaching intervention, the children completed a preference task, a cartoon task, and an oral task. Unlike the results of the adverb-placement study (L. White, 1990, 1991), L. White et al. (1991) found a clear effect for instruction with questions. The question group showed significant improvement in question formation in English compared to the adverb group at the posttest and a follow-up five weeks later. These results make us wonder why the instruction for question formation was more effective than for adverb placement in the same learner population. A possibility is that the intervention was different and more effective in the question studies. Another possibility is that learning word order with question formation is perhaps easier because there is more evidence about question formation in the input than about adverb placement.

4.3.2.2 Form-Focused Instruction and Developmental Readiness

Because French-speaking learners of English tend to assume that, like French, English has optional subject–verb inversion, Spada and Lightbown (1993) examined the effects of form-focused instruction and corrective feedback on the use of questions in an oral communication task.

Learners in two experimental classes received nine hours of form-focused instruction and corrective feedback in English for two weeks. The children completed an oral production task, and videotapes from the classes were also analyzed to follow the children and teachers' production during class. The oral data were analyzed for overall accuracy and for evidence of the developmental stages proposed by Pienemann (1998).

There was improvement after the intervention for the children in the experimental groups at the posttest and later. Unfortunately, the study could not determine which type of corrective feedback (metalinguistic, repetition, focus on error, implicit correction) was more suitable at a given developmental stage because, unexpectedly, the uninstructed comparison group performed as well as, and even better than, the experimental groups in terms of both accuracy and developmental progression. Although the children in the uninstructed comparison group were at the same proficiency level as the children in the experimental groups, examination of the video recording revealed that whereas the teachers in the experimental groups did not correct the children beyond the intervention, the teacher of the comparison group did focus on form and corrected the children on a daily basis. She frequently corrected students' use of questions and other grammatical errors. In other words, contrary to plan, the comparison group ended up being another instructed group. And because these children had received corrective feedback for longer than those in the instructed intervention, they outperformed the children in the experimental groups. It was not possible in this study to distinguish between types of instruction as planned.

A later study, Spada and Lightbown (1999), investigated how learners' developmental readiness in English question formation interacts with instruction to test Pienemann's Teachability Hypothesis. The research questions were

1. Is instruction targeted to the next stage in the learners' L2 development more effective than the instruction targeting a more advanced stage?
2. Is implicit instruction targeted to the learners' next developmental stage sufficient to move the learner into more advanced stages?
3. How does the L1 influence the L2 learners' progress through developmental stages?

Five intact classes in an intensive ESL program in Montreal participated. The children were pretested on questions in English after the first twelve weeks of instruction. Then they were engaged in activities to practice questions for two weeks (four hours per week). They were tested immediately after the intervention and, four weeks later, they were tested again. The measures used were an oral production task to elicit questions, and two paper-and-pencil tasks (a preference task and a scrambled-question task). The study did not include a control or comparison group. Instead, the data for each task was pooled together and analyzed in terms of individual stages of question development, which ranged from Stage 2 to Stage 5, comparing the results of the pretest and the posttest. At the delayed posttest, the children completed a new task: a picture-cued task eliciting written questions. Of the 144 children who participated, 3 percent were in Stage 3, 75 percent in Stage 4, and 21 percent in Stage 5 at the delayed posttest.

Contrary to the predictions of the Teachability Hypothesis, the learners who were in Stage 3 of question formation (as determined by the pretest) did not progress more in their use of questions in the oral production task than the learners who were in Stage 2 at the time of the pretest. The results of the two other tasks revealed that students had knowledge of questions at Stages 4 and 5 at the delayed posttest. The performance of the children in the written tasks was more advanced than in the oral task. In the preference task, the children tended to accept questions with subject–verb inversion when the subject was a pronoun, as in French, but not when the subject was a name. In sum, this study shows that question formation in English is easier to acquire than adverb placement and more amenable to instruction. Even though the children made progress, their native language played a role in the process.

4.3.2.3 Instruction and Feedback during Interaction

A series of studies have also been conducted to examine the role of instruction and feedback during interaction, focusing on question formation in English. Mackey (1999) tested the interaction hypothesis (Long, 1983), which states that taking part in conversational interactions can facilitate second language development (see Box 4.2).

Mackey (1999) also examined whether the developmental outcomes were related to the nature of the conversational interaction and the level of the learner involvement. The prediction was that learners who actively participated in interaction would receive the most benefit compared to learners who observed interactions or took part in scripted interactions. The question forms targeted in the treatment conformed to Pienemann's developmental stages (Table 4.6), and development was operationalized as movement through the sequence. The learners had to show at least two examples of the structures at a particular stage in two different posttests for the researchers to ascertain that development had occurred.

The study found that conversational interactions did facilitate development. The interactor group (the learners who more actively participated in the interactions) produced a significantly higher number of advanced questions than those learners who did not participate actively in interactions (observers, scripters) and those who participated in the interaction but were of lower proficiency (unreadies).

McDonough (2005) investigated whether negative feedback to the learners and the modified output that results from this feedback predict the development of question formation in ESL learners. As in the previous studies, question formation was chosen because it is a linguistic phenomenon with well-defined developmental stages, and the focus of McDonough's study was on the relative contributions of negative feedback and modified output during production. Negative feedback through interaction may contribute to L2 development by informing learners about the comprehensibility of the utterances and by raising their awareness of language. Producing modified output may contribute to L2 development by strengthening representations and by encouraging automatic retrieval of linguistic forms.

The participants were adult learners of English as a foreign language (EFL) in Thailand. The pretest identified a group of learners who were at the same developmental stage of question formation in Pienemann's framework. Six

BOX 4.2 Mackey (1999)

Publication Title: Input, interaction and second language development. An empirical study of question formation in ESL

Research Question: Does participating in interaction lead to second language development?

Participants: 34 beginner and lower intermediate ESL adult learners and 6 native speakers of English, who acted as conversational partners for the participants in the experimental groups

Groups:

ESL participants were assigned to three treatment groups and a control group. The four experimental groups were "interactors," interactionally modified input through tasks (higher level; $n = 7$) in Figure 4.7; "unreadies," interactionally modified input through tasks (lower level; $n = 7$); "observers," observers of interactionally modified input ($n = 7$); "scripted," premodified scripted input through tasks ($n = 6$); and a control group who received no treatment ($n = 7$), "control" in Figure 4.7.

Study Timeline:

- Day 1: pretest
- Days 2, 3, and 4: intervention
- Day 5: posttest 1
- Posttest 2 one week later
- Posttest 3 in week 5

Pre/Posttests: a picture-differences task eliciting wh-questions and yes/no questions, including questions with negation and adverbs

The Intervention: 4 different tasks eliciting wh-questions and yes/no questions, including questions with negation and adverbs

- Information-gap task
- Story-completion task
- Picture-sequencing task
- Picture-difference task

Results:

Overall, the results showed that conversational interaction facilitates second language development. Only the groups that actively participated in the interaction demonstrated evidence of development: These groups increased in developmental stages over time and produced more advanced questions.

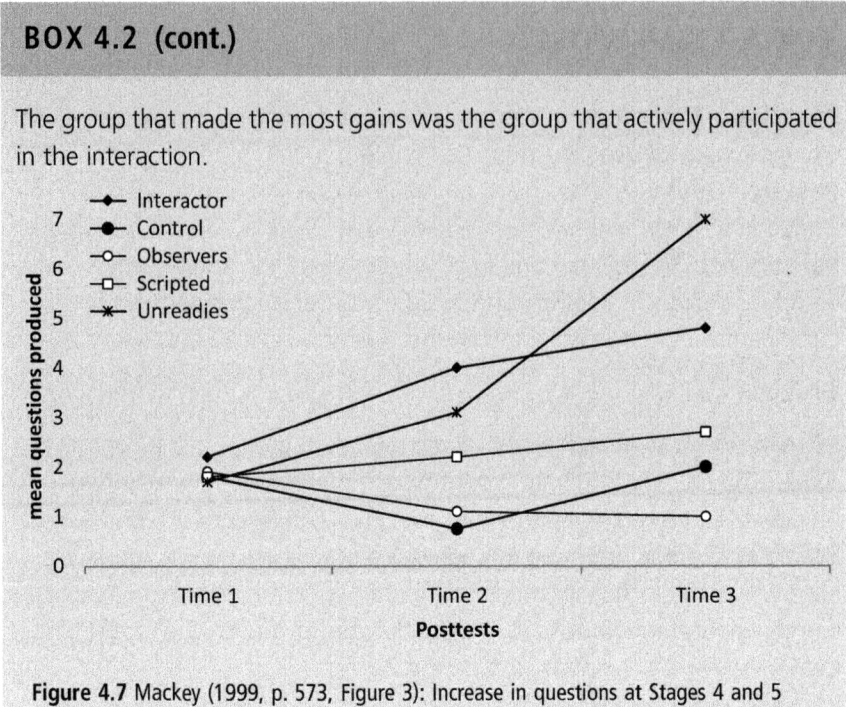

BOX 4.2 (cont.)

The group that made the most gains was the group that actively participated in the interaction.

Figure 4.7 Mackey (1999, p. 573, Figure 3): Increase in questions at Stages 4 and 5 produced by each group in the posttests

native speakers of American and British English were recruited as interactors and were asked to participate in collaborative dialogue with the learners and to respond to the learners' nontarget-like question forms as needed. The participants were divided into four groups: enhanced opportunity to modify, opportunity to modify, feedback without opportunity to modify, and the control group (no feedback). The treatment and test materials included information-exchange and information-gap activities that elicited questions. During each treatment session, the learners took notes about their awareness of what they were learning in a learning journal.

The entire study was carried out over eight weeks. In Week 1, all the groups completed the pretest followed by three treatment sessions over a week. The posttests took place during Weeks 2, 5, and 8. During the treatment sessions, learners in the enhanced-opportunity-to-modify group received the most negative feedback, followed by the opportunity-to-modify group, and the feedback-without-opportunity-to-modify group. The oral data were transcribed and coded for types of questions. Because the learners were at Stage 4 of question development, only modified output involving Stage-5 questions was considered as evidence of development. The no-feedback group received no correction or recasts on their responses.

The difference in the amount of modified output produced by the two opportunity groups was not significant, and they did not produce Stage-5 questions in response to feedback. The test data was examined to identify learners in the treatment groups who had advanced from Stage 4 to Stage 5 in the developmental sequence of question formation. In all, 60 percent (n = 9) of the learners in the enhanced-opportunity-to-modify group advanced to Stage 5, 33.3 percent (n = 5) of learners in the opportunity-to-modify group advanced to Stage 5, and only 13.3 percent (n = 2) in the remaining two groups advanced to Stage 5. Modified output was the only significant predictor of questions in L2 English. Negative feedback in the form of clarification requests may indirectly contribute to question development by creating opportunities for learners to modify their output, a finding that supports the output hypothesis (Swain, 1993). Unlike most studies of instructional interventions, this study did not analyse the data by time or show the results of the pretest and the four posttests separately.

4.3.2.4 Using Priming to Teach Question Formation

McDonough and Mackey (2008) also tested question formation and development along Pienemann's stages using a primed production paradigm. **Syntactic priming** (also known as structural priming) is a well-studied phenomenon in psycholinguistics (Bock, 1986) and occurs when a speaker immediately uses or repeats a structure they have been exposed to in recent discourse (see also Chapter 8). Syntactic priming may lead to the formation of abstract syntactic representations (F. Chang, Dell, & Bock, 2006). By facilitating the production of developmentally advanced structures, syntactic priming might strengthen the knowledge representations that learners already have stored and encourage retrieval of linguistic forms. McDonough and Mackey (2006) found that primed production during conversation was positively associated with question development. McDonough and Mackey (2008) asked whether primed production without interactional feedback facilitates L2 learning.

Participants were adult EFL learners in Thailand. They interacted with six scripted interlocutors who were students with advanced English proficiency from the same university. The design consisted of pretest, intervention, and posttest, as in Table 4.7. The entire study was carried out over a seven-week period, with the pretest in Week 1, treatments in Week 2, and posttests in Weeks 3 and 7. The testing and treatment materials were the same communicative information-gap activities for eliciting questions used in prior studies (McDonough, 2005; McDonough & Mackey, 2006).

The data were audiotaped, transcribed, and coded according to the Pienemann (1998) developmental sequence for ESL questions. Syntactic

Table 4.7 Design of the McDonough and Mackey (2008) study

Week	Priming group	Control group
1	Pretest and biodata questionnaire	Pretest and biodata questionnaire
2	20-minute session with a scripted interlocutor	No interaction
3	Posttest 1	Posttest 1
7	Posttest 2	Posttest 2

priming was demonstrated when participants produced developmentally advanced questions more often after the scripted interlocutor's developmentally advanced questions than after the interlocutor's same-level or lower-level questions. Although not all the learners showed evidence of advancement to a higher stage of question development after the priming treatment, overall, the study found a positive relationship between syntactic priming and question development in English. However, this study reported global results instead of the results of the two posttests.

Table 4.8 provides a summary of the studies on question formation covered in this chapter.

4.4 Summary and Implications

We have seen that the placement of adverbs with respect to the verb in English is very challenging to learn, especially if the native language of the learners allows more flexibility with the position of adverbs with respect to the verb. Since Spanish allows more options for word order, English-speaking learners seem to acquire adverb orders more readily, without the need for negative evidence or significant input manipulation in the classroom. Studies of input manipulation in the classroom yield improvement in Spanish but not in English, maybe because it is easier to learn adverb placement in Spanish than in English, even in the absence of interventions (Bruhn de Garavito, 2003; Guijarro-Fuentes & Larrañaga, 2011; Mandell, 1996).

As for the acquisition of question formation in English, different types of intervention studies in the classroom suggest that these structures are more suitable to different types of interventions and that L2 learners who receive feedback advance more readily than learners who do not. Although the stages of development of question formation in English cannot always be changed with instruction, eventually learners make progress, regardless of the feedback and intervention.

Table 4.8 Summary of intervention studies on question formation in English

Paper	Structures/ phenomena under instruction	Participants' linguistic background	Nature of the intervention	Length of intervention	Major findings
L. White et al. (1991)	Question formation in English	French-speaking grade 5 and grade 6 ESL learners in Montreal, Canada	Input enhancement activities on question formation	2 weeks, in the classroom	Explicit instruction contributed to syntactic accuracy; the group exposed to input-enhancement activities outperformed the uninstructed group
Spada & Lightbown (1993)	*Do*-support and subject–auxiliary–verb inversion in English questions	French-speaking grade 5 ESL learners in Montreal, Canada	Five hours of form-focused instruction and corrective feedback	2 weeks, in the classroom	The two experimental groups and the "uninstructed" control group gained accuracy in question formation from pretest to posttest, to follow-up test
Spada & Lightbown (1999)	Stages of development of questions in English	150 French-speaking grade 6 ESL learners in Montreal, Canada, who were at Stage 2 of question formation development	Exposure to English questions consistent with Stage 4 and Stage 5 of development	2 weeks, in the classroom	Regardless of whether they were in Stage 2 or 3, the learners produced Stage-5 questions in English when the subjects were pronouns, as in French

Table 4.8 (cont.)

Paper	Structures/phenomena under instruction	Participants' linguistic background	Nature of the intervention	Length of intervention	Major findings
Mackey (1999)	Wh- and yes/no questions in English	34 ESL learners from a private English language school in Australia	The L2 learners interacted with native speakers in different input conditions depending in the interactions; one group did not interact but just watched	1 session per day for a week, 1 session 1 week later, 1 session 3 weeks later	Conversational interactions facilitated L2 development in the groups that interacted with native speakers compared with the group who did not participate in the interactions
McDonough (2005)	ESL question development	109 ESL students in Thailand	The L2 learners were divided into 4 groups, interacted with a native-speaker interactor, and received different types of negative feedback and modified output	A pretest and 3 twenty-minute treatment sessions and 3 posttests completed over 8 weeks in lab sessions	Support for the output hypothesis; learners who had the opportunity to modify their output showed greater development in ESL question formation than those receiving implicit negative feedback
McDonough & Mackey (2008)	The role of syntactic priming in ESL question development	46 ESL learners in Thailand	Communicative activities with a more advanced English-speaking interlocutor	Oral pretests, 2 twenty-minute sessions, 2 posttests	Participants who engaged in syntactic priming showed higher levels of development of questions in English

Together, the studies discussed in this chapter raise the question of why some properties of language are more acquirable than others and whether the efficacy of input manipulation is limited to properties of language that are easier to acquire. The answer to this question is still the subject of much investigation, speculation, and debate in second language acquisition. It points to an interaction of the organization of the grammar, psycholinguistic processes, and input evidence, which we continue to explore in the rest of the chapters.

4.5 DISCUSSION QUESTIONS

1. White's (1990, 1991) studies on adverb placement included follow-up studies a year later. What did the follow up studies reveal about what the children have learned? Long, Inagaki, and Ortega (1998) found successful acquisition of adverb placement in Spanish, but compared to White's studies, the study in Long, Inagaki, and Ortega (1998) had a very short intervention. Can Long et al.'s results be taken as definitive in the absence of a follow-up study a year later? Why or why not? What other factors could explain the success of learning verb movement in Spanish and the difficulty of learning that verbs do not move in English? Discuss.
2. Spada and Lightbown (1993) could not determine which type of corrective feedback (metalinguistic, repetition, focus on error, implicit correction) was more suitable at a given developmental stage because the uninstructed comparison group performed as well as, and even better than, the experimental groups in terms of both accuracy and developmental progression. What could they have done to avoid the unexpected error? How valid are the results of this study if the comparison group ended up being an instructed group?
3. McDonough and Mackey (2006, 2008) implemented a design with pretest, intervention, and two posttests but ended up discussing the results of the posttest as a single posttest measure. What do you think of this approach? What are the advantages and disadvantages of presenting the results of each posttest individually rather than all collapsed?

4.6 APPLICATIONS QUESTIONS

1. Design a study of adverb placement in English using an interactionist approach with adult French-speaking learners of English. Describe the design (pretest, intervention, posttests), the control and comparison

groups, and the type of intervention. What type of evidence will you use to conclude that the learners have reset the parameter?
2. The stages of development of questions identified by Pienemann (1984, 1998) are based on production data. Supposing that you also want to know whether those stages reflect the learners' linguistic competence, design an intervention study using grammaticality judgment data. How would you start and implement it? What would you expect to find?

4.7 FURTHER READING

- Pienemann, M. (1998). *Language processing and second language development: Processability Theory.* Amsterdam: John Benjamins.
  This book explains Processability Theory in detail and spells out which grammatical forms are processable at which developmental stage of second language acquisition in different languages.

- White, L. (2003). *Second language acquisition and Universal Grammar.* Cambridge, UK: Cambridge University Press.
  This is an authoritative treatment of the theory of Universal Grammar and of second language studies conducted within generative second language acquisition. It offers a summary and discussion of the verb-movement studies presented in this chapter, written by the author of the studies.

5 Inflectional Morphology

In this chapter we address the second language acquisition (SLA) of **inflectional morphology**, in particular, the markers of tense, agreement, and grammatical gender. Inflectional morphology is known to be particularly challenging for adult L2 learners in all the second languages tested and has been termed the "bottleneck" of the L2 acquisition process by Slabakova (2008). As a result, this area of the grammar has been subject to many experimental SLA and classroom **intervention studies**.

After a review of the relevant terminology, we discuss the debate on whether L2 learners' difficulty with inflectional morphology is due to deficits of linguistic representations or more "surface" problems such as memory retrieval or processing. We then go into and evaluate classroom **intervention** research studies that have been done on verbal inflectional morphology (primarily in English but also in some Romance languages) and on grammatical gender (primarily in Romance languages).

5.1 Terminology

The linguistic subfield of **morphology** studies word formation. A **morpheme** is the smallest linguistic unit that has meaning; morphemes can combine together to form words, but a word may also consist of a single morpheme. For example, in English, *cat* is a morpheme and also a word. It has meaning (denoting the species of domesticated mammals whose members have whiskers, meow, hunt mice, and consider themselves superior to humans), and it cannot be broken down into smaller meaningful units. For example, the /k/ sound in *cat* has no meaning, nor does *ca* without the *t*, and so on. In contrast, *cats* (plural) is a word but not a morpheme. It can be broken down into two meaningful units, *cat* (which has the meaning given above) and -*s* (which means 'plural'). Here, we have two morphemes combining to form a single word.

While *cat* is an example of a **free morpheme** (a morpheme that can stand on its own, i.e., a morpheme which is also a word), the plural -*s* suffix is an example of a **bound morpheme** (a morpheme that must attach to another morpheme and cannot stand on its own). There are two types of bound morphemes: **derivational** and **inflectional**. Derivational bound morphemes are used to derive new words: for example, the *-ness* in *sadness* is a derivational morpheme, which attaches to an adjective (*sad*) in order to create a noun. We do not address derivational morphology in this chapter but focus instead on inflectional bound morphemes, which do not derive new words but rather inflect words for particular grammatical properties.

In English, the plural *-s* inflects a noun for number (turning a singular noun into a plural one, as in *cat – cats*). The past tense marker *-ed* inflects a verb for tense (turning a present-tense verb into a past-tense one, as in *walk – walked*). The *-ing* suffix inflects a verb for progressive aspect, which emphasizes the duration of the event (as in *I was walking for an hour*). And the third-person present tense singular *-s* inflects a verb for person and number agreement with the subject (so that we say *I/we/you/they walk*, but *She/he/it walks*).

In Standard American English, the only type of agreement that exists is **person/number agreement**: The verb must agree with the subject in person and number. The agreement paradigm in English is quite poor compared to other languages. Number agreement is marked only in the present tense, and only in the third person, as shown in (21a–b). It is not marked in the past tense, where both singular and plural subjects occur with the same form of the verb, as shown in (21c–d). There is no number agreement for the first or second person (21e).

(21) a. My cat likes vegetables.
 b. My two cats like vegetables.
 c. My cat liked vegetables until recently.
 d. My two cats liked vegetables until recently.
 e. I/we/you like vegetables.

The one exception is the verb *be*, which exhibits number agreement for both first and third person in the past tense, as shown in (22a–b) (note that modern English only has the plural form of the second-person pronoun, so *you* takes a plural verb). In the present tense, the verb *be* exhibits both person and number agreement, resulting in three distinct forms, as shown in (22c–e). The verb *be* in English has two uses: It is an auxiliary or "helping verb" when occurring with another, lexical verb (as in (22a–b)) and a **copula** or "linking verb" when it links the subject to a nonverbal predicate (as in (22c–e)).

(22) a. I/she/he was swimming in the ocean.
 b. We/you/they were worrying about sharks.
 c. I am sure I see a fin in the water.
 d. Fortunately, it is a dolphin and not a shark.
 e. The dolphins are quite friendly.

Other languages, such as Spanish, German, Hindi, Finnish, and Russian, have much richer verbal agreement paradigms, with different bound morphemes marking various tense/number/person combinations for all verbs, not only the verb *be*. Other languages also have agreement paradigms outside of the verbal domain. In particular, many Romance, Germanic, and Slavic languages have **gender agreement**. In gender-marking languages, every noun is assigned to a particular nominal gender class, and other elements in the sentence (such as adjectives, determiners, pronouns, and/or verbs) must agree with the noun in gender. Among the more familiar languages, some have two-gender systems (feminine vs. masculine in Spanish; common vs. neuter in Dutch) while others have three-gender systems (feminine vs. masculine vs. neuter in Russian and German). There are also languages with more complex gender systems: For example, Swahili is analyzed as having six different genders (see Spinner, 2013 on the L2 acquisition of gender and number and Swahili).

For illustration, consider the Spanish system of grammatical gender. For animate nouns, grammatical gender in Spanish often corresponds to semantic or biological gender. For example, *hombre* 'man' is masculine while *mujer* 'woman' is feminine. In the case of inanimate nouns, grammatical gender has no biological basis: e.g., *libro* 'book' is masculine while *mesa* 'table' is feminine. Indeed, the correspondence between the meaning of an inanimate noun and its grammatical gender is completely arbitrary: For example, in Russian, *kniga* 'book' is feminine while *stol* 'table' is masculine, the opposite of Spanish. What is typically not arbitrary, however, is the correspondence between grammatical gender and phonology as well as orthography. In Spanish, masculine nouns typically end in *-o* while feminine nouns typically end in *-a*. However, there are also many exceptions, both nouns which follow the opposite pattern (e.g., *mano* 'hand' is feminine, while *problema* 'problem' is masculine), nouns which end in *-e* (e.g., *puente* 'bridge' is masculine while *noche* 'night' is feminine), and nouns which end in a consonant (e.g., *pincel* 'brush' is masculine while *flor* 'flower' is feminine). Languages such as French or Dutch have less transparent gender systems than Spanish; while there are phonological and/or orthographic cues to grammatical gender, they are less consistent than the ones available in Spanish.

In Spanish (and many other gender-marking languages), determiners and adjectives are marked for both gender and number agreement. Where English has only one definite determiner, *the*, which is used with both singular and plural nouns, Spanish uses *el* with masculine singular nouns, *la* with feminine singular nouns, and *los* and *las* with masculine and feminine plural nouns, respectively. The indefinite determiner 'a/some' similarly has four distinct forms (*uno, una, unos, unas*). Many adjectives are also marked for both gender and number, with *-o* and *-a* corresponding to the prototypical masculine and feminine singular adjectival endings, respectively. Thus, in Spanish, 'the red house' is *la casa roja* (feminine) but 'the red car' is *el auto rojo* (masculine). Other adjectives are invariant, ending in *-e* for both masculine and feminine (e.g., *inteligente* 'intelligent', *interesante* 'interesting', *transparente* 'transparent', *verde* 'green') or in a consonant (*feliz* 'happy', *azul* 'blue').

In this chapter, we will focus on studies that address inflectional morphology and agreement. In the case of English, our primary focus is the L2 acquisition of the verbal inflectional paradigm (third person *-s* and past tense *-ed*), while in the case of Spanish and other Romance languages, we consider both studies on verbal morphology and those on grammatical gender.

5.2 Inflectional Morphology in Second Language Acquisition: Experimental Findings and Theoretical Implications

Inflectional morphology is known to be one of the most challenging areas in SLA, with learners showing high rates of inaccuracy and variability (optional use of inflectional morphemes in required contexts). At least in some cases, difficulties persist even for very advanced, end-state L2 learners (see, e.g., the case studies of Lardiere, 1998a and L. White, 2003a). Numerous studies on Germanic and Romance languages have found L2 learners omitting inflectional morphemes and overrelying on **default forms**. Default forms are forms that are used by learners across syntactic environments, regardless of tense/person/number (see, among many others, Lardiere, 1998a, 2000 on verbal inflectional morphology in L2 English; Prévost and White, 2000 on verbal inflectional morphology in L2 French and L2 German; Montrul, Foote, and Perpiñán, 2008 on grammatical gender in L2 Spanish).

For example, child L2-English learners in Ionin and Wexler (2002) produced utterances such as *girl play with toy* (instead of *plays*) and *one time I watch this movie* (instead of *watched*). Similarly, adult L2-Spanish learners (as well as Spanish heritage speakers) in Montrul, Foote, and Perpiñán (2008) sometimes produced incorrect gender marking on determiners and adjectives. Bound inflectional morphology is particularly challenging to learners, compared to freestanding inflectional morphemes. For example, in English, learners tend to be more accurate in supplying forms of *be* (*is, are, am, was, were*) than in supplying third person *-s* and past tense *-ed* (Ionin & Wexler, 2002, among others). Learners have also been found to overuse forms of *be* in place of bound inflectional morphology, producing utterance such as *He is want* in place of *He wants* (Ionin & Wexler, 2002).

In this section, we discuss the major theoretical accounts of the SLA of inflectional morphology and the relevant experimental evidence, prior to moving on to intervention studies in section 5.3.

5.2.1 Errors with Inflectional Morphology as a Representation vs. Processing Problem

A major source of debate in the generative SLA literature on inflectional morphology is whether errors with morphology indicate a "deep" impairment to the learners' syntax at the level of mental representation or a more "shallow" impairment to the surface morphology during production. When a learner omits a past-tense marker, is that because the syntactic category **Tense** is absent from their grammar (see also Chapter 4 on functional categories that underlie tense and agreement marking)? Or is the Tense category present, and the omission due to processing or retrieval difficulties during language use? When an L2-Spanish learner misuses a masculine adjective with a feminine noun, is that because she has miscategorized the noun as masculine (a **gender assignment** error) or because she knows that the noun is feminine yet exhibits a gender agreement error? And in the case of the latter, does the problem with gender agreement indicate lack of the grammatical gender category in her grammar, or is the category present, with the error once again due to processing or lexical retrieval difficulties?

There are many different proposals about deep vs. shallow impairments (for an overview, see Ionin, 2012b). Generative SLA proposals that treat problems with morphology as indicative of syntactic impairment include the Minimal Trees Hypothesis (Vainikka & Young-Scholten, 1996), the Failed Functional Features Hypothesis (R. Hawkins & Chan, 1997), the Representational Deficit Hypothesis (R. Hawkins, 2003), and the Interpretability Hypothesis (Tsimpli & Mastropavlou, 2008), among others. While differing in the specifics, all of these proposals argue for missing or impaired categories or syntactic features in learners' developing grammars. On some proposals, such impairment is temporary and can be overcome with proficiency, while on others, it is permanent. In contrast, generative SLA proposals that adopt the Full Transfer/Full Access Model of Schwartz and Sprouse (1994, 1996) assume that learners' developing grammar contains all syntactic categories and **features**. These categories and features are transferred from the learners' L1, but the combination of L2 input and access to **Universal Grammar** allows learners to reset **parameters** and to acquire the categories and features of their L2. On this view, difficulties with inflectional morphology are not indicative of a deeper syntactic impairment. According to the Missing Surface Inflection Hypothesis (MSIH; Haznedar & Schwartz, 1997; Prévost & White, 2000; Lardiere, 2000), omission of verbal morphology is a "surface" problem, due to difficulty with retrieval of inflectional morphemes under the pressure of production. According to the Prosodic Transfer Hypothesis (Goad & White, 2006), the problems with inflectional morphology are prosodic rather than syntactic in nature.

Proponents of the MSIH strive to show that even when learners omit tense morphology, syntactic markers of Tense are still in place (see Lardiere, 1998b, 2003; Prévost & White, 2000; Ionin & Wexler, 2002; L. White, 2003a). Such syntactic markers include overt, **nominative-case** subjects (since Tense licenses nominative case) and correct verb placement with respect to adverbs and negation (see also Chapter 4). Furthermore, learners' errors with verbal morphology are largely errors of omission rather than commission. L2-English learners overuse bare stem forms such as *play* in place of *plays* or *played*, while L2 French and L2 German learners overuse the **infinitival verb form**. Misuse of incorrect **finite verb** forms (e.g., the second-person ending for the third person) is quite rare. MSIH proponents argue that this means that learners overrely on defaults, using the bare or infinitival form whenever they cannot retrieve the correct tense/agreement marker from memory. This account, by reliance on problems with retrieval, predicts that learners' errors should be largely limited to spontaneous production and not evident in other task types.

There is some support for this prediction. For example, Goad and White (2006) found that L1-Chinese ESL learners had very high accuracy in the suppliance of past-tense morphology in a controlled oral sentence-completion task. In contrast, studies that looked at spontaneous production with L1-Chinese ESL learners (R. Hawkins & Liszka, 2003; Lardiere, 1998b) found much omission of past-tense marking with this population. However, Jiang et al. (2011) argue that the explicit task format in Goad and White (2006) was likely targeting learners' explicit rather than implicit knowledge (more on this in the next section).

In the domain of grammatical gender, Bruhn de Garavito and White (2002) and L. White et al. (2004) also argue for the MSIH, proposing that learners have a grammatical category of gender, but have difficulty retrieving the right gender forms during production. While L2-Spanish learners were found to make gender errors in oral production in these studies, they did quite well in a written comprehension task, providing evidence for gender errors as a "surface" production problem. However, other studies have found different results. McCarthy (2008) found that L2-Spanish learners made errors in oral production as well as written comprehension, leading McCarthy to argue that difficulty with gender is at the level of representation. Montrul, Foote, and Perpiñán (2008) compared adult L2-Spanish and heritage Spanish speakers on grammatical gender and found that while the L2 learners' results were consistent with the MSIH, those of the heritage speakers were not. The L2 learners performed better with written comprehension than with oral production, while the heritage speakers exhibited the opposite pattern. Montrul, Foote, and Perpiñán (2008) concluded that that L2 learners do better with explicit, metalinguistic tasks, while heritage speakers have better command of implicit, automatized knowledge (see Chapter 1).

5.2.2 Psycholinguistic Studies on Inflectional Morphology in Second Language Acquisition

In more recent years, researchers have begun to use psycholinguistic methods such as **self-paced reading, eye tracking** and event-related potentials (ERPs; a brain-based measure) in order to examine learners' online sensitivity to inflectional morphology. As we discussed in Chapter 1, online methods have been argued to tap into learners' implicit or at least automatized knowledge more than traditional offline tasks.

With regard to grammatical gender, Grüter, Lew-Williams, and Fernald (2012) examined how highly proficient adult L2-Spanish learners performed across a variety of tasks. Grüter, Lew-Williams, and Fernald (2012) showed that learners differed from native speakers not only in oral production but also in online processing. Unlike native speakers, the learners failed to use gender marking on determiners to predict what noun was coming next in an eye-tracking-while-listening task. Grüter, Lew-Williams, and Fernald (2012) interpreted this finding as indication that L2 difficulty with grammatical gender lies at the level of lexical representation.

In the case of verbal agreement, Jiang, 2004 found that L1-Chinese L2-English learners failed to slow down for errors with verb-agreement morphology in a self-paced reading task. Since Chinese does not have verbal agreement, this result was taken as evidence that learners cannot integrate agreement into their L2 grammar when it is absent in their L1. Jiang (2007) and Jiang et al. (2011) found a similar lack of slowdown for errors with plural marking on the part of L1-Chinese and L1-Japanese L2-English learners, respectively. In contrast, L1-Russian L2-English learners in Jiang et al. (2011) did slow down for missing plural marking. Since Russian has obligatory plural morphology but Chinese and Japanese do not, this pattern was taken as further evidence that learners cannot integrate new inflectional categories into their **interlanguage** grammar. An ERP study by Chen et al. (2007) supported this conclusion, by showing that L1-Chinese L2-English learners did not show the same kind of brain response to agreement errors as native English speakers did.

In contrast, a later ERP study by Armstrong, Bulkes, and Tanner (2018) found similar brain responses to agreement errors from L1-Chinese L2-English learners as from native English speakers, suggesting that native-like processing is possible at least for more proficient learners. In the domain of plural marking, Choi and Ionin (2021) found that L1-Chinese and L1-Korean L2-English learners did slow down for missing plural marking in at least some conditions, despite the lack of obligatory plural marking in their L1s.

In sum, as we can see, there is much evidence that L2 learners have difficulty with inflectional morphology but disagreement as to whether this difficulty indicates problems with syntactic representation. The experimental evidence is contradictory. Some studies find difficulties largely limited to oral production, which is consistent with retrieval problems online. Other studies find difficulties across tasks, including written tasks, indicating a problem with the syntactic representation. Some psycholinguistic studies find that learners are able to integrate inflectional morphology fully into their interlanguage grammar, while others do not.

Ultimately, even if learners do not become fully native-like in their oral production, written and oral comprehension, or processing of inflectional morphology, there is evidence that they can improve with proficiency. In the next section, we discuss what instructional techniques are most effective in this domain.

5.3 Intervention Research Studies on Inflectional Morphology

Intervention studies with inflectional morphology generally start from a more applied rather than a more theoretical perspective. In particular, many intervention studies in this domain either examine the effects of **input processing instruction** (see Chapter 2 for more on this approach) or address the efficacy of different types of explicit vs. implicit instruction as well as different types of corrective feedback. We group the publications in this section both by grammatical area (verbal morphology vs. grammatical gender) and by approach (processing instruction vs. focus on the explicit/implicit distinction).

5.3.1 Processing Instruction Studies on Tense Marking

A number of studies have used processing instruction (PI) in order to improve learners' performance on tense morphology; see Table 5.1 for a summary of these studies. As we discussed in Chapter 2, PI (VanPatten, 1996, 2004) manipulates the input in specific ways, in order to move learners away from default strategies and to improve learners' processing of grammatical forms. One such default strategy is the lexical processing strategy (VanPatten, 1996;

Table 5.1 Summary of intervention studies targeting inflectional morphology using processing instruction

Publication	Structures/phenomena under instruction	Participants' linguistic background	Nature of the intervention	Length of intervention	Major findings
Cadierno (1995)	Spanish past tense (preterit) verbal morphology	61 native English speakers in third-semester Spanish classes in the USA	Traditional output-based instruction vs. processing instruction	2 consecutive class days	On interpretation, the PI group outperformed both the output and the control no-instruction groups. On production, the PI and output groups performed similarly, and both outperformed the no-instruction group.
Benati (2001)	Italian future tense verbal morphology	39 native English speakers in second-semester Italian classes in the UK	Traditional output-based instruction vs. processing instruction	2 consecutive class days	On interpretation, the PI group outperformed the output group, which outperformed the no-instruction group. On production, the PI and output groups performed similarly, and both outperformed the no-instruction group.
Benati (2005)	English past-tense morphology	47 secondary school EFL learners in China and 30 secondary school EFL learners in Greece	Traditional output-based instruction vs. modified output instruction vs. processing instruction	3 consecutive class days	On interpretation, the PI group outperformed the other two groups. On interpretation, all three groups improved to the same extent.
Benati & Angelovska (2015)	English past-tense morphology	36 fifth graders and 13 adult EFL learners in German	Processing instruction	3 consecutive class days	Both children and adults improved equally on production and on the less demanding interpretation task. On the more cognitively demanding interpretation task, adults improved more than children.

J. F. Lee et al., 1997), by which learners overrely on lexical items such as temporal adverbs (*yesterday, today, last week,* etc.) rather than on tense morphology (*-ed, was/were*) in order to determine the temporal interpretation of the utterance. The goal of PI is to increase the saliency of the form–meaning mappings between tense morphology and temporal interpretation. This goal is achieved by exposing learners to structured input in which temporal adverbs are absent so that learners are forced to rely on tense morphology rather than adverbs for temporal interpretation. Unlike traditional output-based instruction, in which learners practice using tense morphemes, PI gets learners to process the meaning of tense morphemes and to ultimately fully incorporate tense morphology into their grammars: The goal of PI is to transform input into intake.

5.3.1.1 Processing Instruction on Tense Marking in Romance Languages

The effects of PI on learners' acquisition of tense marking have been studied across languages. One of the first studies in this area, Cadierno (1995), focused on past-tense marking in Spanish. The participants were three intact classes of English-speaking college students in third-semester Spanish language classrooms in the United States. The three classes were assigned to a PI group, a traditional instruction (TI) group, and a control no-instruction group (abbreviations ours). The TI group was taught about the preterit (perfective) form of the Spanish past tense and subsequently completed oral production activities. The activities for the PI group, in contrast, focused the participants' attention on preterit tense endings and required comprehension instead of production. In one type of activity, participants had to determine whether the action of the sentence that they heard occurred in the present or the past; in the absence of temporal adverbs, they had to rely on verbal morphology. Other activities involved answering comprehension questions about written or aural content. The instruction took place over two consecutive class days, with a pretest immediately prior to the intervention and a posttest immediately after. Two delayed posttests were administered a week and a month after the intervention, respectively. The pre/posttests included both production and interpretation tasks, in order not to bias in favor of either PI (which focuses on interpretation) or TI (which focuses on production). The results were as follows. On the interpretation tasks, the PI group outperformed both the TI and the no-instruction groups. On the production tasks, the PI and the TI groups did not differ, and both outperformed the no-instruction group. These patterns largely held across all three posttests. Thus, overall, PI was found to be superior to TI: It led to greater improvement on interpretation without any detriment to production.

While Cadierno (1995) found a strong advantage for PI over TI, a possible criticism of this study, noted by Benati (2001), is that the activities performed by the two instructed groups were very different. They differed not only with regard to whether comprehension or production was involved but also with regard to the actual content of the tasks. Thus, it is possible that the results reflect something other than an advantage of PI over TI; for example, perhaps the activities performed by the PI group were more engaging or interesting. To control for this possibility, Benati (2001) conducted a more stringently controlled study comparing the effects of PI vs. TI on the L2 acquisition of future tense morphology in Italian.

The participants in Benati's study were second-semester students of Italian at a UK university, with three groups. Similarly to Cadierno (1995), one group received PI, one received output instruction (OI), and one was a no-instruction control group (abbreviations ours). The activities performed by the PI and OI groups were closely matched so that the main difference was that the activities were receptive in the PI group but productive in the OI group. For example, while the PI group had to classify each sentence that they heard as present vs. future, the OI group had to conjugate each verb into the future tense. As in Cadierno's study, both interpretation and production tasks were included in the pre/posttests. The instruction took place over two consecutive days, with the pretest administered three weeks prior to the intervention, the immediate posttest right after the intervention, and a delayed posttest three weeks later. The results paralleled those of Cadierno (1995). The PI group improved more than the OI group on the interpretation tasks; on the production tasks, the PI and OI groups both improved equally relative to the no-instruction group. However, while Cadierno found no improvement in the TI group on the interpretation tasks, Benati found that the OI group improved on interpretation relative to the no-instruction group (though still exhibiting less improvement than the PI group). A major difference between the studies is that the OI group in Benati (2001) engaged in meaning-based output activities. Benati speculates that this could lead to learners in this group providing meaningful input to each other.

5.3.1.2 Processing Instruction on Tense Marking in English

Another study in the same vein, comparing PI and OI, was conducted by Benati (2005) on English past-tense marking (see Box 5.1). The participants were secondary-school students in China and in Greece, which allowed Benati to examine possible effects of the learners' L1 (Greek has past-tense marking, while Chinese does not). Each group (L1 Greek vs. L1 Chinese) was further split into three experimental groups, one receiving PI, one receiving TI, and one receiving meaning-based output instruction (MOI). The rationale

BOX 5.1 Benati (2005)

Publication Title: The effects of processing instruction, traditional instruction, and meaning-output instruction on the acquisition of the English past simple tense

Research Questions:

1. What are the relative effects of processing instruction, traditional instruction, and modified output instruction on the acquisition of English past simple tense as measured on an interpretation task at sentence level?
2. What are the relative effects of processing instruction, traditional instruction, and modified output instruction on the acquisition of English past simple tense as measured on a production task at sentence level?

Participants:

47 secondary school students in China and 30 secondary school students in Greece, all 12–13 years old and studying English at school

Groups:

Processing instruction (PI) groups (n = 15 in China, n = 10 in Greece); traditional instruction (TI) groups (n = 15 in China, n = 10 in Greece); modified output instruction (MOI) groups (n = 17 in China, n = 10 in Greece)

Study Timeline:

- Two weeks prior to instruction: pretests
- Two hours of instruction per day on three consecutive days (six hours in total)
- Immediate posttests immediately at the end of the instructional period (all groups)

Pre/Posttests: two different tests administered each time

- An interpretation tasks: Students listened to sentences and indicated whether the action of each sentence occurred last week or is occurring right now.
- A written production task: Students looked at pictures and wrote a sentence describing what happened, using verbs and nouns from the list provided.

BOX 5.1 (cont.)

The Intervention:

All three groups: explicit information about English past tense

- PI group: information about strategies (do not rely on temporal adverbs, pay attention to the tense ending), followed by structured input activities (for example: classify each sentence as happening in the present or in the past; read sentences about what the school did last year, and indicate if you agree or disagree with each one)
- TI group: output practice, with both mechanical and meaning-oriented activities (for example: put each verb in the past tense; list positive and negative things that the school did for the students last year)
- MOI group: information about strategies (same as in the PI group), followed by structured output activities (for example: listen to instructor's sentences about their holiday and put each verb in the past tense; write about how you spent your holiday)

Results: All groups improved on production, but only the PI group improved on comprehension. The results were very similar in China and in Greece.

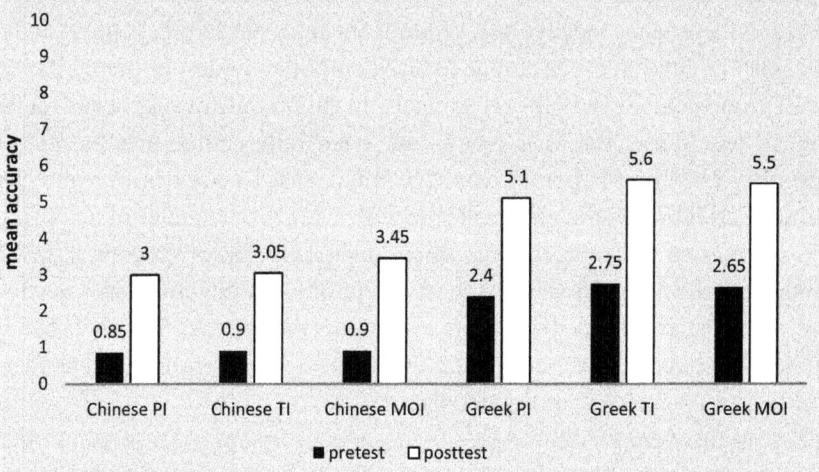

Figure 5.1 Mean accuracy on the production task by group and instructional treatment (based on data from Benati, 2005)

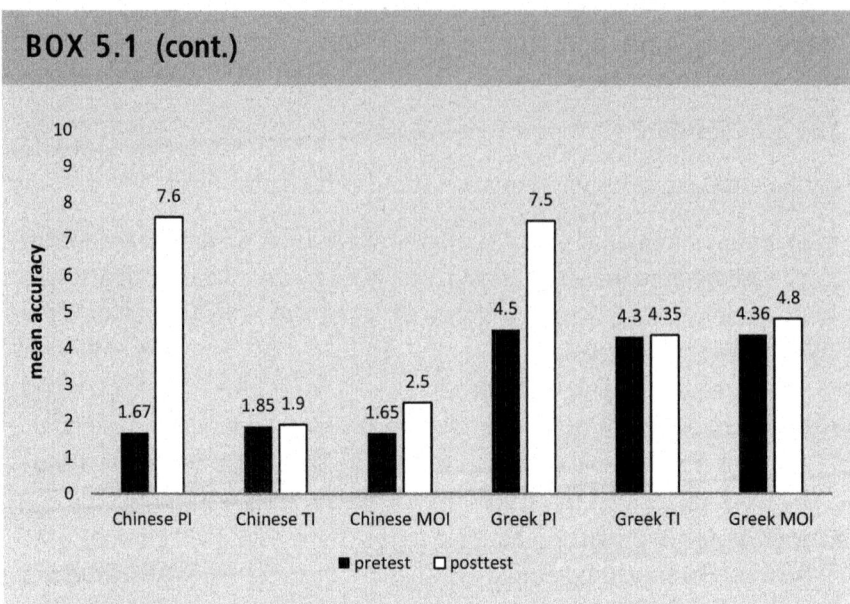

Figure 5.2 Mean accuracy on the interpretation task by group and instructional treatment (based on data from Benati, 2005)

for including two different output-instructed groups (TI and MOI) was to tease apart the focus of input vs. output from the nature of activities as more meaning focused vs. mechanical. While TI includes mechanical output activities, MOI includes more meaning-focused output activities. In Benati (2005), the TI group completed both mechanical and communicative activities on the English past tense, the MOI group completed only communicative output activities, and the PI group completed input-based activities that directed learners' attention to the *-ed* marker. (See Box 5.1 for examples of activities). The instruction took place over three consecutive days. The pretest was administered two weeks before the intervention, and the immediate posttest was administered immediately after the intervention. As in the other PI studies described above, the tests included both interpretation and production tasks (see Box 5.1 for the details).

The results were as follows (see the figures in Box 5.1). On the interpretation task, only the PI groups but not the TI and MOI groups improved, both in China and in Greece. On the production task, all three groups improved equally, in both China and Greece. Thus, the results with English past-tense marking followed the same patterns as those on Spanish and Italian tense marking, discussed above. PI and output instruction were equally effective with regard to production, but PI was superior when it came to interpretation; MOI was not found to be superior to TI. The fact that the same results obtained in Greece and in China indicates that the findings are generalizable across learner populations. At least in this case, the presence or absence of tense marking in the learners' L1 does not appear to matter for the success of the intervention. As shown in Box 5.1, the Greek participants started with better knowledge of English tense marking in the pretest than the Chinese participants did, which could potentially be due to the presence of tense marking in Greek but not in Chinese. Crucially, both groups exhibited the same patterns of improvement. For examples of other studies that compared PI and MOI instruction, see Farley (2004) and J. F. Lee and Benati (2007) on the subjunctive, discussed in Chapter 6.

The study by Benati and Angelovska (2015) probed the effects of PI further, by comparing whether both child and adult learners benefit from PI. Like Benati (2005), this study selected the English past tense *-ed* as the structure under investigation. The study participants were native speakers of German, both children (fifth graders, about ten years of age) and adults, learning English in a formal setting in Germany. Only participants with poor knowledge of the *-ed* marker (scoring no more than 60 percent correct on the pretests) were included in the study. All participants had a low level of overall English proficiency (A1/A2 proficiency level under CEFR, the Common European Framework of Reference for Languages, which corresponds to intermediate low to mid proficiency in ACTFL, American Council for the Teaching of Foreign Languages).

The intervention spanned two consecutive class days, with the pretest administered one week before the intervention, the immediate posttest immediately after the intervention, and a delayed posttest two weeks later. The child and adult participant groups were all instructed using PI. There was no uninstructed control group and no control group receiving traditional instruction, unlike in prior studies. This was because Benati and Angelovska were not interested in overall efficacy of PI instruction (already demonstrated by prior studies) but rather in how child vs. adult learners would respond to PI instruction and to cognitive task demands, which are related to age.

The pretest and posttests included one production task and two interpretation tasks, one of which was specifically designed to increase the cognitive demands on the learners. The less cognitively demanding task was adopted from Benati (2005): For each sentence that they heard, participants had to indicate whether the action happened "last year" or "right now," where the tense marker was the only temporal cue. The modified, more demanding interpretation task included distractor sentences in the present perfect, which works differently in German and in English. For each sentence, participants had to decide whether the action may have continued into the present (correct for the present perfect in English) or was completed in the past (correct for the simple past tense in English). On both the less complex interpretation task and the production task, the child and adult groups improved equally from pretest to posttest and retained the improvement over time. In the case of the more cognitively demanding interpretation task, on the other hand, the adults improved more than the children did, and this effect was retained over time.

The findings of Benati and Angelovska (2015) replicate prior findings showing the efficacy of PI for both interpretation and production. PI was shown to be just as effective with German English-as-a-foreign-language (EFL) learners, including children, as with Chinese and Greek EFL learners in Benati (2005). The child/adult difference on the more cognitively demanding interpretation task suggests that younger learners improve more when tasks are better suited to their cognitive maturation level.

5.3.1.3   Processing Instruction on Tense Marking: Summary

Overall, the PI studies summarized above provide converging evidence that PI is quite effective (and more effective than output instruction) in improving L2 learners' production and comprehension of tense marking. This finding holds across learner ages (elementary-school students, high-school students, and adults), across **target languages** (TLs; Spanish, Italian, and English), and across native languages (English, Chinese, Greek, and German).

It is important to note that the studies using PI have largely focused on tense marking to the exclusion of other types of verbal morphology, such as agreement marking. This is not accidental: PI uses meaning-based instruction, attracting learners' attention to the contribution that a given grammatical element makes to sentence interpretation. While tense markers make a clear and unambiguous contribution to sentence meaning (*I walk* and *I walked* clearly differ in meaning), agreement markers typically do not. For example, *I walk* and *She walks* describe the same action that happens in the present. The difference in meaning is about who does the action (*I* vs. *she*), but this information is already available on the pronoun. By definition, verbal agreement reflects the properties of the subject (the verb agrees with the subject) and does not contribute any new meaning by itself. In a language like English, learners would need to be instructed to pay attention to the agreement morphology even though it is always redundant. In contrast, in null-subject languages such as Spanish or Italian, verbal morphology is the only source of information about who is doing the action in the absence of an overt subject. For example, in Spanish, *Como una zanahoria* means 'I eat (am eating) a carrot' while *Come una zanahoria* means 'She or he eats (is eating) a carrot'. In the absence of an overt subject, only the verb ending (*-o* for first person singular, *-e* for third person singular) provides information about who is doing the eating. One might envision a PI activity in which learners of Spanish are asked to classify null-subject sentences with regard to who is doing the action, based on verbal morphology alone. This said, we are not aware of any study that has used PI with verbal agreement in null-subject languages.

5.3.2 Explicit vs. Implicit Knowledge and Instruction in the Domain of Verbal Morphology

Several studies have examined the development of verbal morphology from the perspective of the explicit/implicit distinction; see Table 5.2 for a summary of these studies. See also R. Ellis et al. (2009) for papers addressing the explicit/implicit distinction with regard to the L2 classroom. As discussed in Chapter 1, the explicit/implicit divide applies to instruction, to learning, and to knowledge. One should not assume that explicit vs. implicit instruction necessarily leads to explicit vs. implicit learning or to the development of explicit vs. implicit knowledge, respectively. Some studies compare the efficacy of more explicit vs. more implicit instructional approaches on learners' development. Some studies measure whether learners develop explicit and/or implicit knowledge as a result of an intervention. And some studies do both, manipulating the type of instruction as well as using different measures to examine what knowledge learners develop.

5.3.2.1 Explicit vs. Implicit Instruction with Tense Marking

R. Ellis, Loewen, and Erlam (2006) examined the effects of implicit vs. explicit corrective feedback on L2-English learners' development of past-tense *-ed*. The study participants were adults learning English in New Zealand; the learners came from a variety of backgrounds, with the majority being of East Asian origin (the L1s of the learners are not specified in the paper). Participants were randomly assigned to two experimental groups or a control group. The two experimental groups were instructed for one hour over two consecutive days, while the control group proceeded with their normal instruction. The two experimental groups completed communicative tasks and received corrective feedback whenever they omitted the past-tense marker. The tasks involved picture description and story retelling, both conducive to the use of the past tense. One group received implicit feedback in the form of recasts: For example, when a learner said "they follow," the researcher recast this as "followed." The other group received explicit feedback in the form of metalinguistic information: for example, when a learner said "He kiss her," the researcher said "Kiss – you need past tense," after which the learner corrected the form to "He kissed" (examples from R. Ellis et al., 2006, p. 353).

Table 5.2 Summary of intervention studies targeting inflectional morphology using a variety of explicit vs. implicit instructional techniques and feedback types

Publication	Structures / phenomena under instruction	Participants' linguistic background	Nature of the intervention	Length of intervention	Major findings
Han (2002)	English past tense -ed	8 ESL learners in the USA, with a variety of L1s	Recasts	11 sessions over 2 months	The recasts group improved in tense consistency relative to the control group
Leeman (2003)	Spanish gender agreement with adjectives	74 first-year college students of Spanish in the USA	Recasts vs. implicit negative evidence vs. enhanced salience	A single 20-minute session	The recasts and enhanced salience groups outperformed the implicit negative evidence and control groups in a production task
Lyster (2004a)	French gender agreement	179 L1-French fifth graders learning English in Quebec	Form-focused instruction (FFI) incorporated into content classes, plus recasts or prompts or no feedback	5 weeks, in the classroom	All three groups receiving FFI improved relative to the control group on both written and oral production tasks; the prompts group improved the most on the written tasks
R. Ellis, Loewen, & Erlam (2006)	English past tense -ed	34 ESL learners in New Zealand, from a variety of L1s (mostly East Asian)	Corrective feedback: recasts vs. metalinguistic information	2 consecutive days, in the classroom	The group receiving metalinguistic feedback outperformed both the recasts group and the control group in both oral imitation and an untimed grammaticality judgment task (GJT), in the delayed posttest

Study	Target feature	Participants	Treatment	Duration	Results
Ammar & Spada (2006)	Gender agreement with English possessive determiners	64 L1-French sixth graders learning English in Quebec	Rule presentation plus recasts or prompts or no feedback	12 sessions over 4 weeks	Both groups receiving corrective feedback improved more than the control group, and the prompts group improved the most
Tode (2007)	English copula *be*	89 seventh-grade EFL learners in Japan	Explicit vs. implicit instruction	A single class period	The explicit group outperformed both the implicit group and the control group, at least in the short-term
Loewen et al. (2009)	English third person singular -s	32 ESL learners in New Zealand, from a variety of L1s (mostly East Asian)	Incidental exposure	2 consecutive days	No improvement in the experimental group relative to the control group in either oral imitation or untimed GJT
Lichtman (2013)	Spanish verbal agreement morphology	30 L1-English elementary school students and 36 L1-English high school students in the USA	Existing instruction: TPRS (implicit instruction) for children and adolescents; explicit instruction for adolescents only	1–3 years for adolescents, 2–8 years for children	Implicit task (story rewriting): all groups performed the same Explicit task (verb conjugation): the adolescent explicit group outperformed the two implicit groups

The learners completed a pretest five days before the intervention, an immediate posttest immediately after the intervention, and a delayed posttest twelve days later. All the tests included both tasks designed to target implicit knowledge (oral imitation) and those designed to target explicit knowledge (untimed **grammaticality judgment task [GJT]** and a metalinguistic knowledge test). Thus, the study addressed the explicit/implicit divide with regard to both instruction (feedback) and measured knowledge.

In the oral imitation test, the three groups did not differ on the immediate posttest, but the group receiving explicit feedback outperformed the two other groups on the delayed posttest. The same pattern held for the untimed GJT, with the explicit-feedback group performing the best on the delayed posttest. The results of the metalinguistic knowledge test were inconclusive, as all groups already performed quite well on the pretest. In sum, this study showed that explicit metalinguistic feedback was more effective than recasts and that such explicit feedback had an effect on the learners' development of implicit knowledge (as measured by the oral imitation task) as well as their explicit knowledge (as measured by the untimed GJT).

5.3.2.2 Explicit vs. Implicit Instruction with Agreement

Another study that focused on the explicit/implicit distinction, this time with regard to agreement morphology, is Loewen, Erlam, and Ellis (2009). This study was also conducted in New Zealand, with ESL learners from a variety of L1 backgrounds (with East Asian L1s – Japanese, Chinese, Korean, and Taiwanese – predominating). There was an experimental group and a control group. The intervention took place over two consecutive days, with a pretest prior to the intervention, a posttest the day after the intervention, and a delayed posttest two weeks later. The experimental group received extensive incidental exposure to third person singular -s through input flooding while being taught about a different structure, the indefinite article *a*. (The effects of instruction on the indefinite article for this group is reported in Erlam, Loewen, and Philp, 2009, discussed in Chapter 3). The participants in the experimental group were exposed to multiple exemplars of third person -s without any explicit instruction about -s, thus making the intervention fairly implicit in nature. Like the participants in R. Ellis et al. (2006), the participants in the Loewen, Erlam, and Ellis (2009) study were tested on measures of both implicit and explicit knowledge (oral imitation and untimed GJT, respectively). Both the experimental and the control group improved from pretest to posttests on the oral imitation task, with no group differences. There was no improvement for either group in the GJT. Loewen, Erlam, and Ellis (2009) concluded that the lack of incidental learning of third person -s, at either implicit or explicit level, was due to the fact that learners' attention was directed toward a different linguistic feature (the indefinite article).

Tode (2007) is another study that manipulated explicit vs. implicit instruction, focusing on the copula *be*. The participants were junior high-school EFL learners in Japan. The verb *be* had previously been shown by Tode (2003) to be problematic for Japanese L2-English learners. Beginner learners would both omit *be* in obligatory contexts (e.g., *My father a teacher*) and overuse it with lexical verbs (e.g., *He is like music*). In Tode (2007), three intact classes were assigned to an explicit group, an implicit group, and a no-instruction control group, respectively. The intervention took place during a single class period, with the pretest administered in the preceding class, the immediate posttest in the following class, and a delayed posttest three weeks later. Three more delayed posttests took place over the following five months. The tests required participants to complete missing elements in English sentences and were therefore quite explicit. The explicitly instructed group was taught about English copular sentences and completed practice activities, including translations from Japanese to English. The implicitly instructed group was presented with the same example sentences as the explicitly instructed group but without Japanese translations or explicit explanations; they repeated and memorized the sentences.

The explicit group outperformed both the implicit group and the control group on all of the posttests, though the differences only reached significance on some of the posttests. The implicit group performed no differently from the control group. Thus, explicit instruction was more effective than implicit instruction in this domain, though the benefit was not necessarily retained in the long term.

5.3.2.3 Explicit vs. Implicit Instruction with Verbal Morphology: Short-Term vs. Long-Term Effects

Taken together, the above studies indicate that explicit instruction is generally more effective than implicit instruction in the domain of verbal morphology. Nevertheless, it is important to remember that all of these studies were very short term, taking place over one to three days, and implicit instruction might be more effective if it were spread over a longer period of time. Two studies potentially demonstrate this point. The first is Han (2002), a very small-scale study which, like R. Ellis et al. (2006), examined the effect of recasts on English tense morphology. The participants were eight ESL learners in the United States, from a variety of L1s. The participants took part in eleven sessions over a period of two months, with a pretest at the beginning, a posttest immediately after the intervention, and a delayed posttest a month later. All participants completed written and oral narratives, but only half of them (the experimental group) received recasts when they made tense errors, while the control group received no recasts. The recast group, but not the control group, improved in their tense consistency. This study thus provides some evidence that implicit feedback can be effective when provided over a long period of time. However, given the very small sample size, the results must be interpreted with caution.

Another study that shows the long-term effects of implicit (vs. explicit) instruction is Lichtman (2013). This was not an intervention study, and participants were tested in a single session. However, by carefully controlling for the type of instruction that the participants had received prior to the testing, Lichtman was able to examine the effects of more explicit vs. more implicit instruction. This study also examined whether younger and older participants differ in their development of explicit vs. implicit knowledge under explicit vs. implicit instruction.

Lichtman (2013) tested both children and adolescents on Spanish verbal agreement morphology. All of the participants were native English speakers studying Spanish at school. The children (ages 8 to 12) were all receiving Spanish instruction at an elementary school through the Teaching Proficiency through Reading and Storytelling (TPRS) method. This method involves whole-language activities with very little grammar instruction and is therefore primarily implicit. The adolescents (ages 14–17) were studying Spanish in high school. The implicit adolescent group was also instructed through TPRS, while the explicit adolescent group was receiving traditional explicit grammar instruction. There was no child explicit group, since one could not be found. The three groups in the study were similar in their overall Spanish proficiency, despite the children having studied Spanish longer than the adolescents. This difference is not surprising, given that older learners tend to have an advantage over younger learners in early stages of acquisition, progressing faster.

All three groups were tested using both a task targeting implicit knowledge (rewriting a story from memory) and a task targeting explicit knowledge (verb conjugation). Both tasks included the same Spanish verbs. The two implicitly instructed groups (both child and adolescent) performed better on the story task than the verb-conjugation task, while the opposite was the case for the explicitly instructed adolescent group. Thus, each group did better on the task that matched the type of instruction that the group had received. Furthermore, the adolescent explicit group outperformed the other two groups on the verb-conjugation task, while the three groups performed similarly on the story task. The findings of this study suggest that explicit instruction is more effective than implicit instruction even when the instruction spans months or years rather than days (the participants in both adolescent groups had had between one and three years of Spanish instruction) and that explicit instruction can lead to the development of implicit knowledge.

5.3.3 Differential Effects of Corrective Feedback Types on Grammatical Gender

There have been considerably fewer classroom intervention studies on grammatical gender than on verbal morphology; the studies discussed in this section are included in Table 5.2. While differing in the specifics, all of these studies examined the effects of corrective feedback on the acquisition of grammatical gender.

5.3.3.1 Corrective Feedback with Gender and Number Agreement in Spanish

Leeman (2003) looked at the effects of recasts, salience, and negative evidence on the development of grammatical gender in Spanish. The participants were first-year undergraduate students of Spanish, native English speakers at a US university. They were randomly assigned to three experimental groups and a control group. The participants completed the pretest, intervention, and immediate posttest in a single one-hour session and a delayed posttest a week later. The tests consisted of picture-difference tasks, in which participants had to list all the differences between two similar pictures (e.g., "in picture A the chair is yellow, but in picture B the chair is red"). This format required participants to use many adjectives, which were analyzed for gender agreement.

During the twenty-minute intervention, participants in each group completed information-gap activities that required them to produce noun–adjective agreement. In the first part of the task, participants provided directions to the researcher. The groups differed with regard to how the researcher reacted to errors. In the recast group, participants were provided with recasts in response to errors with gender or number agreement. For example, suppose that a participant used a masculine adjective with a feminine noun such as *taza* 'cup', as in (23a). The researcher would then recast the utterance as (23b), with the correct form of the adjective. Such a recast provided implicit negative evidence: The fact that the researcher recast the learner's response indicated that the learner may have made an error. At the same time, the recast also enhanced the salience of the positive evidence: that is, the evidence that the correct adjective was *roja*. In the negative-evidence group, participants were provided with information that they made an error but without a correction, as in (23c). The enhanced-salience group and the control group received no feedback on the error at all.

(23) a. En   la   mesa   hay   una   taza rojo.
       on   the   table there   a.FEM   cup red.MASC
       'On the table there's a red cup.'
    b. Um hmm, una   taza   roja.   [recast]
       um hmm   a.FEM   cup   red.FEM
       'Um hmm, a red cup.'
    c. Um hmm, pero tú   dijiste   'una   taza rojo.'   [negative evidence]
       um hmm   but you said   'a.FEM   cup red.MASC'
       'Um hmm, but you said 'a red cup'.'

In the second part of the task, the researcher gave the directions, and participants acted on the basis of this direction: Thus, they were receiving input but not providing output. In this part, the enhanced-salience group received enhanced input, with the salience of the adjective ending (e.g., the 'a' in *roja*) enhanced via stress and intonation. The other three groups received unenhanced input.

The study findings were that with regard to both gender and number agreement, the recast and enhanced-salience groups both improved in the immediate posttest relative to the control group. The negative-evidence group scored in between and did not outperform the control group. The same pattern held at the delayed posttest, with minor variations. Thus, both recasts and enhanced salience were more effective than implicit negative evidence alone.

An important finding of this study has to do with the nature of the benefits provided by recasts. It had previously largely been thought that the effectiveness of recasts had to do with the fact that they provided implicit negative evidence. However, Leeman's study showed that implicit negative evidence by itself (as in (23c)) did not lead to improvement, whereas recasts (as in (23b)) did. This suggests that the effectiveness of recasts lies, at least in part, in the fact that they enhance the salience of the positive evidence, in addition to providing implicit negative evidence.

5.3.3.2 Corrective Feedback with Gender Agreement in French

Lyster (2004a) (see also Lyster, 2015) conducted a form-focused intervention with French grammatical gender, with fifth-grade English-speaking students of French in Montreal (see Box 5.2). In French, as in Spanish, articles and adjectives exhibit gender agreement with the noun. Grammatical gender was integrated into content classes over a five-week period for the six experimental classrooms. For example, in language-arts classes, students were asked to identify the gender of some words in the story. In social studies, students had to fill in missing articles in a text about the history of Quebec. In science class, students had to add articles while responding to a "true or false" lesson review. The six classrooms were further divided into three groups (two classrooms each). One group received form-focused instruction (FFI) on gender that was integrated into the content material, as described above. The other two experimental groups received the same FFI on gender but also received feedback following gender errors, with one group receiving recasts and the other receiving prompts. Finally, there was a fourth group, a control group, which did not receive FFI on gender at all; the control group consisted of two classrooms from the same grade level.

Prompts included teacher responses to errors such as clarification requests, repetitions, or elicitation. Unlike recasts, prompts do not include the correct target form. For example, if a student mistakenly said *la chocolat* instead of *le chocolat*, misusing the feminine definite article with a masculine noun, a recast would involve the teacher providing the correct form. In contrast, a prompt could include the teacher repeating the student's error, stating that it is an error, or saying *Pardon?* 'Sorry?'. All of these served as clues to the students that something was wrong and invited them to restate what they said initially.

The students took a pretest prior to the intervention, an immediate posttest at the end of the intervention, and a delayed posttest two months later. The tests included both written and oral production tasks. The results differed somewhat across tasks, but, overall, all three groups receiving FFI improved on their performance with grammatical gender relative to the non-FFI control group (see Box 5.2 for the specifics). The FFI group receiving prompts did particularly well relative to the other two FFI group, especially on the written tasks. The three FFI groups performed fairly similarly on the oral tasks, outperforming the control group.

Lyster concludes that FFI is quite effective in facilitating students' improvement with grammatical gender. The reason prompts were more helpful than recasts could be because they required students to retrieve and produce the target forms themselves (as opposed to hearing the teacher produce them) or because they were easier to notice. While this study was not specifically concerned with the explicit/implicit distinction, we note that prompts, as defined in Lyster (2004a), provided somewhat more explicit feedback than recasts did. The findings are consistent with findings of other studies (e.g., R. Ellis et al., 2006, see section 5.3.2) that explicit feedback is more effective than implicit feedback.

5.3.3.3 Corrective Feedback with Gender Agreement on English Possessive Determiners

Finally, Ammar and Spada (2006) examined a different aspect of gender marking, focusing on third-person possessive determiners *her* and *his* in the L2 English of French-speaking children. English and French differ in the

BOX 5.2 Lyster (2004a)

Publication Title: Differential effects of prompts and recasts in form-focused instruction

Research Questions:

1. Will Form-Focused Instruction (FFI) improve French immersion students' ability to accurately assign grammatical gender?
2. Is FFI more effective with feedback than without feedback?
3. Which type of feedback is more effective in FFI - recasts or prompts?

Participants: Eight classes of 10-to-11-year-old fifth-grade students in Montreal, L1-English L2-French learners, and their four Francophone teachers; 60 percent of Grade 5 content was taught in French; 22 to 28 students per class, average 25

Groups:

Four groups, each consisting of two classes taught by the same teacher; three groups received form-focused instruction (FFI): FFI-prompt group (n = 49); FFI-recast group (n = 38); FFI-only group (n = 41); control group (n = 51). The oral tasks in the pre/posttests were completed by fifteen participants from each group, while all the participants completed the written tasks.

Study Timeline:

- January: pretests
- February and early March: 8–10 hours of instruction (experimental classrooms only), spread over 5 weeks
- March: immediate posttests (posttest 1)
- May: delayed posttests (posttest 2)

Pre/Posttests: four different tests administered each time

1. Binary-choice test (written): Students had to select the correct article (feminine or masculine) for each noun.
2. Text-completion test (written): Students completed a cloze exercise in which they selected the correct article for each noun in the passage, and a text-completion task in which they had to write a recipe, with singular definite articles for all the nouns.
3. Object-identification task (oral): Students had to name a drawing using a noun with an indefinite article.

BOX 5.2 (cont.)

4. Picture-description task (oral): Students had to describe a picture, which involved using a variety of nouns, with articles.

The Intervention:

The three experimental groups received FFI in their content courses, on sixteen noun endings that serve as reliable cues to gender in French; typographical enhancement in the students' workbooks was used to highlight the endings of the target nouns; a variety of activities on grammatical gender were integrated into the curriculum. There was no FFI on gender for the control group.

- FFI-recast group: teachers provided recasts of gender errors
- FFI-prompt group: teachers provided prompts intended to push students to self-correct their gender errors
- FFI-only group: no corrective feedback
- Control group: no FFI on gender

Results: All FFI groups improved relative to the control group, with the largest improvement for the FFI-prompt group.

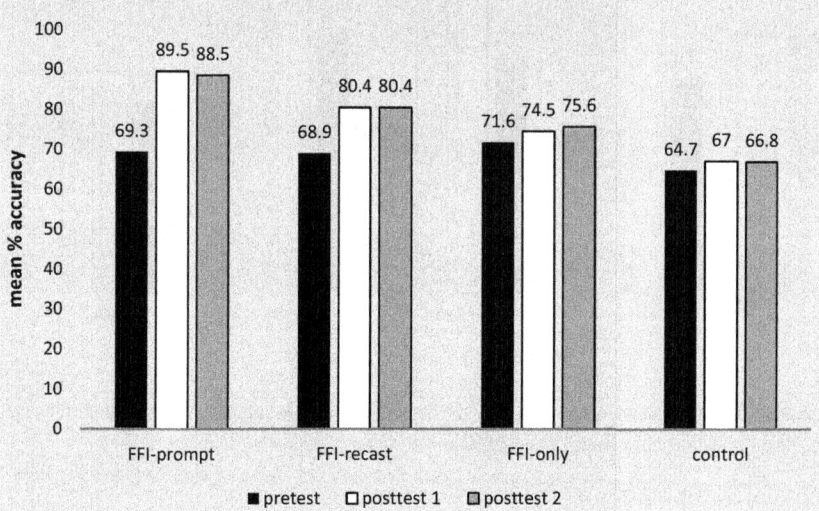

Figure 5.3 Mean percentage accuracy on the written binary-choice test by instructional group (based on data from Lyster, 2004a)

BOX 5.2 (cont.)

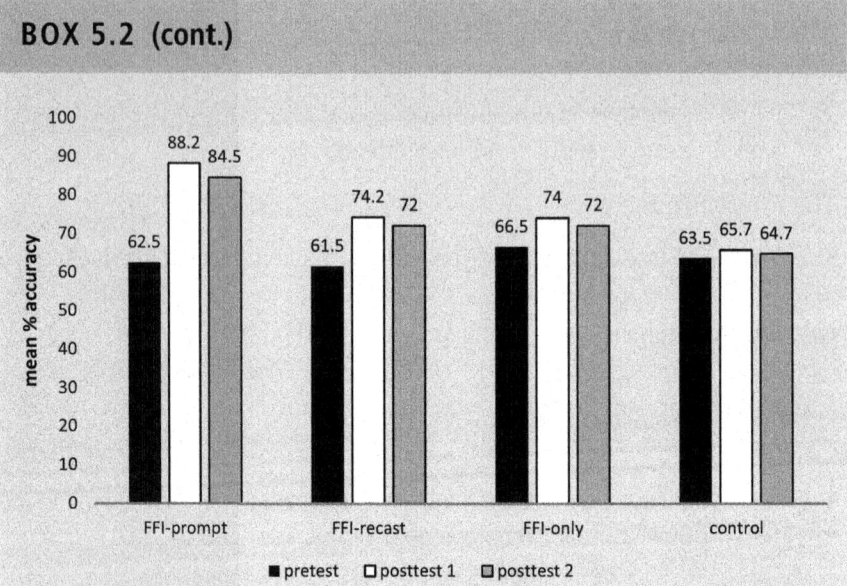

Figure 5.4 Mean percentage accuracy on the written text-completion task by instructional group (based on data from Lyster, 2004a)

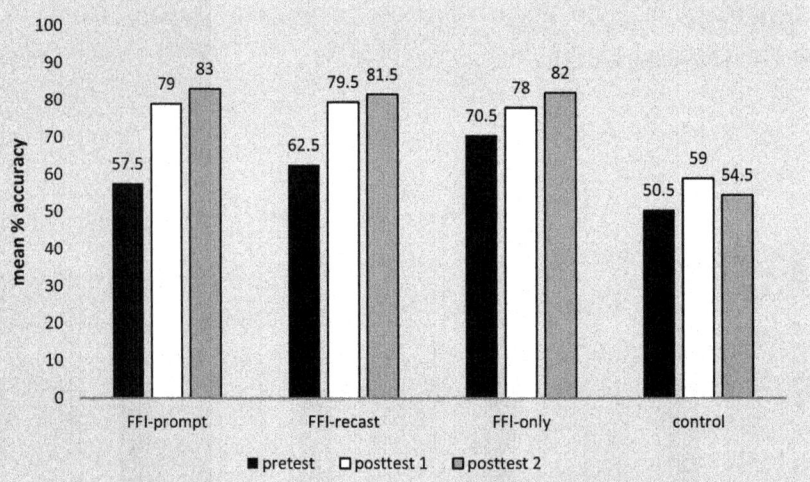

Figure 5.5 Mean percentage accuracy on the oral object-identification test by instructional group (based on data from Lyster, 2004a)

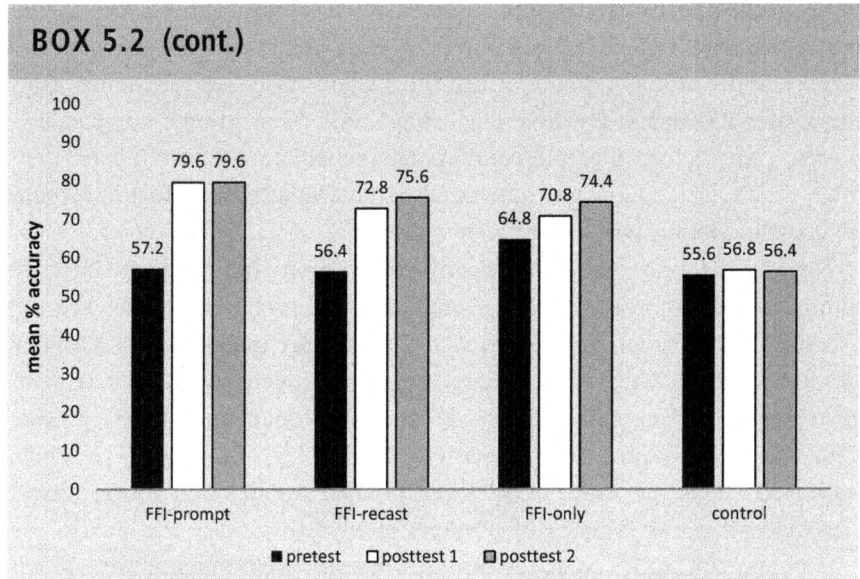

Figure 5.6 Mean percentage accuracy on the oral picture-description task by instructional group (based on data from Lyster, 2004a)

nature of gender agreement with possessive determiners, which makes this a challenging property for L1-French L2-English learners. In English, the determiner agrees with the possessor in gender, while in French, it agrees with the gender of the noun that follows the determiner (which refers to the possessed object or person). Thus, in English, the choice of *her* vs. *his* in front of the noun *book* in (24a) is determined by whether the possessor of the book is female or male. In French, in contrast, since *livre* 'book' is masculine, it always occurs with the masculine possessive determiner *son* 'his', regardless of the possessor, as shown in (24b). If instead of a book we were talking about *clé* 'key', which is feminine, the possessive determiner would be *sa* 'her', regardless of the possessor.

(24) a. Anna read her book. George did not read his book.
   b. Anna a lu son livre. George n'a pas lu son livre.

Ammar and Spada (2006) manipulated instruction on English possessive determiners with three intact classes of L1-French sixth graders in Quebec. The intervention lasted for twelve sessions spread over four weeks, an instruction session about English possessive determiners, and eleven practice sessions. In the practice sessions, the children completed communicative activities maximized to allow for production of possessive determiners. One group received prompts in response to errors, one received recasts, and a third group (the control group) received no feedback. The teacher in the recasts group provided recasts of errors with possessive determiners. The teacher in the prompts group pushed the student to self-correct, much as in the Lyster (2004a) study described above. All three groups completed a pretest right before the intervention, an immediate posttest immediately after, and a delayed posttest four weeks later. The tests consisted of an oral picture-description task and passage correction.

The study found that both experimental groups (prompts and recasts) improved more than the control group, and the prompts group showed the greatest improvement. The results were furthermore modulated by learners' proficiency level, which was obtained through an independent measurement. The efficacy of corrective feedback, and of prompts in particular, was greatest for low-proficiency learners, while high-proficiency learners improved about the same in all three groups. Ammar and Spada (2006) concluded that the efficacy of prompts relative to recasts was due to the explicitness and saliency of the prompts. Recasts were much more implicit and may not have been perceived as corrective within a communicative classroom setting.

5.3.3.4 Corrective Feedback with Gender: Summary

To summarize, we have seen that the intervention studies on grammatical gender reviewed above examined the effect of different kinds of corrective feedback on acquisition of grammatical gender and that they generally found that participants improved more with corrective feedback than without. Both Lyster (2004a) and Ammar and Spada (2006) found prompts (which are more explicit) to be more effective than recasts (which are more implicit). At the same time, Leeman (2003) found recasts to be more effective than implicit negative evidence. Notably, in Leeman's study, the learners receiving implicit negative evidence were not prompted to provide a response, as the learners exposed to prompts in Lyster's and Ammar and Spada's studies did. Thus, the effectiveness of a given method has to do both with the type of evidence it provides (enhanced salience of positive evidence or implicit negative evidence), as well as with whether it prompts learner output. Importantly, the studies taken together provide evidence for the efficacy of FFI and feedback in the domain of gender agreement.

While the studies described above conducted interventions on grammatical gender with students already studying the TL, several other intervention studies on grammatical gender have worked with novice learners, that is, learners with no prior exposure to the TL. The goal of such studies is to examine what kind of instruction, cues, feedback, and so on, is most effective in leading learners to acquire grammatical gender from scratch. In this textbook, our focus is on the relationship between instructional approaches and L2 knowledge in learners who are in the process of learning an L2. Studies with novice learners have a very different focus, as the participants in such studies receive no exposure to the TL beyond the highly constrained input provided during the training sessions. It is an open question whether the cues and instructional techniques that are optimal in this highly constrained setting would generalize to an L2 classroom. We therefore do not include studies with novice learners in this book. The interested reader is referred to the following studies: Davidson and Indefrey (2009) on L1-Dutch novice learners of German; Presson, MacWhinney, and Tokowicz (2014) on L1-English novice learners of French; Morgan-Short et al. (2010) and Lichtman (2016), among others, on L1-English novice learners of artificial mini-languages. The studies by Davidson and Indefrey (2009) as well as Morgan-Short et al. (2010) used ERPs (event-related potentials) in order to examine changes in learners' brain responses with learning. Both Morgan-Short et al. (2010) and Lichtman (2016) examined the effects of explicit vs. implicit instruction with mini-languages and found an overall advantage for explicit instruction, consistent with studies on real languages discussed earlier.

5.4 Summary and Implications

In this chapter we have covered intervention studies on inflectional morphology. We have seen that studies that address the explicit/implicit divide in SLA, with verbal morphology as well as with grammatical gender, generally find that explicit instruction and more explicit corrective feedback are more effective in improving learners' performance than more implicit instruction and feedback. This is attested across languages, across grammatical domains (tense, agreement, and gender morphology) and across ages (a number of studies discussed in this chapter tested children in elementary school, middle school, or high school). While some studies are fairly short term (with interventions lasting only one or two days), similar results obtain for longer-term studies that span weeks or months. A clear conclusion that emerges from all of these studies is that form-focused instruction, integrated into communicative classrooms, is quite effective in improving learners' performance with inflectional morphology. One cannot, and should not, expect learners to exhibit "perfect," error-free performance after days, weeks, or even months of instruction. Crucially, even if learners do not perform in a fully target-like manner, they do show evidence of improvement upon receiving FFI. Still, variation among learners, and fluctuations in performance over time, are to be expected.

A number of studies discussed in this chapter address a particular type of FFI, processing instruction, in the domain of tense morphology. These studies uniformly show that PI is more effective than traditional output-based instruction, leading to improvement not only in processing the input but also in the production of tense marking. This conclusion is consistent with PI studies in other linguistic domains (see Chapters 6 and 9 in particular).

As we see it, there is a disconnect between the generative SLA approach to inflectional morphology, discussed in section 5.2, and the intervention studies in this domain, discussed in section 5.3. Researchers in generative SLA are interested in the source of learners' difficulties with inflectional morphology (impairment to grammatical representations, difficulties with processing, etc.). In contrast, intervention studies take the existence of such difficulties as a given and focus on the optimal way to improve learners' performance, rather than on the deep reasons behind learners' difficulties.

How can the two approaches be reconciled? One way is to consider the finding that explicit instruction improves learners' performance on tasks that measure implicit knowledge, such as oral imitation tasks and production tasks (see in particular R. Ellis et al., 2006; Lichtman, 2013). If this finding is robust and replicable, it would provide support for the interface positions in SLA (see Chapter 1), indicating that explicit instruction can lead to true acquisition of implicit knowledge. However, this still does not answer the question of whether explicit instruction leads learners to overcome a representational problem or a more surface one. In order to address this question, it would be necessary to conduct intervention studies that focus on both syntactic and morphological phenomena. For example, does learners' improvement with tense morphology go hand in hand with improvement on the syntactic reflexes of Tense, such as verb placement? Does instruction on gender agreement in a Romance language lead to improvement on agreement with both articles and adjectives? These are potentially interesting questions to pursue in further research.

5.5 DISCUSSION QUESTIONS

1. Examine the studies listed in Table 5.2, many of which look at the efficacy of different types of corrective feedback. What might be concluded about which types of feedback are more vs. less effective? What might account for the somewhat different findings across studies?
2. Some of the intervention studies discussed in this chapter control for learners' L1s, while others include learners from a variety of L1s.

Inflectional morphology is known to be an area in which learners have difficulty in all L1–L2 combinations; nevertheless, a rich morphological system in the L1 could facilitate acquisition of L2 morphology. Looking across the studies summarized in this chapter, discuss whether the L1 seems to make a difference in learners' performance. Why might a researcher or teacher want to include only participants from one L1 in a study vs. learners from various L1s?

3. Consider the study by Lyster (2004a), summarized in Box 5.2. Examine the different tasks used in the pre/posttests in this study. Which kind of knowledge (explicit or implicit) does each task target, and why? Why do you think there were more pronounced group differences on some tasks than on others?

5.6 APPLICATIONS QUESTIONS

1. Read the publication by Benati and Angelovska (2015) and identify the various components of processing instruction in this study. What was the explicit instruction? What is the strategy that learners need to overcome? How does the intervention succeed in helping learners overcome these strategies? Discuss why the two interpretation tasks in this study are considered to be less vs. more cognitively demanding; what makes the second task more demanding?

2. Section 5.3.1.3 notes that agreement morphology would be compatible with PI in a null-subject language such as Spanish. Based on the idea laid out in this section, propose a study that would use PI to help L2-Spanish learners attend to agreement morphology on the verb instead of to the form of the subject. Identify the strategy that PI would be helping the learners overcome in this case. Provide samples of exercises that could be used as part of PI in such a study.

3. All of the studies about gender agreement discussed in this chapter manipulated the type of feedback that learners receive. Suppose that instead of manipulating the type of feedback, we were to manipulate the type of instruction. Review the components of explicit vs. implicit instruction discussed in Chapter 1 and propose how you might teach learners of a gender-marking language using more explicit vs. more implicit approaches. Pick any gender-marking language with which you have familiarity (Spanish, French, Russian, Dutch…). For ideas, consult Lichtman (2016), which manipulated explicit vs. implicit instruction about gender marking in an artificial mini-language.

5.7 FURTHER READING

- Benati, A., & Angelovska, T. (2015). The effects of processing instruction on the acquisition of English simple past tense: Age and cognitive task demands. *International Review of Applied Linguistics in Language Teaching, 53*(2), 249–269.
  This paper examines whether processing instruction (PI) affects both child and adult L2 learners in the same way.

- Ellis, R., Loewen, S., Elder, C., Reinders, H., Erlam, R., & Philp, J. (2009). *Implicit and explicit knowledge in second language learning, testing and teaching.* Bristol, UK: Multilingual Matters.
  This book examines both implicit and explicit knowledge that L2 learners have and how this knowledge can be affected by instruction; inflectional morphology is one of the topics addressed (see chapter 11 in particular).

- Ionin, T. (2012b). Morphosyntax. In J. Herschensohn & M. Young-Scholten (Eds.), *The Cambridge handbook of second language acquisition* (pp. 75–103). Cambridge, UK: Cambridge University Press.
  This book chapter provides an overview of theoretical approaches and findings in the L2 acquisition of morphosyntax, with a focus on the verbal domain.

- Slabakova, R. (2016). *Second language acquisition* (chapter 7, pp. 175–207). Oxford: Oxford University Press.
  This textbook chapter provides an overview of the L2 acquisition of functional morphology.

6 Subjunctive Mood

In Chapter 5 we discussed the difficulty **inflectional morphology** poses to L2 learners, and in this chapter we turn to a special type of inflectional morphology on the verb: morphology that marks the **subjunctive mood**. As a grammatical category, mood plays a role only in some languages.

Why is the subjunctive mood so difficult to learn in second language acquisition? Not only does the subjunctive mood take substantial time for learners to acquire, but it is also a challenging phenomenon for linguists to describe and theorize. This is because the uses and meanings of the subjunctive depend on the interplay of syntactic, semantic, and discourse-pragmatic factors. As we will see, in some sentences, the subjunctive is obligatory and it is the only correct choice of verb form, whereas in other sentences the use of the subjunctive is optional, depending on the meaning the speaker wants to convey. It is no surprise, then, that acquiring all the uses and meanings of the subjunctive is a protracted process, even in first language acquisition, as we will cover as well.

This chapter examines the second and heritage language acquisition of the subjunctive mood in Spanish and other Romance languages in obligatory and variable contexts. Although the subjunctive is introduced early in the L2 curriculum of Romance languages (at the end of the first year of instruction), it is not learned until much later, and confusion and hesitancy about its use linger even in advanced learners. **Heritage speakers**, who, like monolingual children, are exposed to their language since birth, typically do not reach the level of subjunctive mastery of L1 children by early adulthood.

The types of instruction that best bring about acquisition of the subjunctive in beginner and intermediate-level learners have been the focus of intense investigation in Spanish, Italian, and French as a second language (Collentine, 2010; J. F. Lee & Benati, 2007). This chapter will examine two main strands of research: linguistically oriented SLA studies of the subjunctive and classroom **intervention studies** on the subjunctive in Spanish, Italian, and French. We focus on these languages because most research to date on the L2 acquisition of the subjunctive has been conducted on these languages, especially Spanish.

As we will see, the vast majority of the intervention studies follow the **input processing instruction** (PI) model (VanPatten, 1996, 2002, 2004). While most of the instruction research on the subjunctive has examined low- and intermediate-proficiency learners in the classroom, linguistically oriented SLA studies of the subjunctive, none of which are interventions, have focused on more advanced learners. These SLA studies have examined the acquisition and processing of functional morphology, the relationship between **morphology** and **semantics**, and the integration of other interfaces. In general, however, because the linguistic SLA approach to the subjunctive and the PI approach have focused on different proficiency levels and different aspects of the subjunctive learning problem, these two strands of research have been, for the most part, disconnected from each other.

6.1 Terminology

Before discussing the studies related to the acquisition of the subjunctive, we must review some important linguistic concepts in this area.

6.1.1 Indicative vs. Subjunctive Mood

Mood is one of the ways of expressing modality. All languages express modality. **Modality** is a semantic notion that determines the contexts in which an observation or proposition is possible, probable, likely, certain, permitted or prohibited. Mood encodes the probability, obligation, or necessity of what is stated, according to the point of view of the speaker (Comrie, 1976). Languages that express modality in the grammar do so with a variety of grammatical devices, such as modal verbs (*might, could*), the future tense (expressed with *will* in English), and conditionals (expressed with the modal *would* in English). Due to the limited number of intervention studies on modal verbs, future tense, and conditionals, we will only cover studies of the subjunctive in this chapter.

Many languages distinguish **indicative** and **subjunctive mood** through inflectional morphology on the verb. In general, the indicative expresses facts and affirmations (*realis*) while the subjunctive conveys doubt, opinion, hopes, preferences, hypotheses, and possibilities (*irrealis*). For example, all the Romance languages – Spanish, Catalan, Portuguese, French, Italian, and Romanian – have subjunctive morphology in the form of verbal inflection. Slavic languages such as Polish and Bulgarian also have subjunctive forms. The subjunctive typically appears in subordinate (embedded) clauses, while the indicative appears in main clauses as well as in some types of subordinate clauses. Below, we illustrate the indicative/subjunctive distinction with French.

In French, verbs of saying (*dire* 'say', *observer* 'observe') and epistemic predicates (*réaliser* 'realize', *se rappeler* 'remember') typically select subordinate sentences with the embedded verb in the indicative. In contrast, emotive-factive (e.g., *regretter* 'regret'), desire (e.g., *préférer* 'prefer', *souhaiter* 'wish', *vouloir* 'want'), and **directive** or **mandative** (e.g., *suggérer* 'suggest', *insister* 'insist') **predicates** take subordinate clauses with the verbs in the subjunctive. For example, in (25), the verb of the **main clause**, *penser* 'think', requires the indicative in the embedded clause (enclosed in brackets), whereas the main verb *vouloir* 'want', in (26), triggers the subjunctive in the embedded clause (examples from Dudley, 2020).

(25)   Les étudiants *pensent* [que la première ministre *est* incompétente.]
       the students think.IND that the first minister is.IND incompetent
       'The students think that the prime minister is incompetent.'

(26)   Le gouvernement *veut* [que la 4G *soit* disponible partout.]
       the government wants.IND that the 4G is.SUBJ available everywhere
       'The government wants 4G to be available everywhere.'

It is often believed that native speakers of English have significant difficulty learning and mastering the subjunctive in Romance languages because English does not grammaticize mood on the verb. Many uses of the subjunctive have pragmatic implications, when the speaker expresses possibility and presupposition (as in the example in Table 6.1 *No creo que haya estado aquí* 'I don't believe he might have been here'). However, the status of the subjunctive in English is widely debated. The subjunctive, expressed by a bare stem, can appear in nominal subordinate clauses as a complement of mandative or directive (giving orders) predicates, such as *suggest* in (27a). However, it is often expressed with modals, such as *should* in (27b), especially in British English (Crawford, 2009).

(27)   a. Nate suggested that Sam *receive* detention.
       b. Nate suggested that Sam *should receive* detention.

Dudley (2020) experimentally investigated the acceptability of the subjunctive in clauses headed by verbs of desire, directives, and emotive-factive predicates for native speakers of British English. She found that the only contexts in which the British English speakers allowed the subjunctive was in complement clauses to directive predicates (*The minister demands that the conference take place before the end of the year*). With desire and emotive-factive predicates they categorically preferred the (for)-to infinitive structure (*I really prefer for Lois to be the main presenter; Cecilia wants for her friend*

Table 6.1 Indicative and subjunctive verbal forms in Spanish

Indicative on *estar* 'be'	Subjunctive on *estar* 'be'
present, future Creo que *está* aquí. 'I believe he/she/it/ is here.' Creo que *estará* aquí. 'I believe he/she/it must be here.'	**present** *No* creo que *esté* aquí. 'I don't believe he/she/it/ is here.'
present perfect, future perfect Creo que *estaba/ha estado* aquí. 'I believe he/she/it was/has been here.' Creo que *habrá estado* aquí. 'I believe that he/she/it must have been here.'	**perfect** No creo que *haya estado* aquí. 'I don't believe that he/she/it has been here.'
conditional, preterite/imperfect Creí que *estaría* aquí. 'I believed he/she/it would be here.' Creí que *estuvo/estaba* aquí. 'I believed he/she/it was here.'	**imperfect** No creí que *estuviera/estuviese* aquí. 'I didn't believe he/she/it would be here.'
past perfect, conditional perfect Creí que *había estado* aquí. 'I believed he/she/it had been here.' *Creí que habría estado aquí.* 'I believed he/she/it would have been here.'	**pluperfect** No creí que *hubiera estado* aquí. 'I did not believe he/she/it would have been here.'

to have more confidence in her abilities) or the indicative (*The dentist likes that his patient is aware of the risks associated with eating sugar*) to the subjunctive. Therefore, at least for British English, there is a very limited instantiation of subjunctive mood in the grammar.

In sum, mood selection is regulated by syntactic, semantic, and pragmatic factors related to speakers' presuppositions or intentions. The syntactic, semantic, and pragmatic conditions that govern the use of indicative vs. subjunctive mood selection are very complex, and it is impossible to summarize them in just a few words here. In the next section, we illustrate some of these complexities by focusing on a description of the subjunctive in Spanish.

6.1.2 The Subjunctive in Spanish

The subjunctive in Spanish and in Romance languages in general is very complex, and we can only give a brief summary of the main characteristics. For more in-depth treatments of the Spanish subjunctive, see Alonso (1999), Haverkate (2002), Saldanya (1999), among others.

There is present and past subjunctive. Table 6.1 shows the forms of the present, future, and past in the indicative and the subjunctive moods in

Spanish with the verb *creer* 'believe' as the main verb and with the verb *estar* 'be' in the subordinate clause. The verb *creer* in the main clause determines the mood of the verb *estar* in the subordinate clause. When *creer* is used affirmatively, the verb in the subordinate clause takes indicative morphology. When *creer* is negated, the verb in the subordinate clause takes subjunctive morphology. There are four simple and four complex verbal forms (with *haber* + infinitive) in the indicative but only two simple and two complex forms in the subjunctive.

6.1.2.1 Syntactic Requirements

As in (25) and (26) with French, indicative verbal forms in Spanish occur in both **main** (28) and **subordinate clauses** (29). In contrast, the subjunctive is mostly restricted to subordinate contexts, as in (31), where it appears inside the subordinate clause, and is not used is indicative contexts such as (30).

(28) Hugo está en un auto antiguo.
      Hugo is.IND in a car old
      'Hugo is in an old car.'

(29) La profesora Gómez cree que Lea *está* en esta sala.
      the Professor Gómez think that Lea is.IND in this room
      'Professor Gómez thinks that Lea is in this room.'

(30) *Lea esté en esta sala.
      Lea is.SUBJ in this room
      'Lea is in this room.'

(31) Salomé espera [que Lea *esté* en el tren.]
      Salomé hopes that Lea is.SUBJ on the train
      'Salomé hopes that Lea is on the train.'

The subjunctive can appear in main clauses, as in commands, and after certain adverbs and expressions, such as *ojalá* 'God willing', *tal vez* 'maybe', *acaso* 'perhaps'. For example, the sentence in (30) can be made grammatical with the addition of the expression *Ojalá* (from Arabic, 'God willing', which means 'I hope' or 'hopefully'): *Ojalá Lea esté en esta sala* 'I hope Lea is in this room').

As we saw above for French, indicative vs. subjunctive mood in Spanish can be lexically selected by the verb (or adjectival predicate) of the main clause. Verbs like *saber* 'know' and *descubrir* 'discover, find out' always select the indicative, as shown in (32). Verbs or expressions that express doubt (*dudar* 'doubt', *ser posible/probable* 'be possible/likely') and volitional verbs (*querer* 'want', *esperar* 'wish') select the subjunctive, as shown in (33), and so do other subordinating expressions of doubt, necessity, obligation, regret, etc., as shown in (34).

(32) La   princesa sabe que la primer prueba es/*sea   derrotar un dragón.
      the princess knows that the first trick is.IND/*is.SUBJ defeat.INF a dragon
      'The princess knows that the first task is to defeat a dragon.'

(33) Clara quiere que la   princesa se   prepare/*prepara   para la prueba muy bien
      Clara wants that the princess self prepare.SUBJ/*prepare.IND for the trick thoroughly
      'Clara wants the princess to prepare for the task thoroughly.'

(34) Es importante que la princesa use/*usa   sus poderes mágicos.
      is important that the princess use.SUBJ/*IND her powers magic
      'It is important that the princess uses her magic powers.'

In these cases, the use of the indicative in (32) and the subjunctive in (33) and (34) is obligatory. As the examples show, the use of the other form is categorically ungrammatical.

6.1.2.2 Variable Use of the Subjunctive in Different Pragmatic Contexts

One of the complicating factors in mood selection is that in many other cases, subjunctive selection appears to be optional. The choice of subjunctive or indicative in the embedded clause is a choice the speaker makes. This choice depends on the speaker's appraisal of the situation or on the degree of assertiveness, **presupposition**, or doubt that the speaker needs to convey. For example, the verb *decir* 'say/ask' can appear with subjunctive or indicative in the subordinate clause, depending on its meaning. When *decir* states a fact, the verb in the embedded clause uses indicative, as in (35), but when *decir* states a request, the verb in the embedded clause is in the subjunctive, as in (36).

(35) Lesley dice que *ayuda*   a   Diego.
      Lesley says that help.IND   DOM Diego
      'Lesley says that he helps [is helping] Diego.'

(36) Lesley dice que *ayude*   a   Diego.
      Lesley says that help.SUBJ DOM Diego
      'Lesley asks that I/he/she [someone other than Lesley] help Diego.'

Another typical example of optional or variable uses of the subjunctive is with the verb in **restrictive relative clauses**, as in (37) and (38). **Relative clauses** modify nouns or **noun phrases**, such as the noun phrase *un jugador de fútbol* 'a soccer player' in (37) and (38).

(37) [indicative-presupposition]
      La entrenadora Vázquez busca   a   un jugador de fútbol [que *es*   arquero.]
      the trainer   Vázquez looks for DOM a   player   of soccer that is.IND   goalkeeper
      'Coach Vázquez is looking for a (specific) soccer player who is a goalkeeper.'

(38) [subjunctive-non-presuppositional]
      La entrenadora Vázquez busca un jugador de fútbol [que *sea* arquero.]
      the trainer Vázquez looks for a player of fútbol that is.SUBJ goalkeeper
      'Coach Vázquez is looking for a soccer player who is/could be a goalkeeper.'

The indicative in (37) presupposes that the referent (a goalkeeper) exists, whereas the subjunctive in (38) implies that the referent might not exist. That is, in (37), Coach Vázquez has in mind a specific player who is already a goalkeeper (Marta) and is looking for that specific player, whereas in (38), Coach Vázquez is looking for any player who might be a goal keeper.

Some **adverbial subordinate clauses** have a similar behavior. The subordinating conjunction *para que* 'so that' introduces **purpose clauses** with obligatory subjunctive, as in (39).

(39) Pat cerró la puerta del cuarto [*para que* Lourdes *descansara* tranquila].
      Pat closed the door of bedroom so that Lourdes rest.SUBJ quiet
      'Pat closed the door to the bedroom so that Lourdes could rest quietly.'

With the expression *de manera que* 'so that', the indicative asserts the fact of the main clause, while the subjunctive does not assert it. Thus, in (40) it is implied that all students understand the theorem, while (41) leaves open the possibility that some students will not understand the theorem.

(40) La profesora Olney explica el teorema [*de manera que* todos los
      the professor Olney explains the theorem of a way that all the
            estudiantes lo *entienden*].
            students it understand.IND
      'Professor Olney explains the theorem in a way that all the students understand it.'

(41) La profesora Olney explica el teorema [*de manera que* todos los
      the professor Olney explains the theorem of a way that all the
            estudiantes lo *entiendan*.]
            students it understand.SUBJ
      'Professor Olney explains the theorem so that all the students might understand it.'

Cuando 'when' is another subordinating conjunction that selects indicative or subjunctive in **temporal adverbial clauses** depending on the meaning and time of the event. Indicative is used when *cuando* introduces a habitual event or when an event happens simultaneously with another one, as in (42). The subjunctive is used when the event is likely to occur in the future, and in this case, the verb of the main clause has to be in the future tense, as in (43).

(42) [Cuando la bruja *llega* a su casa] su gato la recibe contento.
      when the witch arrive.IND at her house her cat her greet.PRES happy
      'When the witch arrives at her house, her cat greets her happily.'

(43) [Cuando la bruja *llegue* a su casa] su gato la recibirá contento.
      when the witch arrive.SUBJ at her house her cat her greet.FUT happy
      'When the witch arrives at her house, her cat will greet her happily.'

Other variable uses of subjunctive occur with negation (see Table 6.1), in questions and with other adverbials such as *quizás* or *tal vez* 'maybe'.

Once again, the facts of the subjunctive are too complex to be able to give a more thorough description in a few pages.

6.1.3 The Subjunctive Mood in Linguistic Theory

We saw in Chapter 4 that in generative grammar (Chomsky, 1995) a distinction is made between lexical categories and functional categories. **Lexical categories** refer to verbs, nouns, adjectives, adverbs, and some prepositions. **Functional categories** correspond to inflectional morphology and closed-class words with grammatical meaning such as determiners, complementizers, person, number, gender, tense, aspect, mood, etc. Functional categories such as Tense Phrase (TP) or Aspect Phrase (AspP) are represented above the verb in a syntactic tree, as we saw in Chapter 4 with the **verb-movement** parameter. The lexical verb moves to these syntactic nodes to check (a technical syntactic term) the syntactic and semantic formal features of these categories through overt inflectional morphology.

Just as with tense or agreement, Giorgi and Pianesi (1997), among others, proposed that *mood* is represented in a functional category, MoodP (higher than the Tense Phrase if you recall the syntactic structure in Chapter 4, Figure 4.1), where the feature [+MOOD] is checked through subjunctive morphology when the verb raises from V-to-MoodP to be interpreted. Indicative clauses are assumed not to project MoodP. Assuming an expanded projection for complementizer phrases (CP) (that includes other categories such as ForceP), Kempchinsky (2009) and Quer (2009) proposed that the modal feature is in the head of ForceP. Volitional subjunctives, those subcategorized by verbs like *querer* 'want' in Spanish or *vouloir* 'want' in French, trigger subjunctive in the subordinate clause; the main verb (*querer* 'want' in Spanish or *vouloir* 'want' in French) moves to ForceP. In contrast, epistemic verbs like *recorder* 'remember' in Spanish or *se rappeler* 'remember' in French, select indicative and do not move to ForceP.

Languages may vary with respect to the realization of particular functional categories in the clausal structure or with respect to the feature values or **feature strength** of a given functional category. Since some varieties of English do not grammaticize mood, the functional category MoodP is assumed not to be instantiated, although Dudley (2020) established that it might be active in very limited contexts in British English (see section 6.1.1). If English does not have a category MoodP, or verbs do not move to ForceP to check mood features, this would explain the difficulty in acquiring the MoodP projection and its syntactic, semantic, and morphological consequences for L2 learners of Romance languages whose L1 is English.

Thus, two questions arise. The first one is whether the L2 acquisition of a new functional category such as MoodP is, in principle, possible. The second is whether knowledge of morphology and knowledge of semantics are related or dissociated in **interlanguage** grammars. These questions have largely driven the available linguistic research on the acquisition of the subjunctive.

6.2 First and Second Language Acquisition Studies on the Subjunctive

The subjunctive is one of the most difficult and protracted aspects of the grammar of Spanish to be acquired in L1, L2, and bilingual acquisition (Montrul, 2004a). Native-like mastery of this form requires several years of rich input (in quality and quantity). Even for monolingual children, the acquisition of the subjunctive takes several years. Since the subjunctive is also unlikely to be fully acquired by heritage speakers, and because heritage speakers were exposed to the heritage language since birth, it is important to understand how long it takes monolingual children to master the subjunctive. L2 learners are expected to know the subjunctive because it is taught and emphasized in classrooms, so understanding how long it takes to learn the subjunctive for young children might put the problem of the L2 learner in a broader perspective. Therefore, we cover the acquisition of the subjunctive in the monolingual acquisition of Spanish by young children first.

6.2.1 The Subjunctive in First Language Acquisition

According to Montrul (2004a), subjunctive morphology emerges quite early in Spanish. Data from López Ornat et al. (1994) and Hernández Pina (1984) show that two-year-old children already produced subjunctive morphology in some obligatory contexts. These contexts include imperatives and adverbial clauses with *para que* 'so that' and *cuando* 'when', as well as verbs that subcategorize for subjunctive complements (*querer* 'want', *dejar* 'allow'). Yet, according to Gili Gaya (1972), monolingual Spanish speakers do not master mood selection until adolescence. Blake (1983, 1985), a study of subjunctive development in children between the ages of four and twelve, found that children between the ages of five and seven displayed significant morphological variability with the use of the subjunctive, especially with verbs of doubt (*dudar* 'doubt', *no creer* 'not believe') and attitude, and with assertion expressions (*ver* 'see', *pensar* 'think', *decir* 'say'). Blake (1983, 1985) found what appeared to be a developmental order, according to which subjunctive is mastered first in indirect commands (*Le pide que salte a la cuerda* 'He asks him to jump the rope'), then in adverbial clauses (*Va a abrir el paraguas cuando llueva*, literally 'She will open the umbrella when it will rain'), then in relative clauses (*Necesito un libro que explique bien el subjuntivo* 'I need a book that explains the subjunctive well'), and lastly in **sentential complements** (or **nominal clauses**) (*Es necesario que las cosas sigan así* 'It is necessary that things stay the same').

Pérez-Leroux (1998) noted that the developmental pattern attested by Blake cannot be solely derived from optionality of subjunctive in the input since subjunctive is optional in adverbial clauses (second stage) and mostly obligatory in sentential complements (last stage). It appears that there are other cognitive factors that contribute to the acquisition of subjunctive by children. Pérez-Leroux tested three- to six-year-old monolingual Spanish children on their knowledge of presupposition in subjunctive relative clauses in an oral elicitation task. Presupposition is information that is assumed to be true, even though it is not directly asserted by the utterance. For example, *Joan no longer writes fiction* asserts that Joan does not write fiction now and presupposes that she wrote fiction in the past. Pérez-Leroux found that children's ability to produce the subjunctive was correlated with their ability to entertain false beliefs, which improved significantly with increased age.

More recently, Dracos, Requena, and Miller (2019) examined Spanish-speaking children's acquisition of mood selection in sentential complements (nominal clauses). This study looked both at complements to factive-emotive predicates involving mental state adjectives (*El padre está contento de que su hijo cante* 'The father is happy that his son sings') and the negated epistemic verb *creer* 'believe' (*La mamá no cree que su hija esté en la fiesta* 'The mother does not believe her daughter is at the party'); see Table 6.1. The first is an example of a presupposition ('The father is happy that his son sings' presupposes that his son sings) while the latter is a nonassertion ('The mother does not believe her daughter is at the party' negates the assertion that her daughter is at the party). Results of an oral sentence-completion task with four- to ten-year-old children and adults indicated adultlike mood selection by ages six to seven in the presupposition condition and ages nine to ten in the nonassertion condition. Taken together, all these studies confirm that it takes children several years to produce and understand the meanings of the subjunctive like adults. They reveal that the rate of development is context specific as a function of semantic, syntactic, and cognitive complexity. If the subjunctive takes so long to master in L1 acquisition, why is it implicitly expected that adult L2 learners will grasp it in less time? And why do heritage speakers of Spanish not seem to know all the uses? We turn to studies of the subjunctive in SLA next.

6.2.2 The Subjunctive in Second Language Acquisition

The body of research on the acquisition of the Spanish subjunctive is very extensive, but there are also several studies attesting to the difficulty that

English-speaking learners face when learning subjunctive in L2 French. The latter include Ayoun (2013); Bartning, Lundell, and Hancock (2012); Dudley (2020); Howard (2008, 2012); and McManus and Mitchell (2015). There are also some studies of the subjunctive in L2 Italian (Benati, 2000) and in L3 Portuguese (Cawalho & Da Silva, 2006).

6.2.2.1   Second Language Production of the Subjunctive

One of the earliest studies on the L2 acquisition of the Spanish subjunctive is Terrell, Baycroft, and Perrone (1987), who investigated the written and oral production of subjunctive forms in beginner learners of Spanish. The learners produced subjunctive forms with 90 percent accuracy in a written production task, but when it came to using subjunctive in spontaneous oral production, they were only 12 percent accurate. The difference between the results of the written and oral tasks was explained in terms of the **Monitor model** (Krashen, 1981, 1982; see Chapter 1). In the written task, learners had time to reflect and make use of their "learned" knowledge, but this knowledge had not become "acquisition," and, therefore, learners had serious difficulties retrieving this knowledge automatically in oral production. Collentine (1995) argued that beginner and intermediate learners of Spanish have problems with the morphological realization of the subjunctive because they do not yet control complex syntax, since as we saw the subjunctive is mostly used in subordinate sentences. In oral production, these learners tended to produce simple sentences and coordinated sentences without coordinating or subordinating conjunctions, as well as coordinated structures (with coordinating conjunctions). Collentine (2010) corroborated that instruction on syntax improved beginner and intermediate learners' production of subjunctive morphology. Leow (1995) found that proficiency determined the extent to which L2 learners would pay attention to subjunctive forms in the input.

Studies on the French subjunctive, such as Ayoun (2013) and McManus and Mitchell (2015), used personal narratives and sentence-completion tasks with learners of different proficiency levels (beginners, intermediate, and advanced) and found a few accurate instances of subjunctive in oral narratives but highly inaccurate responses in the written sentence-completion task by all proficiency groups. Ayoun also found that the L2 learners were more accurate with subjunctive with verbs of order (*demander* 'order') and expressions of prohibition (*il est intérdit que* 'it is forbidden that') than with other verbs that subcategorize for subjunctive complements in French (i.e., verbs of judgment, emotion, wish, regret, doubt, and impossibility, as described in section 6.1.1). Still, as found for Spanish, accuracy with the subjunctive is higher, the higher the proficiency of the learners (McManus & Mitchell, 2015).

6.2.2.2 The Subjunctive in Second Language Judgments and Comprehension

Turning away from production and use of subjunctive morphology, studies within the generative linguistic framework have focused on the acquisition of the meanings of subjunctive morphology in advanced to near-native speakers. Unlike all the studies with beginner and intermediate L2 learners examining subjunctive use in oral and written production tasks, the focus of the generative studies has been on the interpretation of subjunctive forms in variable contexts, especially in cases when subjunctive uses are not taught and are underdetermined by the input.

The first study of this kind is Bruhn de Garavito (1997), who tested coreference restrictions on complement clauses in Spanish. With complements of indicative clauses, the subject of the embedded verb can corefer with the subject of the matrix clause, such as *Juan* in (44a). However, this is not possible with the subjunctive in (44b).

(44) a. Juan cree [que no va a llegar a tiempo].
Juan believes that not goes.IND to arrive on time
'Juan believes that he is not going to arrive on time.'
b. (yo) quiero [que vaya a la fiesta].
I want that go.3.SUBJ/*1.SUBJ to the party
'I want him/her/*me to go to the party.'

In (44b) the subjunctive form *vaya* is both first and third person singular. However, with certain subjunctive complements there is a subject coreference restriction, and the (null) subject of the embedded subjunctive verb cannot corefer with the subject of the main clause, which is *yo* 'I' in (44b). For the coreference to be possible, the infinitive form must be used, as in (45).

(45) Yo quiero [ir a la fiesta].
I want go.INF to the party
'I want to go to the party.'

It is usually emphasized in language classes that the subjunctive cannot be used if there is coreference between the subject of the embedded clause and that of the matrix clause. Although presented as a general rule, it is not. With modal verbs such as *poder* 'can, be able to' (46a) and in temporal clauses with *cuando* 'when' (46b) the subject coreference restriction does not hold.

(46) a. (yo) espero [que pueda hablar con él hoy].
I hope that can.SUBJ speak.INF with him today
'I hope that I/he/she will be able to speak to him today.'
b. (yo) voy a llamarte [cuando llegue].
I go to call-you when come.SUBJ
'I am going to call you when I/he/she arrive(s).'

There is a syntactic reason related to the tenseless nature of the subjunctive that explains the different coreference possibilities of sentences (44) to (46). Another property of the subjunctive rarely taught explicitly in the classroom or teaching materials is its temporality. While indicative verbs in embedded clauses can refer to actions anterior, contemporary, and posterior to the time of the main verb, subjunctive complements behave like infinitives and can only refer to contemporary and posterior events. The embedded subjunctive verb has a future interpretation with respect to the tense of the main verb. That is, in (44b) and (46b) the action denoted by the subjunctive verb in the embedded clause (*vaya, llegue*) must occur after the action expressed by the verb of the main clause (*quiero/voy a llamarte*) (*quiero* and *voy a llamarte* are in the present tense; the subjunctive *vaya, llegue* has a future interpretation).

Bruhn de Garavito (1997) tested whether advanced and near-native speakers of Spanish acquire the subject-coreference restrictions with different subjunctive complements using a **truth-value judgment task** (TVJT) and a **grammaticality judgment task** (GJT). The GJT was designed to test the interaction of subjunctive and tense. According to the syntactic assumptions of this study, the coreference restrictions and the future interpretation of the subjunctive are related to the morphological and syntactic properties of subjunctive morphology (a tenseless form) and the syntactic category of the complement clause. Bruhn de Garavito found a correlation between knowledge of tense (future) and coreferentiality. The learners who had acquired the syntactic constraints on coreferentiality also knew the tense restriction.

Another study on interpretations of subjunctive in variable contexts is Borgonovo and Prévost (2003), who investigated the acquisition of the imperfect subjunctive in negative sentences with the verb *creer* (as in Table 6.1) in a TVJT with very advanced French-speaking learners of Spanish. While French has subjunctive like Spanish, subjunctive with negation works differently in French and is more restricted than in Spanish. In Spanish, polarity subjunctive is licensed with epistemic (*creer* 'believe'), perception (*ver* 'see), and communication (*decir* 'say') verbs, while in French it is only possible with epistemic (*croire* 'believe') verbs, as the (b) examples in (47) to (49) show (compare to the (a) examples from Spanish). In the (a) sentences with the verb of the embedded clause (*salir*) in the indicative, the speaker has certainty that Pedro left because somehow the event was witnessed. When the verb *salir* is in the subjunctive, the speaker assumes (thinks) that Pedro left, and there is no certainty.

(47) a. Marta no cree que Pedro ha/haya salido.
      Marta not believe that Peter has.IND/has.SUBJ left
   b. Marta ne croit pas que Pierre est/soit parti.
      Marta not believe not that Peter is.IND/is.SUBJ left
      'Marta does not believe that Peter left.'

(48) a. Marta no vio que Pedro salía/saliera.
      Marta not saw that Peter left.IND/left.SUBJ
   b. Marta n'a pas vu que Pierre est/*soit parti.
      Marta NEG+has not seen that Peter is.IND/*is.SUBJ left
      'Marta did not see that Peter left.'

(49) a. Marta no ha dicho que Pedro salió/ hubiera salido.
      Marta not has said that Peter left.IND/ had.SUBJ left
   b. Marta n'a pas dit que Pierre est /*soit parti.
      Marta NEG+has not said that Peter is.IND/is.SUBJ left
      'Marta did not say that Peter left.'

Taking into account the difference between the semantic-pragmatic notions presupposition or experienced event and nonpresupposition (nonexperienced event), the aim of Borgonovo and Prévost (2003) was to show that participants distinguished between indicative and subjunctive as a function of witnessing or not witnessing an event. Subjunctive was appropriate in both contexts, whereas indicative was only appropriate in presupposed (witnessed) contexts. The task was a truth-value judgment task, testing subjunctive and indicative sentences with epistemic (*creer* 'believe'), perception (*ver* 'see'), and communication verbs (*decir* 'say'). The context of the story set up a presuppositional vs. a nonpresuppositional situation, and participants were to judge whether the following sentence with subjunctive or indicative was true or semantically appropriate in the context provided by the story.

Overall results showed that the L2 learners accepted subjunctive in presupposed and nonpresupposed contexts. Like the native speaker controls, the L2 learners distinguished between indicative in these two contexts: Indicative was judged more acceptable in presupposed than in nonpresupposed contexts by all the groups, while the opposite obtained for subjunctive, which was accepted more often in nonpresupposed contexts only. Another recent study on the variable interpretation of subjunctive with relative clauses by L1-French L2-Spanish learners also found accurate interpretations at advanced levels (Borgonovo, Bruhn de Garavito, & Prévost, 2015). In common with Bruhn de Garavito's study, these results show that the subtleties of subjunctive mood are acquirable in a second language by very advanced learners and that at least some learners can overcome the restrictions imposed by their L1. The functional category MoodP is fully acquirable and operational in interlanguage grammars.

Iverson, Kempchinsky, and Rothman (2008) investigated the knowledge of Spanish subjunctive among intermediate and advanced L2 learners of Spanish. They proposed that English-speaking learners must retrieve the functional projection MoodP and an uninterpretable modal feature on the head of ForceP (see section 6.1.3) via the formal English register of the L1 grammar (*They requested that he not vote at the meeting yesterday*), while delearning the English *for-to* clause (*I would like for you to do your homework*). Findings from a morphology recognition task and a GJT revealed that the advanced learners had knowledge of the morphology and of the obligatory subjunctive complements, while the intermediate learners were developing in the right direction as well. Sanchez-Naranjo (2009), who also focused on advanced learners of Spanish, found that subjunctive adverbial clauses present difficulties even for advanced L2 learners. Although the L2 learners exhibited sensitivity to certain subjunctive features and contextual meanings, convergence and nonconvergence were primarily determined by L1 influence from English, which does not have the subjunctive.

6.2.2.3 Interim Summary: The Subjunctive in Second Language Acquisition

To summarize thus far, we have seen that studies of the acquisition of subjunctive come in two types. Some studies have focused on the production and comprehension of subjunctive by beginner and intermediate instructed learners. Others have examined whether very advanced to near-native speakers understand the meanings of subjunctive and indicative in variable contexts or contexts that depend on semantic-pragmatic notions such as presupposition. Results of advanced speakers, many of whom are French speakers learning L2 Spanish, show that these learners are able to interpret the subjunctive correctly in off-line (paper-and-pencil) tasks.

As we will see next with classroom-based research, much has been said about L2 learners' difficulty noticing and processing subjunctive forms. Therefore, recent studies have implemented online processing tasks to test the validity of these observations. For example, Dudley (2020) conducted an L2 processing study on the acquisition of the subjunctive in obligatory contexts by L1-English learners of L2 French. The study used grammaticality judgments and **eye tracking** during reading. Dudley found that the learners demonstrated native-like ability to distinguish the grammaticality of subjunctive and indicative in the French GJT in different types of sentences, but their processing patterns revealed in the eye-tracking task were not native-like. Online sensitivity to grammaticality violations was affected by L1 influence from English, proficiency in French, and having spent time in a

French-speaking environment (through study abroad). The Fernández Cuenca (2019) study of Spanish, discussed in the next section, found similar nonnative results with online processing during reading. We turn to the intervention studies next.

6.3 Second Language Intervention Research Studies on the Subjunctive

The intervention studies that have been conducted to date have focused on trying different types of instruction to accelerate the way learners notice and process the subjunctive to make form-meaning connections, in different syntactic and semantic contexts. Table 6.2 lists a few of these intervention studies.

Early studies of the classroom acquisition of the subjunctive were deemed unsuccessful by Collentine (2010) because the focus of many studies was the low perceptual salience of subjunctive morphology. In Spanish, the difference between the indicative and subjunctive forms is signaled by a change in the thematic vowel of the verb (*corro-corra, sirve-sirva, duermo-duerma*). Several studies have shown that even with textual enhancement, beginner and intermediate-level classroom learners do not notice the difference in spelling (J. F. Lee, 1987; Leow et al., 2003).

However, Collentine (2013) has argued that L2 learners only notice the morphology and semantics of the subjunctive when they are syntactically ready and have acquired subordination. (Recall that most of subjunctive forms occur in nominal, adjectival, and adverbial subordinate clauses.) Some have found that advanced proficiency and metalinguistic awareness contribute to the use of subjunctive with higher accuracy (Correa, 2011; Lubbers Quesada, 1998). However, this is not always the case. Cameron (2011) found that intermediate and advanced learners with metalinguistic knowledge of the subjunctive were still unable to distinguish indicative and subjunctive forms in subordinate clauses. See also Cheng and Diaz-Mojica (2006) for a study of the Spanish subjunctive from a discourse perspective.

6.3.1 Processing Instruction Studies with the Subjunctive

There are several intervention studies of the subjunctive, as summarized in Table 6.2. Studies of processing instruction (PI) (VanPatten, 1996) have shown that language instruction can help Spanish L2 learners from different proficiency levels better interpret and produce the subjunctive (Pereira, 1996; Farley, 2001b, 2004; Potowski, Jegerski, & Morgan-Short, 2009; Fernández,

Table 6.2 Summary of intervention studies on the subjunctive

Paper	Structures / phenomena under instruction	Participants' linguistic background	Nature of the intervention	Length of intervention	Major findings
Collentine (1998)	Spanish subjunctive in adjectival clauses	54 second-semester L1-English L2-learners of Spanish	Compared processing instruction with output-oriented instruction	Two 50-minute sessions	Instruction groups better than no instruction group. No difference between processing instruction and output-oriented instruction.
Farley (2001b)	Spanish subjunctive with expressions of doubt	129 learners enrolled in fourth-semester Spanish (10 intact classes) assigned to a PI (5 classes) or meaning-based output (MOI) instruction (5 classes) treatments	Formal instruction and practice of the Spanish subjunctive with expressions of doubt; PI group received input processing comprehension activities; MOI received oral practice in meaningful contexts	1 week in the classroom during two consecutive 50-minute classes	All groups substantially improved with accuracy on both interpretation and production of the subjunctive. No differences between the PI and MOI treatments in interpretation or production.
Farley (2004)	Subjunctive in expressions of doubt and certainty	54 fourth-semester L2 learners of Spanish	Compared processing instruction and structured input	1 week in the classroom during two consecutive 50-minute classes	Improvement in sentence-level tasks testing production and comprehension of subjunctive in PI and SI activities. PI improved more than SI, especially with indicative.

Table 6.2 (cont.)

Paper	Structures / phenomena under instruction	Participants' linguistic background	Nature of the intervention	Length of intervention	Major findings
J. F. Lee & Benati (2007)	Subjunctive with verbs of opinion and of doubt in Italian and with verbs of doubt in French	47 learners of Italian (English L1) 61 learners of French (English L1)	Grammatical explanation on the subjunctive and structured input (PI groups) and meaning-based output practice (MOI groups)	4 hours of instruction and practice in two consecutive days	Participants in the PI groups (classroom and computer) made significant improvements in the Italian and French interpretation tasks. The learners receiving MOI did not. There were no differences between PI and MOI in the Italian or French production tasks.
Fernández (2008, experiment 2)	Third person singular of the Spanish subjunctive in expressions of doubt	84 learners enrolled in third-semester Spanish (beginning-intermediate) divided into the PI group and the structured input (SI) group	Exposure explicit information about the subjunctive and practice with PI and SI activities online, following Farley's (2001b) methodology (items)	Pretest, treatment, and immediate posttest took place in three consecutive days	Explicit information was beneficial for the correct processing of the subjunctive online. The PI group reached criterion earlier than the SI group and showed faster response times.
Potowski, Jegerski, & Morgan-Short (2009)	Spanish imperfect subjunctive in relative clauses	127 Spanish heritage speakers (processing instruction, traditional instruction and no instruction groups); 20 L2 learners of Spanish	Explicit information about how the past subjunctive is formed, followed by traditional or input processing instruction practice;	Traditional instruction and processing instruction took place during regular class time one day of the week	Instruction is beneficial for both L2 learners and HL learners. Differential improvement by group and task.

			PI group received explicit information about how the verb form is misprocessed; both groups received feedback		No difference between types of instruction.
Torres (2018)	Spanish subjunctive in relative clauses	44 L2 learners 37 HL learners	The participants in each learner group were assigned to a simple or complex version of a task where they had to decide whether to use the past indicative or subjunctive. Both groups received corrective feedback.	Pretests and treatment (delivered through computerized activities) were completed during one week in 2 two-hour sessions; posttest took place two weeks later in a 45-minute session.	Groups assigned to the simpler task made higher gains than those in the complex task. HL learners benefited from form-focused instruction. L2 and HL learners approached the task differently based on their linguistic experience.
Fernández Cuenca (2019)	Spanish subjunctive in temporal adverbial clauses	39 L2 learners of Spanish (low proficiency) and 20 native speakers of Spanish	Computer-built explicit information tutorial followed by structured input practice	1 hour and 30 minutes	Gains from pretest to posttests in the instructed group compared to the no-instruction group in production, interpretation, and grammaticality judgment measures. Limited support for positive effects of language instruction on online processing during reading.

Table 6.2 (cont.)

Paper	Structures / phenomena under instruction	Participants' linguistic background	Nature of the intervention	Length of intervention	Major findings
Chiuchiù & Benati (2020)	Italian subjunctive with verbs of doubt	18 Chinese-speaking learners of Italian divided into a textual enhancement group and a structured input group	Practice of subjunctive vs. indicative forms in comprehension activities with and without input enhancement (bolded verb forms)	2 hours of instructional activities delivered via computer	Only the learners exposed to structured input showed sensitivity to violations of the Italian subjunctive of doubt on the self-paced reading test.
Fernandez Parera (2021)	Spanish subjunctive in relative clauses	14 HL learners 12 L2 learners	The two groups received instruction with Mindful Conceptual Engagement (MCE)	Three weeks of instruction and homework activities	HL improved on interpretation more than on production. L2 group improved on production more than interpretation, but difference was not statistically significant.

6.3 Intervention Studies on the Subjunctive

2008; Fernández Cuenca, 2019). Farley (2001b) argues that the subjunctive is amenable to input processing instruction based on the principles listed in VanPatten (1996):

1. Learners prefer to process lexical items to grammatical items (e.g., inflectional morphology).
2. They pay attention to more meaningful morphology before less meaningful morphology.
3. They pay more attention to grammatical items (functional elements) at the beginning rather than in the middle of the utterance.

The subjunctive in expressions of doubt, as in *No creo [que sepa la respuesta]* ('I don't believe I/he/she know(s) the answer') presents several challenges. First, the subjunctive is redundant because its morphology expresses doubt and so does the main lexical verb *no creo*. Because L2 learners pay attention to *no creo*, the subjunctive morphology in the subordinate clause has low communicative value. Furthermore, the subjunctive appears in the subordinate clause, which would be medial position in the sentence (if the subordinate clause follows the main clause). The main verb *no creo* appears before the subordinate verb in the subjunctive (*sepa*).

One of the first studies implementing PI to accelerate the acquisition of the subjunctive in Spanish is Pereira (1996). Pereira examined whether language instruction on more difficult or less frequent uses of the Spanish subjunctive (subjunctive in evaluation, as in example (34); temporal, as in example (43); and possibility embedded clauses, such as *Es posible que Juan venga a la fiesta* 'It is possible that Juan will come to the party') would also lead to learning gains on subjunctive uses that were less marked and more frequent (i.e., subjunctive in volition and purpose clauses). A GJT and a contextualized dialogue task were used to assess learning from pretest to posttests. Descriptive results in the dialogue task showed an increase in accuracy in the targeted structured (subjunctive in evaluation clauses) as well as an increase in accuracy in the less marked category (i.e., volition and purpose) from pretest to posttest. Results of the GJT were similar. Positive ratings decreased with ungrammatical sentences and increased with grammatical sentences in the marked and less marked categories from pretest to posttests. Overall, although the statistical analyses did not reveal a significant difference from pretest to posttests for any subjunctive clause type, Pereira concluded that PI led to gains in knowledge and production of the subjunctive among L2 learners.

However, in another study, Collentine (1998) tested knowledge of the subjunctive in relative (adjectival) clauses in third-semester Spanish, as in examples (37) and (38), repeated below.

(37) [indicative-presupposition]
La entrenadora Vázquez busca a un jugador de fútbol [que *es* arquero].
the trainer Vázquez looks for DOM a player of soccer that is.IND goalkeeper
'Coach Vázquez is looking for a (specific) soccer player who is a goalkeeper.'

(38) [subjunctive-nonpresuppositional]
La entrenadora Vázquez busca un jugador de fútbol [que *sea* arquero].
the trainer Vázquez looks for a player of soccer that is.SUBJ goalkeeper
'Coach Vázquez is looking for a soccer player who is/could be a goalkeeper.'

Two classes were part of the PI group, two others were in the output-based instruction group, and another class was the uninstructed control group. According to the findings, the two types of instruction brought about gains in accuracy on interpretation and production of the subjunctive in relative clauses, with no advantage of one type of instruction over the other.

6.3.1.1 Input-Based vs. Modified Output-Based Instruction with the Subjunctive

Farley (2001b) focused on the subjunctive of doubt (*Dudo que* 'I doubt that', *no creo que* 'I don't believe that') in Spanish and asked whether PI and meaning output instruction (MOI) bring about improved performance on sentence-level tasks involving the interpretation and the production of the Spanish subjunctive of doubt. If both PI and MOI bring about improved performance, do both types of instruction result in equally improved performance in interpretation and production?

The hypothesis, based on a pilot study with fewer participants (Farley, 2001a), was as follows. Both PI and MOI would bring improvement in production and interpretation of sentence-level tasks involving the subjunctive of doubt, but PI would be superior to MOI in the interpretation task.

Ten sections of a fourth-semester Spanish course (129 learners) were assigned to one of two treatments, PI and MOI, with five intact courses each. After the pretest, consisting of an interpretation task and a production task, only participants who scored below 60 percent remained in the study. The intervention was administered in two consecutive classes the week immediately after the pretest. Two weeks after the intervention, all classes did the posttest. The results demonstrated significant improvement in accuracy in both comprehension and production, indicating that PI and MOI had an overall greater effect on how learners interpreted and produced the Spanish subjunctive of doubt. Contrary to one of the hypotheses, the PI treatment did not yield higher accuracy in the interpretation task than the MOI treatment.

J. F. Lee and Benati (2007) investigated the acquisition of the subjunctive in Italian (with verbs of doubt and of opinion, as in *Non penso che canti bene* 'I don't think he sings well') and in French (with verbs of doubt, as in *Je doute qu'il vienne* 'I doubt he is coming') by English-speaking university students in the UK. They compared the effects of PI and MOI in the classroom and via computer in two parallel studies: Study 1 was on Italian and Study 2 was on French. The **independent variables** in both studies were the instructional treatment (PI vs. MOI) and the mode of delivery (classroom vs. computer). In each study, the L2 participants were divided into four groups: PI classroom, PI computer, MOI classroom, MOI computer. The participants in the two studies took a pretest and those who scored below 60 percent accuracy were retained in the two studies. The instruction took place on two consecutive days for two hours each day and included grammatical explanations and structured input activities (PI groups) or meaning-based output practice (MOI groups). The posttests measured interpretation and production.

According to the results of the two experiments, the PI groups showed greater gains in the interpretation tasks than the MOI groups, suggesting that the learners of French and of Italian processed the subjunctive better because of the intervention. There were gains in production from pretest to posttest as well, but no differences between the two instruction groups. Lee and Benati consider that the equal gains in production in the two experiments may be due to the explicit nature of the production task but claimed that PI is successful in altering how L2 learners process and interpret sentences containing French and Italian subjunctive of doubt forms.

6.3.1.2 Effects of PI with vs. without Explicit Information

In another study, Farley (2004) tested the effects of explicit information and PI on L2 learners' knowledge of the Spanish subjunctive in doubt and certainty clauses using an aural interpretation task and a production task. One L2 group received PI consisting of explicit information followed by structured-input practice, and the other experimental group received PI that only included structured-input practice. According to the results, both experimental groups showed significant accuracy gains in both tasks over time; however, the L2 learners who received PI with explicit information outperformed the L2 learners in the structured-input-only group. L2 learners in the PI group with explicit information also showed improvements in their use of the indicative mood in the interpretation task from pretest to posttest, whereas the L2 learners in the structured-input-only group did not. Therefore, it seems that explicit information helped promote faster form-meaning connections, which can in turn be reinforced when completing the structured-input portion of the instructional model.

Using Farley's (2004) materials and with the focus on the subjunctive with verbs of doubt, Fernández (2008) also investigated how PI with and without explicit information affects L2 learners' form-meaning connections as they engaged with structured-input activities, except that the instructional intervention was administered to participants individually via computer. Another difference is that Fernández measured **trials-to-criterion,** which she defined as L2 learners responding correctly to three consecutive items that required the subjunctive. Results showed that the L2 learners in the PI-with-explicit-information group also responded faster and were more accurate after reaching criterion compared to L2 learners in the structured-input-only group. Thus, explicit information within the PI module was beneficial as it induced more noticing of the target form, helping L2 learners make connections between the meaning of the verb in the main clause and the verb morphology in the embedded clause. In sum, based on interpretation changes from pretest to posttest, both Farley (2004) and Fernández (2008) found that PI leads to interpretation and production gains with the Spanish subjunctive.

6.3.2. Instruction with the Subjunctive in Adverbial Clauses

Other studies have focused on the subjunctive in adverbial clauses. Isabelli (2007) compared the effects of explicit grammar instruction with two groups of L2 learners' knowledge of subjunctive in adverbial clauses with *cuando* ('when') and *hasta que* ('until') framed within Giorgi and Pianesi's (1997) analysis of MoodP (mentioned in section 6.1.3). One of the groups had recently studied abroad in Spain for one year, and the second group had stayed at home and taken regular Spanish classes at the university. Results of oral interviews used to measure improvement of mood use over time yielded significant differences in learning outcomes between these two experimental groups. The L2 learners who had just returned from a study-abroad program showed significantly larger gains than the stay-at-home group. These findings suggest that recent immersion together with explicit grammar instruction can aid acquisition of Spanish mood with temporal adverbial clauses in L2 learners.

Díaz (2017) studied the effects of PI on L2 learners' knowledge of the Spanish subjunctive and indicative with regular verbs in temporal adverbial (*cuando*) clauses. A sentence-interpretation and a form-completion production task were used as assessment materials, in aural and written modalities, to examine changes from pretest to posttests. The order in which the components of PI appeared was manipulated so that in one group, explicit information preceded structured input, and in the other it followed it. Results showed that L2 learners' understanding and production of the Spanish subjunctive in these adverbial clauses increased significantly over time in both experimental groups, regardless of whether explicit instruction was provided before or after structured-input practice.

6.3.3 The Use of Psycholinguistic Methods in Intervention Studies with the Subjunctive

The findings from the above studies, which examined the effects of language instruction on learners' knowledge of mood, show that language instruction, particularly instruction that contains explicit information about the target form, helps L2 learners interpret and produce the subjunctive. Most of these studies employed an instructional intervention that followed PI guidelines, but none of these studies used an experimental design that could capture changes in L2 learners' input processing. With advances in psycholinguistic methodologies and the growing field of second language psycholinguistics, claims that problems with subjunctive morphology are due to faulty processing strategies and that input processing can change the way L2 learners process subjunctive morphology have recently been reexamined using online methods.

For example, Chiuchiù and Benati (2020) investigated how L2 learners interpret and process subjunctive in real time, that is, as they encounter the input (only) in writing. Chiuchiù and Benati (2020) compared the effects of structured input and textual enhancement by measuring processing of grammaticality violations of subjunctive vs. indicative in Italian with expressions of doubt during reading. The L2 learners of Italian were Chinese students studying in Italy, and the study consisted of a pretest **self-paced reading** task, an instructional period with input enhancement or structured input activities, and a posttest self-paced reading task. The intervention only included comprehension-based activities and no explicit grammatical explanations. The instructional module took place a week after the pretest, and the posttest took place immediately after the online module with the instructional intervention. The results showed that the participants in the structured-input group detected violations of grammaticality due to misuse of indicative or subjunctive as measured by longer reading times at the posttest than in the pretest. By contrast, the enhanced-input group did not show differences in reaction times before and after the intervention.

Eye tracking is also an ecologically valid methodology to examine processing during reading and has been recently used to investigate the subjunctive in French (Dudley, 2020) and in Spanish (Fernández Cuenca, 2019) second language acquisition. During eye tracking, participants sit in front of a computer monitor where visual and auditory (or just visual) stimuli are presented (sentences or pictures, depending on the study). The participant follows visual or auditory instructions, and a small infrared camera takes measurements of the eyes as they move on the screen. In psycholinguistic studies, the measurements of how long the eyes stay on certain words or

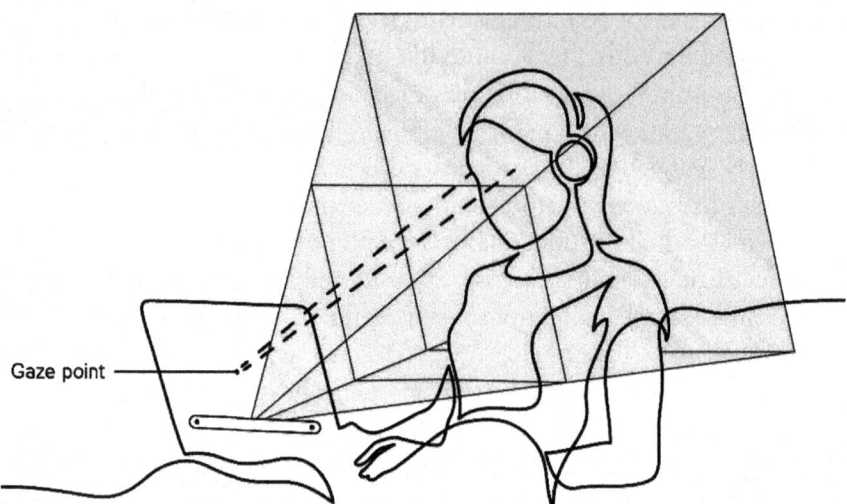

Figure 6.1 Eye tracking during reading and/or listening to linguistic stimuli (picture from Tobii AB: www.tobii.com/group/about/this-is-eyetracking/)

whether they come back to reread some words are indications of noticing linguistic forms during processing. See Figure 6.1.

Fernández Cuenca (2019) examined the effects of language instruction on English-speaking L2 learners' interpretation, production, and input processing of the Spanish subjunctive in adverbial clauses before and after instruction. She examined variable uses of indicative or subjunctive with *cuando* ('when') clauses, where the use of one form or the other implies a difference in tense (Box 6.1). In addition to testing the Lexical Preference Principle (VanPatten, 1996), the study examined whether and how language instruction that considers the psycholinguistic processes that govern L2 learners' input processing can help L2 learners overcome the lexical processing bias and lead them to pay more attention to morphological cues as they read the input in real time.

Fernández Cuenca used a sentence-reading comprehension test with eye tracking to examine L2 learners' changes in processing before and after instruction. At the pretest, the results confirmed that Spanish L2 learners rely more on lexical than inflectional cues when processing adverbial clauses with subjunctive, as measured by accuracy scores on two interpretation tests. Fernández Cuenca found that language instruction can help L2 learners pay more attention to inflectional cues, as measured via eye tracking. Furthermore, the study also found that language instruction led to L2 learners' interpretation and production learning gains, as measured by their responses to two interpretation tests and one production test before and after

BOX 6.1 Fernández Cuenca (2019)

Paper Title: The effects of language instruction on L2 learners' input processing and learning outcomes

Topic: The Spanish subjunctive and indicative in temporal adverbial clauses with *cuando* 'when'

(50) [indicative: cause-effect]
Cuando Ana *canta* se siente feliz.
when Ana sing.IND self feels happy
'When Ana sings she feels happy.'

(51) [subjunctive: future condition]
Cuando Ana *cante* se sentirá feliz.
when Ana sing.SUBJ self feel.FUT happy
'When/if Ana sings she will feel happy.'

Research Questions:

1. Are L2 learners affected by the Lexical Preference Principle, relying more on lexical than morphological cues?
2. If the answer to question 1 is yes, does explicit instruction help L2 learners pay more attention to morphological cues during real time processing?
3. Does explicit instruction lead to interpretation, production, and processing gains on the subjunctive in adverbial clauses in Spanish?

Participants: 39 English-speaking college learners of Spanish recruited from third- and fourth-year classes; 20 monolingually raised native speakers of Spanish

Groups:

- Instruction group (n = 20)
- Noninstruction group (n = 19)
- Native speaker group (n = 20)

Study Timeline:

- Day 1: pretest
- One-day intervention (instructed group only)
- Posttest (both learner groups)
- Delayed posttest three–four weeks later (both learner groups)

BOX 6.1 (cont.)

Pre/Posttests:

1. Event-selection interpretation task
2. Sentence-completion interpretation task
3. Cloze (production)
4. Reading-comprehension task with eye tracking

The Intervention:

A computer-based tutorial with explicit explanations about the subjunctive with *cuando* clauses and accurate processing strategies with *-ar* ending verbs. Comprehension items checked understanding during the lesson. This was followed by a referential activity that required learners to choose the best continuation for sentences.

Results

- At the pretest, the two interpretation tasks showed that all learners were more accurate interpreting the subjunctive in adverbial clauses in sentences with adverbs than without adverbs.
- At the pretest, the L2 learners were very inaccurate with subjunctive in the production task, especially in sentences with adverbs.
- At the pretest, the learners did not show sensitivity to ungrammaticality in the sentence comprehension during the eye-tracking task, although the instructed group showed an unexpected pattern compared to the uninstructed group at the pretest.
- Posttest results showed that the instructed group made significant gains in sentences without adverbs in written production (cloze) and in comprehension (see Figures 6.3 and 6.5) compared to the noninstructed group. It is possible that repeated exposure to these tests, in the pretest, posttest, and delayed posttest might have been enough to bring L2 learners' attention to form–meaning connections. Still, the higher performance of the instructed group indicates that the intervention, in addition to exposure, made a difference in this group.
- Only the instructed group showed a significant decrease in total dwell time from pretest to posttest with sentences without adverbial phrases, but a significant increase in total dwell time from immediate to delayed posttest.

BOX 6.1 (cont.)

- Weak support for language instruction leading to psycholinguistic gains during input processing.

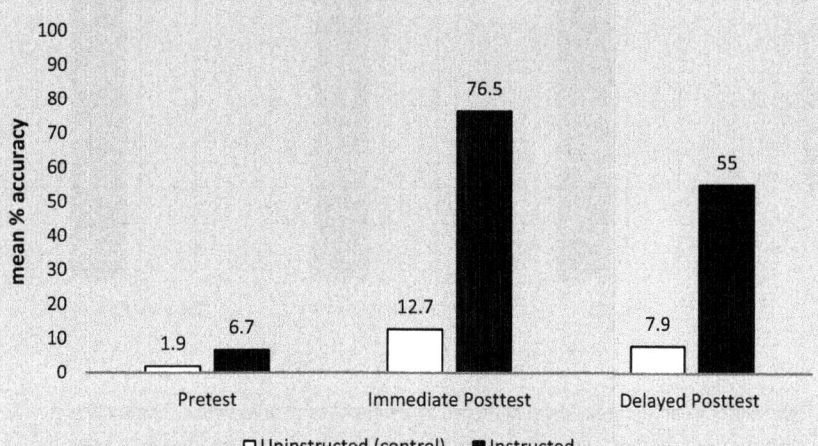

Figure 6.2 Mean accuracy on subjunctive in temporal sentences with *cuando* with adverbs in the cloze (production) task (based on data from Fernández Cuenca, 2019)

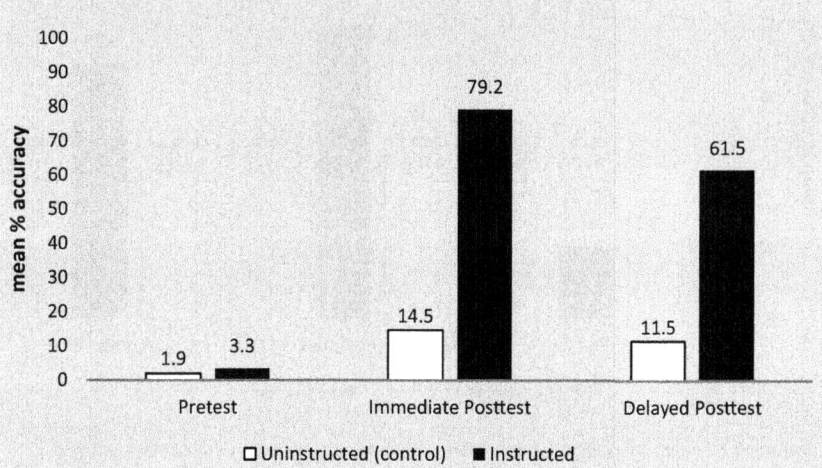

Figure 6.3 Mean accuracy on subjunctive in temporal sentences with *cuando* without adverbs in the cloze (production) task (based on data from Fernández Cuenca, 2019)

BOX 6.1 (cont.)

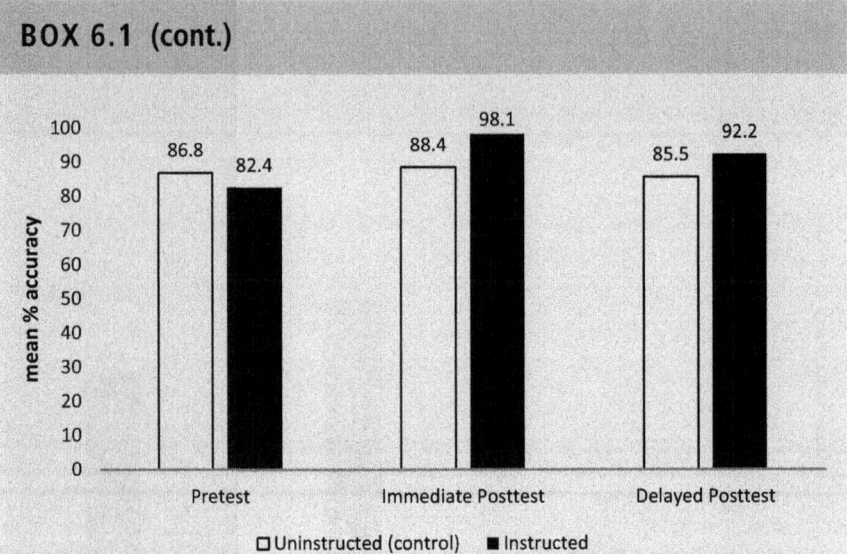

Figure 6.4 Mean accuracy on subjunctive in temporal sentences with *cuando* with adverbs in the event-selection (comprehension) task (based on data from Fernández Cuenca, 2019)

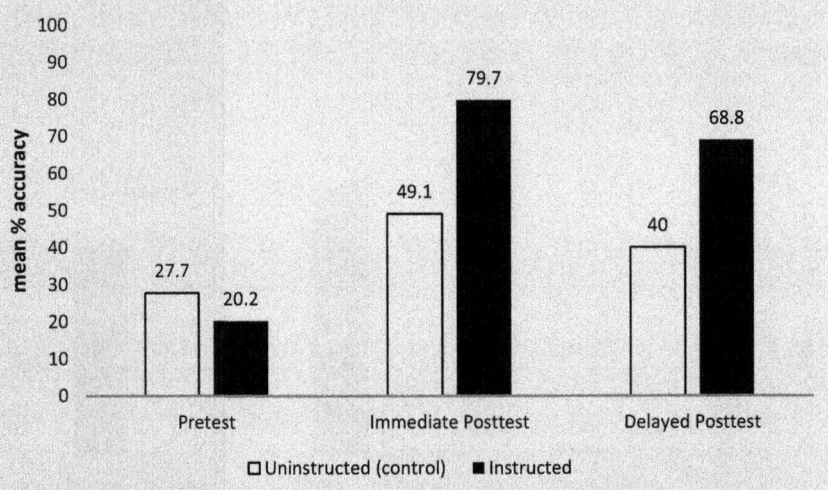

Figure 6.5 Mean accuracy on subjunctive in temporal sentences with *cuando* without adverbs in the event-selection (comprehension) task (based on data from Fernández Cuenca, 2019)

instruction, consistent with previous research. Finally, the results from this study found partial support for the claim that instruction that considers the psycholinguistic processes guiding L2 learners' input processing can help L2 learners become more sensitive to grammaticality manipulations of the target form as L2 learners read for comprehension. Overall, the results provided partial support for this claim, as a grammaticality effect in the direction expected (higher reading time for ungrammatical than grammatical items) in the critical region(s) was only found with one of four eye-tracking measures (total dwell time). Consistent with the findings of Dudley (2020), it seems that even when after instruction L2 learners perform better on off-line measures of comprehension and GJTs, the measures of processing during reading show that the instruction has not yet altered processing routines.

6.4 Studies of the Subjunctive with Heritage Speakers of Romance Languages

We now turn to the few studies that have been conducted with heritage language speakers in the classroom, because, as we discuss next, the subjunctive is also an area of variability and incomplete acquisition in heritage language speakers.

6.4.1 Experimental Studies on Knowledge of the Subjunctive in Heritage Speakers

We saw in section 6.2.1 that the acquisition of the subjunctive in monolingual children spans many years, even when these children receive rich input (in quality and quantity) from their family and social surroundings and through literacy at school. Therefore, it is not surprising that the full spectrum of uses of subjunctive would show a different development in bilingual children, whose exposure to and use of the language is less than in monolingual acquisition. In the United States, bilingual children of Spanish heritage typically never fully acquire, or acquire but later lose, subjunctive morphology. Merino (1983) documented significant loss and deterioration of performance with the subjunctive in Mexican children attending bilingual schools in California after progressive exposure to English. Silva-Corvalán (2014) also showed substantial loss and incomplete acquisition of subjunctive morphology in five bilingual children, two of them followed longitudinally between the ages of two and six. The use, misuse, and underuse of the subjunctive in young adult heritage speakers is well attested.

Heritage speakers of Spanish have been shown to differ from monolingually raised native speakers in (a) their production of indicative mood forms (e.g., *habla* 'speak.IND') where subjunctive mood forms (e.g., *hable* 'speak.SUBJ') are expected, (b) their production of subjunctive mood forms where indicative mood forms are expected, or (c) their use of alternative linguistic structures in places where more fluent Spanish speakers employ subjunctive mood forms. These patterns have been studied as divergences from monolingual norms, and loss and/or incomplete acquisition of subjunctive mood has been amply documented (Giancaspro, 2019; Lipski, 1993; Lynch, 1999; Merino, 1983; Montrul, 2007, 2009; Silva-Corvalán, 1994, 2003). More recent studies have looked at intra-speaker variation and factors such as lexical frequency and morphological regularity (Perez-Cortes, 2022). There are several studies comparing knowledge of subjunctive in heritage speakers and L2 learners of Spanish (Iverson, Kempchinsky, & Rothman, 2008; Lustres, Cuza, & García-Tejada, 2020; Mikulski, 2010; Montrul & Perpiñán, 2011), showing both similar and different patterns between the two groups depending on level and language skills.

Montrul and Perpiñán (2011) compared HL and L2 learners' interpretive and productive abilities and found that the L2 group outperformed the HL group in terms of metalinguistic knowledge. The HL learners with the best performance had received previous formal instruction in Spanish, a finding confirmed by Correa (2011) as well. Montrul and Perpiñán (2011) found that L2 learners (with more previous formal instruction) at all levels were more accurate than their HL peers in distinguishing semantic interpretations with the subjunctive and were statistically more accurate on a morphology recognition task. Mikulski (2010) similarly found that HL learners who had the highest scores on the subjunctive measures were those who had either received formal Spanish instruction or had spent time abroad with a Spanish-speaking family. Because knowledge and use of the subjunctive is so variable in HL learners, it is not surprising, then, that some studies have involved classroom interventions with the subjunctive. These studies aimed to see whether and how heritage speakers can further develop their knowledge and use of subjunctive, and how they react to instruction compared to second language learners.

There are also recent studies of the subjunctive in heritage speakers of Portuguese (Flores et al., 2019; Flores et al., 2017; Silva, 2008). Flores et al. (2019) report protracted development of the subjunctive in Portuguese-speaking children aged seven to sixteen growing up in Germany and in France. Flores et al. found that, as in Spanish, heritage speakers' acquisition of the Portuguese subjunctive is delayed compared to monolinguals, even though higher convergence with the monolingual grammar is observed after twelve years of age. Silva (2008) found that heritage speakers of Brazilian Portuguese had stronger skills in subjunctive production and interpretation than L2 learners of Portuguese.

The few existing intervention studies on the subjunctive with heritage speakers have been done in Spanish, and we turn to those studies next; see also the study summaries in Table 6.2.

6.4.2 Intervention Studies on the Subjunctive with Heritage Spanish Speakers

Potowski, Jegerski, and Morgan-Short (2009) examined the effectiveness of traditional instruction and processing instruction along with feedback on the development of the Spanish past subjunctive, as demonstrated on aural interpretation and written production tasks, as well as a grammaticality judgment test following a pretest to posttest design. See details in Box 6.2.

BOX 6.2 Potowski, Jegerski, and Morgan Short (2009)

Paper Title: The effects of instruction on linguistic development in Spanish heritage language speakers

Topic: The Spanish imperfect subjunctive and indicative in relative clauses with indefinite referents

(52)   Mis padres me buscaban juguetes que ***fueran*** educacionales.
       my parents me look for toys that were.SUBJ educational
       'My parents looked for toys for me that were educational.'

(53)   En esa tienda no había un teléfono que ***costara*** menos de $100.
       in that store no have a telephone that cost.SUBJ less than $100
       'In that store, there wasn't a phone that cost less than $100.'

Research Questions:

1. Does grammatical instruction bring about improvement in performance on sentence-level interpretation, production and GJTs containing obligatory past imperfect subjunctive for heritage Spanish speakers and second language learners?
2. Does improvement differ between heritage speakers and L2 learners and by tasks and by different types of instruction (PI vs. traditional instruction, TI)?

BOX 6.2 (cont.)

Participants:
127 instructed heritage speakers of Spanish recruited from a heritage language program (13 intact classes); 22 English-speaking second language learners of Spanish

Groups:

- HL processing instruction (PI) group
- HL traditional instruction (TI) group
- HL no-instruction group
- L2 PI group
- L2 TI group

Study Timeline:

- Day 1: pretest
- Two-day intervention
- Day 4: posttest

Pre/Posttests:

- Interpretation task: Participants read aloud a clause with imperfect subjunctive or indicative and needed to select the main clause.
- Production task: Participants completed main clauses in writing with a subjunctive or indicative subordinate clause.
- Grammaticality judgment task: Participants judged written grammatical and ungrammatical sentences with subjunctive or indicative in relative clauses.

The Intervention:

- Lab-based lessons with explicit explanations about the subjunctive with relative clauses and nine practice activities for the PI and TI groups.
- The PI activities involved structured input, were presented in written and auditory modalities, were communicative in nature, and required affective responses. Feedback about correct answers was provided.
- The TI output activities were oral (2) and written (7) and ranged from mechanical to communicative. Feedback about correct answers was provided.

BOX 6.2 (cont.)

Results:

Both L2 learners and HL learners improved significantly on the interpretation and production measures after the instructional treatments (PI and TI) compared to the non-instructed HL group.

The L2 learners, but not the heritage speakers, showed significant improvement in the GJT as well.

In both treatment conditions (PI and TI), the L2 learners made substantially more gains than the HL learners.

Type of instruction did not make a difference.

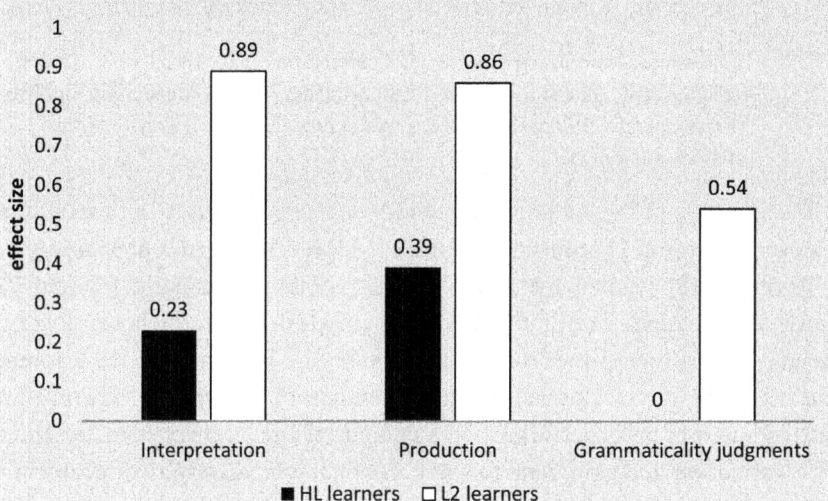

Figure 6.6 Improvement over time by measure and by group (effect size) (based on data from Potowski, Jegerski, & Morgan-Short, 2009)

Their results showed that both HL and L2 learners significantly improved under both types of instruction for interpretation and production tasks; however, only the L2 learners demonstrated improvement on the GJT. Potowski et al. also reported stronger net gains for the L2 learners on both tasks, as revealed by the effect size in the results (see Figure 6.6 in Box 6.2). Both Montrul and Bowles (2010) (discussed in Chapter 8) and Potowski, Jegerski, and Morgan-Short (2009) conclude that HL learners can benefit from form-focused instruction, because they seem to improve in accuracy, at least immediately after exposure to pedagogical interventions. Moreover, HL learners appear to respond well to explicit instruction (i.e., metalinguistic information and traditional/processing instruction), as suggested by the treatment tasks in these studies. Their results also revealed that HL learners do not enjoy the same gains as L2 learners, nor do they reach monolingual native-like performance after one intervention. Therefore, there is need for more research on how HL learners respond to pedagogical interventions in the long term, given that their prior language experience differs from L2 learners (Carreira, 2012).

Torres (2018) conducted a classroom intervention study comparing knowledge and learning of the Spanish subjunctive by L2 and HL learners in adjectival (relative) clauses as the target form, as in (54) and (55).

(54) La empresa contratará a la secretaria que sabe inglés.
      the company hire.FUT DOM the secretary that knows.IND English.
      'The company will hire the secretary who knows English.' [Her name is Rosa].

(55) La empresa contratará a la secretaria que sepa inglés.
      the company hire.FUT DOM the secretary that knows.SUBJ English
      'The company will hire the secretary who knows English.' [They hold the interviews tomorrow.]

The selection of the subjunctive mood in adjectival clauses in this study is relevant because it is problematic for both L2 and HL learner populations.

Torres (2018) studied the effect of task complexity among HL and L2 learners of Spanish. The study employed a pretest/posttest/delayed posttest design. During three intervention sessions, the L2 learners, the HL learners, and a control group completed either a simple or a complex version of a written and oral tasks performed on a computer. The learners were presented with a situation and a problem to solve. For example, they were directors of a university student residence and several problems had been identified with the behavior of the students. The HL and L2 participants were randomly assigned to one of two experimental conditions (i.e., simple and complex) or a comparison (i.e., control) group. The tasks differed in their intentional reasoning demands. Intentional reasoning requires "complex reasoning about the intentional states that motivate others to perform actions" (Robinson, 2011, p. 16).

The simple task provided the participants with one photo depicting the reason for the students' intentions behind their actions. In the complex version of the task, the participants had to figure out the students' intentions by selecting one of four photos. Both task versions required the participants to produce a reason for the students' behavior, using the subjunctive or the indicative depending on the context and what they needed to convey.

Participants interacted by thinking aloud with the computer, and the activity delivered written recasts as corrective feedback.

Learning outcomes were measured using three distinct versions of oral and written assessment tasks, counterbalanced within and across participants and sessions. The control group completed only the assessment tasks whereas the experimental groups additionally engaged in their relevant treatment task.

Like previous intervention studies with HL learners (Montrul & Bowles, 2010; Potowski, Jegerski, & Morgan-Short, 2009), Torres found that HL learners can benefit from different types of instruction, even if their magnitude of improvement is not large. As in Potowski, Jegerski, & Morgan-Short (2009), the L2 group completing the complex version of the task demonstrated larger gains than their HL peers. But, contrary to Potowski et al., the HL and L2 learner groups who completed the simpler version of the task did not differ from each other. Thus, task complexity appears to have a big impact on HL learners' learning outcomes.

Differences between HL and L2 learners also emerged on an exit questionnaire. For example, responses revealed that the HL and the L2 learners approached the task differently. The HL learners were more preoccupied with figuring out the intentions and meanings of the situations they were asked to respond to. They focused more on the content component of the task than on the form of the subjunctive. By contrast, the L2 learners focused more on form or explicit rules as to when to use subjunctive or indicative. In short, the increased reasoning demands pushed the HL learners to derive meaning and solve problems in a communicative and authentic way, while the L2 learners engaged more in hypothesis testing to find out the meanings associated with the grammatical structures.

Finally, in an effort to create new pedagogies suitable for L2 and HL learners, Fernandez Parera (2021) conducted an intervention study to evaluate the efficacy of Concept-Based Instruction (Negueruela-Azarola & Lantolf, 2006), which has its origins in Vygotsky's sociocultural theory (Vygotsky, 1978). The focus of this study was also the subjunctive in adjectival or relative clauses. The measures included a pretest, instruction, class activities, homework, and a posttest conducted three weeks after the homework activities. Feedback questionnaires were given to measure the attitudes and perceptions towards the pedagogical intervention with the posttest. The overall results indicated that both groups substantially improved from pretest to posttest. HL learners improved in their interpretive abilities more than their productive abilities, while the L2 group improved more in their productive abilities than their interpretive abilities. Thus, conceptual instruction can be used in both HL and L2 classrooms.

6.5 Summary and Implications

As we have seen, the acquisition of the subjunctive mood is conditioned by lexical, syntactic, and semantic factors. Because of its complexity, it takes a long time to master in first, second, and bilingual acquisition. Learners must attend to morphological form, syntactic contexts, lexical requirements of the main verb in a complex sentence, and semantic and pragmatic implications of different main and subordinate clauses. Linguistically oriented studies show that, with time and increased proficiency, and in some cases even study-abroad experience (Isabelli, 2007; Dudley, 2020), L2 learners are eventually successful in acquiring the functional category MoodP or ForceP (depending on the analysis) and at reaching target norms.

However, classroom-oriented studies have focused on the early stages of acquisition, when L2 learners are struggling to notice and process morphological forms and before they can integrate them with syntactic and semantic knowledge. Studies of both L2 learners and HL learners demonstrate that explicit instruction with exercises is successful in guiding learners to pay attention to subjunctive forms at beginner and intermediate levels of development. Finally, studies comparing L2 and HL learners have demonstrated that the particular language-learning experience of these two groups plays out differently in how HL learners and L2 learners approach the task. The two groups also show differential improvement depending on the measures used.

Although the linguistically oriented studies and the classroom-oriented studies of the subjunctive seem to be divorced from each other, future research could strive to integrate these two strands of research. This is especially the case now that, with the advent of online methods, specific difficulties with language processing and specific pedagogical interventions to address them can be investigated more directly and fruitfully.

6.6 DISCUSSION QUESTIONS

1. Fernández (2008) conducted the intervention in a lab setting rather than in a classroom setting. Do you think this is a limitation of this study, especially since previous input processing studies on the subjunctive were conducted with actual classrooms? What are the advantages and disadvantages of conducting intervention studies with pedagogical implications in the actual classroom or in the lab? Can studies conducted in the classroom be generalized to other classrooms? How generalizable are the results of lab studies to classroom situations?

2. An unexpected result in Fernández Cuenca's (2019) study was that participants in the noninstructed group also made significant learning gains from pretest to posttest in the two interpretation tests, both with sentences that contained and did not contain an adverbial phrase. What aspects of the design of this study could be responsible for these results?
3. Both Potowski, Jegerski, and Morgan-Short (2009) and Torres (2018) found that instruction is beneficial for heritage speakers. However, heritage language learners were found to perform differently in different tasks or to pay attention to different aspects of the task compared to the L2 learners. Discuss why heritage speakers may respond differently than L2 learners to different tasks. What aspects of their experience could impact these findings? What are the implications of these findings for the classroom and the types of activities that are best for the two types of learners?

6.7 APPLICATIONS QUESTIONS

1. We have seen that most of the studies on the L2 acquisition of the Spanish, Italian, and French subjunctive, with a few exceptions, have been on L2 learners whose L1 is English. How do you think not having subjunctive instantiated in their native language contributes to the difficulty that L2 learners have with the subjunctive at beginning and intermediate stages? Explain your answer. What evidence is there that difficulty with the subjunctive is related to L1 influence? What evidence is there that difficulty with the subjunctive is not strictly related to L1 influence? What other factors may be at play? (You may want to compare the acquisition of the subjunctive in L1 and L2 acquisition).
2. How would you go about testing whether difficulty with the subjunctive is or is not related to L1 influence? What type of study would you design? Think about the L2 learners, the groups you need, the target language(s), and the structures of interest related to the subjunctive. What type of intervention would you use to help L2 learners make progress with the subjunctive (a) if L1 influenced is involved or (b) if L1 influence is not involved with the initial difficulty that learners may experience? What measure or measures will you use to assess the efficacy of the intervention?
3. Most classroom intervention studies on the subjunctive have tested low-intermediate and intermediate-level learners to help them notice, process, and acquire the subjunctive, while most of the linguistically oriented SLA studies have tested advanced and near-native speakers to

show that the acquisition of the subjunctive is possible. Given that, on the one hand, classroom-oriented studies show that L2 learners make gains in their understanding and use of the subjunctive, and on the other hand, linguistic studies show that advanced learners come to know subtleties of the subjunctive at native level, what are the implications of these collective findings for (1) the teaching of the subjunctive, and (2) expectations about the rate and extent of acquisition, especially during the first and second year of instruction?

4. Recall that even when the subjunctive form of the first and third person singular is the same in Spanish, the sentence *Espero que venga a la fiesta* cannot mean 'I hope to go to the party'; rather it means 'I hope he/she (somebody else) goes to the party': the subject of the embedded clause in the subjunctive must be another third-person referent. Most Spanish language textbooks do not mention when to use infinitives as opposed to subjunctive clauses with desire and volitional predicates, as studied by Bruhn-Garavito (1997). They also do not mention the relationship between the coreference restriction and temporal clauses of *cuando*. (See section 6.2.2, examples (44) and (45)). Think of an instruction intervention that explains the constraints on coreference with different verbs and on temporal reference in adverbial clauses with *cuando*. Include pretest and posttest measures to assess gains in knowledge. Learners at which proficiency level would you test and why? Based on what you have read about the effects of different types of instruction on different types of learners, what do you expect to find and why?

6.8 FURTHER READING

- Collentine, J. (2013). Subjunctive in second language Spanish. In K. L. Geestlin (Ed.), *The handbook of Spanish second language acquisition* (pp. 270–286). Oxford: Wiley.

    This chapter considers the role of instructional interventions in the acquisition of the Spanish subjunctive. It considers the complex inflectional and syntactic factors that regulate the acquisition and use of the subjunctive by speakers of English as a first language (L1).

- Cheng, A. C., & Diaz-Mojica, C. (2006). The effects of formal instruction and study abroad on improving proficiency: The case of the Spanish subjunctive. *Applied Language Learning, 16*(1), 17–36.

    This paper focuses on the development of the subjunctive in oral discourse competence. It presents empirical data on how formal instruction during study abroad may help learners make progress with the subjunctive.

- Silva, G. V. (2008). Heritage language learning and the Portuguese subjunctive. *Portuguese Language Journal, 3,* 1–28.

    The study reported in this article supports differentiated instruction for heritage speakers and L2 learners of Portuguese, given that both groups have difficulties with subjunctive morphology and syntax but to different degrees.

7 Argument Structure

Have you ever wondered why the sentence *I painted the house red* sounds good but *I saw the house red* does not? Or why *The plane was delayed until noon* is fine but *The plane was arrived at noon* is ungrammatical? These differences have to do with the meaning of the verbs, which determines their syntactic behavior and morphological expression. It turns out that acquiring the syntactic behavior of different verbs presents nontrivial learnability challenges both for children acquiring their native language and for second language learners, as we discuss in this chapter. An important assumption in linguistics is that the syntactic and morphological behavior of verbs, with respect to how the participants in the event are expressed, is to a large extent determined by the verb meaning (Levin, 1993). Crosslinguistically, languages vary as to how aspects of verb meaning determine syntax, and all learners must discover, based on **positive evidence**, what the constraints on meaning are. We will see that in second language acquisition, positive evidence may not be sufficient and that **negative evidence** and instructional interventions are necessary to guide learners to abandon grammatical analyses rooted in their native languages.

More specifically, in this chapter we consider the difference between **transitive** and **intransitive verbs**, different types of intransitive verbs, and the constraints on **passivization**, which only apply to transitive verbs. A common learner error is overgeneralizing the **passive voice** to intransitive verbs in English, as in **My mother was died when I was nine years old*. Another common learner error is the underuse or overgeneralization of the clitic *se* in Spanish (**Juan movió* 'Juan moved'; **Juan se lloró* 'Juan cried'). We present the available classroom intervention research studies on passives and transitive and intransitive verbs in English and in Spanish as second languages because these are the languages that have been more researched in this area. We discuss these findings' implications for learnability, type of input, the role of L1 transfer, and linguistic universals.

7.1 Terminology and Linguistic Background

Before discussing the details of linguistically oriented second language studies and classroom **intervention studies** on different types of transitive verbs and on passive sentences, we must first introduce some critical terminology related to the **argument structure** of different verb types.

7.1.1 Transitivity

Verbs are syntactically and morphologically classified by their transitivity. **Transitivity** is a property of verbs that determines how many participants take part in the event described (Hopper & Thompson, 1980). Obligatory participants are called **arguments** of the verb.

Transitive verbs such as *treat* or *kill* in (56) and (57) take two arguments, an agent and a theme, that map onto the syntactic positions of subject and direct object, respectively. The **agent** is the doer or causer of the action or event. The **theme** or **patient** is the entity undergoing or being affected by the action or event. The subject is the **external argument** (external to the **verb phrase**) and the direct object is an **internal argument** (internal to the verb phrase).

(56) [Dr. Humfrey] treated [a patient].
      agent   theme
      S   V   O

(57) [The cat] killed [a bird].
      agent   theme
      S   V   O

In Chapter 8 we will cover **ditransitive verbs**; that is, verbs that have two internal arguments (theme and **goal**) mapped to the direct and the indirect object positions, such as *give, pass, promise,* etc. We will see in Chapter 8 that these verbs have different ways of expressing the two arguments in the syntax and participate in the **dative alternation** (*I gave a birthday card to Peter/I gave Peter a birthday card*).

But this chapter deals with intransitive verbs. Intransitive verbs are verbs that have only one argument mapped to the subject **noun phrase** (NP) in the syntax: *I leave, I cry, They breathe, They fall,* etc. There are other verbs that alternate in transitivity; that is, they can appear in a transitive or in an intransitive configuration, such as the verbs *break, freeze, open*. In English, the verb form is the same in the transitive (58a) and intransitive (58b) versions. It has **zero morphology**: The two forms are related but use the same morphological form, instead of morphemes marking transitive and intransitive verbs differently, as in other languages.

(58)   a. The strong wind/the fox opened the trap door.
         b. The trap door opened.

The two ways of expressing the same event described in (58) are called the **causative/inchoative alternation** (Levin, 1993). The transitive use of the verb can be paraphrased as causing the action and a result of the event expressed by the verb. The intransitive version has a resultative or inchoative meaning. This means that the event happens almost instantaneously, and the verb denotes both the action and the resulting state of the subject, which is affected.

Many languages mark one of the two forms of the verb with special morphology. For example, in Spanish these same verbs appear with the **clitic pronoun** *se* in the intransitive form, as in (59).

(59)   a. El viento fuerte/ el zorro abrió la puerta de la trampera.
           the wind strong/ the fox opened the door of the trap
           'The strong wind/the fox opened the trap door.'
         b. La puerta de la trampera se abrió.
           the door of the trap self opened
           'The trap door opened.'

In Turkish, some verbs have causative morphology on the transitive form: With the verb *batmak* 'sink', for example, the causative suffix *-dir* or any of its allomorphs attaches to the verb root to form the causative form, as in (60b) (compare to (60a)).

(60)   a. Gemi bat-mış.
           ship sink-PAST
           'The ship sank.'
         b. Düşman gemi-yi bat-ır-mış.
           enemy ship-ACC sink-CAUS-PAST
           'The enemy sank the ship/made the ship sink.'

Turkish also has verbs that, as in Spanish, add the **anticausative marker** *-Il* (or any of its variants) to the intransitive form, such as the verb *kırmak* 'break' in (61b) (compare to (61a)). The anticausative morpheme *-Il* is also the passive marker in Turkish.

(61)   a. Hırsız pencere-yi kır-dı
           thief window-ACC break- PAST
           'The thief broke the window.'
         b. Pencere kır-ıl-dı
           window break-PASS-PAST
           'The window broke.'

It is important to bear in mind that not all transitive verbs alternate in transitivity: only those that have a causative meaning and whose intransitive form expresses a change of state. For example, the verb *sign* does not alternate: *The Robinsons signed the contract/*The contract signed.* The intransitive form of causative verbs is unaccusative, as we explain below. Not all **unaccusative verbs**, even when they indicate a change of state, participate in this transitivity alternation either (*The package arrived/*The delivery service arrived the package*). Some transitive verbs, such as *sing* or *drink* or *eat*, can be intransitive or transitive, but when they are intransitive, the object, which is related to the action of the verb (e.g., *sing a song, drink a drink*, etc.), is left unexpressed. However, these verbs denote activities and do not imply causation. That is why verb meaning determines syntactic behavior, and learners must discover what those aspects of meaning are.

7.1.2 The Passive

Human languages exhibit the syntactic operation of passivization, which is a syntactic process that applies to transitive verbs. In a sentence in the **active voice** like (62), the agent *the firefighter* is mapped to the subject position in the syntax, and the theme *the brown bear* is mapped to the direct object position.

(62) [The firefighter] caught [the brown bear].
      agent   theme
      S   V   O

7.1.2.1 The Syntax of the Passive

In the passive construction, the relationship between thematic roles and syntactic relations is reorganized, as shown in (63).

(63) [The brown bear] *was* caught (by [the firefighter]).
      theme   agent
      S   V   PP

Passivization in generative grammar is a syntactic operation that moves the theme to subject position and displaces the agent to an adjunct optional **prepositional phrase** (PP; the *by*-phrase). This is also called **A-movement**, for argument movement (see Chomsky, 1993, 1995). In English, the form of the verb changes to the auxiliary *be* + past participle. (Sometimes the auxiliary can be *get*, as in *The thief got caught by the police*.) The past participles of regular verbs take the suffix *-ed*, while irregular verbs have different forms. In many languages that have gender and number agreement, such as Spanish, the participle must agree in gender and number with the theme-subject (example (63) would be *El oso$_{[MASC\ SG]}$ marrón fue cazado$_{[MASC\ SG]}$ por el bombero*).

But things are more complicated because there are different types of passives. At the most basic level, we have **verbal passives,** like the ones exemplified in (63) and (64), and adjectival passives, as in (65). **Adjectival passives** often express a state and do not occur with the *by*-phrase; English adjectival passives are compatible with the negative prefix *un-* (65a) and/or degree words such as *very* (65b) (O'Grady, 1997). As shown in (64), such prefixes and degree words are not possible with verbal passives.

(64) [verbal passive]
 a. The book was (*un)put on the shelf.
 b. The player was (*very) hit by the ball.

(65) [adjectival passive]
 a. The island is uninhabited.
 b. The crowd was very annoyed.

Ditransitive verbs like *give* (which will be discussed in Chapter 8) can appear in what are called **indirect passives.** In these passives, the indirect object or the goal NP is promoted to the subject position instead of the theme or direct object NP. So, double object verbs like *send* in a sentence such as *Somebody sent a suspicious package to the congresswoman* can have two options for passives, depending on whether the focus is the direct object, as in (66), or the indirect object, as in (67).

(66) [direct passive (the direct object NP moves to subject position)]
 A suspicious package was sent to the congresswoman.

(67) [indirect passive (the indirect object NP moves to subject position)]
 The congresswoman was sent a suspicious package.

Indirect passives are possible in English because many dative verbs appear in the **double object construction** (a double object construction is a sentence with a dative verb and two objects; see Chapter 8). However, indirect passives are ungrammatical in Spanish (example (67) would be **La representante del congreso fue mandada un paquete sospechoso*) and in many other languages. Nevertheless, many L2-Spanish learners whose native language is English produce indirect passives or accept them in **grammaticality judgment tasks (GJTs)** due to transfer from their L1 (Montrul, 1999a).

7.1.2.2 The Passive in Spanish

Like English, Spanish has verbal and adjectival passives. The main difference is that verbal passives are expressed with the **copula** *ser* in the preterite past tense, as in (68b) (from the active sentence in (68a)), while adjectival passives take the copula *estar* in the imperfect past tense, as in (69) (Sánchez-Walker, 2019).

(68) a. Los   meseros   sirvieron   la   cena.
       the   waiters   served   the   dinner
       'The waiters served the dinner.'
     b. [verbal passive]
       La   cena   fue   servida   (por   los   meseros).
       the   dinner was.PRET   served   by   the   waiters
       'The dinner was served (by the waiters).'

(69)   [adjectival passive]
       La   cena   ya   estaba   servida.
       the   dinner already   was.IMPERF   served
       'The dinner was already served.'

Spanish also has the reflexive or morphological passive, which is expressed with the **reflexive pronoun** *se* in subject position, as in (70). This is the same clitic pronoun that appears with intransitive verbs that participate in the causative/inchoative alternation (see example (59b)).

(70)   Se   sirvió   la   cena   a   las   8:00pm.
       REFL   served.PRET   the   dinner   at   the   8:00pm
       'The dinner was served at 8:00pm.'

The Spanish verbal passive (also known as a periphrastic passive) is considerably less frequent than the morphological passive or *se*-passive, which is the preferred option for downgrading agency in Spanish. Unlike verbal passives in English, verbal passives in Spanish are quite infrequent in the input (Green, 1975) and are most often used in writing (newspapers, scientific reports, literature, etc.). Spanish-speaking children acquire the verbal passive at about age five in Spanish (Pierce, 1992) and do not use it in writing and speech productively until well into the school years, through exposure to written expository texts (Tolchinsky & Rosado, 2005).

7.1.2.3 The Passive in Japanese and Korean

There are many crosslinguistic differences in passive formation. For example, Japanese has two types of passives: the direct passive, which is equivalent to the English verbal passive and is formed with the morpheme -*rare*, as in (71), and an indirect or adversative passive, as in (72). The adversative passive does not have a translation in English, and means that the patient was adversely affected by the action of the verb (S. Izumi & Lakshmanan, 1998).

(71)   John-ga   Bill-ni/niotte   yob-(r)are-ta.
       John-NOM   Bill-by   call-pass-past
       'John was called by Bill.'

(72)　　Hanako-ga　　John-ni　　jitensha-o　　nusum-(r)are-ta.
　　　　Hanako-NOM　John-by　　bicycle-ACC　steal-PASS-PAST
　　　　Literally: 'Hanako was stolen her bicycle by John.' (= 'Hanako was adversely affected by John stealing her bicycle.')

In Korean there are different types of passives, and the passive constructions are not as productive as in English. One type of passive, the periphrastic passive, applies to almost all transitive verbs. It takes the verbal form *V-e ci-ess-ta*: *-e* on the verb is one of several complementizers and the morpheme *ci-* 'become' is the passive auxiliary (preceded by -e/a), as in (73) (Yeon, 2015).

(73)　a.　John-i　　　namu-lo　　　cip-ul　　　mantul-ess-ta.
　　　　　Jon-NOM　　wood-INST　　house-ACC　make-PAST-DEC
　　　　　'John made (built) the house with (of) wood.'
　　　b.　cip-i　　　　namu-lo　　　mantul-e　　　ci-ess-ta.
　　　　　house-NOM　wood-INST　　make-PASS　　become-PAST-DEC
　　　　　'The house was made of wood.'

However, the Korean passive tends to have an animacy restriction on the surface subject, which English does not have. For example, animate NPs are typically subjects. Therefore, the morphological passive (*cap-ta* 'catch' vs. *cap-hi-ta* 'be caught') is favored when the affected NP is higher in animacy than the subject NP. In sentences with two animate NP arguments, both the active and the passive are acceptable, as in (74).

(74)　a.　kyengchal-i　　　totwuk-ul　　　cap-ass-ta.
　　　　　policeman-NOM　thief-ACC　　　catch-PAST-DEC
　　　　　'The policeman caught the thief.'
　　　b.　totwuk-i　kyengchal-eykey　　cap-hi-ess-ta.
　　　　　thief-NOM　policeman-by　　　catch-PASS-PAST-DEC
　　　　　'The thief was caught by the policeman.'

However, in (75b) and (76b), the passive constructions are dispreferred when the agent phrases are overtly expressed because the syntactic subjects are inanimate.

(75)　a.　John-i　　　kapang-ul　　cip-ess-ta.
　　　　　John-NOM　bag-ACC　　　lift-PAST-DEC
　　　　　'John lifted (picked up) the bag.'
　　　b.　?Kapang-i　John-eykey　　cip-hi-ess-ta.
　　　　　bag-NOM　　John-by　　　lift-PASS-PAST-DEC
　　　　　'The bag was lifted (picked up) by John.'

(76)　a.　namca-ka　kong-ul　　　ccoch-nun-ta.
　　　　　man-NOM　ball-ACC　　chase-PRES-DEC
　　　　　'The man is chasing the ball.'

b. ?kong-i   namca-eykey   ccoch-ki-n-ta.
   ball-NOM   man-by   chase-PASS-PRES-DEC
   'The ball is chased by the man.'

In sum, although the passive structure exists in many languages, the types of passive constructions vary from language to language, and as we will see, this is a source of difficulty in second language learners that can be addressed with instruction.

7.1.3 Intransitive Verbs and the Unaccusative Hypothesis

Recall that it is common for L2 learners to say things like *The plane was arrived at noon*. But this sounds odd. Why? Well, because *arrive* is an intransitive verb and cannot appear in the passive structure in English. **Intransitive verbs** have only one argument, which is mapped in the syntax to the subject NP. A major discovery in linguistics is that intransitive verbs do not form a monolithic class and that there are at least two broad categories of intransitive verbs.

According to the **Unaccusative Hypothesis** (Perlmutter, 1978), intransitive verbs are broadly classified into **unergative verbs**, such as *walk* in (77a), and unaccusatives, such as *arrive* in (78a), depending on the semantic characteristics of their only argument.

(77)   a. The bride walked.   [unergative]
       b. [The bride [VP walked]]

(78)   a. The bride arrived.   [unaccusative]
       b. [e [VP arrived the bride]]
       c. [The bride$_i$ [VP arrived t$_i$]]

Intransitive verbs project their sole argument to the subject NP position in the sentence, which in English is always preverbal. Yet semantically, the argument of *walk* is an agent, while the argument of *arrive* is a theme. Here again the meaning of the verb, or of the arguments of the verb, determines their syntactic behavior. Therefore, the argument of unergative verbs like *walk* in (77b) is an agent and originates as the subject. In contrast, the argument of an unaccusative verb like *arrive* in (78b) is a theme and originates as the object of the verb and then moves to subject position to receive **nominative case,** leaving a trace behind, as in (78c).

Hence, sentences with unaccusative verbs display A-movement of the theme argument to the subject position, just like passive sentences. However, unlike in passives, the form of the unaccusative verb does not change in English: It does not become "auxiliary + past participle" as in the passive construction. The fact that the morphology of the verb does not change in English apparently confuses some learners.

7.1.3.1 Unaccusativity and the Resultative Construction

It is interesting to note that the unaccusative/unergative distinction is universal (i.e., all languages have unaccusative and unergative verbs). At the same time, languages vary as to the syntactic reflexes of unaccusativity or the specific constructions in which these verbs can appear. For example, the difference between unaccusative and unergative verbs is related to perfect auxiliary selection (*be* vs. *have*) in Italian, French, and Dutch, and the use of the partitive clitic *ne* in Italian. Unlike French, Italian, and Dutch, the two English auxiliaries (*be* and *have*) distinguish between the progressive (*I am working*) and the perfect (*I have worked*) aspectual forms but not between unaccusative and unergative verbs in the past. The form **I was arrived* is ungrammatical: Both unaccusative and unergative verbs take the auxiliary *have* in the present perfect (*I have arrived, I have run*) and no auxiliary in the simple past (*I arrived, I ran*). English does not have partitive clitics either, unlike Italian.

However, there are a several constructions in English that do appear to be sensitive to the syntactic distinction between the two classes of verbs. For example, **the resultative construction** (a **small clause** describing the effect on the object of the event denoted by the verb) has been used as a syntactic diagnostics for unaccusativity in English (Carrier & Randall, 1992). Resultatives can only be predicated of the object, so they are possible with transitive verbs as in (79), where the metal became flat as a result of the pounding. They are also possible with unaccusative verbs, whose sole argument expressed as a subject is in fact underlyingly an object, as in (80): The lake became solid as a result of the freezing. However, resultatives are impossible with unergative verbs, whose sole argument is a subject: That is, sentence (81) cannot mean that the choir director became hoarse as a result of the singing. (But unergative verbs *can* occur in resultatives when they take a fake reflexive which as a syntactic object, as in (82)).

(79)   The blacksmith pounded the metal *flat*.   [transitive]

(80)   The lake froze *solid*.   [unaccusative]

(81)   *During the choir rehearsal, the choir director sang *sore*.   [unergative]

(82)   The politician was so angry that he shouted himself *hoarse*.
        [unergative with fake reflexive]

However, the resultative construction does not work with all unaccusative verbs. Verbs of inherently directed motion (*come, arrive, go*) and statives (*be*) are incompatible with this construction. The **adjectival phrase** that follows these verbs in (83) and (84) is not interpreted as a result of the action/state described by the verb but as a depictive predicate (Levin & Rappaport Hovav, 1995).

(83)   Sam arrived *breathless.*

(84)   ?Chris stayed after school *bored.*

Example (83) can only mean that Sam was breathless when she arrived (depictive meaning), *not* that she became breathless as a result of arriving (resultative meaning). Similarly, to the extent that (84) is acceptable, it can only mean that Chris was bored while staying after school, not that he became bored as a result of staying after school.

Because verbs like *arrive, come,* and *go* already have an endpoint, they cannot take another delimiter (the resultative phrase). And since stative verbs do not have endpoints, they are also incompatible with the resultative construction (Tenny, 1987). Once again, the meaning of the verb determines its syntactic behavior, and it is this hidden meaning and its syntactic consequences that learners must figure out.

7.1.3.2 Unaccusativity, Pseudopassives and the Cognate Object Construction

Two other constructions in English that appear to be related to the Unaccusative Hypothesis are **pseudopassives**, as in (85), and the **cognate object construction**, as in (86). Pseudopassives are formed by moving an object of a preposition to subject position (Perlmutter & Postal, 1984). The examples in (85) show that unergative verbs are grammatical in the pseudopassive construction (85a) while unaccusatives are ungrammatical (85b). (The pseudopassive is not grammatical in Spanish.)

(85)   a. This hall has been lectured in by three Nobel laureates.   [unergative]
        b. *This hall was arrived at by ten first-year students.   [unaccusative]

In the cognate object constructions, unergative verbs, as in (86a), can take objects that are semantically compatible with the verb. Unaccusative verbs as in (86b), by contrast, cannot take cognate objects.

(86)   a. The child dreamed a scary dream after staying up late.   [unergative]
        b. *This time, the Heathrow Express arrived a timely arrival.   [unaccusative]

In sum, intransitive verbs are not a semantically uniform class, and as such, different verbs have different syntactic behaviors. Although the phenomenon of unaccusativity is universal, different languages carve semantic space differently and have different morphological and syntactic reflexes of this semantic distinction, which L2 learners must learn and sort out. At least syntactically, there seems to be a relationship between passives and unaccusative verbs because they both involve the operation of A-movement.

We will see that L2 learners seem to be sensitive to these underlying structures, as revealed in their **interlanguage** grammars. We turn to an account of the acquisition of these structures in English and in other languages next.

7.2 The Acquisition of Passives

Due to their complexity, diversity, and centrality in linguistic theory, passives have been the focus of many language acquisition studies (Armon-Lotem et al., 2016; Crain, Thornton, & Murasugi, 2009; Deen, 2011; Fox & Grodzinsky, 1998; O'Grady, 1997; Pierce, 1992; Pinker, Lebeaux, & Frost, 1987). English passives have been claimed not to be acquired until age five in monolingual English-speaking children. Factors that contribute to the difficulty of the verbal passive include their low frequency in the input, the complexity of syntactic movement, and the optionality of the *by*-phrase. In L1 acquisition, passives are acquired earlier with actional (*kick, touch*) than nonactional verbs (*think, see*). Borer and Wexler (1987, 1992) have argued that the difficulty stems from the biological maturation of A-chains (related to A-movement), an account supported by Pierce (1992) for the acquisition of passives in Spanish. In contrast, for Fox and Grodzinsky (1998), the acquisition difficulty is due to children's inability to assign a semantic role to the agent in the *by*-phrase with nonactional verbs.

Adjectival passives in Spanish-speaking monolingual children are acquired by four years of age (Berman & Slobin, 2016). Verbal full passives in Spanish with animate arguments of different genders (e.g., *La muñeca fue lavada por el niño* 'The doll$_{[FEM\ SG]}$ was washed$_{[FEM\ SG]}$ by the boy$_{[MASC\ SG]}$') are acquired by around three years of age. And verbal full passives with arguments of the same gender (e.g., *La muñeca fue lavada por la niña* 'The doll$_{[FEM\ SG]}$ was washed$_{[FEM\ SG]}$ by the girl$_{[FEM\ SG]}$') by five or six years of age (Pierce, 1992). Although verbal passives are acquired relatively early, full command and use of verbal passives are achieved during the late school-age years in Spanish, when children are exposed to text (Jisa et al., 2002; Pierce, 1992; Tolchinsky & Rosado, 2005). Overall, the acquisition schedule of passives in child language is determined by the formal and semantic complexity of the construction.

For the rest of this section, we focus on passives in L2 acquisition, crosslinguistically and in intervention studies.

7.2.1 Passives in Second Language Acquisition

Similarly to the L1 acquisition studies mentioned above, several SLA studies have also acknowledged the challenge involved in learning the English passive due to its structural complexity (S. Izumi & Lakshmanan, 1998; Kuiken & Vedder, 2002; Sadri Mirdamadi & De Jong, 2015). However, since the passive voice is a structure that occurs in every language, the learnability issue for L2 learners stems primarily from the fact that passives vary semantically, morphologically, and syntactically across languages. The challenge is to figure out which verbs, according to their meaning, undergo which type of passivization in the second language.

Studies on the L2 acquisition of passives in Spanish show that L2 learners have difficulty with verbal and adjectival passives because of the use of the copulas *ser* and *estar* with the two passives. They also have difficulty with the aspectual difference between the two types of passives, which also depends on the verb tense used. As illustrated in (68) above, adjectival passives take the copula *estar* in the imperfect and are stative; verbal passives are formed with the copular *ser* in the preterite and are eventive. Spanish has reflexive and impersonal passives (see (70)), and L2 learners often struggle with the distinction between these two passives as well (Bayona, 2009; Bruhn de Garavito, 2009; Bruhn de Garavito & Valenzuela, 2008; Tremblay, 2006). To our knowledge, however, most available intervention studies on the passive have been conducted on English as a second language, and to a lesser extent on Spanish.

7.2.2 Classroom Intervention Studies of the Passive

There have been relatively few intervention studies on the English passive. Some of them tested the efficacy of **input processing instruction** to guide learners into processing passive morphology, while others tested linguistic knowledge of the passive rule and its lexical semantic constraints. The studies discussed in this section are summarized in Table 7.1.

7.2.2.1 The Morphosyntax of the Passive and Input Processing Instruction: English

Many low- and intermediate-proficiency L2 learners misinterpret passive sentences like *Harry was hugged by Eunice* as active sentences meaning *Harry hugged Eunice*. That is, they don't process the verbal morphology and the reversal of arguments. Several intervention studies have tested the efficacy of input processing instruction to change the way L2 learners interpret passive sentences in English, Japanese, and Spanish (Benati, 2015; J. F. Lee, 2015, 2019; J. F. Lee & Doherty, 2019; Qin, 2008; Uludag &

Table 7.1 Summary of intervention studies on passives and unaccusative and unergative verbs

Paper	Structures/phenomena under instruction	Participants' linguistic background	Nature of the intervention	Length of intervention	Major findings
Yip (1994)	Ergative (unaccusative) verbs in English	10 university-level advanced L2-English learners of different L1 backgrounds	Consciousness raising sessions to direct learners' attention to the syntactic and morphological features of these verbs	Two 45-minute class sessions during one week	Some of the participants receiving the treatment improved significantly on certain categories.
S. Izumi & Lakshmanan (1998)	The English passive	15 Japanese-speaking university-level L2-English learners in Illinois	Formal instruction on the English passive and the impossibility of indirect passives with positive and negative evidence, and examples of breakdown in communication	One week in the classroom during two consecutive 90-minute classes	The four participants in the instructed group improved their knowledge of the passive in English and came to realize that indirect passives are not allowed in English (unlike in Japanese). The uninstructed group showed no improvement on realizing the impossibility of the indirect passive in English.
Qin (2008)	The English passive	110 EFL Chinese 13–15-year-old learners of English in China divided into PI group, DG group, and no-instruction (control group)	Instruction on the verbal morphology and word order differences between active and passive sentences	Two class periods (90 minutes total) split into two days	PI group performed better than group instructed with Dictogloss at the first posttest in comprehension and production. No differences between the groups in the delayed posttest (a month later).

Uludag & VanPatten (2012)	The English passive	60 native speakers of Turkish in a preintermediate-level professional English language class in Turkey	Instruction on the verbal morphology and word order differences between active and passive sentences to avoid First Noun Strategy	Two class periods (90 minutes total) split into two days Delayed posttest was 8 days after immediate posttest	PI and DG groups better than control. PI group performed better than the DG group on the two interpretation posttests (immediate and delayed). DG group outperformed the control group on the delayed interpretation posttest but not on the immediate posttest. The PI and DG groups performed equally well on the immediate and delayed sentence production and text reconstruction posttests.
Hirakawa (2013)	English unaccusative and unergative verbs and passives	27 university-level Japanese L2-English learners in Japan 12 native speakers of English	Explicit teaching that passive unaccusative verbs are ungrammatical in English	Four weeks during regular English class time Two 30-minute explicit teaching lessons per week	The learners in the instructional group improved on their knowledge of three ungrammatical passive structures, while the non-instructed showed some improvement with one or two ungrammatical passives but not three
Jung (2019)	The English passive	99 Korean-speaking L2-English learners	Exposure to written text with input enhancement (implicit instruction group) or grammatical explanations and exercises with consciousness raising (explicit instruction group)	Five 2-hour treatment sessions, one every three days, for three weeks	Both implicit and explicit instruction groups gained knowledge of the form, meaning and function of the passive voice in English compared to the no instruction group.

Table 7.1 (cont.)

Paper	Structures/phenomena under instruction	Participants' linguistic background	Nature of the intervention	Length of intervention	Major findings
Toth (2006)	The clitic se in Spanish with impersonal, passive, middle constructions, inchoative, and emotion verbs	80 second-semester English-speaking L2-Spanish learners	Explicit explanations with oral communicative activities (communicative output group) and with comprehension-based practice (processing instruction group)	One week of explicit teaching and practice	The two instruction groups improved on their use of the clitic se compared to the no instruction (control group). Oral communicative practice group better than input processing group.
Toth & Guijarro-Fuentes (2013)	The clitic se in Spanish with unaccusative verbs and impersonal passives	35 high-school L2-Spanish learners 31 native speakers of Spanish	Communicative, explicit instruction on the use of nonagentive se	Three 90-minute lessons during one week	The instructed group increased target-like uses of se on a written production and a timed GJT. Overgeneralization errors were observed along the unaccusative/unergative verb distinction.
Benati (2015)	Japanese passives	55 adult learners of Japanese in the UK assigned to PI, PI with reexposure, and no-instruction control groups	Explicit instruction on verb morphology and First Noun Strategy Structured-input activities	Three hours in one day Reexposure one week after immediate posttest Delayed posttest four weeks after immediate posttest	The two PI groups improved in comprehension and production compared to the control group. PI with reexposure group maintained and improved performance from immediate to delayed posttest compared to PI only group.

J. F. Lee (2015)	Spanish verbal passive (primary), object and subject pronouns (secondary)	51 intermediate-level L1-English learners of Spanish in Australia	Explicit grammatical explanation of the Spanish passive voice with *ser*, verbal morphology, and First Noun Principle Structured-input activities	One month: 2-hour intervention and first posttest took place two weeks after the pretest Second posttest two weeks after first post-test	PI group improved on the interpretation and production of passives compared to the control group. Gains were maintained from immediate posttest to delayed posttest (two weeks later).
J. F. Lee (2019)	Spanish verbal passive (primary), object and subject pronouns (secondary)	38 intermediate-level (PI group) and 21 advanced English-L1 learners (uninstructed, classroom experience group) of Spanish in Australia	Explicit grammatical explanation of the Spanish passive voice with *ser*, verbal morphology and First Noun Principle Structured-input activities	Two months: 2-hour intervention and first posttest took place two weeks after the pretest Second posttest five weeks after first posttest	Advantages for advanced group with greater classroom experience on all three structures tested at the pretest. PI group improved on passives and null subjects after instruction.
J. F. Lee & Doherty (2019)	The Spanish verbal passive (with *ser*)	22 English-speaking advanced students of Spanish 11 native Spanish speakers	Explicit information on word order, the verb *ser*, and the past participle with gender and number in Spanish Structured input activities with feedback	One 75-minute lab session Self-paced PowerPoint presentation and structured input activities with eye tracking	Pretest and posttest measured processing during reading and listening with eye tracking. Learners' processing of passive sentences improved after the treatment. At the posttest, L2 learners were no different from the native speakers.

VanPatten, 2012). All these studies conducted an intervention in which learners are informed about the change of morphology in the verb and the different order of patient and agent arguments in active and passive sentences. More specifically, the learners in the processing instruction (PI) treatment group are trained to avoid the First Noun Principle (the idea that learners assume that the first noun phrase of the sentence is the subject in a SVO sentence). Overall, results of all these studies report that PI has positive effects on leading L2 learners to modify their initial processing and misinterpretation of passive sentences compared to active sentences.

Qin (2008) tested Chinese learners of English in China on the acquisition of the English passive measured by interpretation and production tasks. The efficacy of structured input practice (common in PI) was compared to text reconstruction or **dictogloss practice** (DG) using a pretest–treatment–immediate-posttest–delayed-posttest design. Dictogloss practice involves learners listening to a text read by the teacher while writing down important words related to the text; subsequently, the students work in small groups to reconstruct the text using the target grammatical form (see also Vasiljevic, 2010). Qin's results showed that the two groups scored higher after the treatments at the posttests than at the pretest, confirming a positive effect for instruction. However, the PI group performed significantly better than the DG group on interpretation and as well as the DG group on production in the immediate posttest. The delayed posttest a month later showed no significant differences on either interpretation or production between the two groups' scores.

As a partial replication of Qin (2008), Uludag and VanPatten (2012) also investigated the effects of PI and DG on the acquisition of the English passive as measured by interpretation, sentence-level production, and text-reconstruction tasks using a pretest–treatment–immediate-posttest–delayed-posttest design. The participants were adult native speakers of Turkish enrolled in a preintermediate-level professional English language class at a Turkish university; they had not studied the passive in the curriculum. Uludag and VanPatten (2012) found that both instructed groups (PI and DG) outperformed the uninstructed control group. Among the instructed groups, the PI group performed significantly better than the DG group in interpretation on the immediate and delayed posttests. The DG group outperformed the uninstructed control group in interpretation at the delayed posttest. There were no differences between the PI and DG groups on the immediate and delayed sentence production and text reconstruction posttests. Thus, PI helps learners change how they interpret passive sentences.

7.2.2.2 The Morphosyntax of the Passive and Input Processing Instruction: Japanese and Spanish

The grammatical subject, agent, and verb are marked in Japanese passives with overt morphology. Benati (2015) examined the effects of PI on the acquisition of Japanese passive in production and comprehension. The participants were native speakers of English, enrolled in intermediate-level university Japanese L2 classes in the United Kingdom. There were a PI and an uninstructed control group. The PI group's accuracy scores improved significantly from pretest to posttest on all assessment tasks while the control group's scores did not.

A series of studies (J. F. Lee, 2015, 2019; J. F. Lee & Doherty, 2019) with learners of Spanish in Australia used a pretest-treatment-immediate-posttest-delayed-posttest design to examine the effects of PI on the acquisition of the Spanish verbal passives, again, looking at the initial misinterpretation of passives as actives. The verbal passive in Spanish uses the copula verb *ser* and the past participle bears gender and number agreement (see section 7.1.2), as measured by a sentence-level listening-based interpretation test.

J. F. Lee (2015) investigated whether PI on the Spanish verbal passive yielded transfer-of-training to two other word-order-based processing problems: **accusative-case** object pronouns in OVS order, with gender-cued null-subject pronouns. The main assessment tool was an auditory interpretation task. The results indicated that all learners benefitted from instruction and improved in their interpretation of passive sentences, compared to the control group of uninstructed learners. There was also improvement on the structures testing pronouns. The PI group's immediate and delayed posttest scores were significantly higher than the pretest scores, although the delayed posttest scores were significantly lower than the immediate posttest scores.

J. F. Lee (2019) used the same research design and materials to see how a PI group compared to an uninstructed control group of more advanced proficiency with classroom learning experience. Again, the focus of the instruction was on the form and meaning of the verbal passive with *ser*. At the pretest, the advanced group had better scores on the interpretation of passives than the lower proficiency PI group, but after the treatment, the PI group showed higher accuracy than the advanced group in the posttests. Finally, J. F. Lee and Doherty (2019) compared native and nonnative processing of active and verbal passive sentences in Spanish. The native speakers were tested once and provided a baseline for comparison. **Eye tracking** during visual sentence comprehension was used to capture changes in processing after the instructed intervention with passives. At the pretest, there were significant differences in accuracy and reaction times between the native speakers and the L2 learners, but differences between the two groups disappeared in the posttest. This study did not include a delayed posttest.

To summarize, all these intervention studies found PI to help L2 learners whose L1s are English, Turkish, and Chinese process the verbal morphology and the different word order of the passive structure in English, Spanish, and Japanese. The acquisition of passives supports the findings from PI on other linguistic targets. Recent research has begun to use online methodologies (eye tracking) to measure changes in processing in real time, after the intervention, as we saw in Chapter 6 with the Fernández Cuenca (2019) study of the subjunctive.

The rest of the studies covered in this chapter examine the relationship between syntax and lexical semantics, and the types of verbs that participate or do not participate in the passive structure.

7.2.2.3 Teaching the Passive to Japanese-Speaking Second Language Learners of English

Inspired by the studies of adverb placement conducted by L. White (1990, 1991) discussed in Chapter 4, and the role of negative evidence in second language acquisition, S. Izumi and Lakshmanan (1998) investigated the effects of formal instruction on the acquisition of the verbal passive by Japanese-speaking learners of English. As shown in (71) and (72) in section 7.2.1, a learnability problem arises because such learners may assume that the Japanese morpheme -*rare* is similar to the verb *to be* in English. The passive rule is broader in Japanese than it is in English because Japanese has indirect passives (with both transitive and intransitive verbs) that express adverse actions, as discussed earlier. As a result, Japanese-speaking learners of English may produce passives that are not allowed in English if they do not get these aspects of meaning right. Because their L1 grammar would over-generate passives with all types of verbs, instruction may be necessary to lead the L2 learners to apply the passive rule only with transitive verbs in English.

The participants in the study were Japanese university ESL learners of beginner, intermediate, and advanced proficiency. This group was split into an experimental group that received form-focused instruction on passives in English and a no-instruction comparison group. All learners completed a pretest on the English passive. Three assessments were used: a translation test from Japanese to English, a picture-cued production task, and a GJT. The GJT presented grammatical and ungrammatical passive sentences in the context of a short story.

One week after the pretest, the participants in the instructed group began to participate in the instructed intervention, which lasted one week. Learners were given explicit instruction on how to form passives and the specific types of verbs that can be passivized. They were also told that indirect passives with adversity meaning were not allowed in English: Their use caused breakdown in communication.

The first posttest was administered five days after the instruction, followed by a second posttest seven weeks later. The results of the pretest showed that the Japanese-speaking learners did not have problems with the direct passive in English but that most learners produced ungrammatical indirect passives (e.g., *Taro was cried by his girlfriend yesterday, *I was eaten final cake by friend). Therefore, data analysis in the two posttests focused on the incorrect production or acceptability of indirect passives. According to the results, the participants in the experimental group did not produce or accept indirect passives in the two posttests. By contrast, the participants in the no-instruction group showed little to no improvement. Izumi and Lakshmanan concluded that negative evidence was highly effective in making the participants realize that indirect passives are not grammatical and are even incomprehensible in English. Given the very small sample sizes (See Table 7.1), the success of this early study cannot be generalized, however.

7.2.2.4 Teaching the Passive to Korean-Speaking Second Language Learners of English

Most recently, Jung (2019) investigated the effects of implicit and explicit instruction on the L2 acquisition of the English passive by Korean learners of English. As in Japanese, the passive in Korean is also more extended, and has semantic meanings and connotations not usually expressed in English, as we explained earlier. The study employed an experimental design including a pretest, immediate posttest, and delayed posttest, with five treatment sessions between the pretest and posttest. Participants were EFL learners in Korea, randomly assigned to two experimental groups that received implicit or explicit instruction, respectively, and a control group who received no instruction. The implicit-instruction treatment consisted of exposure to typographically enhanced passive constructions to increase the perceptual saliency of the verb form. The group receiving explicit instruction performed grammar activities with consciousness raising.

Five tasks were used to measure changes in the participants' knowledge of and ability to use the passive: a GJT, a sentence-pair task, a discourse-completion task (DCT), and spoken and written production tasks. Results from quantitative and qualitative analyses of the data found that implicit instruction had a more beneficial effect than explicit instruction on the acquisition of the meaning and function of the passive in English. In contrast, the two types of instruction had almost equal benefits on the form of

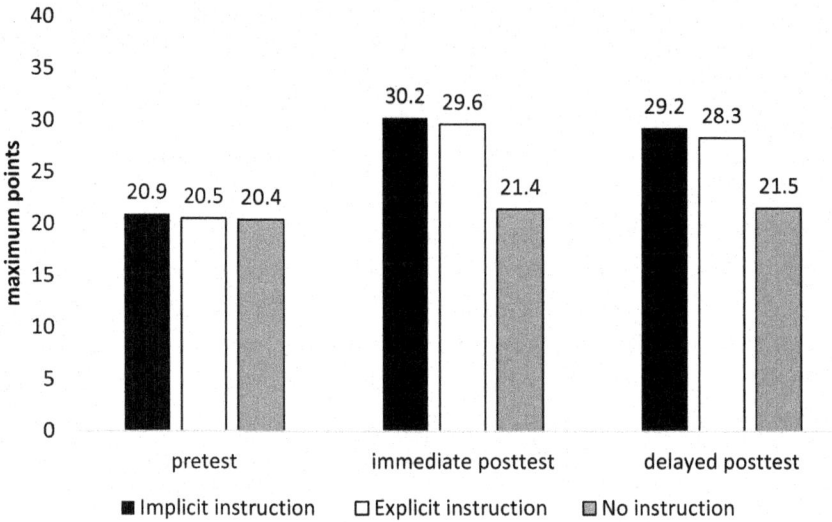

Figure 7.1 Mean accuracy judgments on the English verbal passive by instructional group (based on data from Jung, 2019)

the passive, regardless of the proficiency of the learners. For example, Figure 7.1 shows the trends of the GJT.

Overall, these findings suggest that both types of form-focused instruction are beneficial for the L2 acquisition of the passive in English. When learners are informed about the relationship between meaning and syntactic behavior, they seem to be able to grasp it.

7.3 The Acquisition of Unaccusativity

As mentioned earlier, intransitive verbs come in two varieties, unaccusative and unergative verbs. Recall that the subject of unaccusative verbs is a theme or patient, whereas the subject of unergative verbs is an agent. There is also an aspectual difference between unaccusative and unergative verbs. Unergative verbs (*walk, sing, run, pray*) denote activities or events that are dynamic but have no implicit end (*I ran for a while, I always prayed at night*). By contrast, unaccusative verbs describe a spontaneously occurring situation (Haspelmath, 1993) or internally caused eventuality (Levin & Rappaport Hovav, 1995). Aspectually, many unaccusative verbs are **telic** achievement verbs that have an endpoint; they also express instantaneous events: *fall, appear, leave, arrive*.

Some languages have overt syntactic reflexes of unaccusativity. For example, unaccusative verbs in Italian appear with the perfective auxiliary *essere* 'be' (87a) and are grammatical with the partitive clitic *-ne* (87b). In

Russian, unaccusative verbs can appear with the genitive of negation (87c), but unergative verbs cannot (87d). In Dutch unergative verbs, but not unaccusatives, appear in impersonal passives (87e). Unaccusative verbs in this Dutch construction are ungrammatical (87f).

(87) a. I turisti   sono / *hanno   partiti   durante   la   note.   [Italian]
         the tourists were/ *have   left   during   the night
         'The tourists left during the night.'
     b. (Turisti), ne   sono   partiti   molti   durante   la   note.   [Italian]
        tourists   PART were   left   many   during   the night
        'Tourists, many of them left during the night.'
     c. Ne   pryšlo   nikakix   pisem.   [Russian]
        NEG   arrived.NEUT.SG   no-GEN   letters-GEN
        'No letters arrived.'
     d. *Ne   tancevalo   nikakix   ballerin.   [Russian]
        neg   danced.NEUT.SG   no-GEN   ballerinas- GEN
        'No ballerinas danced.'
     e. Er   werd   door   de   jonges geworkt.   [Dutch]
        there become.PRES.3SG   through the boys   worked
        'The boys worked.'
     f. *Er   werd   door   de   jonges gevallent. [Dutch]
        there become.PRES.3SG   through the boys   fallen
        'The boys fell.'

Unlike Italian, Spanish does not have different perfective auxiliaries and uses just one: *haber* 'have'. So, perfective auxiliaries are not relevant in Spanish as a test of unaccusativity. Spanish doesn't have partitive clitics either. In Spanish many unaccusative verbs are marked with the clitic *se*, which indicates aspect (**telicity**): *marcharse* 'leave', *irse* 'leave', *caerse* 'fall', *derretirse* 'melt', *asustarse* 'frighten'. In general, unaccusative verbs have postverbal subjects in presentational sentences: *Llega el tren* 'The train arrives', while unergatives prefer preverbal subjects, *María camina mucho* 'Mary walks a lot' (Hertel, 2003; Lozano, 2006).

7.3.1 Unaccusatives and Overpassivization

A common developmental error observed in English as a second language is **overpassivization**: the application of the passive structural rule to intransitive verbs (Fukuda, 2017; Hwang, 1999; Ju, 2000; Montrul, 1999b; Oshita, 2001; Zobl, 1989). Recall that only transitive verbs can be passivized in English. However, the interlanguage patterns in (88) are common (Zobl, 1989: 204, examples 1–3).

(88) a. *The most memorable experience of my life was happened 15 years ago.
     b. *Most of people are fallen in love and marry with somebody.
     c. *My mother was died when I was just a baby.

This phenomenon was first discussed by Zobl (1989), who noticed inappropriate uses of *be + -en* morphology (past participles often end in *-en*, as in *brok-en*) in English with unaccusative verbs in written production. These L2 productions cannot be traced back to the learners' first language. Nor is there any evidence from English that these intransitive verbs can occur in passive constructions, since intransitives cannot be passivized. Zobl interpreted such errors as support for the Unaccusative Hypothesis (Perlmutter, 1978) because unergative verbs in passive constructions were not observed. Zobl (1989) concluded that L2 learners treated the two classes of intransitive verbs differently, overpassivizing mostly unaccusatives and only rarely unergatives.

Various accounts have been proposed for the overpassivization of unaccusative verbs. The Causativization Hypothesis states that the primary source of overpassivization is incorrect lexical causativization (Balcom, 1997; Ju, 2000; Montrul, 1999b; Yip, 1995). The proposal is that L2 learners first create a nontarget causative construction with unaccusative verbs by adding a causer to the event, as in the analysis of transitive alternating verbs (Montrul, 2000). These causative verbs are then passivized, as in (89a–b), from J.-H. Lee (2010).

(89)   a. *Someone happened the accident. (overcausativization)
           b. *The accident was happened (by someone). (passivization)

Once the causative is generated, the syntactic movement of passivization is legitimate. Recall that **alternating verbs**, like *break, melt, open*, etc. have a transitive-causative and an intransitive-inchoative version. The intransitive version of these verbs is in fact unaccusative (Levin & Rappaport Hovav, 1995). Many L2 learners may treat unaccusative verbs that do not alternate in transitivity as alternating because they fail to acquire the lexical-semantic meaning of the different types of verbs and the semantic constraints on argument structure alternations (Montrul, 2000).

Studies of the causative/inchoative alternation in Spanish, Turkish, Greek, Japanese, and English as second languages (Cabrera & Zubizarreta, 2003, 2005; Matsunaga, 2005; Montrul, 2000, 2001a, 2016b; Zyzik, 2006) showed that overgeneralization of the alternation (the transitive form) to intransitive verbs is common. Usually, such overgeneralization affects unaccusative more than unergative verbs. Therefore, the learnability problem occurs at the lexical level rather than syntactic level when learners have incomplete or fuzzy lexico-semantic representation for these verbs in the L2. Once again, it is the meaning that determines the syntactic behavior of these verbs.

Another account for overpassivization is the NP-movement Marker Hypothesis, according to which the passive morphology that marks the syntactic movement of the argument (A-movement) is overgeneralized (Hirakawa, 1995; Zobl, 1989). That is, L2 learners correctly project the single argument of an unaccusative verb in the object position and then move it to the subject position. The problem occurs when the *be* + participle is added as an indicator of the syntactic movement. This is probably because of an incorrect analogy with agentless passives (*The student was scolded*), which also involves an NP-argument movement from the object to the subject position (J.-H. Lee, 2010). However, the overpassivized sentence is different from a genuine passive because it does not have any external argument suppressed since there is no agent to suppress in the first place.

Regardless of the cause of overpassivization errors, these errors reveal that interlanguage grammars observe the Unaccusative Hypothesis. This means that passivization mainly affects unaccusative verbs. So, at some implicit level, L2 learners show sensitivity to aspects of lexical semantics.

7.3.2 The Unaccusativity Hierarchy

Yet another source of crosslinguistic variation in the syntactic expression of unaccusativity has been noticed by Sorace (2000). Sorace uncovered that many verbs (*arrive, talk*) display consistent unaccusative and unergative behavior within and across languages, whereas other verbs (*run, decay*) show variable syntactic behavior depending on aspectual elements in the sentences in which they appear. Sorace proposed a semantic hierarchy of unaccusative and unergative verbs, as in Figure 7.2, with some verbs being "more"

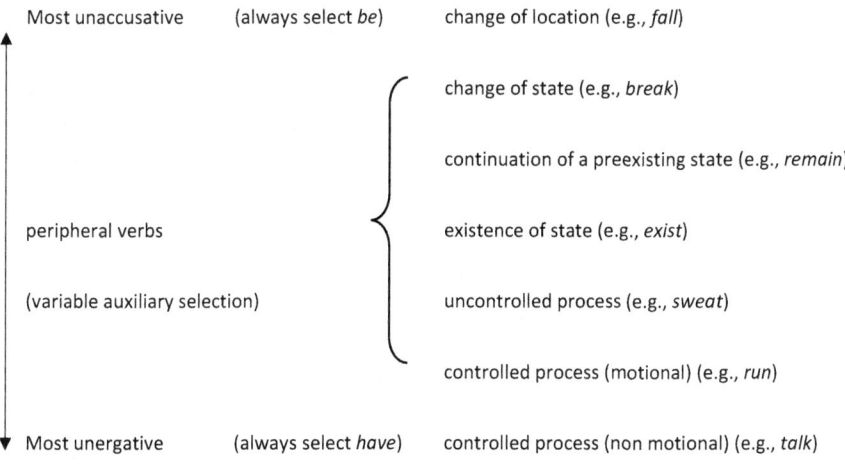

Figure 7.2 The Unaccusativity Hierarchy (based on Sorace, 2000)

unaccusative or "more" unergative than others, depending on their lexical meaning. The verbs in the extremes of the hierarchy (unaccusative *fall*, unergative *talk*), for example, have stable behavior with perfective auxiliaries (in languages that use different perfective auxiliaries) crosslinguistically. In contrast, those in the center (*exist, sweat*) are more peripheral and display unstable behavior.

Several studies on L1 acquisition and others with native speakers and L2 learners of different proficiency levels learning Italian, Spanish, and Japanese have provided empirical support for the psycholinguistic validity of the Unaccusativity Hierarchy. These studies have used language-specific constructions as diagnosis for unaccusativity (Montrul, 2004b, 2006; Sorace, 1995, 2000; Sorace & Shomura, 2001).

Montrul (2004b) found that Spanish monolinguals and L2 learners of Spanish were sensitive to the Unaccusativity Hierarchy in an online sentence-processing task. They rated verbs along the unaccusative-unergative hierarchy significantly differently from each other. Montrul (2006) found that heritage speakers of Spanish showed sensitivity to the hierarchy, again, based on their accuracy ratings on an acceptability judgment task, in English and Spanish. Regarding overpassivization errors, Ju (2000) found that learners tend to accept passivized unaccusative verbs involving external causation (i.e., which have the agent or cause available), more than those involving internal causation. However, the unaccusativity factor may not be the only factor playing a role in these errors. Another factor that has been argued by Ju (2000) to lead to overpassivization errors is the animacy of the argument. Because in Korean passives have different meanings, including adversity (similarly to Japanese, see example (72)), Korean EFL learners tend to overpassivize a sentence that carries an adversative connotation (Jung, 2019).

In sum, there is evidence that the Unaccusativity Hypothesis is psycholinguistically real, and L2 learners observe it. The types of errors learners make with these verbs and with the passive structure appear to reflect, in some way, that they do have the correct syntactic analyses for these verbs. Learnability issues remain at the level of lexical semantics and with the morphological expression of the distinction crosslinguistically (Montrul, 2001c).

7.3.3 Intervention Studies with English Unaccusatives

Now that we understand what the problem is for L2 learners when it comes to the syntactic and morphological expression of unaccusative verbs, let us see what interventions can do to lead learners to retreat from overgeneralizations. The intervention studies discussed in this section are summarized in Table 7.1.

7.3.3.1 Overpassivization and Consciousness Raising

One of the first studies to investigate the role of instruction on the acquisition of unaccusative verbs is Yip (1994). She asked, How can learners be made to notice that some structures generated by their interlanguage grammars are not in fact grammatical in the target language? The purpose of the study was to find out whether the technique of consciousness raising (Sharwood Smith, 1981) is effective in guiding learners with the acquisition of structures that may be difficult to acquire from exposure to input only. The passive unaccusative seems to be one of those structures. Yip considered that the causativization rule underlies these errors: That is, passive unaccusatives occur because some unaccusative verbs do have transitive counterparts and can be passivized (e.g., *The cup broke/The cup was broken*). Since unaccusative verbs involve A-movement of the theme to the subject position and lack an agent, they are perceived as being very similar to the passive voice by L2 learners. Despite apparent similarities, unaccusative verbs in English do not have any overt morphology, while passive verbs do, through the change of the verb form and the participle form. Thus, the lack of overt morphology may be a contributing factor for these errors in English. The learners need to know the difference between the passive and unaccusative verbs.

Yip (1994) recruited advanced L2 learners of English from different language backgrounds. They were administered a GJT that included grammatical passive sentences with transitive verbs and ungrammatical passive sentences with unaccusative verbs. The participants were asked to make corrections to those sentences that they judged ungrammatical. Immediately after taking the pretest, a 45–60-minute consciousness raising session was held, where learners were told about the meanings of verbs and their syntactic possibilities. Two weeks after the session, the learners completed the same GJT again.

The results indicated that most learners did not show any changes from pretest to posttest, whereas some showed significant decrease of acceptance of ungrammatical sentences from pretest to posttest. The participants came from two different classes, and the few showing improvement over time were in the same class. A difference between the two classes was that in one of the classes there was no discussion of the correct answers of the pretest in class, whereas in the other class there was an in-class review of the answers to the GJT after the pretest. The participants who showed improvement were in the class that went over the answers to the GJT after the pretest and before the consciousness-raising session. Yip concluded that focus on form through consciousness raising is effective at addressing overpassivization errors with unaccusative verbs in English. However, the study included a very small group of participants, among other methodological shortcomings, and because of this it is hard to generalize the results.

7.3.3.2 Teaching Learners about Different Types of Intransitives

Given previous studies on the acquisition of unaccusativity and their implications for the classroom, Hirakawa (2013) considered that perhaps students should be taught about transitive, unergative, and unaccusative verbs, rather than the typical instruction on just transitive and intransitive verbs. In this way, learners could be informed about the semantic difference between different types of intransitive verbs.

Three groups of participants were recruited for the study (see Box 7.1). The Japanese-speaking learners of English were administered a GJT twice (as pretest and posttest), five weeks apart. The instruction group received five weeks of instruction on the passive in English, including information and practice on the fact that unaccusative verbs are ungrammatical in the passive in English. The written, untimed GJT included transitive, alternating, and nonalternating unaccusative and unergative verbs on different points of the Unaccusativity Hierarchy (Sorace, 2000).

The results showed that all learners knew the passive construction with transitive verbs, but rejection of ungrammatical passive unaccusatives in the pretest was not as strong as it was for the native English speakers who also completed the pretest. There were no statistical differences between the instructed and noninstructed groups at the pretest. At the posttest, the learners in the instructed group rejected ungrammatical passive unaccusative sentences significantly more than the noninstructed group. Furthermore, there was evidence that the learners did not faithfully observe the Unaccusativity Hierarchy, since they were less accurate rejecting ungrammatical +telic unaccusatives than −telic unaccusatives and −control unergatives (see section 7.1.3). They were also more accepting of −telic unaccusatives than of −control unergatives, which goes against the Unaccusativity Hierarchy. In general, while the instruction was successful in informing the learners about the ungrammaticality of passive unaccusatives, it was not equally successful with all verbs and constructions included in the study.

We turn to studies of Spanish next, where we will see that similar tendencies are found.

7.3.4 Acquisition of Spanish Unaccusatives

We next consider the properties of Spanish unaccusatives, the challenges that they pose to L2 Spanish learners, and how they are influenced by instructional interventions.

BOX 7.1 Hirakawa (2013)

Publication Title: Alternations and argument structure in second language English: Knowledge of two types of intransitive verbs.

Research Question: Does negative evidence help learners who make "passive" unaccusative errors to expunge such incorrect structures from their interlanguage grammars?

Participants: 27 Japanese learners of English (first-year university students in Japan) and 12 native speakers of English

Groups:

- Instruction group (n = 14)
- Noninstruction group (n = 13)
- Control group of native English speakers (n = 12)

Study Timeline:

- Day 1: pretest
- 4 weeks of instruction on unaccusatives and passives (instructed group) vs. regular English instruction (noninstructed group)
- Posttest

Pre/Posttests: Scaled written GJT with six verb types in two tenses (past, present) and two syntactic constructions:

- intransitive S-V (Trains arrive on time, The plane arrived very late)
- ungrammatical passives *S-be+Ved (*Trains are arrived on time, *The plane was arrived very late.)

Verbs included in the test:

- Type 1: +telic unaccusative: *arrive, (dis)appear, happen/occur*
- Type 2: −telic unaccusative: *survive, stay, last*
- Type 3: −control unergative: *cough, sneeze, shine* (see uncontrolled process verbs in Figure 7.2)
- Type 4: +control unergative: *play, run, walk* (see controlled process verbs in Figure 7.2)
- Type 5: alternating verbs: *melt, increase, dry*
- Type 6: transitive verbs: *read, build, cut, see, hit/attack*

BOX 7.1 (cont.)

The Intervention: Instructional activities with transitive and intransitive verbs, and explanations that the passive voice is ungrammatical with intransitive verbs.

Results:

- Comparison of the English native speakers and the experimental groups on the pretest showed that the learners accepted grammatical sentences but failed to reject ungrammatical sentences with passive unaccusatives, unlike the English native speakers.
- The L2 learners had difficulty rejecting passive with +/−telic unaccusatives and −control unergatives
- After the instruction, the learners in the instructed group improved with +telic unaccusatives and −control unergatives, unlike the learners in the noninstructed group.
- Teaching the "ungrammaticality" of passive intransitives ("negative evidence") has some positive effects on knowledge of L2 English.

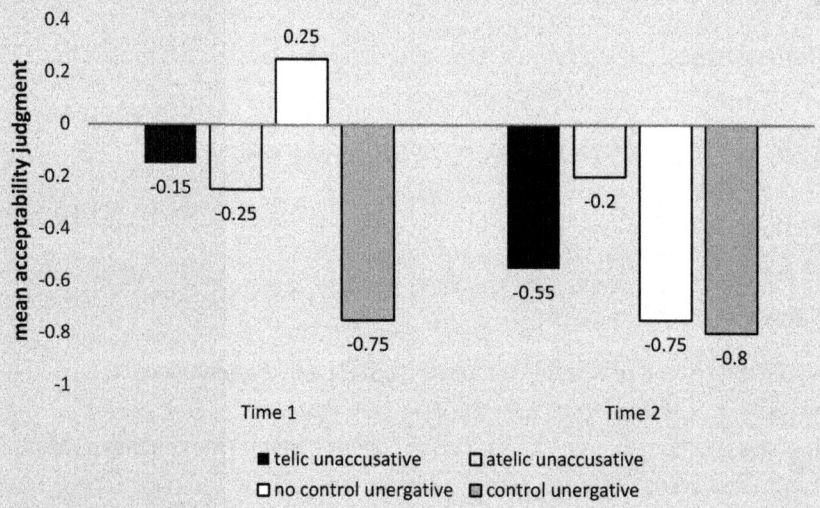

Figure 7.3 Acceptance of ungrammatical passives in the past tense with unaccusative and unergative verbs, instruction group (based on data from Hirakawa, 2013)

BOX 7.1 (cont.)

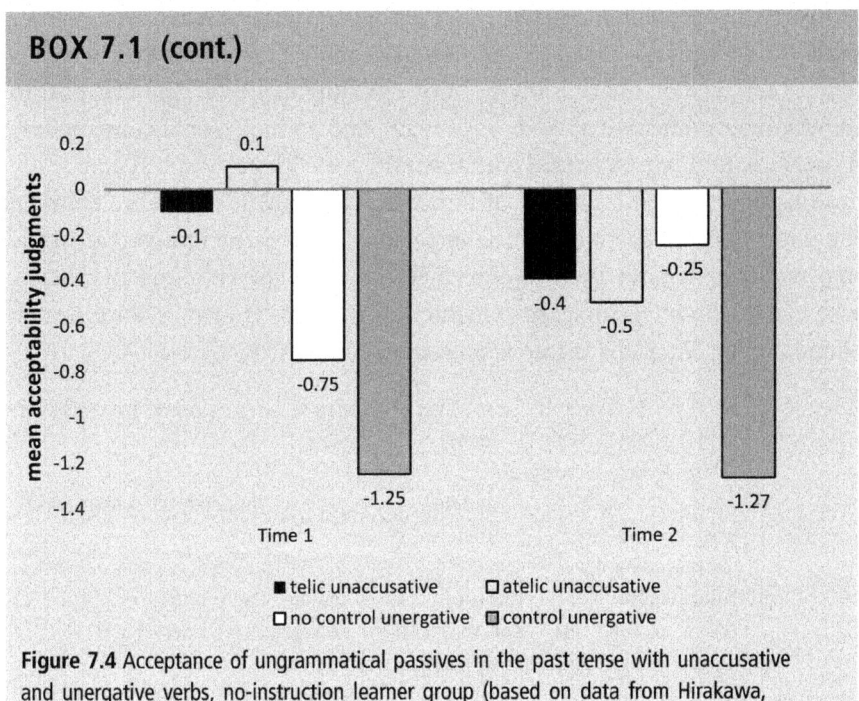

Figure 7.4 Acceptance of ungrammatical passives in the past tense with unaccusative and unergative verbs, no-instruction learner group (based on data from Hirakawa, 2013)

7.3.4.1 Unaccusativity in Spanish

As mentioned earlier, both the passive structure and unaccusativity are universal, occurring in every language. Spanish has verbal (90b) and adjectival passives (90c), and transitive (90a), unaccusative (90e) and unergative (90d) verbs:

(90)   a. Juan empacó la maleta.   [active transitive verb]
         Juan packed the suitcase
         'Juan packed the suitcase.'
    b. La maleta fue empacada (por Juan).   [verbal passive]
         the suitcase was packed (by Juan)
         'The suitcase was packed (by Juan).'
    c. La maleta está empacada.   [adjectival passive]
         the suitcase is packed
         'The suitcase is packed.'
    d. Juan viaja muy/seguido.   [unergative verb]
         Juan travels frequently/often
         'Juan travels frequently/often.'
    e. La maleta se cayó y se abrió.   [unaccusative verbs]
         the suitcase REFL fell and REFL opened
         'The suitcase fell and opened.'

However, different languages have different types of passive constructions, as we saw for Japanese and English, and the syntactic and morphological reflexes of unaccusativity vary crosslinguistically. Spanish has an impersonal or reflexive passive, as in (91a), and an impersonal construction, as in (91b). Both are expressed with the reflexive clitic *se*, which syntactically absorbs the external argument of transitive clauses. The difference between the impersonal *se* passive and the impersonal *se* construction is that in the impersonal *se* passive there is agreement between the verb and the theme, whereas in the impersonal *se* construction the verb is always third person singular even when the theme is plural.

(91)   a. Se vendieron muchos boletos. [impersonal passive]
REFL sold.3PL many tickets
'Many tickets were sold'
b. Se vende boletos. [impersonal construction]
REFL sell.3SG tickets
'Tickets are sold'
c. Alicia abrió la maleta./ La maleta se abrió.
Alicia opened the suitcase/ the suitcase REFL opened
'Alicia opened the suitcase/The suitcase opened.'
[causative/inchoative alternating verb]
d. *Alicia cayó la maleta/ ✓La maleta se cayó.
Alicia fell the suitcase/ the suitcase REFL fell
'Alicia fell the suitcase. / The suitcase fell.'
[non-alternating unaccusative verb]
e. Alicia empacó la maleta/ *La maleta se empacó.
Alicia packed the suitcase/ the suitcase REFL packed
'Alicia packed the suitcase/The suitcase packed.'
[non-alternating transitive verb]
f. Alicia (*se) viajó por toda América Latina.
Alicia (*REFL) traveled all over America Latin
'Alicia traveled all over Latin America.'
[unergative verb]

This clitic *se* also appears with the intransitive form of alternating verbs that participate in the causative/inchoative alternation (91c), and with other unaccusative verbs that do not alternate in transitivity (91d), for which *se* is like an aspectual morpheme that implies telicity. Finally, many transitive verbs do not alternate in transitivity (91e), and the clitic *se* is ungrammatical with unergative verbs (91f).

As you may imagine, the acquisition of different constructions with the clitic *se* is very confusing for L2 learners of Spanish, especially those with English L1 background. The *se* construction has therefore received attention in the L2 acquisition literature (Bruhn de Garavito, 1999; Suarez Cepeda,

2000; Tremblay, 2006). Target-like implicit knowledge of the distribution of the reflexive clitic *se* requires sensitivity to verb argument structure, to transitivity, to unaccusativity, and to aspect. For English-speaking learners, whose language does not have impersonal passives or morphology on unaccusative verbs, the multifunctionality of the clitic *se* in Spanish is a daunting puzzle. What makes matters worse is that structures with the clitic *se* can be translated in different ways, because the clitic *se* also has reflexive and reciprocal meaning, as in (92a,d), in addition to being an indirect object, as in (92b), or an aspectual marker, as in (92c,d,e); this last category includes an external argument absorber of alternating and some non-alternating unaccusative verbs, as in (92e).

(92)   a. Dora   se   peinó.   [reflexive]
          Dora   REFL   combed
          'Dora combed herself.'
       b. Dora   se   lo   dió.   [indirect object]
          Dora   him   it   gave
          'Dora gave it to him.'
       c. Dora   se   cayó.   [aspectual marker of unaccusative verb)
          Dora   REFL   fell
          'Dora fell.'
       d. Los   niños   se   secaron.   [reflexive, reciprocal, aspectual]
          the   children   REFL   dried
          'The children dried themselves/each other.'
       e. Los   niños   se   asustaron.   [alternating unaccusative, aspectual]
          the   children   REFL   frightened
          'The children got frightened.'

7.3.4.2   Intervention Studies with the Spanish *se*

Most studies examining the acquisition of clitic *se* appearing with passive, middle voice, and impersonal constructions in the classroom aim to contribute to pedagogical debates as to what type of instruction brings about more development in L2 learners. The studies also examine the type of linguistic knowledge (implicit vs. explicit) that L2 learners develop as a result. Like the L2 English studies discussed in section 7.3.3, the L2 Spanish studies also reveal that underlying learner errors is the L2 learners' linguistic knowledge of the unaccusative/unergative distinction. The intervention studies discussed below are summarized in Table 7.1.

For example, Toth (2006) compared the relative efficacy of input processing instruction (VanPatten, 1996) and meaning-oriented output-based instruction following a communicative methodology. A total of fifty-five English-speaking L2 learners of Spanish in second-semester classes were divided into two experimental treatment groups: One received input processing instruction and the other performed oral production activities following the natural approach method (Terrell et al., 1994). The study also included a group of uninstructed learners as a control group.

All groups took a pretest, and the following day the instructional groups were introduced to and practiced impersonal *se* (Day 2), passive *se* (Day 3), middle voice *se* (Day 4), middle voice *se* with indirect object clitics (Day 5), and *se* with verbs of emotion (Day 6). On Day 7 they had a review session and took the immediate posttest. The delayed posttest was administered twenty-four days after the instruction ended. Even though the experimental groups performed comprehension and oral production activities, the assessment instruments for pre- and posttests were a GJT and a written sentence-level picture-description task.

The results showed that the instructed groups made linguistic gains on accepting and using the clitic *se* with the target verbs, compared to the control group. The three groups produced 0 percent *se* clitics at the pretest, but their use of *se* with **inchoative verbs** jumped to 40 percent and 60 percent in the two experimental groups at the immediate posttest. However, the results revealed no advantage for input processing instruction compared to communicative output instruction. In fact, the group practicing *se* constructions in oral communicative tasks performed better in the GJT than the input-processing group. At the pretest, the L2 learners largely rejected inchoative verbs with the clitic *se*, but after the instruction their acceptance of these grammatical sentences increased significantly for both groups, and some of the gains were maintained at the delayed posttest. The control groups rejected the verbal forms with the clitic *se* in all three testing sessions (preferring zero-derived forms as in English instead).

A frequent error that English speaking learners of Spanish make is to produce intransitive alternating verbs without *se* (**La puerta abrió* 'the door opened'), because in English the causative/inchoative alternation is zero-derived, or has no overt morphology (Cabrera & Zubizarreta, 2003, 2005; Gómez Soler, 2015; Montrul, 1999b, 2000, 2001c; Toth, 2006; Zyzik, 2006).

Toth and Guijarro-Fuentes (2013) conducted another classroom-based study to investigate whether instruction to help learners of Spanish figure out the different meanings and uses of *se* can counteract L1 transfer and generalize beyond the exposure received in the classroom (see details in Box 7.2). The instruction intervention included 270 minutes of exposure to the passive *se*, the impersonal *se*, and the spontaneous or inchoative meanings of *se* with explicit information about each structure and equivalent English translations. The learners practiced recognizing when to use or not to use *se* with nonalternating transitive, nonalternating unaccusatives, unergatives, and alternating verbs. Toth and Guijarro-Fuentes (2013) found that

BOX 7.2 Toth and Guijarro-Fuentes (2013)

Publication Title: The impact of instruction on second-language implicit knowledge: Evidence against encapsulation

Research Questions:

1. Does communicative language teaching contribute to raising awareness, and does it facilitate implicit knowledge of the Spanish clitic *se* with intransitive verbs?
2. Do explicit information and guided interaction contribute to shape this type of UG-based knowledge?

Participants: 43 high-school students at beginner and lower-intermediate (third-semester) level of L2 Spanish and 31 adult native speakers of Spanish from different Spanish-speaking countries

Groups:

- Instructed group (n = 19)
- Control group (n = 24)

Study Timeline:

- Day 1: pretest
- Days 2, 4, and 6: Explicit instruction on *se* with unaccusative and unergative verbs every other day for 90 minutes (instructed group) vs. regular Spanish instruction (noninstructed group)
- Day 7: immediate posttest
- Week 6: delayed posttest

Pre/Posttests:

- Written sentence-level picture-description task
- Timed picture-based grammaticality judgment task

The Intervention:

- Materials for instructed intervention included culturally authentic texts that present impersonal *se* (text 1), passive *se* (text 2), and inchoative *se* (text 3). Lessons included communicative tasks, a grammar explanation, teacher-led oral practice, and information-exchange activities in groups.

Results: Instruction increased target-like use of *se* with unaccusative and alternator verbs. Instruction also led to overgeneralizations of *se* to

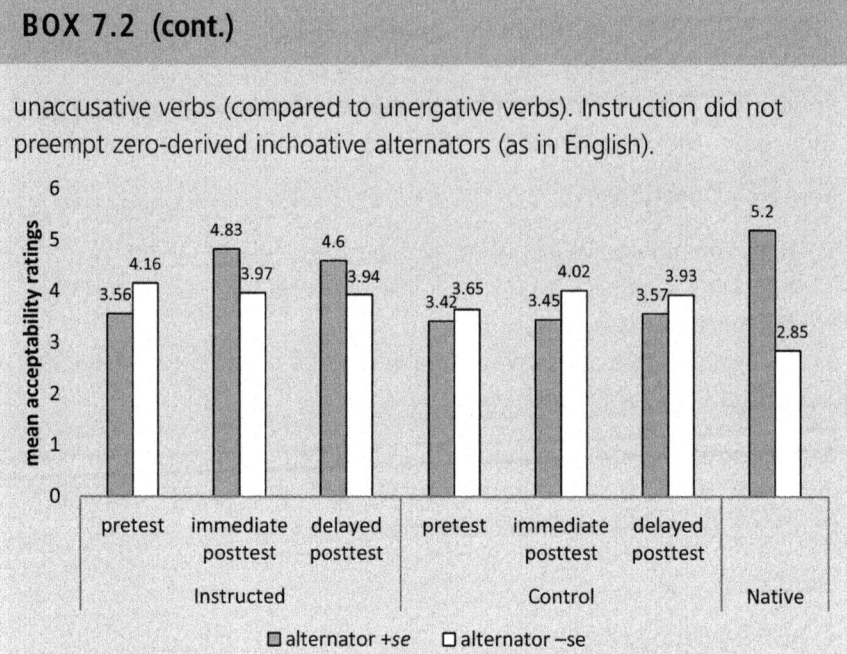

Figure 7.5 Mean acceptability ratings on alternator intransitive verbs with *se* (*se secó* 'dried out') and ungrammatical versions without *se* (**secó* 'dried out') (based on data from Toth & Guijarro Fuentes, 2013)

the instruction increased the learners' use of target-like *se* with alternating verbs. And the instructed group improved on production, even though their practice was on input comprehension activities.

At the same time, it appears that the instruction encouraged incorrect overgeneralizations of the clitic *se*, especially with unaccusative verbs. Finally, the instruction did not cause the learners to eliminate or expunge zero-derived inchoative alternating verbs as in English altogether. In fact, scores for producing and accepting this ungrammatical form remained relatively unchanged across test administrations. So, L1 influence persisted at this level despite the instruction, and it is the main force behind the patterns of result found. Toth and Guijarro-Fuentes (2013) acknowledge that the effects of instruction were indirect and incomplete because linguistic factors (knowledge of unaccusativity) contributed to overgeneralizations in the interlanguage grammars and L1 transfer could not be preempted altogether. Toth (2006) found overgeneralizations of *se* that could only be explained by implicit linguistic knowledge exceeding the information available from explicit instruction, L1 transfer, and L2 input data.

7.4 Summary and Implications

We have seen that verb meaning is related to syntactic behavior and the morphological form of verbs. The passive voice and the classification of intransitive verbs into two broad classes (the Unaccusativity Hypothesis) are universal and attested in all languages. However, languages vary as to the aspects of verb meaning that allow different types of passive constructions as well as the syntactic and morphological reflexes of unaccusativity. Discovering aspects of meaning that are critical for syntactic operations poses a complex learnability challenge. Nevertheless, it is clear that in this domain of argument structure, learners' interlanguage grammars are guided by universal syntactic operations (A-movement) and by the morphology of their L1. The few existing classroom intervention studies on this topic, discussed in this chapter, all show that focus on meaning and form with passives and unaccusatives, explicitly or implicitly, does in fact help learners eliminate incorrect generalizations generated by positive evidence and their own grammars.

7.5 DISCUSSION QUESTIONS

1. Yip (1994) used the same grammaticality judgment task, with the same items, in the pretest and the posttest. Is this methodological choice sound? Discuss how the use of the same items in the pretest and posttest may have affected the results. What other methodological improvements can be made on this study?
2. What is the Unaccusativity Hierarchy, and how does it capture variability within the unaccusative and unergative verbs classes within one language and crosslinguistically? Why do you think the results of Hirakawa (2013) show that the L2 learners did not always follow the Unaccusativity Hierarchy? What may the reasons be? Consider the distinction between implicit and explicit knowledge.
3. All the studies covered in this chapter used written grammaticality judgment tasks as assessment measures. Discuss the suitability of the GJT to investigate knowledge and improvement in passives and unaccusative verbs in a classroom environment. What are the pros and cons of using this methodology? What methodologies could be used to assess syntactic knowledge of verbs and verb classes?

7.6 APPLICATION QUESTIONS

1. Because of the syntactic similarity between unaccusative verbs and the passive voice, Hirakawa (2013) argues that teachers should understand

that it is the unaccusative verbs rather than unergative verbs that are more likely to be used incorrectly in passive constructions. Therefore, the implication is that the ungrammaticality of passive unaccusatives should be taught explicitly, alongside explanations of how the passive is formed in English with transitive verbs. Do you think that language teachers know about the Unaccusativity Hypothesis? Examine a couple of textbooks for English as a second language to see how they cover the passive voice. Do these textbooks mention that intransitive verbs cannot be passivized? Is there mention of the semantic distinction between different types of intransitive verbs? How would you propose addressing this issue in teacher training or materials design? Design a lesson in English for a textbook and include some exercises.

2. In Spanish and in English, some of the same verbs participate in the causative/inchoative alternation (*break, open, frighten,* etc.). At the same time, some unergative verbs that express manner of motion can be made transitive in English with the addition of a prepositional phrase (*The soldiers marched to the tents. / The captain marched the soldiers to the tents.*) However, these same verbs cannot be transitive in Spanish (*Los soldados marcharon hacia el campamento. / *El capitán marchó a los soldados hacia el campamento.*) Many L2 learners of Spanish incorrectly use manner of motion verbs in Spanish in transitive configurations (Montrul, 2001b), and they also use indirect passives (**Pedro fue dado un libro* 'Peter was given a book') in Spanish (Montrul, 1999a), which are also ungrammatical. Propose an intervention study to help English-speaking learners of Spanish overcome these argument-structure errors. What measures will you use as pretest and posttest? How many posttests will you include and why? How many participants and groups will you include and why? What will the intervention look like?

3. Inagaki (2002) investigated whether Japanese speakers can recognize the directional reading of English manner-of-motion verbs (*walk, swim*) with locational/directional PPs (*under, behind*), such as *John swam under the bridge,* where *under the bridge* can be either the goal of John's swimming (directional) or the location of John's swimming (locational). By contrast, the Japanese counterparts allow only a locational reading, as Japanese is more restricted than English in allowing only directed motion verbs (*go*) to appear with a phrase expressing a goal. Inagaki found that the Japanese speakers consistently failed to recognize a directional reading, even when positive evidence from English should be sufficient to trigger this knowledge. Design an intervention study to help Japanese learners of English broaden their interlanguage grammar.

What measures will you use as pretest and posttest? How many posttests will you include and why? How many participants and groups will you include and why? What will the intervention look like?

7.7 FURTHER READING

- Juffs, A. (1996a). *Learnability and the lexicon: Theories and second language acquisition research*. Amsterdam: John Benjamins.
  This is the first and most in-depth theoretical and experimental investigation of argument structure in second language acquisition. It includes an in-depth study of the locative alternation in English (*John loaded hay onto the wagon/ John loaded the wagon with hay*) by speakers of L1 Chinese, which shows that learners initially transfer L1 semantic organization to the L2 but are able to retreat from overgeneralizations and achieve native-like grammar in this area.

- Juffs, A. (1996b). Semantics-syntax correspondences in second language acquisition. *Second Language Research*, 12(2), 177–221.
  This is a shorter version of the main ideas and experiment on the locative alternation presented in Juff's book *Learnability and the lexicon*.

- Montrul, S. (2001b). Agentive verbs of manner of motion in Spanish and English as second languages. *Studies in Second Language Acquisition, 23*, 171–206.
  This paper reports on an experimental study of verbs of manner of motion (*run, march*) that behave differently syntactically in Spanish and English. It includes a bidirectional study of English and Spanish by native speakers and L2 learners of English and Spanish, respectively.

- Slabakova, R. (2016). *Second language acquisition* (chapter 9, pp. 245–270). Oxford: Oxford University Press.

- White, L. (2003). *Second language acquisition and Universal Grammar* (chapter 7, pp. 203–240). Cambridge, UK: Cambridge University Press.
  These two chapters provide well-referenced critical overviews of the L2 acquisition of lexical semantics and argument structure in English and other languages.

8 Direct and Indirect Objects

In this chapter we discuss the position and meaning of the objects of the verb. Objects correspond to the **arguments** (obligatory elements) of verbs. As discussed in Chapter 7, sentences with **transitive verbs** such as *see, touch,* and *discover* require an obligatory noun phrase that functions as a **direct object** (*see a tree, touch a surface, discover a new species*). Sentences with **ditransitive verbs**, such as *give, send,* and *tell*, require a direct object and an **indirect object** to complete their meaning (*give something to somebody, send a message to a friend, tell a story to a child*). Direct and indirect objects can be replaced by **object pronouns** (*see them, tell him, give it to her*), which are case-marked. Direct objects receive **accusative case** and indirect objects **dative case**, and this is more visible in languages that mark case overtly than it is in English.

This chapter discusses the complex grammatical characteristics of constructions with indirect objects in English and with direct and indirect objects and object pronouns in Spanish. These constructions have been widely investigated in **second language acquisition** (SLA) because they pose serious learnability issues, especially at intermediate levels of development. We will see that the **intervention** studies in the lab and in the classroom that have been carried out to date show that explicit instruction and negative evidence are effective in promoting the acquisition of these phenomena.

8.1 Terminology

The direct object is the noun phrase (NP) that is subcategorized by a transitive verb to complete its meaning. In the sentence *Mary bought two puppies, two puppies* is the direct object of the verb *buy* and can be replaced by the pronoun *them* (i.e., *Mary bought them*). The pronoun *them* has accusative case (it contrasts with *they*, which is the **nominative** form of the subject).

Unlike transitive verbs, ditransitive verbs require two NPs to complete their meaning: the direct object and the indirect object. In the sentence *Andrew sent a birthday card to his sister, a birthday card* is the direct object, and *his sister* is the recipient of the event or **goal** of the action of the event, and the indirect object. As we will see next, the indirect object in English can be introduced by the preposition *to* or *for* in a **prepositional phrase** (PP), or without a preposition in an NP.

Direct objects receive accusative case in the syntactic structure, which is usually not overtly marked in Spanish or in English, unlike in many other languages. In Spanish and in English, case is visible with subject and object pronouns, which have different forms. Accusative pronouns in English are *me, us, you, him, her, it, them*. Note that while *you* and *it* have the same form in the nominative and the accusative, the other pronouns have distinct forms in the nominative (*I, we, he, she, they*). The first- and second-person accusative pronouns in Spanish are *me* 'me', *te* 'you-singular', *nos* 'us', and *os* 'you-plural'. Third-person pronouns have gender and number: *lo* 'him/it', *la* 'her/it', *los* 'them-masculine', *las* 'them-feminine'.

Indirect objects receive **dative case** in the syntactic structure. Dative pronouns in English have the same form as accusative pronouns: *me, us, you, him, her, it, them*. Dative pronouns in Spanish first and second person have the same form as the accusative pronouns *me* 'me', *te* 'you-singular', *nos* 'us', *os* 'you-plural'. Third-person dative pronouns have number but no gender: *le* 'him/her/it', *les* 'them'. In Spanish and in English, dative case is usually expressed through a preposition (*to* in English, *a* in Spanish: *I sent a text to Maria, Envié un texto a María.*)

Subject and object pronouns in English are **strong** and phonologically independent (*She came to see me. She did not see me*). Subject pronouns in Spanish are strong, but object pronouns (accusative and dative, or direct and indirect object pronouns) are weak pronouns known as **clitics**. They are phonologically unstressed and must attach to a verb host. Spanish object pronouns occupy different positions with respect to the verb depending on verb finiteness (after nonfinite verb forms: *Ella vino a verme* 'She came to see me'; before conjugated verbs: *Ella no me vio*, literally 'She did not me see.').

Direct and indirect objects present different problems for learners in different languages. We start by discussing direct and indirect objects in English in the context of the **dative alternation**, which is related to the issues of argument structure and lexical semantics covered in Chapter 7.

8.2 The English Double Object Construction in Second Language Acquisition

Some verbs in English allow an alternation in the expression of indirect objects and have two possible syntactic configurations, as in (93) through (95).

(93) a. The witch gave a magic ring to the frog.
　　　b. The witch gave the frog a magic ring.

(94) a. Professor Travis assigned the problem to Lauren.
　　　b. Professor Travis assigned Lauren the problem.

(95) a. Nate promised the prize to Malory.
　　　b. Nate promised Malory the prize.

Indirect objects can be introduced in a PP with the preposition *to* (*to*-datives) and have the frame NP1 V NP2 *to* NP3 (93a, 94a, 95a) or as another object NP, with the frame NP1 V NP3 NP2 (93b, 94b, 95b). This latter construction is called the **double object construction** and is very productive in English. The alternation is known as the **double object alternation** or alternatively, the dative alternation.

8.2.1 Background on Double Objects: Theory and First Language Acquisition

The English double object construction has received significant attention in the syntax, semantics, and language acquisition literature because it presents a genuine learnability problem (C. L. Baker, 1979).

8.2.1.2 Constraints on the Double Object Alternation

What is significant about this alternation is that some verbs can alternate (*give, send, tell*) and allow *to*-datives or double object constructions, as in (93) through (95). Other verbs cannot alternate (*donate, transmit, guarantee*) and appear in the **to-dative construction** only, as shown in (96) and (97). Levin (1993) lists the semantic classes of verbs that can and cannot participate in this alternation.

(96) a. Nicholas donated the antique book to the school.
　　　b. *Nicholas donated the school the antique book.

(97) a. Bella issued an order to other players.
　　　b. *Bella issued other players an order.

How do learners discover, inductively, which verbs participate in the alternation (allowing both *to*-datives and double object constructions) and which ones do not (allowing only *to*-datives)? If learners make overgeneralization errors and extend the double object construction to verbs that do not admit the alternation, how do they retreat from overgeneralizations so that they apply the rule to the appropriate verbs?

Much of the theoretical discussion about the dative alternation has been about the syntactic status of the double object construction and the semantic and morphological constraints on the dative alternation. The majority of the verbs that are allowed in the double object construction (V NP NP) are verbs of change of possession broadly defined (e.g., *give, lend, sell*), and this category also includes some verbs of transmission and of communication (*show, teach, tell, write*). There is also what is called the Latinate restriction. Verbs whose morphological roots are of Anglo-Saxon origin, such as *give* (93), participate in the alternation (appearing in the *to*-dative and the double object construction) whereas verbs of Latin origin, such as *donate* (96), usually do not (there are exceptions, such as *promise*, which is of Latin origin yet allows the double object variant: *Clara promised Harold her help*). Such verbs can only appear with the *to*-dative construction (96a). Another restriction involves the nature of the goal phrase, which has to be animate in the double object variant (98b–c), while there is no animacy restriction on the *to*-dative variant (98a).

(98)   a. Ruby sent a letter to Charles/to Essex.
         b. Ruby sent Charles a letter. [animate]
         c. *Ruby sent Essex a letter. [inanimate]

8.2.1.3 Productivity of the Double Object Construction

The double object construction is very productive in English. When new verbs, such as *text* or *twitter*, enter the language, both the double object and the *to*-dative constructions become instantly available, as exemplified by *Anne texted Bill the news / Anne texted the news to Bill*. Another telling sign that the construction is very productive comes from children's naturalistic production data. English-learning children spontaneously use verbs in the double object construction that are ungrammatical in adult language (at about 5 percent of all tokens). A few naturally occurring examples from Gropen et al. (1989) and Bowerman and Croft (2008) are given in (99).

(99)   a. *Jay said me no.
         b. *I said her no.
         c. *Don't say me that. (Asking adult not to tell him to put on his socks)
         d. *So don't please ... keep me a favor. (Asking brother not to throw up on a ride)
         e. *Shall I whisper you something?
         f. *You put me just bread and butter.
         g. *Mattia demonstrated me that yesterday.

Additionally, both children and adults easily use novel verbs in double object constructions (Gropen et al., 1989). For example, Conwell and Demuth (2007) asked three-year-old children to observe an action that involved transferring an object from the child to a recipient via a conveyor belt or a catapult; the action was described as *pilk* or *gorp*. The experimenter modeled the use of the novel verb in one of the two dative constructions: *You pilked the cup to Toby* (*to*-dative) or *I pilked Petey the cup* (double object). The children were then asked to perform and describe these actions. Conwell and Demuth found that young children are more likely to generalize from double objects to *to*-datives than the other way around. They also found that the children were capable of extending both constructions to different verbs and were not limited to the usage form they were exposed to during the experiment (contra findings from Akhtar & Tomasello, 1997).

In sum, the English dative constructions show the typical pattern in the acquisition of rules in coexistence with exceptions: During L1 acquisition, children overgeneralize before learning lexically arbitrary restrictions, while discovering the productive regularity within certain subclasses (e.g., *fax, text, email*). Pinker (1989) proposed a learning model that entirely relies on universal structural constraints and attempts to explain how children retreat from overgeneralizations through indirect negative evidence. Yang (2016) offers a probabilistic learning framework that assumes a very minor role for universal principles and relies on input frequencies to guide generalizations on rules and exceptions. Regardless of what theory we assume, L1 children eventually recover from overgeneralizations and acquire native knowledge of which verbs allow the dative alternation. As we see next, however, L2 learners of English do not easily acquire the double object construction.

8.2.2 Second Language Acquisition Experimental Research on English Double Object Constructions

The English dative alternation has been a poster child of generative approaches to second language acquisition (Juffs, 1996a, 1996b; Perpiñán & Montrul, 2006; L. White, 2003b). There are several studies of the L2 acquisition by L1 speakers of Spanish (Agirre, 2015), Brazilian Portuguese (Zara, Oliveira, & Souza, 2013), French (R. Hawkins, 1987; Le Compagnon, 1984; Mazurkewich, 1984), Japanese (Bley-Vroman & Yoshinaga, 1992), Chinese (L.-H. Chang, 2004), Japanese and Chinese (Inagaki, 1997), Korean (Oh, 2010), Korean and Japanese (Whong-Barr & Schwartz, 2002), Russian (De Cuypere, De Coster, & Baten, 2014), Turkish (Marefat, 2005), and German (Jäschke & Plag, 2016; Woods, 2015). These studies, most of them experimental, have addressed the role of L1 transfer, the developmental stages L2 learners go through in acquiring the dative alternation, and how L2 learners acquire different subclasses of verbs based on finer-grained semantic and morphological constraints: e.g., goal (*send*) vs. benefactive (*feed*) verbs, and Latinate vs. Anglo-Saxon verbs.

One common SLA finding is that the prepositional *to*-dative construction (*Harriet sent a message to Clare*) is acquired before the double object construction (*Harriet sent Clare a message*) and extended to double object verbs.

This is the opposite of what is found in child L1 acquisition of English. Recall that young children are more likely to generalize from double objects to *to*-datives than the other way around (Conwell & Demuth, 2007). In L2 acquisition, higher preference for *to*-datives than for double objects has been reported at initial, intermediate, and even advanced stages of development. This may occur because in some studies the L1 of the learners has *to*-datives (indirect objects with dative case or a preposition), and only some of the world's languages have double objects (two NPs).

For example, Le Compagnon (1984), Mazurkewich (1984) and R. Hawkins (1987) examined the acquisition of the dative alternation by French-speaking learners of English, with a focus on the Latinate constraint. French is assumed not to have the double object construction, and the three studies found that the learners acquired the *to*-dative construction (*Harriet sent a message to Clare*) earlier than the double object construction (*Harriet sent Clare a message*). Syntactically, Spanish appears to have double object constructions as in English, although double objects seem to have a broader distribution in Spanish than in English. Agirre (2015) investigated the acquisition of the English dative alternation by Spanish-speaking L2-English learners and found that beginner-level learners assigned similar ratings to sentences with double objects (*Harriet sent Clare a message*) and *to*-dative (*Harriet sent a message to Clare*) verbs, while intermediate and advanced learners rated *to*-datives as more acceptable than double objects.

Since double objects and prepositional datives (*to*-datives) are available in Spanish, Agirre interpreted the results of the beginner learners as firmly supporting the Full Transfer/Full Access Hypothesis (Schwartz & Sprouse, 1996; see Chapter 1 for discussion of this model). The intermediate and advanced learners' higher acceptance of prepositional datives than of double objects suggests a stage of extension of *to*-datives to double object constructions. Higher use, acceptance or preference of the *to*-dative over the double object constructions in studies with French-speaking L2-English learners (Le Compagnon, 1984, Mazurkewich, 1984, R. Hawkins, 1987) may occur because French facilitates the acquisition of *to*-datives in English. Since Spanish is assumed to have the equivalents of double objects and *to*-datives, L1-Spanish L2-English learners do not show a pattern of preference for the *to*-dative (*Harriet sent a message to Clare*) over the double object construction (*Harriet sent Clare a message*) until later (intermediate level), when they may have accumulated more exposure to ditransitive verbs in the input.

Other studies finding a preference for, or higher use of, *to*-datives over double object constructions cannot be accounted for by L1 influence, however. L.-H. Chang (2004) found this pattern with Chinese-speaking learners,

De Cuypere, Coster, and Baten (2014) with Russian-speaking learners, and Jäschke and Plag (2016) with German-speaking advanced learners. Chinese, Russian, and German are assumed to have double object constructions similar to English. Jäschke and Plag (2016) examined whether L1-German L2-English learners would prefer the double object construction (*Harriet sent Clare a message*) over the *to*-dative construction (*Harriet sent a message to Clare*) in English and which contextual and syntactic factors regulated their preferences. At the group level, the learners were sensitive to many of the same syntactic and discourse factors as native English speakers, but there was a slight preference for *to*-datives over double object constructions.

To summarize, even though the dative alternation is very frequent and productive with English ditransitive verbs, studies show that the double object construction is quite challenging for L2 learners of diverse language backgrounds and that L2 learners take a different path in their acquisition process compared to L1-acquiring children.

Next, we consider whether interventions are successful in changing the route and accelerating the process of acquisition of the dative alternation in English.

8.2.3 Intervention Studies with English Double Object Constructions

In this section we discuss intervention studies in the classroom geared to manipulating input and feedback, in order to see whether and how L2 learners of English learn the double object construction and discover which verbs participate in the dative alternation. These are summarized in Table 8.2.

8.2.3.1 The Role of Feedback with English Double Object Constructions

The first study to investigate the dative alternation in English with instructed learners was Carroll and Swain (1993) (see Box 8.1).

This study tested the theoretical proposal that language learning is an inductive process that requires problem solving. It also requires feedback to help the learner narrow the range of possible hypotheses that can account for the data. If the input includes negative feedback, Carroll and Swain maintain that natural languages can be learnable in principle. What they intended to demonstrate was whether negative feedback, including implicit and explicit forms of feedback, can help learners learn grammar. Learning in a natural environment involves exposure to heterogeneous and unordered data. But in the language classroom, the teacher presents language rules that may not be entirely accurate with respect to the abstract grammar to be learned.

BOX 8.1 Carroll and Swain (1993)

Publication Title: Explicit and implicit negative feedback. An empirical study of learning of linguistic generalizations

Research Questions:

1. Does negative feedback help learners learn grammar?
2. If it does, are all types of negative feedback equally usable?

Participants: 100 L1-Spanish low intermediate L2 learners of English

Groups:

Group A (n = 20) Explicit Hypothesis Rejection
Group B (n = 20) Explicit Utterance Rejection
Group C (n = 20) Modeling/Implicit Negative Feedback
Group D (n = 20) Indirect Metalinguistic Feedback
Group Z (n = 20) No Treatment (Control)

Study Timeline: Participants were tested individually in two lab sessions, a week apart.

- Session 1: listening tests, background questionnaire, pretest, intervention, recall test 1 at immediate posttest
- Session 2: recall test 2 at delayed posttest

Pretest (Initial feedback session):

Screening grammaticality judgment task
8 item training session (could be repeated twice)
  Training example (on card):
    Either: Peter wrote a letter to Theresa.
    Or: Peter wrote Theresa a letter.

Verbal Instructions: We are doing a study concerned with English as a second language. I will give you a sentence and I would like you to think of a different way of saying the same thing. For example, in English you can say *Peter wrote a letter to Theresa*. Once again, *Peter wrote a letter to Theresa*. But you can also say *Peter wrote Theresa a letter*. I repeat: *Peter wrote Theresa a letter*. These two sentences, *Peter wrote a letter to Theresa* and *Peter wrote Theresa a letter*, have the same meaning; they "alternate."

BOX 8.1 (cont.)

The Intervention:

- Week 1 (Recall 1): 12 feedback items, 12 testing items, 12 feedback items, 12 testing items (48 items) (randomized)
- Week 2 (Recall 2): same 12 feedback items, 12 testing items, 12 feedback items, 12 testing items (48 items) as in Week 1

Results:

- All treatment groups performed better on experimental items than the no-treatment (control) group on the initial feedback session, recall 1, and recall 2 sessions.
- The type of feedback mattered. The performance of the explicit feedback with explicit-information group (Group A) was statistically better than the performance of the groups receiving implicit feedback and negative feedback without explicit information.
- With the guessing items as well, Group A performed significantly better than groups C, B, and D.

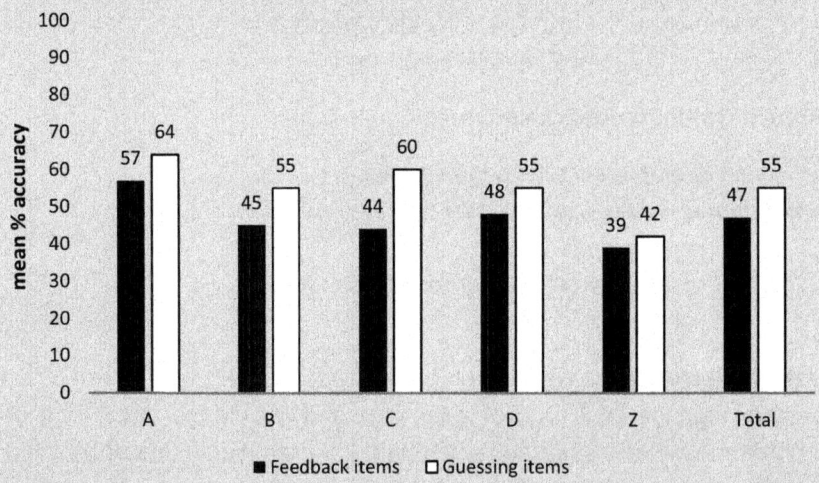

Figure 8.1 Initial feedback session: Percentage accuracy by group for feedback and guessing items (based on data from Carroll & Swain, 1993)

8.2 The English Double Object Construction 241

BOX 8.1 (cont.)

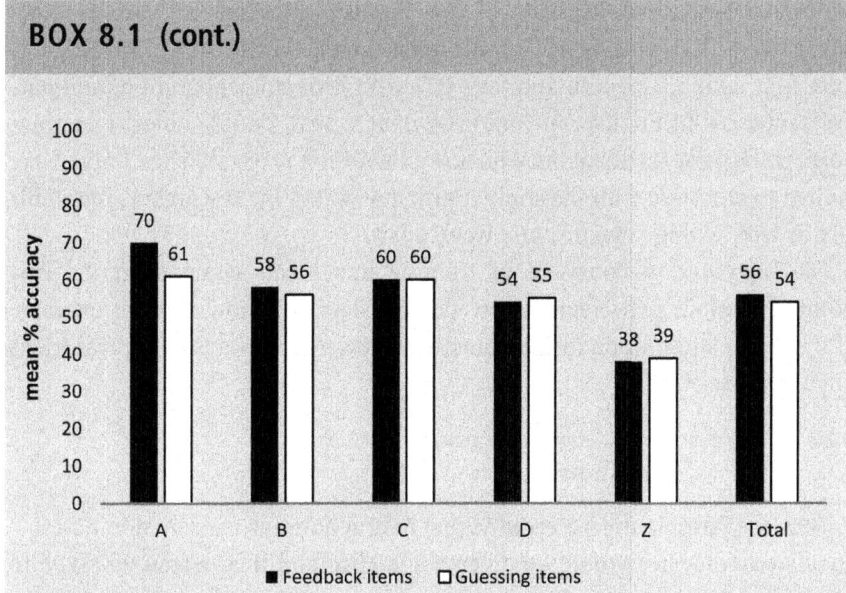

Figure 8.2 First recall session: Percentage accuracy by group for feedback and guessing items (based on data from Carroll and Swain, 1993)

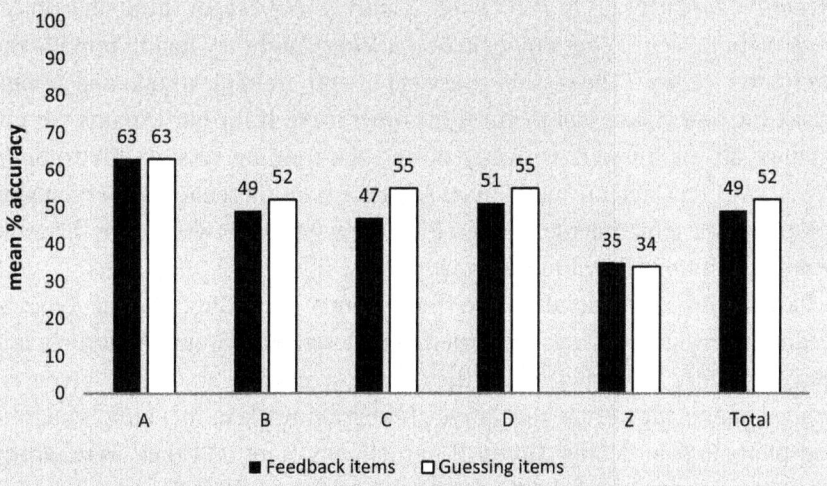

Figure 8.3 Second recall session: Percentage accuracy by group for feedback and guessing items (based on data from Carroll and Swain, 1993)

Classroom research contexts can focus on the specific learning objective: The data are ordered and presented in a more homogeneous fashion, which might lead more straightforwardly to inductive generalizations on the part of learners.

Adult L1-Spanish learners of L2 English enrolled in various low-intermediate ESL classes in Toronto participated in the study. All learners were first administered an auditory GJT with grammatical and ungrammatical sentences in English, including sentences with double object constructions. Only those participants who scored within a preestablished range were invited to continue with the study. Participants met the researchers individually in two testing sessions, one week apart.

The intervention consisted of training and recall sessions. In the first training session, participants were presented with a card with an example of the dative alternation (one ditranstive verb and two ways to express it), as in (100).

(100)   a. Peter wrote a letter to Theresa.
          b. Peter wrote Theresa a letter.

Then the participants received verbal instructions, as presented in Box 8.1. They were told they would be given a sentence and they would be asked to think of a different way of saying the same event. Referring to the card, the experimenter explained how the two sentences had the same meaning and alternated. Participants were given four more sets of alternating sentences (either the *to*-dative, as in *Peter wrote a letter to Theresa*, or the double object construction, as in *Peter wrote Theresa a letter*), and they had to provide the alternative version. The session consisted of both training stimuli and stimuli where the participant had to guess the other form. If the participants did not produce all the answers correctly during the training session, the training session was repeated one more time. After the training session(s), participants completed the experimental session (the intervention). A week later, the same items were administered to the same groups.

Participants were divided into five groups depending on the type of feedback received during the experimental session. Group A participants were explicitly corrected when they made a mistake and were given an explicit statement of how the dative alternation worked, including semantic and phonological details. Group B participants were told they were wrong when they made a mistake. Group C participants were indirectly corrected through a recast when they made a mistake. Group D participants were asked if they were sure about what they had said when they made a mistake. Group Z was the control group that received no treatment.

The null hypothesis was that there would be no significant differences among the groups. If negative evidence contributes to learning the dative alternation, then all experimental groups should perform more accurately than the control group. If the explicitness of the feedback has an effect on learning, Groups A and B (the explicit-feedback groups) would be statistically more accurate than Groups C and D (the implicit-feedback groups).

The results, displayed in Box 8.1, showed that on the initial feedback session, recall 1 (posttest 1) and recall 2 (posttest 2) sessions, all the treatment groups scored significantly higher than the control group. Group A, the group receiving explicit correction and explicit information about the linguistic rules of the dative alternation, performed significantly better than all the other groups. With the guessing items as well, Group A performed significantly better than Groups B, C and D. The results showed that all treatment groups performed better on experimental items than Group Z (the control group) and that the type of feedback mattered. The performance of the group with explicit feedback (Group A) was statistically better than the performance of the groups receiving implicit feedback and negative feedback without explicit information.

In conclusion, Carroll and Swain (1993) demonstrated that feedback contributes to L2 learning and, more specifically, that explicit information about linguistic rules is effective in changing initial incorrect inductive generalizations that L2 learners may make. The fact that the results were maintained a week later suggests that the feedback was effective. Ideally, as the authors acknowledge, more robust confirmation that actual learning took place would be to have participants use these verbs in other contexts or tasks and to test the participants long term.

8.2.3.2 Structural Priming with the English Double Object Alternation

Another intervention study focusing on the dative alternation is McDonough (2006). Instead of manipulating the type of instruction or feedback in receptive and written production tasks, McDonough investigated whether interaction through syntactic priming leads to implicit learning of the double object construction. **Syntactic or structural priming** occurs in production, when a speaker hears and tends to repeat a structure that was used by the speaker or somebody else (Bock, 1986).

The existence of syntactic priming has been demonstrated for adult native speakers and for children learning their L1 (Huttenlocher, Vasilyeva, & Shimpi, 2004). The syntactic priming literature has focused on syntactic structures that have two alternatives, such as the passive/active alternation (as discussed in Chapter 7) and the dative alternation (double object construction, as in *Peter wrote Theresa a letter*, and *to*-dative construction, as in *Peter wrote a letter to Theresa*). The idea is that if somebody says something using the passive voice (*A letter was written by Peter*), the other interlocutor is likely to choose to use the passive voice instead of the **active voice** (*Peter wrote a letter*) when describing something, even when different content words are used. Effects of syntactic priming seem to persist. That is, syntactic priming occurs even when there is time between the prime (the sentence that participants hear and repeat) and the target (the new sentence that participants produce, e.g., as a picture description). Because of these characteristics, syntactic priming has been claimed to be an important mechanism of implicit language learning (F. Chang et al., 2000).

By facilitating the repeated production of a syntactic form across lexical items, syntactic priming might help L2 learners implicitly learn abstract syntactic constructions. McDonough (2006) is the first study to extend the syntactic priming technique to the L2 acquisition of the dative alternation. Most studies of syntactic priming have been done in a lab setting using elicited production or sentence-completion tasks. McDonough went a step further by investigating whether syntactic priming plays a role in L2 development through interaction.

Two experiments took place in a lab setting and consisted of having L2 learners of English interact with a researcher who was nonnative in English acting as a **confederate** (a conversational partner following a script). The design of the experiments followed a confederate scripting technique that elicited comprehension and production priming. In the first experiment, college-age ESL learners (speakers of different L1s) were divided equally between two priming groups (comprehension vs. production) through random assignment. The materials consisted of picture cards with depicted actions and a verb printed in one corner. The experiment had three phases: the baseline phase, the priming (or intervention) phase, and the postpriming phase with double object dative verbs, nonalternating verbs, and filler verbs, as shown in Table 8.1.

When each participant met with the confederate, the two sat opposite each other. The participant and the confederate had to talk about the cards they were given as in a picture-matching activity, taking turns to describe their pictures using the verbs written on each card. There was a barrier between the participants so that they could not see each other's cards. The participants in

Table 8.1 Distribution of materials in the McDonough (2006) priming study

Phase	Confederate	Participant
Baseline	13 fillers	5 datives + 8 fillers
Priming	6 prepositional datives 6 double object datives 26 fillers	12 datives 26 fillers
Postpriming	9 fillers	5 datives + 4 fillers

the comprehension-priming group listened to the confederate's primes and then described their target pictures. In the production-priming group, participants repeated the confederate's primes before they described their own target pictures.

According to the results, the participants in the comprehension-priming and in the production-priming groups produced significantly more *to*-dative targets (*Peter sent a letter to Theresa*) after prepositional primes than following double object primes. The production of double objects (*Peter sent Theresa a letter*) was numerically higher after double object primes than after prepositional primes, although not statistically significant. Therefore, the study found evidence of syntactic priming for *to*-datives but not for double object constructions, unlike studies of adult native English speakers, which found priming with double object constructions as well (Branigan, Pickering, & Cleland, 2000).

A second experiment was carried out to see whether syntactic priming for double object constructions would occur if participants were exposed to double object primes (*Peter sent Theresa a letter*) exclusively. Another group of participants were recruited from the same courses where the participants in Experiment 1 were recruited. The methodology was exactly the same as in Experiment 1 except that the confederates were scripted with double objects (*Peter sent Theresa a letter*) only. As in Experiment 1, the results revealed that priming type (comprehension vs. production) was not significant. Furthermore, the participants produced significantly more *to*-datives (*Peter sent a letter to Theresa*) than double object targets even when the priming included only double object constructions. Therefore, there was no syntactic priming of the double object construction.

In conclusion, this study found evidence of syntactic priming of *to*-datives only. This may be because the participants had incomplete knowledge of the morphological and semantic constraints on the dative alternation. Something that is not considered or discussed by McDonough (2006) is that the double object construction does not occur in many other languages and that the L2 learners may be constrained by the syntactic representation of their L1. This is especially likely in the case of low-intermediate and intermediate proficiency learners.

In a more recent study, Kaan and Chun (2018) investigated the nature of priming and learning during the course of an intervention in English native speakers and L2 learners of English with Korean L1. This study only included two phases, the baseline and the priming, and used a written task with a sentence-completion protocol to probe the use of the double object construction and *to*-datives. According to the results, both groups showed cumulative learning (adaptation) effects for both constructions. Priming was sensitive to the frequency of the construction, such that there was more priming for the less frequent construction as established in the baseline phase: the *to*-dative (*Peter sent a letter to Clare*) for the native English speakers, and the double object construction (*Peter sent Clare a letter*) for the L2 learners. Although the L2 learners were not primed to the same level as the native speakers, Kaan and Chun's conclusion was that L2 learners and native speakers use similar processing mechanisms; differences in the extent of priming and learning arise from differences in the relative frequency of structures for the different types of speakers.

8.2.4 Summary and Implications: English Double Object Constructions

To summarize, the studies of the English dative alternation show that this particular syntactic alternation presents a genuine learnability problem in L1 and L2 acquisition. Learners must discover inductively the broad-range and narrow-range rules that constrain the alternations, such as the types of verbs (semantics), the morphological characteristics of the verbal roots (Germanic or Latinate), and characteristics of the affected object (such as animacy). The double object construction is very productive in English and is acquired before the prepositional construction by L1 children, who eventually recover from overgeneralizations without needing negative evidence. By contrast, several studies of L2 acquisition show that the *to*-dative is acquired before the double object construction and is preferred in use.

Intervention studies of implicit learning through priming show that the double object construction is not learned as well as the prepositional construction (*to*-dative). The intervention studies that have shown more success with the acquisition of the double object construction are those that provided learners with explicit feedback, correction, and information about the linguistic rules that regulate the alternation. Knowledge of grammatical or linguistic rules helps learners notice and acquire the double object construction. Table 8.2 summarizes intervention studies on the dative alternation in English.

8.3 The Expression of Objects in the Second Language Acquisition of Spanish

Although under some analyses Spanish appears to also have a dative alternation, difficulty in Spanish arises from the overt marking of some direct objects and the use and position of object pronouns. This section first reviews the properties of Spanish object expression, and then discusses SLA and intervention studies in this domain.

Table 8.2 Summary of intervention studies on double object constructions in English

Study	Structures/phenomena under instruction	Participants' linguistic background	Nature of the intervention	Length of intervention	Major findings
Carroll & Swain (1993)	Double object construction	100 L1-Spanish L2 learners of English	Participants were trained with an elicited-production task on the dative alternation with different verbs. Groups received different types of feedback: A explicit feedback, B explicit utterance rejection, C implicit negative feedback (modeling), D indirect metalinguistic feedback, Z no treatment	One single testing session with two feedback and two guessing sessions	The group that received explicit feedback with semantic or phonological explanation (A) outperformed all other groups (B, C, D, Z)
Radwan (2005)	Double object construction	42 learners of ESL (Arabic, Chinese, Korean, and other L1s)	Textual-enhancement group Rule-oriented group Content-oriented group Control group	One week Pretest (GJT) Interventions Posttest (GJT) Debriefing questionnaire	The rule-oriented group scored the highest
McDonough (2006)	Double object construction	Experiment 1: 50 ESL learners with different L1s (to-datives and double object primes); Experiment 2: 54 ESL learners with different L1s (double object construction primes)	Comprehension priming Production priming	One session Baseline Priming Postpriming	No difference between comprehension and production priming. Syntactic priming with prepositional to-datives only No priming of double object construction in Experiment 2.
Kaan & Chun (2018)	Double object construction	71 American English native speakers 75 Korean L1 learners of English	Priming with written elicited completion task	One session Baseline Priming	Evidence of cumulative priming effects for both groups. Groups primed by frequency of construction: native speakers to-datives, L2 learners double object construction.

8.3.1 Background: Object Expression in Spanish

In Spanish, direct and indirect objects can be expressed with prepositional phrases or noun phrases, or with pronouns, as in (101) and (102). Object pronouns are clitics, i.e., syntactically independent words or constituents that depend phonologically on a stressed host. In Spanish, the host is the verb. Accusative clitics (e.g., *la*) are direct objects, as in (101b), and dative clitics such as *les* in (102b) and *se* in (102c) are indirect objects. Both animate and inanimate objects are replaced by the accusative clitics *lo* and *la*, as (101b) and (102c) show.

(101) a. Roberto vio su dormitorio/ a la directora de la residencia
Roberto saw his dorm/ DOM the head of the residence
estudiantil por primera vez.
student for first time
'Roberto saw his bedroom/the head of his student residence hall for the first time.'
b. Roberto la vio.
Roberto she/it.ACC.FEM.SG saw
'Roberto saw it/her.'

(102) a. El decano mandó la carta de admisión a los nuevos estudiantes.
the dean sent the letter of admission to the new students
'The dean sent the admission letter to the new students.'
b. El decano les mandó la carta de admisión.
the dean them.DAT sent the letter of admission
'The dean sent them the admission letter.'
c. El decano se la mandó.
The dean them.DAT it.ACC.FEM.SG sent
'The dean sent it to them.'

The syntactic status of clitics has been studied a lot in Romance linguistics. Debate has centered on whether clitics are phrases in argument positions that then move to preverbal position (Kayne, 1975; Borer & Grodzinsky, 1986) or whether they are morphological (agreement) affixes heading their own functional projections (Franco, 1993; Sportiche, 1996). Crucially, since English has strong pronouns and lacks object clitics, if clitics are functional projections in Spanish, these functional projections are not instantiated in English.

8.3.1.1 Clitics and Differential Object Marking

In addition to syntax, semantics plays a role in the realization of objects and their corresponding clitics in Spanish. Examples (103a–b) show that animate and specific direct objects, both NPs and strong pronouns, are marked with the dative preposition *a*. Other direct objects (animate, nonspecific (103c); inanimate, specific (103d), and inanimate, nonspecific (103e)) receive no marking.

8.3 The Expression of Objects in Spanish

The marking of some direct objects that are more semantically or pragmatically prominent than others is called **Differential Object Marking** (DOM) (Aissen, 2003). The term used in pedagogical grammars is the **a-personal**. Many languages have DOM, but English does not, and this causes a learnability problem for L2 learners and bilinguals whose dominant language is a non-DOM language. In (103a) the object is an animate noun phrase and is preceded by *a*. In (103b) the object is a strong pronoun (*ella*). When the object is a strong pronoun, the pronoun must be doubled by a clitic, such as *la* in (103b).

(103)   a. Anna busca   a   su   maestra   favorita.
           Anna looks for   DOM   her   teacher   favourite.
           'Anna looks for her favorite teacher.'   [animate, specific]
        b. Anna <u>la</u>   busca   a   ella.
           Anna her   looks for   DOM   she
           'Anna looks for her.'   [animate, specific]
        c. Anna busca   una   maestra.
           Anna looks for   a   teacher
           'Anna looks for a teacher (any teacher).'   [animate, nonspecific]
        d. Anna busca   su   libro   azul.
           Anna looks for   her   book   blue
           'Anna looks for her blue book.'   [inanimate, specific]
        e. Anna busca   un   libro   azul.
           Anna looks for a   book   blue
           'Anna looks for a blue book.'   [inanimate, non-specific]

Indirect objects, as in (104a–b), are PPs (like *to*-dative constructions in English, as discussed earlier), which are always preceded by the dative preposition *a*, and replaced by the dative clitic *le/les*. **Clitic doubling**, the cooccurrence of the clitic and the PP, is a possible option in all Spanish dialects, as in (104a), with indirect objects.

(104)   a. El   decano   les$_i$ mandó   la   carta   de   admisión
           the dean   them.DAT   sent   the   letter   of   admission
           a   los nuevos   estudiantes$_i$
           to the   new   students
           'The dean sent the admission letter to the new students.'
        b. El   decano   les   mandó   la   carta   de   admisión.
           The dean   them.DAT   sent   the   letter   of   admisión
           'The dean sent them the admission letter.'
        c. El   decano   se   la/las   mandó.
           the dean   them.DAT   it.ACC.FEM.SG/them.ACC   sent
           'The dean sent it/them to them.'

Spanish has more flexible word order than English and objects can appear in preverbal position (105b–c). In sentences with finite verbs and object pronouns, the clitic precedes the verb, and because Spanish allows postverbal subjects, as in (105c), L2 learners whose L1 is English sometimes misinterpret object pronouns as subject pronouns. So, they think that (105c) means 'He saw Rosa', when in fact it means 'Rosa saw him'.

(105) a. Rosa vió a Juan por primera vez.
Rosa saw DOM Juan for time first
'Rosa saw Juan for the first time.'
b. Rosa lo vió.
Rosa him.ACC saw
'Rosa saw him.'
c. Lo vió Rosa.
him.ACC saw Rosa
'Rosa saw him.'

There are other topicalizations in Spanish that have obligatory clitic doubling: This is when the clitic pronoun and the direct object NP that it refers to cooccur in the same sentence, as in (106a). These are called **clitic left dislocation constructions**. They are used to emphasize the object and make it the focus in discourse.

(106) a. A Rolo$_i$ finalmente lo$_i$ conoció Laura.
DOM Rolo finally him.ACC met Laura
'Rolo, Laura finally met.'
b. *A Rolo finalmente conoció Laura.
DOM Rolo finally met Laura

8.3.1.2. Object Expression in Spanish Ditransitive Sentences

Clitic doubling is very common with **ditransitive sentences** (sentences with a direct object and an indirect object). Such sentences are also characterized by the presence of a dative clitic (*le/les*) and a case marker (*a*), as in (107a). However, the clitic doubling in some dative constructions is optional (compare (107a) to (107b)).

(107) a. El decano le$_i$ dió el galardón a Sofia$_i$.
the dean her.DAT gave the award to Sofia
'The dean gave the award to Sofia.'
b. El decano dió el galardón a Sofia.
the dean gave the award to Sofia
'The dean gave the award to Sofia.'

The indirect object of such ditransitive sentences can have different thematic roles: **recipient, possessor** (or source), **beneficiary,** and **locative**. Ditransitive sentences with recipients express transfer or transmission, as in (107), where *an award* is given to *Sofia* by *the dean*. Sentences with possessors, as in (108a), imply that the direct object (the possessum) on which the action is performed belongs to or is an integral part of the direct object

NP. In (108a), *the ear* is an integral part of *Natalia* (part of her body). Thus, *Natalia* is the possessor of *the ear*. In sentences with beneficiaries, as in (108b), the indirect object benefits from the action: *Laura* is the beneficiary of *a sandwich*. Lastly, sentences with locatives, as in (108c), have an indirect object that expresses where the action was performed: *my mother's window* was the location where *flowers* were put.

(108) a. La enfermera le$_i$ curó el oído a Natalia$_i$.
    The nurse her.DAT cured the ear to Natalia
    'The nurse treated Natalia's ear.'
 b. Kathy le$_i$ preparó un bocadillo a Laura$_i$.
    Kathy her.DAT prepared a sandwich to Laura
    'Kathy prepared a sandwich for Laura.'
 c. La Sra Diaz le$_i$ puso flores en la ventana$_i$ a mi madre$_i$.
    the Mrs Diaz her.DAT put flowers in the window to my mother
    'Mrs. Diaz put flowers in my mother's window.'

These four ditransitive constructions can also be expressed as prepositional constructions, as shown in Table 8.3. In all cases, the alternation between the ditransitive construction and the prepositional construction involves no dative clitic and a different preposition (*a, de, para, en*). In the prepositional constructions, the indirect object is not an internal argument of the verb; rather, it is an external argument (a prepositional object) (Cuervo, 2003; Fernández-Alcalde, 2013). According to some syntactic proposals (Cuervo, 2003; Demonte, 1995), the dative constructions with clitic doubling are structurally similar to the double object construction in English discussed earlier. So, in some sense, Spanish also has a dative alternation (see section 8.2.1).

Table 8.3 Alternation between ditransitive and prepositional constructions in Spanish

Thematic role	Ditransitive construction	Prepositional construction
recipient	El decano le$_i$ dió el galardón a Sofia$_i$.	El decano dió el galardón a Sofia.
possessor/source	La enfermera le$_i$ curó el oído a Natalia$_i$.	La enfermera curó el oído de Natalia.
beneficiary	Kathy le$_i$ preparó un bocadillo a Laura$_i$.	Kathy preparó un bocadillo para Laura.
locative	La Sra Diaz le$_i$ puso flores a la ventana$_i$ de mi madre.	La Sra Díaz puso flores en la ventana$_i$ de mi madre.

8.3.2 Studies on Object Expression in Spanish as a Second Language

Studies show that L2 learners of Spanish at beginning and intermediate levels omit clitics or tend to avoid them in production (Malovrh & Lee, 2014; VanPatten, 1990; Sánchez & Al-Kasey, 1999; Zyzik, 2008). Eventually, L2 learners learn clitics, and they know early how to place clitics with respect to the finiteness of the verb (Bruhn de Garavito & Montrul, 1996; Liceras, 1985; Montrul, 2010b). In Spanish, object pronouns appear before a finite verb (*lo vio* 'She/He saw him') or after an infinitive (*quiero verlo* 'I want to see it/him').

The acquisition of Differential Object Marking, by contrast, is quite challenging for English-speaking learners of Spanish (Arechabaleta Regulez, 2019; Bowles & Montrul, 2009; Guijarro-Fuentes, 2012) compared to learners whose L1 instantiates DOM, such as Turkish (Montrul & Gürel, 2015) and Romanian (Montrul, 2019). English-speaking L2 learners of Spanish often omit obligatory DOM with animate, specific direct objects in production and tend to accept unmarked animate, specific direct objects as grammatical in acceptability judgment tasks. A sentence-processing study conducted by Jegerski (2018) also showed that L2 learners of Spanish are not sensitive to grammatical violations of DOM with animate objects during **self-paced reading**. Studies have also found that even though clitic doubling is very productive in Spanish with dative constructions, L2 learners of Spanish do not exhibit the same degree of productivity as native speakers and do not often double clitics.

There are studies of how speakers of English and French produce and interpret Spanish clitics. Montrul (1999a) investigated knowledge of dative clitics and clitic doubling using a written GJT. Results showed that the French-speaking group, whose L1 has clitics but no clitic doubling, did not have problems with clitic doubling constructions in Spanish, while the English group, whose L1 lacks clitics, did.

In another study, Perpiñán and Montrul (2006) investigated whether L1-English L2 learners of Spanish transferred the English double object construction into Spanish. Participants completed a sentence-interpretation task in which a situation was provided (in English) and two possible answers were presented (in Spanish). The task tested different conditions, one of them being the clitic doubling construction, as in (109). Results revealed that intermediate L2 learners of Spanish often chose the wrong option (109b), while the advanced L2 learners of Spanish were native-like. Perpiñán and Montrul concluded that at the intermediate level, there is still transfer from English into Spanish with these constructions.

(109)   María, Juan's friend, had a baby. So Juan decided to send flowers to his friend:
  a. Juan   le   envió   flores   a   su   amiga.
     Juan   her.DAT sent   flowers to   his   friend
     'Juan sent his friend flowers.'
  b. *Juan   envió   su   amiga   flores.
     Juan   sent   his   friend   flowers

Bruhn de Garavito (2006) examined the interpretation of dative constructions with clitic doubling by Spanish monolinguals, Spanish–English bilinguals, and Spanish L2 speakers (L1 English) at the near-native level. Results showed no differences between the bilingual and the native groups. In contrast, the L2 group had problems interpreting clitic-doubling constructions when the indirect object was human, even though the learners had a near-native level of proficiency.

Cuervo (2007) tested semantic and syntactic knowledge of Spanish dative constructions with intermediate L2 learners of Spanish (L1 English). Like Bruhn de Garavito (2006), Cuervo found that intermediate learners had mastery of morphosyntactic aspects but only accepted clitic-doubling constructions as grammatical when the indirect object was animate. Overall, it seems that L2 learners of Spanish whose L1 does not have clitics go through different phases in their acquisition of clitic doubling. They seem to acquire the morphosyntax of the construction before its semantics.

Finally, studies that have tested knowledge of clitic left dislocations (CLLD) have found initial difficulty (Montrul, 2010b; VanPatten & Cadierno, 1993) and discrepancies in eventual mastery at advanced levels (Leal, Slabakova, & Farmer, 2017; Valenzuela, 2006). These structures are quite informal and frequent in spoken Spanish. Leal and Slabakova (2019) found that they are also not common in classroom discourse, and some teachers perceive them as too informal to be an object of instruction. Still, these structures are eventually acquired, apparently without much instruction.

8.3.3   Intervention Studies of Spanish Object Expression

Given the challenges that Spanish object expression poses to L2 learners, there have been a number of intervention studies in this domain, some focusing on clitics and others on DOM. The studies discussed in this section are summarized in Table 8.4.

8.3.3.1   Processing Instruction on Spanish Word Order with Clitics

VanPatten and Cadierno (1993) investigated the acquisition of clitic pronouns in Spanish and different word orders for subjects and objects as exemplified in (105) and (106). Details of this study are summarized in Box 8.2.

Table 8.4 Summary of intervention studies on object expression in Spanish

Study	Structures/phenomena under instruction	Participants' linguistic background	Nature of the intervention	Length of intervention	Major findings
VanPatten & Cadierno (1993)	Direct object clitics and word order (clitic left dislocation)	80 L1-English L2 learners of Spanish	Participants were taught about object pronouns through output-based instruction or input processing instruction	A month Pretest Instruction intervention Immediate posttest Posttest 2 (a week later) Posttest 3 (a month later)	The L2 learners learned object pronouns in Spanish, but only those in the input-processing group made gains in production and comprehension.
Leeser & DeMil (2013)	Direct and indirect object clitics in OVS and SVO sentences	123 learners of Spanish	Learners were divided into processing instruction, traditional instruction, and no-instruction groups. Instruction groups were taught about accusative (direct object pronouns only).	One month Pretest Intervention (one day, one class time) Immediate posttest and delayed posttests one month after pre-test Post-tests examined comprehension of accusative and of dative clitic pronouns	The two instruction groups improved their interpretation of accusative and dative clitic pronouns with OVS sentences, but PI was more effective with SVO sentences as well.
J. White (2015)	Direct and indirect object clitics in OVS and SVO sentences	460 beginner learners of Spanish divided into seven experimental groups and a control group	All groups received processing instruction but differed on the number of token items received during the treatment (40, 60, 80, 100, 120, 140)	About 10 days in total Pretest a week before intervention (one class of either 50 or 80 minutes) Immediate posttest and delayed posttests 3 days after; immediate posttest examines comprehension of accusative and of dative clitic pronouns	All treatment groups made gains compared to the no-instruction control group. No differences between groups at the immediate posttest. At the delayed posttest (3 weeks after treatment), the 140-token group outperformed the 100-token group.

Study	Topic	Participants	Treatment	Timeline	Findings
Farley & McCollam (2004)	Differential object marking	29 learners of Spanish (L1 English)	Participants assigned to instruction conditions: explicit information, structured input, processing instruction, no treatment (control)	A month Pretest a week before intervention Immediate posttest (in 3 sessions a week apart)	All treatments resulted in development of DOM to some extent.
Bowles & Montrul (2009)	Differential object marking	146 L2 learners of Spanish (L1 English) 12 native speaker controls	Intervention online module with explicit rule presentation and feedback of differential object marking and dative case in Spanish	One month Pretest Intervention Posttest	Improvement in ability to distinguish between grammatical and ungrammatical sentences involving DOM and to produce those sentences
Montrul & Bowles (2010)	Differential object marking and dative case	32 heritage speakers of Spanish	The instructed group completed an online module with explicit rule presentation and feedback on differential object marking and other uses of dative case.	One month Pretest Intervention Posttest	Improvement in ability to distinguish between grammatical and ungrammatical sentences with inanimate objects but less sensitivity to omission of DOM with animate objects
Hurtado & Montrul (2021a)	Dative clitic doubling and verbal passives	28 L2 learners of Spanish (L1 English) 23 native Spanish speakers	Participants described pictures orally	One 90-minute lab session Baseline Priming intervention Postpriming task	Priming increased L2 speakers' production rates of the target constructions
Hurtado & Montrul (2021b)	Dative clitic doubling with recipient and nonrecipient construction	23 Spanish native speakers 28 L2 learners of Spanish 26 heritage speakers of Spanish	Participants described pictures orally	One 90-minute lab session Baseline Priming Immediate posttest (5 minutes later) Delayed posttest (a week later)	Structural priming was effective in different ways for all the groups but had most effect in the L2 learners, who produced 0 clitics in the baseline phase

> **BOX 8.2 VanPatten and Cadierno (1993)**
>
> **Paper Title:** Explicit instruction and input processing
>
> **Research Questions:**
>
> 1. Does altering the way in which learners process input have an effect on their developing systems?
> 2. If there is an effect, is it limited solely to processing more input or does instruction in input processing also have an effect on output?
> 3. If there is an effect, is it the same effect that traditional instruction has (assuming an effect for the latter)?
>
> **Participants:** 80 L1-English low intermediate L2 learners of Spanish
>
> **Groups:**
>
> No instruction (n = 27)
> Input processing instruction, PI (n = 27)
> Traditional output-based instruction, TI (n = 26)
>
> **Study Timeline:**
>
> - Day 1: pretest
> - Day 2: instruction
> - Day 3: instruction and immediate posttest
> - 1 week after instruction: 2nd posttest
> - A month after instruction: 3rd posttest
>
> **Pre/Posttests:** Production and interpretation tasks
>
> The interpretation task: 15 sentences presented auditorily with pictures (*Al chico lo saluda la chica./Lo saluda la chica.* literally 'DOM the boy him says hi the girl/Him says hi the girl'). Learners had to indicate who was doing what.
>
> The production task: 5 written completion sentences (*El chico piensa en la chica y entonces* 'The boy thinks about the girl and therefore' _____ [expected response: *la llama* 'her he calls']).
>
> **The Intervention:** Instructional packets with input processing and output-based instruction
>
> **Results:** In the interpretation task, the PI group outperformed the TI and control groups on all three posttests. There was no difference between TI and control group. In the production test, both PI and TI groups outperformed the control group on all three posttests.

BOX 8.2 (cont.)

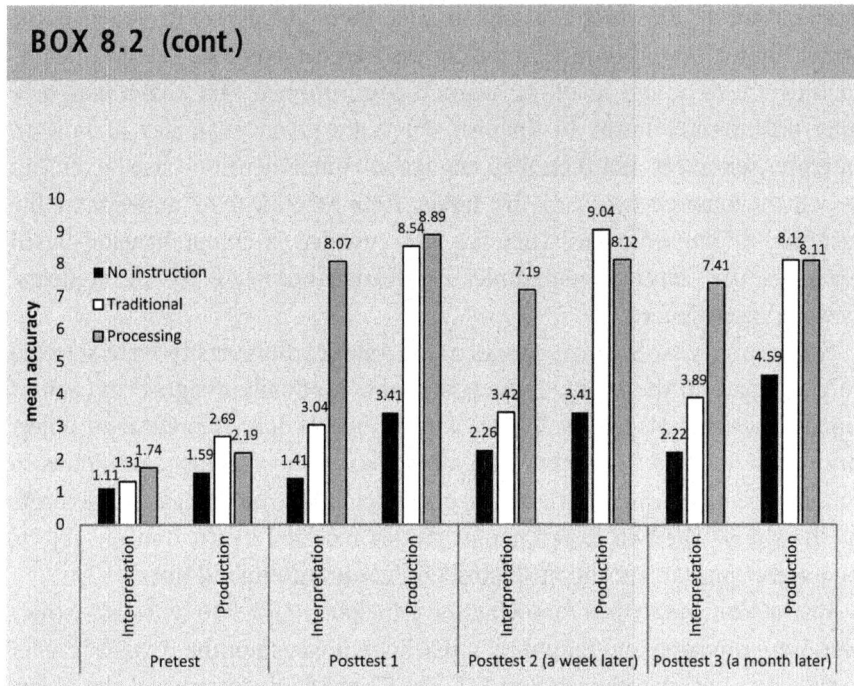

Figure 8.4 Mean raw scores (out of 10) on the interpretation and production tests (based on data from VanPatten & Cadierno, 1993)

VanPatten and Cadierno noted that beginning and intermediate learners of Spanish (with English L1) tend to misinterpret object pronouns in Spanish as subjects when the sentence has postverbal subjects (*Lo besa la mujer* 'The woman kisses him'). They assumed that L2 learners follow a processing strategy by which they assign the agent role to the first NP in the sentence, likely because English has a strict SVO word order. That is, learners of Spanish assume that the clitics *lo* and *la* ('him' and 'her') in sentence-initial position are subjects (*he* or *she*). To modify this initial strategy, processing instruction (PI) (VanPatten, 1996) was implemented. PI draws L2 learners' attention to how their processing strategies often lead them to make incorrect form–meaning connections (see Chapter 2 for more discussion). Thus, the purpose of this study was to modify how learners initially process input, which becomes intake and feeds the developing interlanguage system.

The study set out to contrast two different ways of teaching grammar in the L2 classroom. The target structures were clitic pronouns with finite verbs, and different words orders (SOV vs. OVS). The two teaching methods compared were input processing instruction (PI) and traditional output-based instruction (TI). In traditional instruction, L2 learners receive a grammatical explanation of the target grammar and then are asked to practice the structure in elicited production during mechanical exercises devoid of communicative meaning. In PI, L2 learners are informed that sometimes they may misinterpret forms in Spanish. They are given examples of how to interpret sentences and then they engage in comprehension-based exercises in which comprehension of the target form is critical to understand the meaning of the sentences. They are also engaged in comprehension-based exercises that have a communicative focus and relate to the students' personal experiences.

Six second-year Spanish classes at an American university were selected to participate in the study. Two classes were randomly assigned to each of three experimental groups: PI, TI, and no instruction. A pretest on object pronouns eliminated students who already knew how to place pronouns in Spanish, reducing the final number of participants who completed all facets of the study. The two experimental groups received instruction on objects and object placement; the no-instruction control group did not.

Instructional materials following the principles of the two types of instruction were prepared and taught by a teacher who was not the regular teacher assigned to the classes: see Box 8.2. The TI materials introduced the object pronouns and explained how they have different orders in the sentence. The practice consisted of an elicited-production task where students had to replace NPs with clitic pronouns and place them in the correct order. The PI materials included information about how to interpret different word orders in Spanish and had the students respond to the communicative content of sentences with OVS order. Activities after the presentation included listening to or reading sentences and answering questions demonstrating that the objects and subjects of the sentences were interpreted correctly. The group receiving PI was not asked to produce clitics during the practice activities.

There was a pretest before the instruction intervention, an immediate posttest, and two delayed posttests. The pretest and posttests consisted of both written production and interpretation tasks, as described in Box 8.2. The instructional intervention took place on two consecutive class days, and the first posttest was administered immediately after instruction, the second posttest a week after instruction, and the third posttest a month later.

The results of the interpretation task showed significant effects of test and of instruction and a significant interaction between structure and test. That is, there were no significant differences between the TI and PI groups in the written production task, but the PI group outperformed the TI group in the interpretation task. So, the PI group made gains both in interpretation and in production, while the TI group only made gains in production. This study showed that PI is superior to TI. Most importantly, this study showed that intermediate L2 learners of Spanish learn how to process direct object pronouns when they appear in different orders in the sentence.

Leeser and DeMil (2013) used a very similar design as VanPatten and Cadierno (1993) to investigate whether an intervention focused on accusative clitics (direct object pronouns), the primary treatment, would also extend to the correct interpretation of dative clitics (indirect object pronouns) with secondary structures, such as psych verbs (e.g., *gustar* 'like') in object-verb-subject (OVS) sentences. The verb *aburrir* can appear with indirect objects (assuming that the NP preceded by *al* and the clitic *le* are indirect objects) or with direct objects, when the verb has a more agentive meaning in subject-verb-object (SVO) sentences. In the structure with indirect objects, the dative NP and the clitic must appear in the sentence together (clitic doubling) (*Al chico le aburre el profesor* 'The boy, he is bored with this professor'), or the NP can be omitted and the sentence must have the dative clitic (the indirect object) in initial sentence position, object-subject-verb (OSV) (*Le aburre el profesor* 'he is bored with this professor'). The same verb can also occur in an SVO sentence where *el chico* 'the boy' is the direct object and is replaced by *lo* (*El profesor aburre al chico* 'The professor bores DOM the boy'/*Lo aburre el profesor* 'him bores the professor') in Spanish. The goal was to test if there was transfer of training from a primary structure to a secondary structure. Intermediate-level English-speaking L2 learners of Spanish completed a pretest, immediate posttest, and a delayed posttest on the interpretation of direct and indirect object pronouns, but the PI and TI treatments focused only on direct object pronouns. The results showed improvement on dative and accusative clitics with both OVS sentence types (*Le aburre el profesor* and *Lo aburre el profesor*) for the PI group. The TI group only showed improvements with dative clitics in OVS sentences (*Le aburre el profesor*). Therefore, PI is successful in helping learners process and acquire object pronouns in Spanish.

J. White (2015) used the same methodology and materials as Leeser and DeMil (2013) with very beginning (first-semester) learners of Spanish. At issue was the amount of exposure and practice during the PI intervention conducted during one class period, so groups were divided according to how many tokens they were exposed to during instruction and practice (40, 60, 80, 100, 120, and 140). According to the results, all instructed groups made gains with both direct and indirect object pronouns in comprehension compared to the no-instruction groups, suggesting that even forty tokens are sufficient to effect learners' comprehension of different word orders with accusative and dative clitics in Spanish. At the delayed posttest, the group exposed to 140 tokens maintained the gains more than the other groups.

8.3.3.2 Intervention with Differential Object Marking in L2 Spanish

There are studies investigating the effects of instruction on Differential Object Marking (DOM), the obligatory use of the preposition *a* with animate specific objects, as in *Harold vio a Anna Maria* 'Harold saw Anna Maria', in L2 learners and Spanish heritage speakers. Both L2 learners and heritage speakers omit the preposition *a* and produce and accept as grammatical sentences like **Harold vio Anna Maria*, which are ungrammatical in Spanish.

Farley and McCollam (2004) tested learners of Spanish enrolled in a fifth-semester course, who were randomly assigned to either a control group or one of three instruction groups that were exposed to varying degrees of explicitness and practice with DOM. Learners' knowledge of DOM was assessed based on their performance on a pretest and immediate posttest consisting of a GJT and a picture-description task. The study's results showed that learners in all instruction groups improved in their ability to recognize and produce grammatical sentences on the posttest compared to the control group that received no instruction on DOM. However, the small number of participants who completed the pretest, instruction, and posttest (fewer than ten per group) limits the generalizability of the study's findings.

Bowles and Montrul (2009) examined the role of explicit instruction and feedback (delivered via online modules) in the acquisition of DOM by L2 learners of Spanish. A written GJT was used to determine whether learners could distinguish between grammatical and ungrammatical sentences involving DOM (*Marisa conoce a mi hermana* 'Marisa knows my sister' vs. **Marisa conoce mi hermana* 'Marisa knows my sister'), and a controlled written production test was used to evaluate their ability to use DOM productively. In Week 1, a group of 12 native speakers and a group of 12 L2-learners completed a language-background questionnaire, followed by the written production and GJT pretests. Then, in Week 2, the L2 learners completed the instructional module online, followed by the immediate posttests. Three weeks later, the L2 learners completed the delayed posttests.

The intervention consisted of an explicit grammatical explanation of the *a*-personal with transitive verbs, indirect objects with ditransitive verbs, and dative experiencers with *gustar* verbs (positive evidence), followed by a practice exercise in which immediate, explicit corrective feedback (negative evidence) was provided. The learners were specifically alerted about the contrast between Spanish, which requires *a*-marking in these constructions, and English, which does not differentially mark objects on the basis of animacy, allows double objects, and has nominative experiencers with the verb *like*. In Spanish, *gustar* verbs have dative experiencers, preceded by the preposition *a* (*A Juan le gusta bailar* 'John likes to dance'). An elicited written production task (PT) and a written GJT were used to elicit participants' knowledge of DOM and dative experiencers. Two versions of the two tasks were prepared, one for the pretest and one for the posttest.

Results of the GJT showed that after instruction learners became more accepting of grammatical sentences with DOM (*Marisa conoce a mi hermana*) and less accepting of ungrammatical ones without DOM (**Marisa conoce mi hermana*). The largest differences were found for animate ungrammatical sentences, indicating that instruction had the greatest impact on sentences that require DOM in Spanish. The production scores increased over time, with a significant difference between the pretest and the immediate posttest but no significant differences between scores on the two posttests on sentences with animate, specific direct objects. The gains were quite substantial, with learners averaging just 17 percent use of the *a*-personal in obligatory contexts on the pretest but between 39 and 42 percent use on the posttests. Furthermore, there was only a slight tendency to overgeneralize the rule, with 9 percent use of the *a*-personal with inanimate objects on the delayed posttest.

Overall, the results of this study indicated that intermediate-level L2 learners of Spanish were able to improve in their ability to distinguish between grammatical and ungrammatical sentences involving DOM. They were able to produce those sentences, after receiving explicit instruction and practice involving corrective feedback, although they still scored significantly differently from native speakers. Furthermore, the online instruction in this study was modeled after the types of instructional modules used throughout a hybrid-delivery Spanish course that uses online modules as a unit of grammar instruction, reserving face-to-face class time for communicative activities. Therefore, the study found that students made gains with respect to the target structure from interacting with the self-instructional grammar unit. Although this study provides only written measures of learning and tests the efficacy of just one module of instruction, it seems to provide support for this type of hybrid instruction.

8.3.3.3 Intervention with Differential Object Marking in Heritage Spanish

Like L2 learners of Spanish, heritage speakers of Spanish often omit DOM and are insensitive to grammatical violations of DOM with animate, specific direct objects (Montrul, 2004c; Montrul & Bowles, 2010; Montrul & Sánchez-Walker, 2013). Figure 8.5, using data from Montrul and Bowles

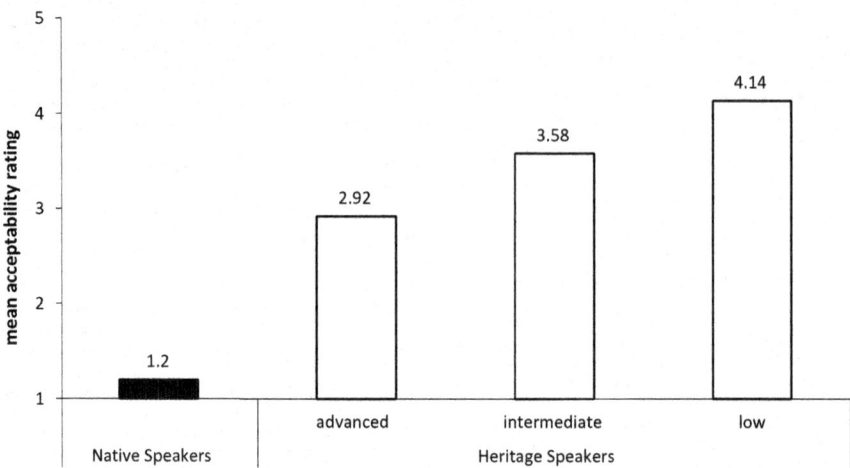

Figure 8.5 Mean acceptability ratings (from 1-unacceptable to 5-acceptable) on ungrammatical sentences without DOM (based on data from Montrul & Bowles, 2010)

(2010), shows that heritage speakers of low, intermediate, and high proficiency Spanish have difficulty rejecting ungrammatical sentences without DOM in Spanish.

Montrul and Bowles (2010) extended the methodology used in Bowles and Montrul (2009) to investigate whether heritage language (HL) learners also benefit from explicit instruction. See supplementary online materials for details about the intervention in this study. The initial pool of participants consisted of twelve Spanish native speakers from various Spanish-speaking countries (baseline group) and eighty-six HL learners enrolled in Spanish-for-heritage-speakers classes in a metropolitan university in Chicago. Of this initial pool, forty-five Spanish HL learners completed written production and acceptability judgment tests both before and immediately after instruction, which began with an explicit grammatical explanation of the targeted structures.

Due to technical problems and lost data, the results of the production task are based on two groups of HL learners tested on two occasions. The uninstructed group (n = 16) was made up of learners who completed the pretest but not the instructional module or the posttest, while the instructed group (n = 16) were learners who only completed the instructional intervention and the posttest. Montrul and Bowles (2010) showed that instructed HL learners made significant gains on the production test on all sentence types. However, instructed HL learners' gains were not equal in all areas or on all sentence types. Most notably, instruction did not affect learners' acceptability ratings in the GJT as much as their production. On most sentence types, instruction affected acceptability ratings in the expected direction. However, on ungrammatical sentences with animate objects (missing the *a*-personal), as in *Pedro conoce el chef* 'Pedro knows the chef', instructed HL learners' pre- and post-instruction acceptability ratings were not significantly different from each other.

Overall, Montrul and Bowles (2010) found that explicit instruction and feedback was highly beneficial to HL learners. In fact, the magnitude of the gains on all of the structures was higher for HL learners than for the L2 learners in Bowles and Montrul (2009), which followed the same design. This study suggests that negative evidence plays a role in both instructed L2 acquisition and instructed HL acquisition, and that explicit instruction is beneficial for both groups, although the studies' design did not allow the researchers to determine the individual contributions of explicit grammatical information and negative evidence.

8.3.3.4 Structural Priming with Spanish Dative Constructions

We now turn to an intervention study of dative constructions in Spanish, using structural priming. Hurtado and Montrul (2021b) investigated the effectiveness of structural priming to promote the acquisition of clitic doubling with dative constructions in Spanish, as in examples (107) and (108). Spanish native speakers often produce recipient dative (*Pedro le da un lápiz a Julio* 'Pedro gives Julio a pencil') and nonrecipient dative constructions (*Antonia le lava la camiseta a Carmen* 'Antonia washes Carmen her T-shirt') doubled by a dative clitic. This alternation resembles the English dative alternation (McDonough, 2006). Furthermore, the study investigated the potential roles of L1 transfer, lexical priming, and the long-term effects of structural priming in promoting implicit learning of clitic doubling constructions in Spanish.

Native speakers of Peninsular Spanish and Mexican Spanish, L2 learners of Spanish (intermediate level), and heritage speakers of Spanish were tested. At the onset (in the baseline portion of the study), the heritage speakers were expected to produce clitics closer to the rate of native speakers and at higher rates than L2 learners. The L2 learners were expected to produce fewer clitic constructions than native speakers and heritage speakers overall. After the priming intervention, L2 learners were expected to show a higher rate of clitic production than native speakers and heritage speakers because more gains were expected in this group (for whom clitics are less frequent) than for the heritage speakers (who use clitics already). The study also tested whether priming effects would last several days after the intervention, as this would have implications for L2 instruction. It also tested whether lexical repetition enhanced structural priming and whether the type of construction (recipient vs. nonrecipient) and the animacy of the indirect object played a role in priming clitics.

Figure 8.6 Sample picture stimuli for the oral elicitation task (with priming) (from Hurtado & Montrul, 2021b)

The intervention took place in a lab setting. In the first session, the L2 learners and the heritage speakers were administered a Spanish proficiency test and a clitic production pretest to make sure they had basic knowledge of clitics. All groups then completed a baseline task that measured the use of clitics in a picture-description task (following Bock, 1986), followed by a priming treatment and an immediate posttest. A delayed posttest took place a week later. During the baseline phase, the participants completed a picture-description task with dative constructions. They saw pictures accompanied by verbs on a computer screen and were asked to describe the picture using the verb. The target stimuli sentences included dative verbs with recipient indirect objects, such as *regalar* 'give', and dative verbs with nonrecipient indirect objects, such as *robar* 'steal', as shown in in (110); see Figure 8.6 for the corresponding pictures.

(110) Target responses for (a) and (b) in Figure 8.6
    a. El hombre (le) regaló perfume a la mujer.
       the man (her) gave perfume to the woman
       'The man gave the perfume to the woman.'
    b. El ladrón robó la billetera al joven.
       the thief stole the wallet to/the young guy
       'The thief stole the wallet from the young guy.'

Right after the baseline phase, the intervention phase began. Participants were presented with pictures accompanied by full sentences in Spanish. They had to read the sentences (primes) (e.g. *La mamá le entregó un paquete al niño* 'The mother gave a package to the boy'), and they also had to produce their own description for the slides where only a verb was provided (targets). The immediate posttest took place five minutes after the priming intervention. As in the baseline, the participants were shown pictures with verbs and were asked to describe the pictures. The delayed posttest (with no priming) was conducted a week later in a separate session, following the same structure as the baseline and the immediate posttest.

The results of the baseline showed that, as expected, the Spanish native speakers produced the highest number of dative clitic constructions compared to the heritage speakers and the L2 learners. The results of the structural priming intervention showed that structural priming was effective in different ways for all the groups. The native group increased its production of dative clitic constructions by more than 10 percent, while the heritage group and the L2 group increased by almost 20 percent. The increase of the L2 learners is very telling, because many of these participants produced 0 percent clitics in the baseline phase, despite being familiar with clitics, as tested in the clitic pretest. The results of the L2 learners were further analyzed to see whether priming rates were higher in those learners who had produced at least one clitic construction in the baseline (+Clitic) compared to those who did not (−Clitic), and this difference was confirmed statistically.

Furthermore, lexical repetition enhanced priming: When the verb was repeated in the prime and in the target, speakers showed a higher rate of priming. The clitic increase effect was maintained a week later, and the highest increase occurred for the L2 speakers. The native speakers and the heritage speakers produced more clitic constructions when the indirect object was a nonrecipient than when it was a recipient, but the L2 group behaved in the opposite way. This group-by-construction interaction could be possibly explained by construction frequency, which could be different in the three groups as they were exposed to different input. L2 speakers were more primed with the construction that is most frequent for native speakers and heritage speakers, which happens to be the most infrequent for them.

Finally, the animacy of the indirect object was also found to have an effect on the degree of priming: Native speakers and heritage speakers produced more clitic constructions when the indirect object was [+animate], while the L2 speakers were not sensitive to animacy. Perhaps these L2 speakers had not yet acquired the semantic features of the construction, given that even advanced Spanish L2 learners have problems with this (Bruhn de Garavito, 2006; Cuervo, 2007).

Overall, the study showed that structural priming was effective in the three groups considered and lasted at least a week. The priming had the most effect in the L2 learners, who barely produced any clitics in the baseline phase, and suggests that priming could be used in the classroom to promote implicit language learning.

Hurtado and Montrul (2021a) tested intermediate L2 learners of Spanish (L1 English) on clitic doubling dative alternations and the passive/active alternation. Participants completed a baseline task and a postpriming task following a picture-description methodology. Priming increased the L2 speakers' production rates of both passives and clitic doubling, but the increase was higher for clitic doubling in Spanish, even though passives are more frequent in English than in Spanish. The L2 learners were sensitive to the frequency of the constructions in Spanish.

8.3.4 Summary and Implications: Object Expression in Spanish

Table 8.5 summarizes intervention studies of object expression in Spanish. The available studies have found that, regardless of the type of intervention, in the classroom or in the lab, there is evidence that instruction facilitates acquisition in this domain. This finding holds for explicit instruction with negative feedback, input processing instruction, and even priming interventions. Instruction facilitates the acquisition of object clitics and their interpretation in sentences with different word orders, raises learners' awareness on the use of the preposition *a* to mark animate specific direct objects, and leads learners to produce more clitic-doubling constructions with datives. Difficulty with DOM persists into advanced levels of proficiency with learners who may have been instructed on the clearest cases of DOM, with human, specific direct objects. It is an open question whether further instruction or a priming intervention would be successful with more advanced learners as regards some other subtleties of this phenomenon, such as indefinites, quantifiers, and animate (nonhuman) objects.

8.4 DISCUSSION QUESTIONS

1. Look back at the examples in (99) (these were the child L1-English learners' errors with datives) and explain why these overgeneralizations happen. Can you explain why these overgeneralization errors happen? Can you explain how and why they go away, eventually?
2. The studies of the dative alternation in English show that explicit instruction and negative feedback are the only ways L2 learners pay attention to and learn the double object construction. Why do you think implicit interventions are not generally successful? What type of

linguistic knowledge (implicit or explicit) do you think these interventions engage and why?

3. McDonough (2006) found that interaction with priming did not work for the acquisition of the double object construction in English, whereas Hurtado and Montrul (2021b) found that a priming intervention was successful at making L2 learners of Spanish use more dative constructions with clitics (equivalent to the English double object construction) in Spanish. What could explain the difference in results between these two studies?

4. The study by VanPatten and Cadierno (1993) found that the L2 learners who received processing instruction actually advanced their grammatical development of different word orders in Spanish sentences with preverbal object clitics more than those who received traditional, output-based instruction. If this is true, what type of learning (implicit, explicit) do you think that input-based instruction promotes and why?

8.5 APPLICATIONS QUESTIONS

1. An intervention study conducted by Radwan (2005) also found positive effects of explicit feedback on the acquisition of the dative alternation in English. Read Carroll and Swain (1993) and Radwan (2005) and compare and contrast the two studies in terms of participants, type of intervention, methodology, and results. Explain how and in what ways Radwan confirms and expands Carroll and Swain's findings and what both studies suggest for the learning and teaching of the dative alternation in English.

2. Although the studies reported by Bowles and Montrul (2009) and Montrul and Bowles (2010) were part of the same overall project, a series of circumstances with participant attrition resulted in the studies being methodologically deficient and not fully comparable. Still, taken together, the two studies found that explicit focus on form with negative evidence helped both L2 learners and heritage speakers improve on their knowledge and production of differential object marking in Spanish. Suppose that you had the opportunity to redo these two studies so that the results could be compared more directly. The aim would be to determine who benefits more from explicit instruction, L2 learners or heritage speakers, and whether the gains are long-lasting. Read the two articles and provide the design of the intervention study to include the two groups.

3. Read Leal, Slabakova, and Farmer (2017) and Leal and Slabakova (2019). Leal and Slabakova (2019) explain that the Spanish clitic left dislocation

construction, shown in (106), is frequent in informal spoken Spanish and learnable in advanced levels of Spanish (see Leal, Slabakova, and Farmer, 2017), especially when L2 learners study abroad and have opportunities to interact with Spanish native speakers in an immersion context. At the same time, Leal and Slabakova (2019) find that these structures are not frequent in classroom discourse or instruction, but they should be. Do you agree with their claim that intermediate-level students of Spanish should receive more linguistic information and focused practice with the Spanish clitic left dislocation construction? If these structures are eventually learnable, how would learners benefit from this information and practice earlier?

4. To what extent does (or should) classroom discourse mirror that of native speakers? You may discuss ESL or Spanish classes and focus on any of the structures with direct and indirect objects discussed in this chapter, based on your own experiences as a learner and/or a teacher. There are corpus studies that show how frequent double object vs. *to*-constructions are in English, for instance, and there have been some studies in addition to the work by Leal and colleagues that show that L2-Spanish classroom discourse underuses structures (in their case CLLD but also word orders other than SVO). See, for example, LoCoco (1987).

8.6 FURTHER READING

- Leal, T., & Slabakova, R. (2019). The relationship between L2 instruction, exposure, and the L2 acquisition of a syntax–discourse property in L2 Spanish. *Language Teaching Research, 23*(2), 237–258.
  This article discusses the acquisition of topicalizations and clitic left dislocations constructions in Spanish, which are difficult for L2 learners of English.

- Leal, T., Slabakova, R., & Farmer, T.A. (2017). The fine-tuning of linguistic expectations over the course of L2 learning. *Studies in Second Language Acquisition, 39*(3), 493–525.
  This article is about the syntactic processing of structures with clitics (object pronouns) in Spanish.

- Radwan, A. A. (2005). The effectiveness of explicit attention to form in language learning. *System,* 33(1), 69–87.
  This article reports on another intervention study on the dative alternation in English.

9 Word Order and Related Syntactic Phenomena

Throughout this textbook we have seen that languages differ in a great variety of ways. In this chapter we focus on crosslinguistic differences in structures that affect word order (syntax) and on concomitant changes in meaning. Whenever the learners' L1 and their L2 use different word order for a particular syntactic configuration, this presents a potential challenge to the learners, and may be subject to classroom instruction. We have already discussed a number of studies that instructed learners about the specifics of L2 word order. Chapter 4 covered studies about the relative ordering of verbs and adverbs inside a **verb phrase** (VP), as well as about the correct word order in question formation. Chapter 7 examined word order manipulations related to argument structure, including passivization and the placement of subjects with unaccusative verbs. Chapter 8 included studies about the relative ordering between direct and indirect objects. The present chapter discusses other word order phenomena that have been the subject of **intervention studies** and that fall beyond the scope of the topics covered in prior chapters.

This chapter is divided into four parts: (i) sentence-level word order, (ii) adjective ordering, (iii) relative clauses (RCs), and (iv) quantifier scope. While quantifier scope is not directly about surface syntactic word order, it is about the order in which sentential elements are interpreted, and hence is included in this chapter. For each of these four topics, we provide an overview of the linguistic phenomena, briefly mention experimental studies in **second language acquisition** (SLA), and discuss the intervention studies that have been done in this area. All of the **intervention studies** discussed in this chapter are summarized in Table 9.1.

9.1 Sentence-Level Word Order

We begin this chapter by looking at different word-order configurations at the level of the sentence. We have already seen that languages differ in the relative position of the verb and the adverb (Chapter 4) or the direct and

Table 9.1 Summary of intervention studies targeting word order and relative clauses

Publication	Structures/phenomena under instruction	Participants' linguistic background	Nature of the intervention	Length of intervention	Major findings
Eckman, Bell, & Nelson (1988)	English RCs (focus on subject- vs. direct-object vs. indirect-object RCs)	36 ESL learners at a US university, with a variety of L1 backgrounds	Explicit instruction on subject, direct object, or object-of-preposition RCs	A single one-hour session	Groups taught about subject and direct-object RCs improved on these two RC types, relative to the control group. The group taught about object-of-preposition RCs improved on all three RC types.
Doughty (1991)	English RCs (focus on object-of-preposition RCs)	20 ESL learners in an intensive English institute in the USA, with a variety of L1 backgrounds	Rule-oriented vs. meaning-oriented instruction	Ten days	Both experimental groups improved relative to the control group, both on object-of-preposition RCs and on less marked RCs (subject, direct object and indirect object).
Long, Inagaki, & Ortega (1998)	Japanese adjective ordering	24 second-semester learners of Japanese at a US university	Recasts vs. modeling	A single 40-minute session	Both recasts and modeling groups improved relative to the control group.
S. Izumi (2002)	English RCs (focus on object-of-preposition RCs)	61 ESL learners at a US university, with a variety of L1 backgrounds (Arabic most common)	Enhanced vs. unenhanced instruction, and output vs. nonoutput instruction	Six sessions	Enhanced input led to greater noticing, while output groups showed greater improvement, with no effect of enhancement.

Study	Target feature	Conditions	Duration	Results
Y. Izumi & Izumi (2004)	English RCs (focus on object-of-preposition RCs)	24 ESL learners at a US university, with a variety of L1 backgrounds	Aural/oral format, output vs. nonoutput	Three days, 25 minutes per day	No major differences among groups, but greater improvement for nonoutput than for output group.
Yabuki-Soh (2007)	Japanese RCs (focus on oblique-object RCs)	60 first-semester university students of Japanese in Canada, with a variety of L1s (predominantly English, Korean, and Chinese)	Form-based instruction, meaning-based instruction, and mixed form-/meaning-based instruction	Three 50-minute sessions spread out over a week	The form-based instruction group improved the most relative to the other two groups.
VanPatten et al. (2013)	Canonical vs. noncanonical word orders in Spanish, German, Russian, and French	Native English speakers, third-semester students of a foreign language at a US university: 42 learners of Spanish; 46 learners of German; 44 learners of Russian; 48 learners of French	Processing instruction with vs. without explicit rule presentation	A single 60-minute session	Spanish and Russian: no effects of explicit instruction, no relationship with grammatical sensitivity. German and French: explicit instruction led to learners reaching criterion faster; for German only, grammatical sensitivity correlated with performance for the explicit-instruction group.
Hirakawa, Shibuya, & Endo (2018)	English adjective ordering	Study 1: 25 Japanese EFL learners in Japan, of upper-elementary and low-intermediate proficiency. Study 2: 44 learners from the same population as Study 1	Study 1: naturalistic exposure (study abroad) vs. explicit instruction. Study 2: naturalistic exposure (study abroad) vs. artificial input flooding (study abroad)	Study 1: 5 weeks of study abroad vs. 3 weeks, 3 hours per week of instruction; Study 2: five weeks of study abroad vs. 3 weeks of study abroad + input flooding. A single session	Study 1: the explicit-instruction group improved, but the naturalistic-exposure group did not. Study 2: neither group improved relative to the control group.

Table 9.1 (cont.)

Publication	Structures/phenomena under instruction	Participants' linguistic background	Nature of the intervention	Length of intervention	Major findings
Wu & Ionin (2022a)	Inverse scope in English scopally ambiguous sentences	48 L1-Mandarin ESL learners at a US university	Explicit instruction on either the double-quantifier or the quantifier-negation configuration		Both experimental groups improved in their acceptance of inverse scope on the configuration which they were taught but did not generalize to the configuration which they were not taught
Henry (2022)	Canonical vs. noncanonical word order in German	51 students of third- and fourth-semester German in the USA	Processing instruction vs. traditional instruction on German word order	A single session (with an earlier session for vocabulary learning)	The PI but not the TI group improved on the interpretation task and on the self-paced reading task. Both groups improved on production task.

indirect objects (Chapter 8). In this section, we consider the relative positioning of the main sentential elements: the subject, the verb, and the object.

9.1.1 Noncanonical Word Orders Crosslinguistically and in Second Language Acquisition

Languages have different underlying word order for declarative sentences: for example, English, Russian, and Mandarin Chinese are subject–verb–object (**SVO**) **languages**, while Turkish and Japanese are subject–object–verb (**SOV**) **languages**. Thus, a sentence such as *Rachel saw Mary* is expressed with the order *Rachel Mary saw* in an SOV language. The underlying word order of a language is the **canonical word order:** It is typically the most frequent word order, and the word order more commonly used "out of the blue," e.g., in answer to "what happened?".

Languages also allow **noncanonical word orders**, to differing degrees. English is a rigid-word-order language which does not readily allow noncanonical word orders: *Mary saw Rachel* cannot be turned into *Mary Rachel saw*, which is completely ungrammatical. English does allow topicalization, however. This is when the object is moved to the front of the sentence, emphasized prosodically and often interpreted contrastively, as in, *Soup, Jenny likes (unlike beans, which she hates!)*. However, such topicalizations are fairly infrequent and highly marked because they have particular discourse and prosodic constraints, as noted in the above example. In contrast, many other languages readily allow noncanonical word orders and also allow a great variety of word orders: e.g., Russian, a SVO language, allows all possible permutations of the subject, verb, and objects (SVO, SOV, OVS, OSV, VSO, VOS), though some are more frequent than others. Although not as flexible as Russian, Spanish allows more word orders than English, especially with regard to the position of the subject, which can appear after the verb (VS, VSO, VOS).

The availability of flexible word order is closely related to the availability of case marking. In languages that use different endings for the subject and object (the **nominative** and **accusative** case markers, respectively – see also Chapter 8), a **noun phrase**'s (NP) role in the sentence is identifiable from the case markers, regardless of the word order. In contrast, in English, a language without overt case marking (except on some pronouns, as in *she/her, he/him,* etc.), word order is the primary cue as to which NP is the subject vs. the object. Case-marking languages include Korean, Japanese, Russian, German, and Finnish, among many others. All of these languages have fairly flexible word order. When the object moves to a position in which it precedes the subject, the process is often called **object scrambling**. This is illustrated in (111) for Russian: Both (111a), with canonical SVO order, and (111b), with scrambled OVS order, convey the same basic meaning. Who did the seeing vs. who was seen is determined by the case markers, not by word order. The two word orders occur in different discourse contexts: For example, (111a) is more likely to answer an object question, "Who did Anne see?", while (111b) is more likely to answer a subject question, "Who saw Mary?". Crucially, both orders are fully acceptable, and both can be produced with neutral prosody, unlike English topicalization, as discussed above.

(111) a. Anna videla Mariju.
Anne.NOM saw.FEM Mary.ACC
'Anne saw Mary.'
b. Mariju videla Anna.
Mary.ACC saw.FEM Anne.NOM
'Anne saw Mary.'

There are many studies on the production, comprehension, or processing of noncanonical word order and object scrambling by L2 learners of languages with flexible word order. See, among many others, Hopp (2005, 2009) on L2 German; Unsworth (2005, 2007) on L2 Dutch; Mitsugi and MacWhinney (2010) on L2 Japanese; Erdocia, Zawiszewski, and Laka (2014) on L2 Basque; M. H. Kim (2019) on L2 Korean; Ionin et al. (2021) on L2 Russian. There are also many studies on sentence-level word order in L2 Spanish (e.g., Lozano, 2006; Leal, Destruel, & Hoot, 2018). While Spanish does not have widespread overt case marking (except for dative and differential object marking, discussed in Chapter 8), it has greater word-order flexibility than English does, as explained above, with regard to the position of the subject. For example, the sentence *Hoy Mario trajo un regalo* 'Today Mario brought a present', with the subject *Mario* preceding the verb, can also be expressed as *Hoy trajo un regalo Mario* or *Hoy trajo Mario un regalo*, with postverbal subjects, even though there is no overt case marking in these sentences.

The specifics differ across studies, but in general, noncanonical word order presents a challenge to L2 learners, especially when the learners' L1 is a rigid-word-order language such as English or Mandarin Chinese. In production, learners tend to overrely on canonical word order, which is never exactly ungrammatical. Rather, canonical word order tends to be dispreferred by native speakers in particular discourse contexts because word-order changes correlate with some subtle discourse-related differences. In comprehension, learners may misinterpret noncanonical word order, e.g., misinterpreting OVS as SVO due to an overreliance on word order rather than case-marking cues. Therefore, word order is a good candidate for focus on form in the classroom.

9.1.2 Processing Instruction Studies on the Comprehension of Noncanonical Word Orders

The interpretation of noncanonical word order in the L2 has been the subject of several studies that use the processing instruction (PI) approach (VanPatten, 1996, 2004; see Chapter 2). The present section focuses on studies across several different L2s whose goal is to teach learners about noncanonical word orders using structured input activities.

9.1.2.1 The Use of Structured Input to Teach Learners about Noncanonical Word Orders

As discussed in Chapter 2 and the sample studies in Chapters 5, 6, and 8, the goal of PI is to change how learners process the input, moving them away from their preferred strategies and focusing their attention on the target linguistic structure. In the case of word order, the strategy in question is the First Noun Principle (VanPatten, 1996, 2004), according to which learners generally interpret the first noun that they hear or read in a sentence as the subject of the sentence and the agent of the action. It is not clear whether this strategy is a universal default strategy adopted by all learners or a result of L1 transfer from English, a rigid-word-order language in which this strategy works quite well. Given that all PI studies on word order have English as the learners' L1 (while varying the L2), this question does not have an answer at present.

As discussed in Chapter 8, VanPatten and Cadierno (1993) conducted a PI study with L2-Spanish learners on Spanish word orders with clitic pronouns. While Spanish is a SVO language, sentences with an object clitic can have OVS word order, in which case learners may misinterpret the object clitic as the subject of the sentence. VanPatten and Cadierno (1993) found that PI was more effective than traditional instruction (TI), improving learners' comprehension as well as production of OVS sequences in Spanish. In later work, VanPatten and colleagues tested the efficacy of PI on noncanonical word orders in several different L2s. VanPatten et al. (2013) report on four separate intervention studies with noncanonical word orders in L2 Spanish; in L2 German (also reported in VanPatten & Borst, 2012a); in L2 Russian (also reported in VanPatten, Collopy, & Qualin, 2012); and in L2 French (also reported in VanPatten & Price, 2012). The specifics of all four studies are given in Box 9.1.

Given that VanPatten and Cadierno (1993) already showed the efficacy of PI over traditional instruction for noncanonical word order, the four studies in VanPatten et al. (2013) do not compare PI to TI. Instead, these studies examine the following two questions: (1) whether including explicit

BOX 9.1 VanPatten et al. (2013)

Publication Title: Explicit information, grammatical sensitivity, and the first-noun principle: A cross-linguistic study of processing instruction

Research Questions:

1. Does explicit information make a difference in processing instruction (PI), as measured by trials-to-criterion (how soon learners begin processing correctly) during online performance?
2. Does grammatical sensitivity correlate with outcomes of PI, independently of the presence or absence of explicit information?

Participants: Native English-speaking US college students, in their third semester of language study for Spanish (n = 42), German (n = 46), Russian (n = 44), and French (n = 48)

Groups: For each language, two groups: both groups received processing instruction (PI) but differed in whether they also received explicit instruction (+/−EI groups). Spanish: 23 +EI, 19 −EI; German: 24 +EI, 22 −EI; Russian: 23 +EI, 21 −EI; French: 23 +EI, 25 −EI

Study Timeline: A single session in the lab, 60 minutes or less, consisting of:

- Pretest (10 trials)
- Grammatical sensitivity and spelling sections of the MLAT (25 minutes)
- For +EI groups only: explicit instruction about word order
- Intervention (50 trials, with the last 10 trials treated as the posttest)

Format of Both Pretest and Intervention:

- Each item was a sentence with either canonical or noncanonical word order (e.g., SVO vs. OVS); participants listened to the sentence while looking at two drawings and selected the drawing that matched the sentence.
- Pretest: participants responded to 10 items, with no feedback.
- Structured input intervention: participants responded to 50 items, with feedback (correct vs. incorrect answer); the last 10 items were the same as in the pretest but in reverse order, and constituted the posttest.
- Trials-to-criterion scoring: The number of items that preceded the criterion, where the criterion is providing at least four correct answers in a row to three target noncanonical items and at least one distracter canonical order item.

BOX 9.1 (cont.)

Results: Mean trials-to-criterion and pretest vs. posttest results (VanPatten et al., 2013)

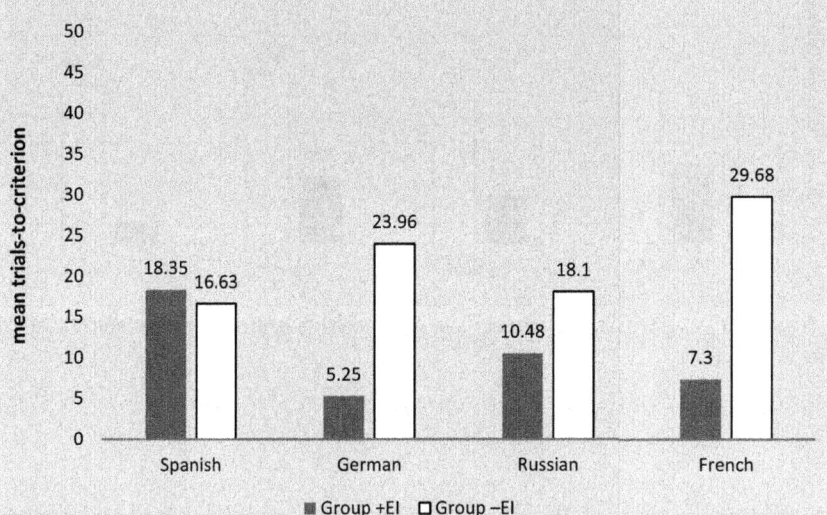

Figure 9.1 Mean trials-to-criterion by instructional group for the four studies in VanPatten et al. (2013)
Note: Lower score means faster learning

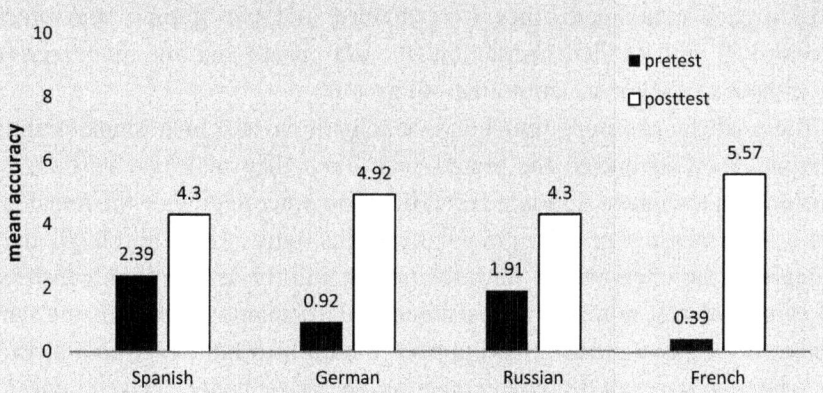

Figure 9.2 +EI groups' mean accuracy (out of 10 trials) (based on data from VanPatten et al., 2013)

BOX 9.1 (cont.)

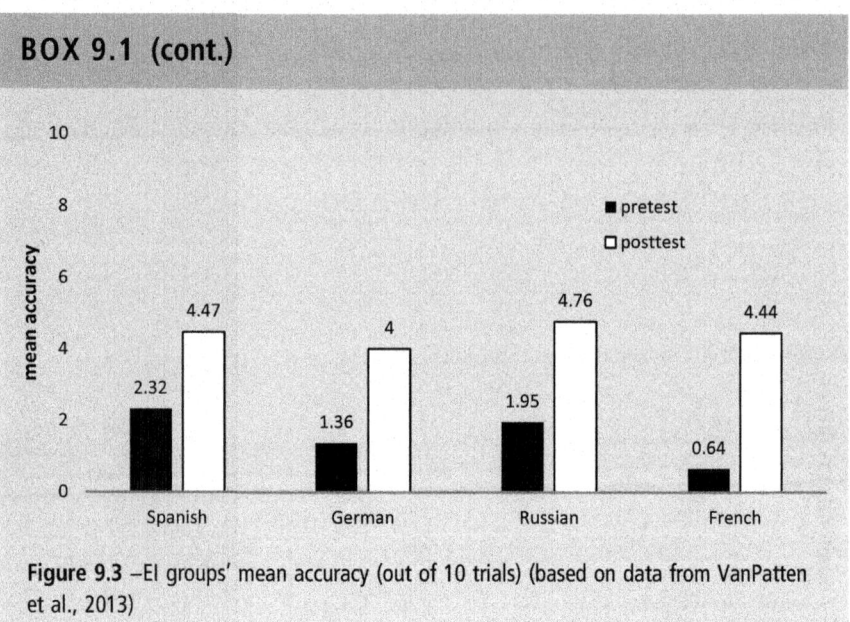

Figure 9.3 –EI groups' mean accuracy (out of 10 trials) (based on data from VanPatten et al., 2013)

information as part of PI affects performance, and (2) whether learners' individual grammatical sensitivity correlates with the outcome of PI. All four experiments reported in VanPatten et al. (2013) had the same structure. The participants were native English-speaking US college students studying the target language in the classroom, in their third semester of language study. Within each experiment, they were divided into two groups, one which received PI with explicit instruction (the +EI group) and one that received PI without explicit instruction (the –EI group).

The participants were tested individually in a lab, in a single testing session. They completed the pretest first. Then they took two portions of the Modern Language Aptitude Test (MLAT), in order to provide the researchers with a measure of their grammatical sensitivity. After the MLAT, they completed the intervention. Both the pretest and the intervention consisted of canonical and noncanonical sentences. Participants listened to the sentence, viewed two pictures, and pressed a button to indicate which picture matched the sentence. In the intervention, the participants received immediate feedback of "correct/incorrect" after their response. For the +EI groups, this structured input intervention was immediately preceded by explicit information about the structure in question; otherwise, the +EI and –EI groups' interventions were identical.

In place of a traditional posttest, the study used a **trials-to-criterion** scoring method, as follows. The intervention consisted of fifty trials, some with canonical and others with noncanonical word orders. The researchers scored how many trials it took for a given participant to reach criterion, which consisted of correctly answering three noncanonical order items and at least one canonical order item in a row. The lower the score, the better: A participant who reached the criterion after twelve trials had a better score than one who reached it after twenty-five trials. A participant who never reached criterion over the entire fifty trials was given a score of fifty. In addition to the trials-to-criterion measure, the researchers also examined performance on the last ten of the fifty intervention items for accuracy, treating them as a measure of final outcome similar to a posttest.

9.1.2.2 The Effectiveness of Processing Instruction with and without Explicit Instruction, across Languages

What did the results of the four experiments in VanPatten et al. (2013) show? Before answering this question, we need a bit more background on the experimental items. In the Spanish experiment, all sentences contained an object-pronoun clitic (e.g., 'The professor sees him'). The word order varied between canonical (SOV, with the object clitic in front of the verb, *El professor lo ve*) and noncanonical (OVS, with preverbal object pronouns, *Lo ve el profesor*). In the German and Russian experiments, all sentences contained two animate NPs (e.g., 'The cat hears the dog'), with the word order varied between canonical SVO and noncanonical OVS. Case-marking (on the determiner in German, on the noun in Russian) indicated the syntactic roles. The OVS orders for German and Russian, respectively, are illustrated in (112a-b). The French experiment was a little different. French has fairly rigid word order, but in causative sentences such as (112c), the word order in the embedded clause has the object (*a song*) appearing before the agent (*the girl*); this noncanonical order was contrasted with two other sentence types that had canonical order.

(112) a. Den   Hund   hört   die   Katze.
         the.MASC.ACC dog hears the.FEM.NOM cat
         'The cat hears the dog.'   [German]
     b. Sobaku   slyšit   koška.
         dog.ACC   hears   cat.nom
         'The cat hears the dog.'   [Russian]
     c. Le   garçon   fait   chanter   une   chanson   à   la   fille.
         the   boy   makes   sing.INF   a   song   to   the   girl
         'The boy makes the girl sing a song.'   [French]

The results were as follows (see Box 9.1 for the specifics). In both the Spanish and the Russian experiments, the +EI and −EI groups did not differ in how quickly they reached criterion or in the final outcome, and grammatical sensitivity did not correlate with performance. In the German experiment, in contrast, the +EI group reached criterion much faster than the −EI group (replicating prior findings by Henry, Culman, & VanPatten, 2009, on the same linguistic phenomenon). In the German experiment, grammatical sensitivity correlated with performance for the +EI group only: Learners with higher sensitivity reached criterion faster but only in the group receiving explicit instruction. In the French experiment, the +EI group reached criterion much faster than in the −EI group, just as in the German experiment, but there was no correlation with grammatical sensitivity. Even though the +EI group outperformed the −EI group in the German and French experiments with respect to trials-to-criterion, the +EI and −EI groups did not differ in the final outcome (as measured by performance on the final ten items of the intervention), for either language.

Why did explicit information speed up learning for German and French but not for Spanish or Russian? VanPatten et al. (2013) propose that the explicit instruction was easy to apply to input processing in the case of German and French. In German, the explicit instruction directed learners to attend to the form of the definite determiner (*der* vs. *den*, nominative vs. accusative), while in French, it directed learners to attend to which noun was marked with *à* 'to'. In contrast, the explicit instruction was less effective for learners of Spanish and Russian. In the case of Spanish, plural and feminine singular object pronouns have the same forms as definite determiners (*los, las, la*); in Russian, nouns have a variety of nominative and accusative endings. Given the complexity of the paradigm in both cases, explicit information was less helpful. The conclusion of this study was that explicit instruction affects input processing only if "the information is easy and portable enough to use during real time processing" (VanPatten et al. 2013, p. 524).

9.1.2.2 Processing Instruction and Psycholinguistic Measures

Until recently, intervention studies on PI, such as the ones discussed above, have mostly used offline measures in order to investigate learners' production and interpretation. As pointed out by Henry (2022), off line measures may not tap into learners' **implicit knowledge** and do not provide information about real-time processing. In order to study real-time processing, psycholinguistic measures such as **self-paced reading** (SPR) or **eye tracking** should be used (see also Chapter 1 of this book on the use of psycholinguistic tasks to study implicit knowledge). In Chapter 6 we did see some studies that combined off-line with on-line methodologies (Chiuchiù & Benati, 2020; Dudley, 2020; Fernández Cuenca, 2019) to investigate the acquisition of subjunctive forms. Here, we briefly discuss Henry (2022), a study that used the SPR task in conjunction with offline production and comprehension tasks in order to compare the efficacy of PI and TI in the domain of word order. The participants were third- and fourth-semester students in German courses in the United States, and the target structure was OVS in German, as in earlier studies on German discussed above. In German OVS sentences, the presence of accusative case on the definite article, as in example (112a), indicates that the first noun is the object rather than the subject of the sentence.

When assessed on sentence interpretation, the group of students receiving PI improved from pretest to posttest, but the group receiving TI did not. Both groups improved from pretest to posttest on written production, with the PI groups making greater gains. The advantage of PI over TI, especially with regard to interpretation, is consistent with what many other PI studies have found (e.g., the PI studies on tense marking discussed in Chapter 5). The novel component of Henry's study was the inclusion of the SPR task among the pretest/posttest materials. On the pretest, the PI and TI groups read the first NP in SVO and OVS sentences equally fast in the SPR task. On the posttest, the PI group read OVS sentences significantly more slowly than SVO sentences when the article in the first NP was unambiguously accusative vs. nominative. The TI group made no such distinction. Henry interprets this result as indicating that the PI group started to pay attention to case-marking on the first NP in the sentence and slowed down when the case-marking (accusative) went against the learners' expectation that the first NP is the subject. (However, the PI group did not make a distinction between OVS and SVO when the disambiguating article form occurred on the second NP, suggesting only partial sensitivity to case marking). Overall, Henry's study shows that PI affects learners' real-time processing system and provides additional evidence in favor of PI.

9.2 Adjective Ordering

Having discussed sentence-level word order, we now move on to word order within the noun phrase. This section examines the ordering of adjectives within an NP, while the following section moves on to noun-modifying **relative clauses**. (Relative clauses were also mentioned in Chapter 6 in some examples of subjunctive use).

9.2.1 Adjective Ordering in Linguistic Theory and in Second Language Acquisition

A noun can be modified by multiple adjectives, as in *a big green plastic box* or *a tall beautiful leafy tree*. There are constraints on the order of adjectives within the NP. For example, in English, size adjectives come before shape adjectives: *a tall circular table* sounds much better than *a circular tall table*. There is much theoretical linguistic literature aimed at explaining the constraints on adjective ordering (e.g., M. C. Baker, 2003; Laenzlinger, 2005; Cinque, 2010).

One distinction that is commonly made is between absolute and nonabsolute adjectives. **Absolute adjectives** name properties that are binary, such as shape adjectives (*round*) or material ones (*glass*). An object either is round or it is not, and it is either glass or not. **Nonabsolute adjectives** name gradient properties, such as size (*small*) or height (*short*): One object can be smaller or shorter than another, something can be very short or just a little short, etc.

Languages like English, Spanish, and Arabic impose ordering restrictions on adjectives (for example, nonabsolute adjectives precede absolute adjectives) but differ in the placement of the adjective relative to the noun. Modifying adjectives come before the noun in English, after the noun in Arabic, and either before or after, depending on the adjective and/or the intended meaning, in Spanish and other Romance languages. In contrast, Korean and Japanese do not have direct modification by adjectives, using relative clause markers instead (Sproat & Shih, 1991; M. C. Baker, 2003), so that 'a beautiful picture' is expressed, roughly, as 'a picture which is beautiful' (see section 9.3 for more on relative clauses). Such indirect modification is not subject to ordering constraints: Japanese and Korean allow both 'small wooden table' and 'wooden small table', unlike English, in which the former is strongly preferred. Finally, Chinese falls in between, allowing both direct modification as in English (which is subject to ordering constraints) and indirect modification as in Japanese and Korean (which is not subject to ordering constraints).

Relatively little is known about SLA of adjective ordering. Stringer (2013) reports on a study that compared adjective ordering in the L2 English of Arabic, Korean, and Chinese speakers. The learners' L1s differ from each other and from English with regard to adjective ordering (see above). Stringer tested a large sample of learners from the four different L1s and found a high degree of similarity in their performance and no clear evidence of transfer effects. For example, all learner groups displayed robust knowledge of the distinction between nonabsolute and absolute adjectives, even though not all of the learners' L1s had the corresponding ordering constraint, as described above. Stringer's conclusion is that the teaching of adjective ordering does not need to be tailored to the specific L1 of the learners.

9.2.2 Intervention Studies with Adjective Ordering

We are aware of only two published classroom intervention studies on adjective order, both of which contrast English and Japanese. Japanese resembles Korean and Chinese in not having restrictions on adjective ordering (Sproat & Shih, 1991), as described above.

Long, Inagaki, and Ortega (1998) examined whether L1-English L2-Japanese learners would be able to learn two facts about Japanese adjective ordering. The first fact is that color adjectives can precede size adjectives (which is not good in English). The second fact is that the first adjective in the sequence is required (or at least strongly preferred) to appear in a gerundive form, as illustrated in (113) (from Long, Inagaki, and Ortega 1998, p. 360). (In addition to this experiment on adjective ordering, Long, Inagaki, and Ortega, 1998, also report on an experiment with adverbs, discussed in Chapter 4).

(113) aka-kute ookii hako
  red-gerund large box
  'a large red box' [Japanese]

The participants were second-semester learners of Japanese in a US university, who were divided into two experimental groups and a control group. The intervention (which the control group did not complete) took the form of a communication game. One experimental group received recasts: e.g., if a learner said "large red box" in Japanese, the researcher would recast it with the sequence in (113). The other experimental groups received modeling of the target forms, or models – as in (113) – instead. The pretest and posttest consisted of oral picture-description tasks, designed to elicit adjective sequences. Both experimental groups (recasts and modeling) improved relative to the control group and did not differ from each other. While both techniques were found to be effective, it is not clear how much the intervention really taught students about Japanese adjective ordering. Only the color–size sequence was taught in the study, hiding the fact that Japanese in fact allows both color–size and size–color sequences.

Hirakawa, Shibuya, and Endo (2018) conducted an intervention study in the opposite direction, with L1-Japanese L2-English learners. They asked whether learners would recognize that English allows only one order for adjective pairs (e.g., size before shape) where Japanese allows both. The participants were Japanese college students with upper-elementary to low-intermediate English proficiency. The participants were divided into two groups who completed a pretest, an immediate posttest, and a delayed posttest three months later. The naturalistic-exposure (NE) group completed a five-week study abroad program in the United States between the pretest and the posttest; while they received intensive English instruction during the study-abroad, they received no instruction about adjective ordering. The explicit-instruction (EI) group remained in Japan but received explicit instruction about adjective ordering for three weeks, three hours per week. The focus of the instruction was on differences between Japanese and English, and on the semantic categories of absolute and nonabsolute adjectives. In the pretest and posttests, learners completed a preference task, choosing between sentences with two different adjective orders. The EI group showed a high level of improvement (which was still present in the delayed posttest), while the NE group did not. Hirakawa, Shibuya, and Endo (2018) concluded that a five-week study-abroad did not provide the NE group with enough input of multiple adjective modification. They therefore conducted a follow-up study to see if artificial input flooding (IF) could improve learners' performance with adjective ordering. The learners in the follow-up study came from the same population in the original study and completed very similar tasks as pretest and immediate posttest. Learners in the NE group were in a five-week intensive study-abroad program, as in the original study. Learners in the IF group were in a three-week study-abroad program and received input flooding with adjective sequences but no explicit instruction. Neither group improved from pretest to posttest. In sum, only explicit instruction was found to be effective with regard to adjective ordering.

9.3 Relative Clauses

Relative clauses (RCs) are clauses that modify nouns and have an adjectival function. For example, each sentence in (114) has a RC modifying the noun *cat*; the RC is inside square brackets and begins with a relative pronoun (*that*, as in most examples in (114), or *which/who/whom/whose*). RCs are classified according to the role that the head noun (the noun *cat* in (114)) has inside the RC. In (114a), it is the subject of the RC (the cat came into our back yard). In (114b), it is the direct object (my daughter brought the cat home). In (114c), it is the indirect object (my daughter gave a toy to the cat), and so on. Note that the full NP (*the cat that...*) is the direct object of the verb *fed* in all of sentences in (114), so the classification refers not to the syntactic function of the NP inside the matrix clause, but rather to the type of relativization. The full NP could just as easily be the subject of the matrix clause (*The cat [that my daughter brought home] just came in*).

(114) a. I fed the cat [that/who came into our back yard]. [Subject RC]
b. I fed the cat [that/whom my daughter brought home]. [Direct object RC]
c. I fed the cat [that/whom my daughter gave a toy to]. [Indirect object RC]
d. I fed the cat [that/whom my daughter put a hat on]. [Oblique (object-of-preposition) RC]
e. I fed the cat [whose owner was on vacation]. [Genitive RC]
f. I fed the cat [that my own cat is smaller than]. [Object of comparative RC]

9.3.1 Relative Clauses in Linguistics and in Second Language Acquisition

Keenan and Comrie (1977), a typological investigation of over fifty different languages, proposed that the distribution of different types of RCs is governed by the **noun phrase accessibility hierarchy** (NPAH). According to the NPAH, different RC types have different degrees of **markedness**. The hierarchy is implicational, meaning that the presence of a more marked RC type in a language implies the presence of a less marked RC type: Less marked RCs are more accessible. **Subject RCs** (as in (114a)) are the least marked, which means that they occur in all languages that have RCs. Direct **object RCs** (114b) are next on the scale: If a language has direct object RCs, it necessarily also has subject RCs, but not necessarily any other RC type. The presence of indirect object RCs (114c) entails the presence of subject and direct object RCs, and so on. English has the six RC types in (114), arranged in order from least marked to most marked.

The NPAH has received much attention in acquisition literature, since it makes clear and testable predictions for acquisition. Learners should have more difficulty acquiring more marked RCs, and instruction on more marked RCs should lead to success with less marked RCs. There have been many experimental SLA studies on RCs and the NPAH in particular, and the results have provided partial support for the NPAH while also sometimes challenging it. For sample studies and overviews of early research with RCs in SLA, see the *Studies in Second Language Acquisition* special issue of June 2007, vol. 29, issue 2: "The acquisition of relative clauses and the noun phrase accessibility hierarchy: A universal in SLA?", and in particular the introduction to this special issue (S. Izumi, 2007).

In more recent years, many psycholinguistic studies have examined the processing of RCs in the L2, as well as the L1. Such studies have generally found that subject RCs (SRCs) are easier to process than object RCs (ORCs), both in one's L1 and in one's L2. This has been found both for the processing of RCs in languages like English and Dutch (where the RC follows the head noun) and in languages like Japanese and Korean (where the RC precedes the head noun; see also section 9.3.2 below). See, among others, Baek (2012);

Jackson and Roberts (2010); Kanno (2007); O'Grady, Lee, and Choo (2003); Omaki and Ariji (2005). While the relative ease of processing of SRCs relative to ORCs is fully consistent with the NPAH, there have been many different explanations about the exact reasons for why SRCs are easier to process. The difference has been attributed to structural factors, memory load, and frequency considerations, among others, or some combination thereof (see Staub, 2010, for an overview of different accounts). Reviewing this rich body of SLA literature on relativization goes far beyond the scope of this book. Here, we highlight several intervention studies that have tested different instructional approaches to the teaching of RCs.

9.3.2 Intervention Studies on Relative Clauses and the Noun Phrase Accessibility Hierarchy in English as a Second Language

Several intervention studies have tested the predictions of the NPAH by examining whether teaching learners about a more marked type of relativization leads them to also acquire the less marked structures. Many of these studies have been done on English, including Gass (1982); Eckman, Bell, and Nelson (1988); Doughty (1991); and Ammar and Lightbown (2005); the studies generally find support for the NPAH. We consider two early studies, Eckman, Bell, and Nelson (1988) and Doughty (1991), in more detail below.

9.3.2.1 Explicit Instruction about English Relative Clauses

Adopting the notion of typological markedness (Eckman, 1977), Eckman, Bell, and Nelson (1988) hypothesized that once a learner acquires the most marked aspects of the L2, they should be able to generalize to the less marked aspects. To make this concrete, let us consider how this applies to the acquisition of relative clauses. As discussed in the previous section, the NPAH classifies RCs from the least marked (subject RCs) to the most marked (object of comparative RCs), see (114). The prediction based on markedness is that students instructed on more marked RCs should generalize to less marked RCs, but that the opposite will not necessarily hold. For example, a student instructed about indirect object RCs (114c) should generalize to both subject and direct object RCs, while a student instructed on oblique object RCs (114d) should generalize to all the RC types in (114a–c), and so on.

Eckman, Bell, and Nelson (1988) tested this prediction by comparing ESL learners at a US university who were randomly assigned to four groups. One group was taught to form only subject RCs, another group was taught to form only direct object RCs, and a third group was taught to form only object-of-preposition RCs. This last category combined both indirect object RCs (114c) and oblique object RCs (114d); crucially, both are more marked than subject and direct object RCs (114a–b). The control group was not taught about RCs at all. Each group included participants with Arabic, Spanish, Japanese, and Korean L1s.

All groups completed a pretest prior to the intervention, and a posttest two days after the intervention; the tests explicitly directed participants to combine two sentences (e.g., *Joan likes the professor. The professor gives easy exams to the class.*) using the words *who, whom, which*, or *that* (target response: *Joan likes the professor that/who gives easy exams to the class*). The tests had an equal number of items testing subject RCs, direct object RCs, and object of a preposition RCs. The instruction was quite explicit, directly teaching the students how to combine two sentences into one using words like *that, which* and *who/whom*. Crucially, as noted above, each experimental group was taught about only a single RC type. The explicit instruction was followed by oral and written practice exercises.

All four groups made many errors with all three types of RCs on the pretest, with no group differences. On the posttest, the groups performed largely as predicted. The group taught about object-of-preposition RCs improved the most, making almost no errors on any of the three RC types on the posttest. The groups taught about subject RCs and direct object RCs both improved on subject and direct object RCs, but not on the object-of-preposition RCs, while the control group showed no improvement. Thus, generalization was largely in the predicted direction from more marked to less marked structures. One exception was that the group taught about subject RCs did generalize to some extent to direct object RCs, despite the latter being more marked.

9.3.2.2 Rule-Oriented vs. Meaning-Oriented Instruction about English Relative Clauses

Another early study that tested the effects of instruction on RCs in light of the NPAH was Doughty (1991). The participants in Doughty's study were ESL students at an intensive English institute in the United States. Only participants with little knowledge of relativization in English were selected for the study. The participants came from seven different L1s, with half of the participants having L1 Japanese. Doughty notes that all of the participants' L1s have all types of RCs with the exception of object of comparative. The participants were randomly assigned to two experimental groups (the meaning-oriented instruction group, or MOG, and the rule-oriented instruction group, or ROG) and a control group (COG). All participants completed both written and oral tasks on RC formation as pretest and posttest (administered immediately before and after the intervention, respectively). Each test consisted of two different written GJTs, a written sentence-combination task, a written sentence-completion task, and an oral elicitation task. The intervention lasted ten days, with participants coming to a computer laboratory to complete one lesson per day.

All three groups (MOG, ROG, and COG) were taught via computer-assisted language learning (CALL), with a focus on comprehension; they had to read texts and answer questions about them. All the texts contained object of a preposition RCs (the type in (114d)). While all three groups read for comprehension, the MOG and ROG participants (but not the COG) received additional instruction. The MOG participants received lexical and semantic rephrasings of sentences containing RCs, while the ROG participants received instruction about relativization. The study was interested both in which type of instruction (meaning-oriented or rule-oriented) was more effective and in whether instruction about object-of-preposition RCs would facilitate acquisition of less marked RCs (subject and direct object RCs), as predicted by the NPAH.

All three groups scored similarly on the pretest, with participants exhibiting a better command of subject RCs than of any other RC type. While all three groups improved from pretest to posttest, the two experimental groups improved about twice as much as the control group (across all the different tests combined). There were no differences in improvement between ROG and MOG. The findings provided support for the NPAH, in that participants showed a tendency to improve not only on the RC type on which they were instructed (object-of-preposition RCs) but also on the less marked RC types (subject RCs, direct object RCs, and indirect object RCs). However, the small sample size (only twenty participants across all three groups), and the great variety of L1s combined in this study, mean that the results must be interpreted with caution.

9.3.3 Intervention Studies on English Relative Clauses, and the Role of Learner Output

The studies described above taught relative clauses via input and/or explicit rule presentation. In contrast, S. Izumi (2002) as well as Y. Izumi and S. Izumi (2004) examined the effects of learner-produced output on improvement with English RCs. Unlike the earlier studies, these studies did not address the predictions of the NPAH, focusing entirely on the efficacy of different instructional methods, rather than on the implicational hierarchy among RC types.

9.3.3.1 Teaching Relative Clauses with Written Input and Output

The participants in the S. Izumi (2002) study were ESL students from two US universities. Only students with rudimentary knowledge of English relativization were included in the study, while those with no knowledge or ample knowledge were excluded. The learners included in the study came from twelve different L1s, with Arabic being the most common L1, spoken by over half of the participants. Participants were assigned to four different experimental groups plus a control group. The four experimental groups differed along two parameters: whether they were required to produce output (+/−O) and whether they were provided with enhanced or unenhanced input (+/−IE). Izumi examined both whether participants would notice the target structure and whether they would demonstrate learning of the target structure. Based on prior literature, Izumi hypothesized that both noticing and learning of the target structure would be greater for +O than −O participants, and for +IE than for −IE participants, with the greatest gains being in evidence for the +O+IE participants.

The participants completed the pretest about a week before the intervention, which lasted over a two-week period, during which participants in the experimental groups came to a computer laboratory for six separate sessions. The posttest was completed a few days after the intervention. The control group completed only the pretest and posttest. The tests assessed participants via four different written tasks: two production tasks (a sentence-combination test and a picture-cued sentence-completion test) and two receptive tests (an interpretation test and a GJT).

During the intervention, participants read a text and answered comprehension questions. As in Doughty (1991), the target structure, which occurred multiple times in the text, was object-of-preposition RCs (the type in (114d)). The two +O groups were instructed to reconstruct the text, in writing, based on their notes, while the two −O groups instead answered extension questions about the topic of the text. Participants read the text twice. In the case of the two +IE groups, the second presentation of the text contained typographical enhancement of RC-containing NPs, as well as the individual components inside the NP (the relative pronoun and the preposition). Participants were directed to pay attention to the enhanced portion of the text.

Participants' noticing was measured by scoring the notes that they took on the text, while learning was measured by improvement from pretest to posttest. With regard to noticing, the two +IE groups improved more than the two −IE groups: Enhancement of the various components of relativization led to greater noticing of relativization. In contrast, output production did not play a role in noticing. The two output (+O) groups were similar in their use of RCs in text reconstruction, with not much advantage for the +O+IE group over the +O−IE group.

Turning to the test results, which indicate learning, the two +O groups exhibited greater overall improvement from pretest to posttest than the two −O groups and the control group. While the two −O groups improved less than the two +O groups, they still improved more than the control group, indicating that input flooding with RCs, even without output production, still has a positive effect.

In sum, while input enhancement facilitated noticing of the target structure, noticing was not directly linked to learning. The greatest improvement in learning occurred for groups that produced the target structure in their output, regardless of whether they received enhanced input. S. Izumi concludes that while both input enhancement and output production involve focus on form, output was more conducive to learning in this case.

9.3.3.2 Teaching Relative Clauses with Aural/Oral Input and Output

Y. Izumi and S. Izumi (2004) is a follow-up study to S. Izumi (2002), which examined the conditions under which output best contributes to learning. The study consisted of two different experimental group (output and nonoutput) as well as a control group. The target structure was object-of-preposition RCs, as in Doughty (1991) and S. Izumi (2002). The participants were ESL learners in the United States, from nine different L1s. The pretest took place the day before the intervention, which took place over three days, with a 25-minute session per day; the posttest was administered immediately after the intervention. The control group participants did not take part in the intervention but completed the tests. The whole study took about a week, with all tasks administered in a lab, via a computer.

The two experimental groups were exposed to aural input accompanied by pictures but performed different tasks. The output group completed a picture-description task that elicited RCs, while the nonoutput group completed a picture-sequencing task that required comprehension of the input. The aural input that both groups received contained multiple object-of-preposition RCs. The tests were two of the four tests from S. Izumi (2002), the two that Izumi found to be most successful: sentence combination and interpretation. However, in Izumi and Izumi (2004), these tasks were presented in oral/aural rather than written format, for consistency with the rest of the study. Both tasks targeted three types of RCs: subject, direct object, and object of preposition. The results on both tasks failed to yield major differences among the three groups; the nonoutput group improved the most, and the control group improved the least, but overall, there was no effect of group.

The findings of Izumi and Izumi (2004) thus contradict those of S. Izumi (2002), with no advantage found for the output group in the 2004 study. Izumi and Izumi (2004) consider a number of possible explanations, including the shorter duration of the 2004 study, a lower amount of input, and an effect of modality (aural vs. written). They also suggest that the production

9.3.4 Intervention Studies with Japanese Relative Clauses

While the majority of intervention studies on RCs, including those described above, have focused on English, there are studies on RCs in typologically different languages as well. Yabuki-Soh (2007) is an example of an intervention study that looked at the predictions of the NPAH for L2 Japanese (an earlier intervention study with Japanese RCs is Roberts, 2000). Japanese RCs differ from English ones in several ways. They are prenominal, meaning that the RC precedes rather than follows the head noun. There are no relative pronouns such as *that* or *which* in English. And while Japanese has postpositions (which are like prepositions, except that they come after rather than before the noun), postpositions are not allowed inside the RC. Japanese has five types of RCs, the ones in (114a–e), lacking only the object of comparative RCs. Examples of subject and direct object Japanese RCs are given in (115) below.

(115)   a. [Watashi-ni   hon-o   kure-ta]   hito   [subject RC]
           I-DAT   book-ACC   give-PAST   person
           'the person [who gave me the book]'
       b. [Watashi-ga   kinoo   at-ta]   hito   [direct object RC]
           I-NOM   yesterday   meet-PAST   person
           'the person [whom I met yesterday]'

Prior experimental SLA studies on Japanese have yielded somewhat conflicting findings, with some research supporting predictions of the NPAH and other research contradicting it. Yabuki-Soh (2007) conducted an intervention study in order both to test the predictions of the NPAH for teaching L2 Japanese and to examine the effects of different types of Japanese instruction. The study focused on oblique (object-of-preposition) RCs (the type in (114d)), illustrated in (116) for Japanese. Japanese has locative postpositions, including *ni* (locative) and *e* (directional): 'in the house' is *ie ni* and 'from the restaurant' is *resutoran e*. However, postpositions cannot occur inside RCs, as illustrated in (116a–b).

(116)   a. [Jon-ga   sunde-iru]   ie
           Jon-NOM   lives   house
           'the house that Jon lives in'
       b. [Jon-ga   it-ta]   resutoran
           Jon-NOM   go-PAST   restaurant
           'the restaurant [which Jon went to]'

The participants in the study were first-year learners of Japanese at a Canadian university; their L1s included English, Chinese, and Korean, as well as several other languages. The study used intact classes, with three different classes assigned to three different interventions, respectively. All participants heard a lecture about the target structure, took a pretest the next day, and subsequently took part in three 50-minute intervention sessions spread over several days. A posttest was administered two days after the end of the intervention (ten days after the pretest). The tests consisted of a comprehension task and a sentence-combining task, which tested all five types of Japanese RCs (subject, direct object, indirect object, oblique object, and genitive).

The three classes were assigned, respectively, to three experimental groups: a form-based group (FG), a meaning-based group (MG) and a form-/meaning-based group (FMG). All three groups completed the same number of tasks during the intervention, but the tasks differed. The tasks for FG focused on the grammatical properties of RCs (e.g., identifying the head noun of the RC; combining two sentences together), while the tasks for the MG focused on meaning and production (e.g., answering questions and drawing pictures). The tasks for the FMG were a combination of shortened FG and MG tasks. All tasks were designed around oblique object RCs.

On both the comprehension and the sentence-combination tests, the FG improved the most, with gains twice as large as those for the MG and FMG. The learners' L1s did not influence the results. The highly explicit instruction provided to the FG proved to be the most beneficial. This is consistent with the many other findings discussed in earlier chapters that explicit instruction leads to the greatest gains, at least in the short term.

Turning to the different types of RCs, Yabuki-Soh found that on the comprehension task, the biggest improvement was for oblique and indirect object RCs, with the least improvement on genitive RCs. A similar pattern was attested on the sentence-combination test, but here, learners improved the least on subject RCs, which was also the RC type on which they had performed the best on the pretest. Overall, participants improved the most on the structure on which they were instructed (oblique RCs). The results were partially consistent with the NPAH, but ultimately inconclusive.

9.4 Quantifier Scope

In this last section we discuss the interpretation of sentences with quantifier expressions (*every, all*, and others, see below). While not directly about word order, **quantifier scope** is directly tied to the structural relationships between the words in a sentence. We first discuss the properties of quantifier scope, before moving on to a discussion of SLA and intervention studies on this topic.

9.4.1 Quantifier Scope: Linguistic Background and Terminology

Words such as *every, each, many, some, a, several*, etc. are known as **quantifiers**; when a sentence contains two quantifiers, it is potentially ambiguous, depending on the structural relationship between those two quantifiers. This is illustrated in (117) for a sentence with an indefinite quantifier (the article *a*) in subject position and a universal quantifier (*every*) in object position.

(117)   A witch memorized every spell.
   a. SS reading (a>every): There is one specific witch who memorized all the spells.
   b. IS reading (every>a): For every spell, there is a witch who memorized it (potentially different witches for different spells)

If the two quantifiers are interpreted according to their surface structural configuration (which in this case also matches the linear word order), then the indefinite *a witch* is said to "take scope" over the universal *every spell*, resulting in the "**surface scope**" (SS) reading paraphrased in (117a) (the symbol > stands for "takes scope over"). If instead *every spell* takes scope over *a witch* (i.e., the universal is interpreted before the indefinite), we get the "**inverse scope**" (IS) reading paraphrased in (117b). Thus, (117a) is only true if the same one witch memorized all the spells, while (117b) is true even if different witches memorized different spells.

Scope ambiguity can also obtain in sentences which contain one quantifier and negation. This is illustrated in (118), with a universal quantifier in subject position and sentential negation; the SS and IS readings, paraphrased in (118a–b), respectively, arise based on whether the quantifier scopes over negation or vice versa.

(118)   Every letter didn't arrive on time.
   a. SS reading (every>not): For every letter, it didn't arrive on time (i.e., no letters arrived on time).
   b. IS reading (not>every): It is not the case that every letter arrived on time (possibly some did and some didn't).

There are cross-linguistic differences regarding availability of inverse scope. English allows both SS and IS readings for configurations such as (117) and (118), even though SS readings are generally found to be easier to access and/or process (see, e.g., Anderson, 2004). In contrast, Mandarin

Chinese is a scope-rigid language, which allows only SS readings in configurations corresponding to (117) and (118) (Aoun & Li, 1989, 1993; for experimental evidence confirming the English/Mandarin difference, see Scontras et al. 2017; Wu and Ionin, 2019, 2022b).

9.4.2 Second Language Acquisition and Intervention Studies with Quantifier Scope

SLA studies have found that learners tend to transfer the scope possibilities of their L1 to their L2 (e.g., Marsden, 2009) and that L1-Mandarin L2-English learners in particular do not allow IS readings for (117) and (118) in English, consistent with transfer from Mandarin (Wu & Ionin, 2019, 2022b). This finding led Wu and Ionin (2022a) to conduct an intervention study that examined whether explicit instruction can help L1-Mandarin L2-English learners to acquire inverse scope (for more discussion of quantifiers and L2 instruction, see Gil, Marsden, & Whong, 2013). See supplementary online materials for details about the intervention in this study. Following the logic of verb-raising studies by L. White (1990, 1991; see Chapter 4), Wu and Ionin (2022a) examined whether learners taught on one structure can generalize to a structure which is underlying related. Specifically, they asked whether learners taught about the availability of IS for the double-quantifier configuration in (117) would also allow IS for the quantifier-negation configuration in (118), and vice-versa. On the assumption that IS readings of both (117) and (118) result from the same syntactic mechanism (covert quantifier movement), true acquisition of this mechanism should lead learners to acquire one structure as soon as they have acquired the other.

The details of this study are given in Box 9.2. The participants in Wu and Ionin (2022a) were L1-Mandarin L2-English learners of intermediate to advanced proficiency studying at a US university. The participants were assigned to three groups: The two experimental groups were taught about the configurations in (119a–b), respectively, while the control group received no intervention. All three groups completed a pretest a week prior to the intervention, an immediate posttest right after the intervention, and a delayed posttest a month later. The pretest and posttests consisted of picture-based acceptability judgment tasks. Both configurations in (119a–b) were tested, where each picture matched either the SS reading or the IS reading of the target sentence.

(119)   a. One dog got every bone.
        b. Every pirate didn't leave the ship.

The picture in Figure 9.4 matches the inverse-scope reading of the double-quantifier sentence in (119a): It is true that every dog got a bone (*every*>*one*,

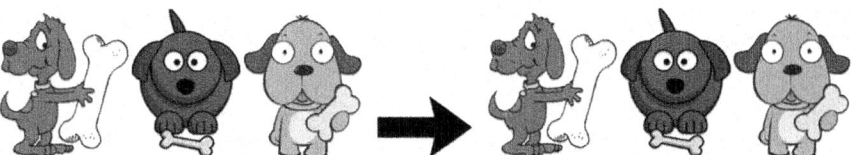

Figure 9.4 Picture matching the inverse-scope configuration of (119a), from Wu and Ionin (2022a)

Figure 9.5 Picture matching the inverse-scope configuration of (119b), from Wu and Ionin (2022a)

inverse scope), but false that one specific dog got every single bone (*one>every*, surface scope). Similarly, the picture in Figure 9.5 matches the IS reading of the quantifier-negation sentence in (119b): It is true that it's not the case that every pirate left the ship (*not>every*, inverse scope), but false that every single pirate failed to leave the ship (*every>not*, surface scope). Thus, acceptance of (119a) in the context of Figure 9.4, or acceptance of (119b) in the context of Figure 9.5, indicates availability of inverse scope in the learner's grammar.

The intervention, which took place in a single session in the lab, consisted of explicit information about interpretation of the sentence type in (119a) or (119b) (depending on the group) and practice items with automatic feedback. The findings (see Box 9.2 for details) were that the two experimental groups successfully learned IS for the configuration which they were taught. In fact, in the posttests, the instructed learners accepted IS readings for the taught configuration even more than the native English-speaker baseline group. While the baseline native-speaker group preferred SS readings to IS readings, the instructed learners came to accept IS readings as much as SS readings after the intervention. At the same time, the learners failed to generalize to the untaught structure. Wu and Ionin concluded that in this case, explicit instruction did not lead to true acquisition, but only to explicit learning. The explicit knowledge gained in the intervention was retained over time, a month after the intervention.

BOX 9.2 Wu and Ionin (2022a)

Publication Title: Does explicit instruction affect L2 linguistic competence? An examination with L2 acquisition of English inverse scope

Research Questions:

1. Do L1-Mandarin L2-English learners learn inverse scope for the configuration on which they are explicitly instructed?
2a. Do L1-Mandarin L2-English learners generalize the availability of inverse scope from one linguistic configuration to another?
2b. Do L1-Mandarin L2-English learners overgeneralize the availability of inverse scope to a superficially similar configuration that does *not* allow inverse scope?

Participants: 48 L1-Mandarin L2-English learners at a US university, and 33 native English speakers as the baseline group

Groups: Two experimental groups (for each group n = 16), instructed on the double-quantifier configuration in (117) and the quantifier-negation configuration in (118), respectively, and a control group (n = 16), plus a baseline group of native English speakers (n = 33)

Study timeline: For the learners (the baseline group completed all tests in one sitting):

- A week before the intervention: pretest
- A single session consisting of intervention + immediate posttest (the two experimental groups only)
- A month after the intervention: delayed posttest

Pre/posttests: Picture-based acceptability judgment tasks, in which participants rated how well a sentence matched a picture, on a 1-to-4 scale; for the target sentences, the picture depicted either the surface-scope or the inverse-scope reading; the configurations in both (119a–b) were tested, to check for generalization. See Figures 9.4 and 9.5.

The intervention: Explicit information about the ambiguity of the sentence type in either (119a) or (119b), depending on the group.
   Practice items in the form of a context followed by a sentence; for the target items, the context matched either the surface-scope or the inverse-scope reading, and participants judged the sentence as either true or false in the context; automatic feedback was provided for each item, which included both information about whether the response was correct or incorrect, and a metalinguistic explanation.

BOX 9.2 (cont.)

Results: Mean ratings for sentences with IS readings. (Only results for sentences with IS readings given here; sentences with SS readings were rated close to ceiling across all tests and all groups.)

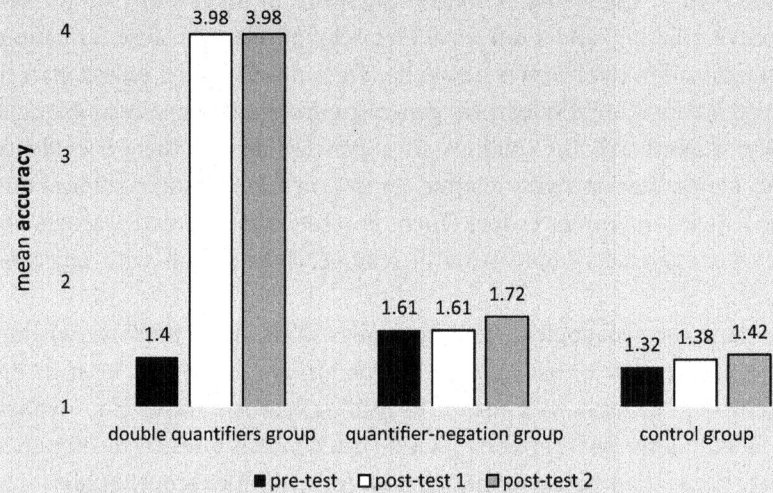

Figure 9.6 Mean acceptability ratings on the double-quantifier configuration by group (based on data from Wu & Ionin, 2022a)

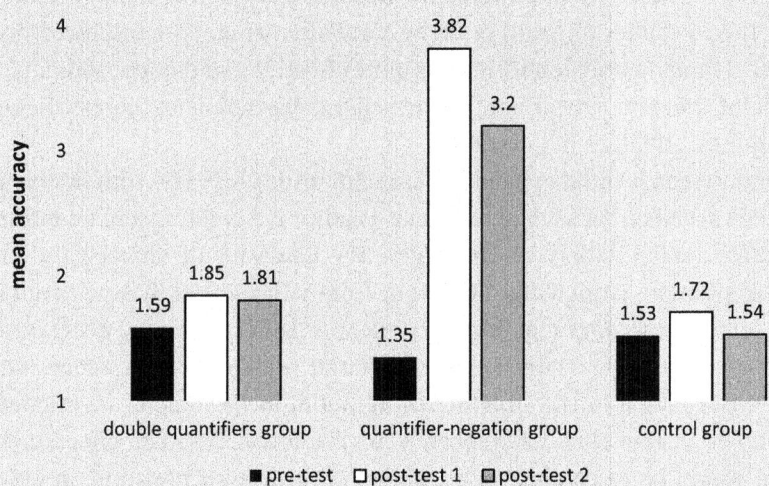

Figure 9.7 Mean acceptability ratings on the quantifier-negation configuration by group (based on data from Wu & Ionin, 2022a)

9.5 Summary and Implications

In this chapter, we have discussed four separate phenomena (sentence-level word order, adjective ordering, relative clauses, and quantifier scope), all of which involve sentence-level or phrase-level syntactic structures. Many of the intervention studies covered in this chapter have their starting point in linguistic theory. These studies address questions of universality (universals of adjective ordering, and a universal hierarchy of relative clause formation) and generalization (do learners generalize from more marked to less marked types of relativization? Do learners generalize from one scopally ambiguous structure to another?). The findings are somewhat mixed: There is evidence both for generalization (with relative clauses, at least in some studies) and against it (with quantifier scope). There is some evidence that learners are sensitive to universals (more so with relative clauses than with adjective ordering).

Turning to the pedagogical side, the studies summarized here overwhelmingly provide evidence that explicit instruction is effective, at least in the short term and at least with regard to leading learners to develop explicit knowledge. Improvement after explicit instruction was attested for adjective ordering, for relative clause formation, and for quantifier scope. Studies that took a more fine-grained look at the nature of explicit instruction paint a more nuanced picture: With regard to relative clauses, S. Izumi (2002) found that output practice played a more important role than input enhancement (though the efficacy of output practice was not replicated in Izumi & Izumi, 2004). The PI studies on word order by VanPatten et al. (2013) showed that structured input instruction by itself is quite effective and that the addition of explicit information may or may not be helpful, depending on the specifics of the linguistic structure in question.

Further research could expand the crosslinguistic coverage, with intervention studies addressing such phenomena as adjective ordering and quantifier scope in a greater variety of languages. The questions of universality and generalization are particularly important from a theoretical SLA perspective and deserve further investigation. At present, it is not clear why generalization is attested with relative clauses but not with quantifier scope, and whether this is due to the structure in question, to the type of instruction, or to other factors such as frequency in the input. Another direction to expand would be to conduct more studies with delayed posttests, in order to examine the retention of knowledge gained from explicit instruction over months or even years.

9.6 DISCUSSION QUESTIONS

1. Consider the various studies about relative clauses covered in section 9.3. Classify each one with regard to whether the instruction is more explicit or more implicit, and whether the pre/posttests target more explicit or more implicit knowledge. What can you conclude about the efficacy of explicit vs. implicit instruction and its relationship to the development of explicit vs. implicit knowledge, in this particular domain?
2. Discuss the findings of VanPatten et al. (2013), summarized in Box 9.1. Address the following points in your discussion. What accounts for the different findings across the four different languages? Which is the better measure of success, trials-to-criterion, or posttest performance, and why?
3. Consider the findings of Wu and Ionin (2022a), summarized in Box 9.2. Explain the patterns in the data: On which structures does each group of learners improve? On which structures does each group not improve? Are there any surprising findings in the data, and if so, what do you think they indicate?

9.7 APPLICATIONS QUESTIONS

1. The studies on German, Russian, and French summarized in VanPatten et al. (2013) are also reported in greater depth in VanPatten and Borst (2012a); VanPatten, Collopy, and Qualin (2012), and VanPatten and Price, (2012), respectively. Read one of these publications and identify the various study components. What is the strategy/default principle that learners need to overcome? What was the nature of the explicit instruction? How was grammatical sensitivity measured? What is the pattern of findings, and how is it explained?
2. Read Stringer (2013) (in particular section 5.4) to obtain more background about the different types of adjectives and the SLA findings on adjective ordering. Explain what makes an adjective absolute vs. non-absolute. Classify adjectives that denote opinions (e.g., *dangerous*) vs. materials (e.g., *wooden*) vs. colors (e.g., *blue*) as absolute vs. nonabsolute. Is your classification the same as the one laid out in Stringer (2013)? What are the criteria for classifying adjectives?
3. Conduct an empirical test of the NPAH (discussed in section 9.3.1). Find speakers of as many different languages as you can and ask them to translate the six RC types listed in (114). If a given language lacks any of

the types in (114), does it always lack the more marked RC types, as predicted by the NPAH? Or do you find any violations of the NPAH? As another possible test of the NPAH, find a low-proficiency L2 English learner and ask them to combine two simple sentences into a complex sentence: For example, for (114a), they would need to put together 'I fed the cat' and 'The cat came into our back yard' into a single sentence; for (114b), they would need to put together 'I fed the cat' and 'My daughter brought home the cat'. And so on. Is the learners' performance consistent with the NPAH? Do they have an easier time putting together complex sentences that contain subject RCs than those that contain direct object RCs? Are comparative RCs the most difficult of all? And so on.

9.8 FURTHER READING

- Izumi, S. (2007). Universals, methodology and instructional intervention on relative clauses. *Studies in Second Language Acquisition, 29*(2), 351–359.
  This introduction to a special issue of the journal provides an overview of L2 acquisition research on relative clauses, with a focus on the noun phrase accessibility hierarchy.

- Gil, K.-H., Marsden, H., & Whong, M. (2013). Quantifiers: Form and meaning in second language development. In M. Whong, K.-H. Gil, & H. Marsden (Eds.), *Universal Grammar and the second language classroom* (pp. 139–159). Dordrecht: Springer.
  This chapter links theoretical and classroom research on quantifiers in the L2, providing an overview of the relevant prior research.

- Stringer, D. (2013). Modifying the teaching of modifiers: A lesson from Universal Grammar. In M. Whong, K.-H. Gil, & H. Marsden (Eds.), *Universal Grammar and the second language classroom* (pp. 77–100). Dordrecht: Springer.
  This chapter provides an overview of ordering constraints on the ordering of modifiers, including adjectives, and presents corresponding findings from L2 acquisition.

10 Where to Go Next

When **second language acquisition** (SLA) emerged as a field in the 1960s, it was strongly linked to pedagogical concerns. Over the years, starting with the ideas of Krashen (1982), the relationship between cognitive, linguistic, and social aspects of SLA and language pedagogy has weakened. The result has been that SLA as a theoretical field and Second Language Teaching (SLT) have become two different fields, in many ways unrelated to each other. Among the few exceptions to link SLA and language teaching during this time have been the **Processability Theory** and **Teachability Hypothesis** of Pienemann (1984, 1989, 1998) and **input processing instruction** (PI) of VanPatten (1996, 2002, 2004). VanPatten's work, covered in many chapters of this textbook, became a model of intervention research design. Another theory that links SLA and SLT is sociocultural theory (Lantolf & Poehner, 2008; vanCompernolle & Williams, 2013), but as this theory is not specifically about grammatical development, we do not discuss it further.

In the past few years there has been growing recognition that linguistics and SLA must do more to inform second language learning in the classroom (see, e.g., Whong, Gil, & Marsden, 2013), and that the two fields must relate to each other fruitfully. In this volume we have explored the relationship between linguistic theory, the SLA of different aspects of morphology, syntax, and semantics, and language teaching. We have examined existing intervention research motivated by linguistic and pedagogical research questions, including but not limited to studies of developmental sequences in the framework of Pienemann (1989) and studies on input processing instruction (VanPatten, 1996). In this closing chapter, we review what we have learned so far in this book. First, we summarize the main themes that have emerged from the studies in this volume. Subsequently, we offer some suggestions for where to go next.

We have organized this chapter differently from the preceding chapters. Instead of asking discussion questions at the end of the chapter, we pose one or two discussion questions for each section or subsection. Our goal with this format is to encourage our readers to engage in reflection and discussion about the themes below. For more advanced students, these themes could generate new ideas for term papers, undergraduate or master's theses, or other research projects.

10.1 Efficacy of Different Instructional Approaches

The studies discussed in this book have examined the efficacy of a variety of both more explicit and more implicit instructional approaches for SLA (see Chapter 1). Our focus is the development of **interlanguage** grammars, and how learners build grammatical representations in time, from initial state to intermediate levels of development and to the final state, which may be native-like or not (recall Figure 1.2 in Chapter 1, repeated below as Figure 10.1).

Although classroom language and instruction is part of the exposure that L2 learners experience, it is still debatable whether this information actually becomes input that feeds the grammatical representation (Schwartz & Gubala-Ryzak, 1992; Leeser, 2021). Nearly all of the studies in this book incorporated explicit grammar instruction with more meaning-based or communicative activities. That is, they adopted, to varying degrees, the principles of focus on form approaches discussed in Chapter 2.

In this section, we reflect on the studies mentioned in this book in order to draw some conclusions about the relative efficacy of different approaches to grammar instruction. In the next section we consider what these findings may tell us about how instruction affects grammatical restructuring at the level of implicit linguistic knowledge, which is what SLA strives to elucidate.

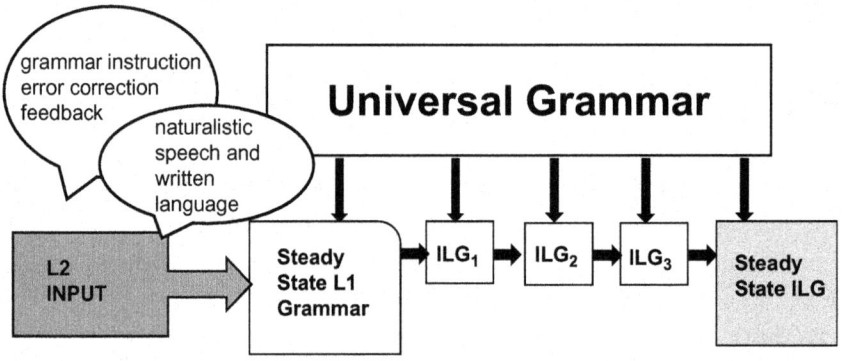

Figure 10.1 A representation of the Full Transfer/Full Access Model of Universal Grammar in L2 acquisition (Schwartz & Sprouse, 1996) with a role for instruction (adapted from L. White, 2003b).

10.1.1 Efficacy of Explicit Output-Based Instruction

The studies discussed in this book that used some form of explicit rule presentation combined with output-based instruction generally found this instructional approach to be effective. More specifically, they found that instruction with explicit grammatical information led to improvement, at least in the short term. In contrast to explicit instruction, implicit grammar instruction involves making some aspects of the input salient (through visual enhancement or frequency of exposure) and letting the learners discover the grammatical rules on their own. Studies that compared explicit and implicit grammatical instruction with instructed adult (or in a few cases, adolescent) learners, for the most part, found explicit instruction to lead to greater improvements (again, in the short term). Let us consider some examples.

In the case of English articles (Chapter 3), Master (1994) found that L2 learners improved in their accuracy of article use (as measured by fairly explicit test instruments) following explicit instruction. In the domain of adverb placement (Chapter 4), L. White (1990, 1991) similarly found improvement in English adverb placement after explicit rule presentation. Turning to verbal morphology (Chapter 5), Tode (2007) found that explicit instruction on the copula *be* was more effective than implicit instruction, at least in the short term (with the explicit advantage decreasing on delayed posttests). Lichtman (2013) found a long-term advantage of explicit instruction in the domain of Spanish verb conjugations. In particular, on an explicit task, high-school students who received explicit instruction at school outperformed those who received more implicit Teaching Proficiency through Reading and Storytelling (TPRS) instruction. In contrast, the two groups performed similarly on a more implicit task.

The efficacy of explicit instruction is confirmed by studies of more complex syntactic phenomena. For example, Torres (2018) (Chapter 6) found form-focused instruction was beneficial in the domain of the Spanish subjunctive (with a simpler task having more success than a complex task). Similarly, S. Izumi and Lakshmanan (1998) and Jung (2019) both found explicit instruction to be effective in teaching about the English passive (Chapter 7); while the former study used explicit rule presentation, the latter used the consciousness-raising technique. Along the same lines, Yip (1994) and Hirakawa (2013) both found improvement on errors with unaccusative verbs after explicit instruction. Communicative explicit instruction was also effective with the use of clitic *se* with Spanish unaccusatives (Toth & Guijarro-Fuentes, 2013); furthermore, this improvement was observed both in a more explicit **grammaticality judgment task (GJT)** and a more implicit task (production).

In the case of **Differential Object Marking (DOM)** in Spanish (Chapter 8), both L2 learners (Bowles & Montrul, 2009) and heritage speakers (Montrul &

Bowles, 2010) were found to benefit from explicit instruction. With regard to double objects in English (Chapter 8), Radwan (2005) found that explicit rule-oriented instruction was more effective than the more implicit approaches of content-oriented instruction and textual enhancement.

Explicit instruction has led to improvement in word-order manipulations as well (Chapter 9). L2 learners have been found to improve in their performance with relative clauses after explicit form-focused instruction, in multiple studies (English: Eckman, Bell, & Nelson, 1988; Doughty, 1991; S. Izumi, 2002 – though Izumi's findings were not replicated in Izumi & Izumi, 2004; Japanese: Yabuki-Soh, 2007). Hirakawa, Shibuya, and Endo (2018) found that L2-English learners improved on adjective ordering with form-focused explicit instruction but did not improve after naturalistic exposure or input flooding. Finally, with regard to quantifier scope, Wu and Ionin (2022a) found that explicit instruction about availability of inverse scope led to improvement for the structure that the learners had been taught.

In sum, we see that across linguistic domains and L1/L2 combinations, explicit form-focused output-based instruction and rule presentation is generally found to be effective in improving target language performance among adult (and adolescent) learners. This is consistent with meta-analyses carried out on the role of instruction, in general, and of the superiority of explicit instruction, in particular, over two decades ago (Norris & Ortega, 2000). While the tasks that measure improvement are in most cases tasks that tend to elicit explicit knowledge and application of grammatical rules, there is at least some evidence that learners gain implicit linguistic knowledge as well. Some of the studies discussed above used production or elicited imitation tasks, which appear to tap more implicit knowledge, in order to measure performance. However, we still don't know whether and to what extent the knowledge gained from explicit instruction is retained in the long term. We also don't know whether explicit instruction contributes to grammatical restructuring and implicit knowledge. Most studies that compare explicit and implicit instruction find a greater benefit from the former (at least in the short term), but once again, we do not know whether this advantage is maintained in the long term. A rare study that included posttests a year later (L. White, 1990, 1991) found that improvement in English adverb placement after explicit rule presentation was not retained a year after instruction.

Discussion Question 1 Pick one or two of the studies mentioned in this subsection and check the form of the pre/posttests used in those studies. (You can find this information in the corresponding chapters.) What do these tests measure? What type of knowledge are learners gaining in the course of the intervention?

10.1.2 Efficacy of Implicit Instruction

As we have seen, explicit instruction on grammar yields important behavioral changes in target language accuracy after treatment. At the same time, some studies do find improvement following more implicit instructional techniques. However, the evidence is mixed.

Going back to the domain of adverb placement (Chapter 4), Trahey and White (1993) found that learners taught with the more implicit approach of input flooding improved, just as the explicitly taught learners in L. White (1991) did. However, while the learners receiving the implicit treatment improved on their acceptance of the target structure (SAVO), they did not unlearn the nontarget structure transferred from L1 French (*SVAO), and they incorrectly assumed that with intransitive verbs, adverbs could not occur between the verb and a prepositional phrase (SVAPP) in English. Furthermore, the knowledge that the learners did gain was not retained a year later (Trahey, 1996). In the case of adverb placement, neither explicit rule presentation, as mentioned earlier, nor the more implicit input flooding led to long-term effects. In a different adverb-placement study, Reinders and Ellis (2009) found that neither input enhancement nor input enrichment led to improvement on tasks targeting either explicit or implicit knowledge.

With regard to question formation in L2 English (Chapter 4), a number of studies have found improvement following implicit instruction, at least in the short term. L. White et al. (1991) found that input enhancement led to improvement with question formation. Mackey (1999) similarly found improvement after an interaction-based treatment, while McDonough and Mackey (2008) found improvement following syntactic priming. Syntactic priming was also found to be quite effective with English double-object constructions (McDonough, 2006 and Kaan & Chun, 2018; Chapter 8) and clitic doubling in Spanish (Hurtado & Montrul, 2021a, 2021b; Chapter 8). For more on syntactic priming in SLA and in language teaching, see Trofimovich and McDonough (2011).

The previous section noted a number of studies in which explicit instruction was more effective than implicit instruction. However, some studies find the two methods to be equally effective. In Jung (2019), a study on the English passive (Chapter 7), the more implicit input-enhancement method yielded as much improvement as the more explicit consciousness-raising method. Similarly, Doughty (1991) found that meaning-focused instruction was as effective as rule-oriented instruction with English relative clauses (Chapter 9).

In sum, such implicit instructional methods as input enhancement, meaning-based instruction and syntactic priming have yielded positive results in at least some studies. In contrast, incidental exposure alone, with no instruction, was found to lead to no improvement in Loewen, Erlam, and Ellis (2009), a study on number agreement (Chapter 5).

Overall, implicit instruction leads to fewer positive results than explicit instruction. One reason for this is likely the fairly short timeline of most intervention studies, which may prevent implicit instruction from having an effect. Structural priming as an instructional tool seems to yield most promising results, but again, information about improvement is mostly confined to the short term. More research needs to be done in this area.

Discussion Question 2 Pick one study discussed in this section that uses input flooding and/or input enhancement and another study that uses syntactic priming. Discuss how these two techniques compare. (You can check the corresponding chapters for study details). What makes each of these instructional approaches an implicit rather than an explicit approach? Which technique seems to be more effective, and why do you think this is the case?

10.1.3 Efficacy of Structured Input and Input Processing Instruction

Many of the studies discussed in this book manipulated the input during the intervention, and/or compared the efficacy of structured input activities relative to more traditional output-based instruction. All of these studies were either done directly in the processing instruction framework (VanPatten, 1996, 2002, 2004) or else were based on this framework.

Multiple studies found that input-based instruction was more effective than either traditional or modified output-based instruction (Cadierno, 1995 and Benati, 2001, 2005 on tense marking in different languages, Chapter 5; multiple studies on the Spanish subjunctive in Chapter 6; VanPatten & Cadierno, 1993 and Leeser & DeMil, 2013 on Spanish clitics, Chapter 8). In particular, these studies typically found that while both input-based and output-based instruction led to improvements in production, the former was more effective in improving comprehension. Additionally, Leeser & DeMil (2013) found that input processing instruction with Spanish clitics led to improvement not only with accusative clitics or direct object pronouns (the primary target) but also with dative clitics or indirect object pronouns that appeared with psych verbs, indicating transfer-of-training. J. F. Lee and Benati (2007) as well as J. F. Lee (2015, 2019) found transfer-of-training effects from passives (primary target) to the interpretation of subject and object pronouns in anaphoric contexts (secondary targets) (Chapter 7). In a different instructional comparison, Chiuchiù and Benati (2020) found that structured input instruction was more effective than textual enhancement with the Italian subjunctive (Chapter 6).

A few other studies found that input-based and output-based approaches were equally effective in leading to improvement (Collentine, 1995; Farley, 2001b, and Farley & McCollam, 2004 on the Spanish subjunctive, Chapter 6) or that input-based instruction was less effective than output-based instruction (Erlam, Loewen, & Philp, 2009 on English articles, Chapter 3; Toth, 2006 on the Spanish clitic *se*, Chapter 7).

Overall, input processing instruction is found to be at least as effective as traditional instruction in production, and often more effective for comprehension. Given the general efficacy of this approach, later studies have manipulated specific aspects of this approach, rather than comparing input-based instruction to other teaching methods. For example, Benati and Angelovska (2015) (tense marking, Chapter 5) showed that both children and adults benefited from input processing instruction, but that task complexity played out differently in these two populations. J. White (2015) (Chapter 8) examined the amount and intensity of input on accusative clitics as measured in number of tokens during the intervention. Farley and McCollam (2004) on DOM in Spanish (Chapter 8), VanPatten et al. (2013) on word order in different languages (Chapter 9), and Fernández Cuenca (2019) on the Spanish subjunctive (Chapter 6) manipulated the presence of explicit information in addition to structured input and found that explicit information matters in some but not all cases.

In sum, processing instruction has been clearly shown to be effective in improving learners' comprehension of grammatical phenomena, and, at least in some studies, their production as well. This is because, according to Leeser (2021), this framework is firmly based on a theory of linguistic knowledge and of language processing. Instruction in this framework seeks to change the way L2 learners convert input into intake, at the precise moment during comprehension when learners are making form-meaning connections that enter the language module and developing interlanguage system.

Discussion Question 3 Pick two of the studies discussed in this subsection (check the corresponding chapters for study details): one which showed a benefit of input processing instruction over output-based instruction, and another that found no advantage for input processing instruction. Read more about these studies in the corresponding chapters and discuss why they yielded different results. Do you think the difference is due to different linguistic phenomena, the specifics of how the intervention was done, the length of the intervention, the learners' proficiency, or some other factor?

10.1.4 Efficacy of Different Feedback Types

Finally, let's reflect on those studies that focused on the relative efficacy of different types of corrective feedback. Throughout this book, we have seen studies that used explicit corrective feedback (such as direct error correction), with and/or without metalinguistic explanation, as well as more implicit feedback (recasts).

Explicit feedback was found to improve performance with articles (Sheen, 2007, Chapter 3) as well as double objects (Carroll & Swain, 1993, Chapter 8): Both studies found that metalinguistic feedback, in which the nature of the error was explained to the learners, was more effective than simple correction. R. Ellis, Loewen, and Erlam (2006) (tense marking, Chapter 5) found metalinguistic feedback to be more effective than recasts, leading to greater improvement in both more a more explicit task (GJT) and a more implicit one (elicited imitation). At the same time, a number of studies found recasts to be quite effective (Long, Inagaki, & Ortega, 1998 on both adverb placement, Chapter 4, and adjective ordering, Chapter 9; Han, 2002 on tense marking, Chapter 5). Leeman (2003) on grammatical gender in Spanish (Chapter 5) was able to pinpoint the source of the effectiveness of recasts as lying in enhanced positive evidence rather than negative evidence alone. Two other studies on grammatical gender (Lyster, 2004a and Ammar & Spada, 2006) found that prompts, which encouraged learners to correct their errors, were more effective than recasts, which did not. McDonough (2005), a study of question formation (Chapter 4), similarly found that learners improved more when they were given opportunity to modify their output, compared to receiving negative feedback without an opportunity to modify.

In sum, corrective feedback is generally quite effective. Two aspects of corrective feedback appear to make it especially effective: (i) providing a metalinguistic explanation of the error; or (ii) pushing learners to modify their output, i.e., to correct the error, rather than simply receiving the negative feedback.

Discussion Question 4 In the context of the studies summarized above, discuss why both metalinguistic feedback and an opportunity to modify output appear to be more effective than correction or feedback alone.

10.1.5 Summary

We have seen that a number of different instructional approaches are effective at least in the short term and at least with regard to gains in explicit knowledge. Some studies provide evidence for gains in implicit knowledge as well (as measured by production or psycholinguistic tasks), but very few studies follow learners for more than a few weeks after the intervention, which means that we still do not know much about long-term gains. With regard to the efficacy of different methods, input processing instruction has perhaps the best track record of improving learners' performance in both production and comprehension of grammatical phenomena. This said, explicit output-based instruction has also led to improvement. Among more implicit instructional techniques, structural priming has led to improvements in some recent studies. With regard to feedback, both metalinguistic feedback and more implicit feedback in the form of recasts and prompts have been found to lead to improvements. For more on the efficacy of different instructional techniques, we refer the interested reader to the meta-analyses of Norris and Ortega (2000), Spada and Tomita (2010), and Goo et al. (2015), among others.

10.2 Intervention Research and Linguistic Representations

The previous section provided a synthesis of the relative effectiveness of different instructional approaches for the linguistic phenomena discussed in this book. It is now time to reflect on the question that opened this textbook: How does intervention research relate to theoretical SLA and to linguistic theory? More specifically, what can intervention studies tell us about the nature of learners' linguistic representations, and, conversely, how can linguistic theories and theories of SLA inform language teaching?

10.2.1 The Role of the First Language

As discussed in Chapter 1, research in formal generative SLA places great importance on the role of learners' first language (or their dominant language, in the case of heritage language speakers), also known as transfer. Many influential theories of SLA, including the Full Transfer/Full Access model (FT/FA) (Schwartz & Sprouse, 1996) and the Feature Reassembly Hypothesis (FRH; Lardiere, 2009), allot a major role to the L1. On the FT/FA, learners transfer the entirety of their L1 grammar, including all functional categories and features, at the initial state of their L2 acquisition; on the FRH, learners have to reassemble features on L2 morphemes when there are differences between the L1 and the L2. Experimental SLA studies often compare L2 learners from two (or more) different L1s, which differ with regard to the linguistic phenomenon in questions; the results often provide support for crosslinguistic influence or L1 transfer (see Slabakova, 2016 for an overview).

Given the importance of the L1 in SLA literature, what can we learn about the role of the L1 from intervention studies? In some domains, the role of the

L1 is largely ignored. In particular, intervention studies on question formation (Chapter 4), inflectional morphology (Chapter 5), and relative clauses (Chapter 9) generally do not isolate the effects of the L1, and do not consider how the corresponding structure behaves in the L1. Similarly, many input processing studies, discussed throughout this book, do not consider how L1 sentence processing may impact the ways in which L2 learners convert input into intake.

At the same time, those intervention studies that are motivated by linguistic theory often do consider the role of the L1, focusing on linguistic structures that work differently in the L1 and the L2. For example, the studies on adverb–verb order discussed in Chapter 4 (L. White, 1991 and beyond) have the syntactic difference in verb-raising between the L1 (French) and the L2 (English) as their starting point. The same is true for studies on passive formation that contrast passives in English and in Japanese (see Chapter 7). The L1 is also addressed by studies on sentence-level word order, adjective placement, and quantifier scope (Chapter 9), which focus on L1–L2 pairs in which the L1 has a different word order (or scope interpretation) from the L2.

Other studies look at L2 phenomena that have no L1 equivalent. This is the case for intervention studies on English articles with learners from article-less L1s (Chapter 3), or on Spanish DOM (Chapter 8) or Spanish subjunctive (Chapter 6) with learners whose L1 or dominant language is English, a language with no DOM and very limited subjunctive morphology.

However, none of these studies compare L2 learners from two L1s that differ in the relevant respect. For example, the study by VanPatten et al. (2013) (Chapter 9) starts with the basic fact that English speakers learning languages with flexible word order tend to assign the role of agent to the first noun in the sentence. This intervention study examined how processing instruction can help learners overcome this default strategy. However, VanPatten et al. (2013) did not consider whether learners whose L1 already has flexible word order (e.g., German-speaking learners of Russian) would adopt a similar strategy or be helped by a similar intervention.

In the same vein, L. White (1991) and Trahey and White (1993) found that French-speaking learners of English allow French verb–adverb order in English; these studies used different instructional techniques to teach these learners the correct order for English. However, these studies did not include learners whose L1 (e.g., Chinese) has adverb–verb order like English, or explore how such learners might respond to the intervention. One exception – a study that did compare L2 learners with two different L1s – was Benati (2005), a study on tense marking discussed in Chapter 5; see discussion question 6 at the end of this subsection for more about this study.

There are many reasons why intervention studies generally do not include comparisons of multiple L1s. Some of these reasons are purely practical and relate to the availability of participants. For example, researchers working with English-speaking college students learning Spanish do not have ready access to a different L1 population of L2-Spanish learners. Given that many intervention studies are conducted with actual classrooms, controlling for the native language is often not ecologically valid. For example, White's studies on adverb placement discussed above were conducted with French-speaking learners of English in Montreal who were in an English immersion program. There was no other L1 population in a similar immersion program in the same location.

On a more conceptual level, researchers who conduct interventions are interested in helping learners acquire aspects of the L2 that are particularly challenging. Such challenging aspects of the L2 often correspond to properties that are absent or different in the learners' L1. The focus, then, is on helping learners acquire novel linguistic properties in the L2, rather than on comparing learners from different L1s. Therefore, we have to keep in mind that the efficacy of a given intervention does not necessarily generalize to learners from other L1s or to other L1–L2 combinations.

In sum, the intervention studies discussed in this book either largely disregard the role of the L1 or focus on L1/L2 pairs where the L1 clearly differs from the L2 in the relevant domain. Virtually nonexistent are intervention studies that compare two different L1 groups, one that behaves like the L2 on a given structure and one that is different, which is the standard design in experimental SLA studies that examine the role of L1 transfer. As a result, intervention studies cannot at present tell us much about L1 transfer. For example, we know from experimental SLA literature that learners whose L1 has articles tend to outperform those whose L1 lacks articles, but we also know that both groups do make article errors. In light of that, it would be interesting to find out whether the same instructional approaches are equally valid for both groups. The same question can be asked about teaching grammatical gender, DOM, quantifier scope, and all the other phenomena discussed in this book.

We encourage the readers of this volume to consider future intervention studies which carefully control for L1 transfer by comparing learners from different L1s. Such comparisons would advance the field in at least two different ways. First, they would provide additional evidence about the role of L1 transfer in SLA. Second, on a practical level, they would provide novel information about whether the same instructional approaches work for L2 learners from different L1s.

Discussion Question 5 Pick one of the studies discussed above; check the corresponding chapters for study details. Propose how the study could be replicated and extended in order to investigate L1 transfer. Specifically, propose a comparison of at least two different L1 groups so that the L1s differ from each other in the relevant respect (e.g., one behaves like the L2 on the target structure while the other behaves differently). If L1 transfer is at work in this linguistic domain, how would you expect the two groups to behave on the pretest? What predictions might you make for the efficacy of the intervention in these two groups?

Discussion Question 6 Consider the study by Benati (2005), discussed in Chapter 5. This is one of very few intervention studies that compared L2 learners from two different L1s. Specifically, this study of tense marking in L2 English compared speakers of Greek (a language which has tense marking) with speakers of Chinese (a language with no tense marking). This intervention study did not set out to investigate the role of L1 transfer, focusing instead on the efficacy of processing instruction across different populations. Nevertheless, the results do potentially inform us about L1 transfer. Discuss what Benati's study tells us about both the role of L1 transfer and about the efficacy of processing instruction across different L1s.

10.2.2 Linguistic Theory and Intervention Research

Next, we consider one of the central questions in this book: How does linguistic theory inform intervention research, and vice versa?

10.2.2.1 Different Approaches to Grammar

First of all, as discussed in Chapter 1, descriptive and theoretical linguistics seek to describe and explain the implicit grammatical system that native speakers have for their native language, regardless of prescriptive or normative grammar rules. Now, pedagogical grammars are grammars that may be related to some extent to abstract linguistic grammars, but often the rules of pedagogical grammars are simplistic at best and incomplete. For example, Spanish has two copula or linking verbs, *ser* and *estar*, both of which correspond to the verb *be* in English. Many grammar books explain the rules and distribution of these two verbs in Spanish as follows: *ser* is used with adjectives that express permanent attributes whereas *estar* is used with temporary attributes or states. However, this explanation does not fully capture the linguistic knowledge and internalized rules that native speakers of Spanish have. For example, *to be dead* is a permanent state, yet it is expressed with *estar* (*estar muerto*). Locations are expressed with *estar* (*La biblioteca está en la esquina* 'The library is on the corner'), but the location of event nominals (*fiesta* 'party', *funeral* 'funeral') is expressed with *ser* (*La fiesta es en la esquina* 'The party is on the corner'). The aspectual properties of *ser* and *estar* are not typically captured in pedagogical grammars.

Many pedagogical rules are not actual rules that govern speakers' linguistic knowledge. For example, Bruhn de Garavito (1997), a study of the coreference restrictions of the subjunctive in temporal clauses, mentioned in Chapter 6, found that the implicit knowledge that advanced L2 learners develop surpasses or goes beyond the misleading and incomplete rules that L2 learners are exposed to in the classroom. A pedagogical grammar that is linguistically informed and that successfully captures (most of) the rules and constraints that actually govern speakers' grammars is likely to be of value in language teaching. Linguistically informed intervention research can thus contribute to the development of more accurate pedagogical grammars. We next discuss how linguistic theory and analysis can enhance intervention research.

10.2.2.2 The Importance of Linguistic Analysis for Intervention Research

Most studies discussed in this book assume a particular analysis of the structure in question based on theoretical linguistic and/or experimental SLA literature. In the absence of an analysis of DOM, for example, or inverse scope, or unaccusatives, or the subjunctive, it would not even occur to researchers to do intervention studies on this topic. Theoretical linguistic analyses, together with experimental research, provide psycholinguistically accurate descriptions of the relevant constructions. Prior SLA studies provide information about the kinds of challenges that learners face and the kinds of errors they tend to make.

For example, several studies of articles reviewed in Chapter 3 adopt particular theoretical analyses of article semantics, which capture the role that semantic notions like definiteness, specificity, genericity, and kind reference play in the distribution and interpretation of articles. The studies on question formation in Chapter 4 have as their starting point the Processability Theory of Pienemann (1984, 1989, 1998), which identifies developmental stages in this domain. All of the studies on the subjunctive in Chapter 6 are informed by a valid linguistic analysis of the subjunctive. However, many of the intervention studies on this topic were done with lower-proficiency learners, while SLA studies generally find that the subjunctive is mastered much later in development.

The intervention studies on unaccusative verbs (Chapter 7) are informed by the Unaccusative Hypothesis (Perlmutter, 1978) and the Unaccusativity

Hierarchy (Sorace, 2000). In the same vein, the studies on double objects and DOM (Chapter 8) are informed by the linguistic literature about the semantic constraints on the syntax of objects.

None of the intervention studies mentioned above would have been possible without prior theoretical linguistic and/or SLA literature that provided a particular linguistic analysis. These analyses can and must inform pedagogical grammars. For example, in order to teach learners that unaccusatives cannot occur in passive form (as in *The plane was arrived*, see Chapter 7), researchers and teachers first need to understand the difference between unaccusative and unergative intransitive verbs. They also need to be familiar with the findings from SLA literature that unaccusative verbs, but not unergative verbs, are overpassivized in SLA (e.g., Zobl, 1989). This knowledge can then help focus the instruction on the verbs that are more likely to be incorrectly passivized. Similarly, the article intervention studies of Snape and Yusa (2013), Lopez (2019), and Umeda et al. (2019) discussed in Chapter 3 are based on prior SLA research on the kinds of challenges that L2-English learners face. These studies would not have been conducted without the prior research that indicated, for example, that learners mistakenly associate the definite article with specificity (Ionin, Ko, & Wexler, 2004).

While linguistic analyses can fruitfully guide teaching interventions, not all of the studies based on linguistic theory we have covered in this textbook were equally successful. In particular, the linguistically informed studies on articles mentioned above did not find much improvement, perhaps because the materials were too complex for the learners. Other studies were more successful: For instance, Bowles and Montrul (2009) as well as Montrul and Bowles (2010), studies informed by linguistic analysis of Spanish DOM, were able to improve L2 learners' and heritage speakers' performance with DOM marking.

We note that not all intervention studies are equally linguistically informed. In particular, many of the studies on inflectional morphology (Chapter 5) and sentence-level word order (Chapter 9) have their starting point in the simple fact that learners make errors (such as omitting tense marking or using incorrect word order). However, these studies often do not adopt a particular syntactic analysis of the structure under consideration or address the question (discussed in Chapter 5) of whether learners' difficulties indicate a deep impairment to the representation or a more "shallow" problem. We suggest that this is another direction for future research: to conduct intervention studies on such topics as tense/agreement marking or word order within a particular theoretical framework. For example, an intervention study looking at both syntactic and morphological reflexes of tense could potentially help address the question of representation vs. surface inflection (see Chapter 5). An intervention study that adopts a particular analysis of object scrambling might consider the relationship between word order and a variety of both semantic and discourse factors (such as scope and information structure).

Discussion Question 7 Why do you think some intervention studies (e.g., the ones on articles or DOM) adopt a particular linguistic analysis while others do not (e.g., the ones on inflectional morphology or sentence-level word order)? What is the benefit of starting an intervention study with a specific linguistic analysis? Are study results more or less informative and important for language teaching when they adopt a linguistic analysis than when they do not? Why?

Discussion Question 8 Some studies have found that even when explicit grammatical rules are informed by linguistic analyses, the intervention is still not effective in changing the interlanguage representation, as in the case of the adverb-placement studies conducted by L. White (1990, 1991), discussed in Chapter 4. Why is that so? Do you think that negative evidence and explicit grammar explanations, even if linguistically accurate, become intake for the developing grammatical system? Why or why not?

10.2.2.3 Generalization in Intervention

We saw that many intervention studies on grammatical phenomena are informed, to a greater or lesser extent, by linguistic theory. What is less common, however, is for linguistic theory to be informed by intervention research. One might ask, how can intervention research inform linguistic theory? One answer lies in generalization. If learners taught about one type of linguistic structure (the primary target) are able to generalize their knowledge to a different structure (the secondary target), this would validate or confirm linguistic analyses proposing that the two structures are related.

At present, the relevant data are fairly limited. In this book, we have seen several domains where generalization was addressed in intervention. The adverb-placement study by L. White (1990, 1991) discussed in Chapter 4 examined whether teaching L2-English learners about question formation would lead them to generalize to adverb placement, given that these two phenomena are both related to the verb-raising parameter. Following the logic of White's study, Wu and Ionin (2022a) (discussed in Chapter 9) examined whether teaching L2 English learners about inverse scope in one construction would lead the learners to generalize to a different construction, given that inverse scope is derived by the same mechanism in both cases. Both studies yielded null results with regard to generalization: The learners in both White's and Wu and Ionin's studies improved on the primary structure (the one that they were taught) but failed to generalize to the secondary structure. The results were more promising in several studies of relative clauses (Chapter 9), which found that learners taught about more marked RC types improved on less marked types as well, consistent with the NPAH. However, as discussed in Chapter 9, the evidence was somewhat mixed, with learners sometimes exhibiting improvement that did not fully align with the NPAH predictions. Furthermore, these studies for the most part failed to take into account the role of the L1, and the possibility that learners could be transferring their knowledge of relative clauses from the L1 to the L2.

There are also several studies that used input processing instruction, discussed in Chapters 7 and 8, that found transfer of training effects. For example Leeser and DeMil (2013) and J. White (2015) instructed learners on accusative object pronouns in Spanish and found that the knowledge learned was generalized to dative clitics with psychological verbs as well. J. F. Lee (2015, 2019) found that instruction on how to process word order in passive sentences in L2 Spanish generalized to similar word-order differences with subject and object pronouns in discourse.

There are many reasons why learners in some intervention studies failed to generalize as predicted. One possibility is that the phenomena in question are not in fact related linguistically. For example, maybe adverb placement and question formation are not part of the same parameter. Alternatively, one might say that learners past the critical age do not have access to Universal Grammar, as discussed in Chapter 1. Unlike children, perhaps adult learners do not have access to the underlying parameters or syntactic mechanisms, and instead learn language in a more "surface" fashion, one structure at a time (cf. Bley-Vroman, 1989, 1990, 2009).

Yet a third possibility, the one advocated by Schwartz (1993), is that explicit instruction cannot lead to true acquisition (of implicit knowledge), only to learning (of explicit knowledge) or surface rules (such as linear word order), as explained in Chapter 1. On this view, learners are capable of true acquisition of parameter settings and syntactic mechanisms, but such acquisition can only happen through exposure to naturalistic input, perhaps eventually through implicit instruction, but most likely not through explicit classroom instruction. As we saw in Chapter 1, this view is part of the noninterface position (Krashen, 1981 and beyond), according to which explicit and implicit learning are completely distinct.

In contrast, weak and strong interface positions argue that explicit knowledge can become implicit knowledge. Indeed, we have seen throughout this book that explicit instruction *can* lead learners to acquire implicit knowledge. We have seen that explicitly instructed learners do improve on both production (e.g., Lichtman, 2013; Toth & Guijarro-Fuentes, 2013) and elicited imitation (e.g., R. Ellis, Loewen, & Erlam, 2006), tasks which are more likely to tap into implicit knowledge than untimed GJTs. We have also seen that explicitly instructed learners improve on psycholinguistic measures such as eye tracking (e.g., Fernández Cuenca, 2019), which are even more likely to target underlying, implicit knowledge.

If learners are in fact capable of acquiring implicit knowledge through explicit instruction, then generalization from taught to untaught phenomena should in principle be possible, as long as the phenomena in question are related. So far, there have been far too few studies of generalization through intervention for any definitive conclusions to be reached.

Discussion Question 9 L. White (1990, 1991), discussed in Chapter 4, found that L2 learners did not learn the relationship between adverb placement and question formation subsumed under the verb-movement parameter. J. F. Lee (2015, 2019), discussed in Chapter 7, found that learners generalized the interpretation of agents and patients in different word orders in passive and active sentences with subject and object pronouns, although these phenomena were not linked to a single syntactic analysis. Finally, Leeser and DeMil (2013) and J. White (2015), discussed in Chapter 8, found that instruction on word-order interpretation of accusative object pronouns transferred to interpretation of dative clitics with psychological verbs in Spanish, even when no specific syntactic analysis was assumed to underlie these two phenomena. Why were the learners successful generalizing knowledge in some studies but not in others? Have the learners restructured their implicit grammatical knowledge in some studies but not in others? Or have the learners merely learned unrelated surface word order patterns in all these studies, as claimed by Schwartz and Gubala-Ryzak (1992), a critique of the L. White (1990, 1991) studies? What would be an argument in favor of one interpretation or the other?

10.2.2.4 Strengthening the Links

As we mentioned in the opening chapter, the theoretical study of second language acquisition seeks to understand the implicit linguistic system that second language learners develop, much like monolingual and bilingual L1 learners, over time. Language teaching and language instruction seek to help this process, and even accelerate it, by manipulating the exposure to the language in the classroom and by providing shortcuts in the form of explicit rule presentation, grammatical explanations, structured practice, and feedback.

We know that language learners change their linguistic behavior after instruction, but we still cannot tell if and how the implicit linguistic system is actually changed as a result of the interventions. Recall that Krashen (1982), Schwartz (1986), and to some extent VanPatten (1996) claim that positive evidence and language experienced in meaningful contexts favor the creation of form–meaning connections that feed into the implicit linguistic interlanguage system. How might links between linguistic theory, SLA, and intervention research be strengthened? We advocate conducting more intervention studies that are linguistically informed, testing for the role of L1 influence, and looking at learners' ability to generalize from one structure to another in a greater variety of linguistic domains. Below, we suggest several methodological points that could be addressed in future work, some of which rely on latest technologies.

10.3 Suggestions for Future Research

In this section, we consider the limitations of existing intervention studies and make suggestions for how these limitations can be overcome in future research.

10.3.1 Issues of Scope, Generalizability, and Study Length

One important criticism of most intervention studies of L2 and heritage language acquisition conducted to date is the fact that the studies are very small, with insufficient numbers of participants (Meurers et al., 2019). When the sample size is small, the likelihood of detecting statistically significant effects is diminished, and even if statistical differences are found, the generalizability of the results to other settings and populations is also limited. In this book, we have discussed studies with fewer than ten participants in total (e.g., Han, 2002) or with fewer than ten participants per group. At the same time, we have also discussed studies with more than thirty participants that, despite the larger sample size, found no effects (e.g., Loewen, Erlam, & Ellis, 2009). Most studies tend to focus on only one, or at most two, targeted linguistic structures. Furthermore, they target only one or at most two levels of proficiency, typically at earlier stages of development.

In sum, the findings of small-scale quasi-experimental studies are difficult to generalize to other contexts and populations, especially to language learning in school contexts. Larger-scale studies and/or large numbers of small-scale studies are needed to ensure that the findings replicate, allowing us to arrive at a better understanding of the phenomenon. Understandably, the nature of intervention studies is such that large-scale implementations may not be feasible, or at least have not been feasible up to now.

Related to scope, and the fact that most intervention studies have been carried out with university students enrolled in semester-long courses, is the length of the study. Most intervention studies discussed in this textbook take at most two to three months from pretest to delayed posttest, and the majority are much shorter than that. As discussed above, most studies have found that explicit instruction and corrective feedback are effective in the short term. When interventions involving implicit instruction are unsuccessful, it is hard to tell whether the lack of success is due to the short study timeline.

Studies of L2 acquisition by primary-school-age children immersed in schooling in the L2 show that it takes a minimum of five to seven years for children to reach native norms in the L2 vocabulary, syntax, and morphology in a natural school environment. This learning happens implicitly because children are learning content through the L2, without focus on form, focus on formS, or much correction (J. Paradis, 2011, 2019). Perhaps the best environment to examine implicit and explicit learning after intervention is in school settings, as in the studies of L. White (1990, 1991), Trahey and White (1993), and Trahey (1996), but with longer interventions than in those studies.

Long-lasting interventions are not always feasible, however. Something that has not been done very often but that could also indirectly tell us more about the length of time needed for implicit knowledge to develop would be interventions with L2 learners of different proficiency levels. The intervention may not work with beginner learners but may be effective with advanced proficiency learners. This could be particularly fruitful with aspects of grammar that are candidates for fossilization in particular language groups. Examples are the acquisition of English tense-marking by Chinese-speaking learners and the acquisition of articles by learners whose languages lack articles. Spanish DOM has been found to be still quite challenging with advanced-proficiency learners whose L1 does not have DOM (e.g. English) (Guijarro-Fuentes & Marinis, 2007).

The study of J. F. Lee (2019) included an experimental group with low proficiency in Spanish and a control group with advanced proficiency in Spanish, who received no treatment. Although comparing instructed low-proficiency level learners with uninstructed advanced learners seems odd, one of the goals of this study was to see how processing instruction with lower-proficiency speakers compared to simply more years of classroom experience. In other words, do you need to teach something early, or will learners eventually learn it implicitly later on just through regular classroom exposure? The alternative that we are proposing is doing the treatment with groups of different proficiency in the language. Will the instruction be more effective in earlier or in later stages of development? And what type of linguistic knowledge would it affect, explicit or implicit?

Discussion Question 10 Choose and contrast two different studies discussed in this textbook: one with a very small sample vs. one with a very large sample, or one with a very short timeline (a few days at most) vs. one with a long timeline (several months). You can use the summary tables in Chapters 3 through 9 to look for relevant studies to contrast. Do the larger-scale and/or longer studies always yield clearer results than the smaller-scale and/or shorter studies? What were some reasons behind the sample size and timeline/Were these always dictated by practical limitations, or were other considerations at play?

10.3.2 Nature of Intervention Activities

Leeser (2013) raises several issues related to the nature of the tasks and the instructions given to learners during intervention studies, and how these affect experimental outcomes. If the goal of second language acquisition is to understand L2 learners' implicit linguistic knowledge, then perhaps the nature of the interventions themselves needs to tap more into implicit knowledge. This is relevant for how the input is manipulated and what activities are used to practice the language structures of interest. As discussed in Chapter 1, we cannot assume that implicit and explicit instruction automatically lead to the acquisition of implicit and explicit knowledge, respectively. It is important to measure linguistic gains using tasks that tap into implicit knowledge as well as those that tap into explicit knowledge.

What are some ways of making the interventions themselves more implicit? The materials could be presented in a way that allows learners to inductively discover the underlying patterns and rules, as in naturalistic language learning environments, rather than being told what the rule is (even if the rule is informed by linguistic theory). Additionally, practice exercises could be created to promote rule discovery in meaningful communicative contexts. Trahey and White (1993) and Trahey (1996) did just that, and the results were discouraging. However, more recent studies utilizing structural priming appear promising (e.g., McDonough, 2006; Hurtado & Montrul, 2021a, 2021b). Structural priming, discussed in Chapter 8, can be used during the intervention itself to encourage implicit learning.

Discussion Question 11 Revisit the noninterface vs. interface positions discussed in Chapter 1. What does each position have to say about the importance of teaching learners using implicit instructional techniques? What are some benefits of doing more explicit vs. more implicit instruction?

10.3.3 New Technologies

As discussed in Chapters 1 and 2, many tasks used to assess linguistic knowledge and gains in second language studies tend to test explicit knowledge. This is especially the case when the tasks are written and give the students plenty of time to reflect on the correct answer or change their answers by consulting their explicitly learned knowledge about the structures in question. Examples of metalinguistic tasks or tasks that elicit explicitly learned forms are fill-in-the-blank and multiple-choice tasks, written grammaticality judgment tasks, and tasks that ask learners to compare two sentences and express a preference for one based on considerations of grammaticality. Some oral production tasks and timed written and auditory comprehension and judgment tasks minimize metalinguistic knowledge, and have been claimed to tap implicit knowledge (R. Ellis, 2005; Godfroid et al., 2015).

In recent years, advances in technology have allowed the implementation of online methods to measure reaction times and to capture processing of linguistic stimuli in real time. Eye-tracking technology, for example, can be used to measure gaze fixations on a reading passage or looks to images on a screen in response to auditory input. Since language acquisition is guided by language processing, the ability to measure language processing in real time, rather than after the fact, is a welcome advancement for both SLA and the study of language teaching. After all, both VanPatten's input processing framework and the Processability Theory of language acquisition (Pienemann, 1984), two linguistic frameworks that have tried to lead to direct instructional applications, claim that interlanguage development is driven by language processing. It is now possible to compare the outcomes of language learning via tasks that appear to tap into implicit knowledge and those that tap into explicit knowledge.

Which measures show changes after the intervention? We have very preliminary results with eye tracking from studies of the subjunctive in French in a nonintervention context (Dudley, 2020) and in Spanish in an intervention context following processing instruction (Fernández Cuenca, 2019). Both studies found acquisition of the subjunctive in the offline measures, but Fernández Cuenca also detected changes in processing after the instruction in the online processing data collected via eye tracking. Fernández Cuenca (2019) captured learners' processing of subjunctive sentences in temporal clauses with and without adverbs and found that the learners who were exposed to stimuli without adverbs changed their processing of morphological subjunctive forms in Spanish after the intervention, as revealed in an eye-tracking-while-reading study. J. F. Lee and Doherty (2019) also detected changes in processing for comprehension of Spanish verbal passives via eye tracking, but this study did not include a delayed posttest measure that would have indicated whether the changes observed were maintained. Detecting changes in online performance as a result of an intervention and assessing their longevity beyond the immediate posttest certainly deserves further investigation.

Leeser (2013) discusses the importance of also controlling the format of the secondary task that participants perform in an online study, which yields measures of participants' final interpretation or acceptance of the stimuli. More specifically, in some sentence-comprehension studies, participants are asked to answer a yes/no comprehension question or to make a grammaticality judgment. These secondary tasks assure the researchers that participants have read/listened to the stimuli during processing. In many studies, the reaction time data are only examined for the correct responses to these secondary tasks, because the assumption is that only the correctly answered sentences were attended to and processed. Leeser (2013) points out that the format of these secondary tasks can in fact influence the learners' performance on the primary processing task.

Leeser, Brandl, and Weissglass (2011) conducted a **self-paced reading** study of morphosyntactic violations in L2 Spanish, contrasting the effects of comprehension questions vs. grammaticality judgment questions as the secondary task. Native Spanish speakers and intermediate L2-Spanish learners read sentences with noun phrases modified by adjectives, which in Spanish require obligatory gender and number agreement. In half of the stimuli, the noun agreed with the adjective, and in the other half there was an ungrammatical mismatch. In one version of the secondary task, the learners answered yes/no comprehension questions on the stimuli; in the other version of the task, they were asked to provide a yes/no grammaticality judgment. The native speakers showed sensitivity to noun-adjective ungrammatical mismatches regardless of the format of the secondary task. The L2 learners, by contrast, showed sensitivity in the region of interest only in the version with grammaticality judgment questions as secondary task and no sensitivity to grammaticality violations in the version of the task with yes/no comprehension questions.

Leeser, Brandl, and Weissglass (2011) also found that the L2 learners showed slower reading times in the region before the grammaticality violation in the task with grammaticality judgment questions but not in the task with comprehension questions. They concluded that when learners are asked to perform grammaticality judgments in real time they process sentences at a slower pace, indicating that they are accessing their explicit knowledge until they detect the violation. Once they detect the violation, they race through the rest of the sentence. This is another intriguing finding that deserves follow-up. Indeed, the standard in studies of language processing, whether with native speakers or with L2 learners, is to use comprehension questions rather than grammaticality judgments as the secondary task (see Jegerski, 2014). This minimizes the possibility that learners are relying on their explicit knowledge during processing.

Finally, another area where advances in technologies could help address many of the limitations of intervention research conducted to date is the advent of new online platforms and mobile-device applications to deliver the intervention and assess its outcomes. Meurers et al. (2019) discuss the use of technology in supporting large-scale intervention studies in primary-school settings. They developed a web-based workbook for seventh grade that replaces a regular printed textbook commonly used in EFL classes in German schools. The web-based e-book provides explanations and immediate scaffolded feedback on form and meaning on a variety of grammatical topics. The results of an intervention study with 205 students (randomly divided into an experimental and a control group) following a pretest–intervention–posttest design confirmed that scaffolded feedback is effective. The intervention group improved significantly more than the nonintervention group. The main conclusion was that providing secondary-school students with immediate scaffolded feedback on grammar while they work on their homework significantly improves their mastery of those grammatical aspects. Since this large-scale study is still ongoing, there was no information about maintenance of the knowledge gained as measured by a posttest.

Discussion Question 12 What other current technologies could be leveraged to improve the current state of intervention research and to gain a deeper insight into the nature of linguistic knowledge in second language and heritage language learners as a result of language instruction? What are the pros and cons of using new technologies?

10.4 Conclusion

The nature of the linguistic knowledge that second language learners develop as a result of language instruction is still a puzzle. We still do not know the impact of explicit grammatical teaching and learning on the acquisition of a second language. Answering these questions requires cooperation among several disciplines – linguistic theory, psycholinguistics, neurolinguistics, second language acquisition, and language teaching – to yield the most fruitful results. The value and importance of intervention research is that it helps bridge the divide between the theoretical and the practical or applied.

We have advocated intervention research that (a) follows theoretically coherent research frameworks, (b) adopts a variety of experimental methodologies (including new technologies), and (c) expands the range of the native languages and the proficiency levels of the participants, both in order to revisit previous findings and to investigate unexplored questions.

In closing, we hope that this book has led you to think more deeply about the nature of intervention research, the relationship between linguistic theory and SLA, and the methodologies that can be used both in language teaching and to measure linguistic knowledge at different stages of development and learning outcomes after an intervention.

10.5 FURTHER READING

- Leeser, M.J. (2021). Why does processing instruction work? In M. J. Leeser, G. Ward, & W. Wong (Eds.), *Research on second language processing and processing instruction: Studies in honor of Bill VanPatten* (pp. 295–323). Amsterdam: John Benjamins.

  This chapter provides a recent overview of the input processing instruction approach and discusses the integration of language processing with language acquisition.

- Meurers, D., De Kuthy, K., Nuxoll, F., Rudzewitz, B., & Ziai, R. (2019). Scaling up intervention studies to investigate real-life foreign language learning in school. *Annual Review of Applied Linguistics, 39,* 161–188.

  This article reports on a recent study that uses new technology (a web-based workbook) to increase sample size.

- Trofimovich, P., & McDonough, K. (Eds.).(2011). *Applying priming methods to L2 learning, teaching and research: Insights from psycholinguistics.* Amsterdam: John Benjamins.

  This edited volume presents an overview of priming techniques and their place in SLA and language teaching; chapter 1 by the editors discusses how priming methods can be used to study language learning and teaching.

Glossary

A-movement: In generative syntax A-movement is an abstract transformation that moves arguments (subjects, objects) from their base position in the syntax to another position in the clause. Examples of A-movement are the passive structure and preverbal subjects with unaccusative verbs.

A-personal: This is the descriptive and pedagogical grammar term for Differential Object Marking (DOM) in Spanish. It refers to the preposition *a* that appears before animate, specific direct objects in Spanish.

Absolute adjective: An adjective that names a binary property, such as adjectives which name shapes or materials.

Accusative case: The case of the direct object of a sentence; accusative case **marking** can be overt – as in Turkish, Korean and Russian – but it is not overt in English (except with some pronouns: e.g., *me, her, him*).

Acquisition: The implicit development of language; depending on the theoretical view, acquisition may result only from naturalistic exposure to the language, or it could result from explicit instruction as well.

Action research (in the classroom): Research in which the teacher is the researcher and conducts the study in order to address specific questions in their classroom, without aiming for generalization beyond the classroom.

Active voice: In the active voice, the subject of the sentence performs the action described by the verb. An example is *The wizard cast a spell.* The wizard is the subject of the sentence and the one who performed the action of casting a spell.

Adjectival passives: A sentence with a copular verb (like *to be*) followed by a past participle. The past participle describes the state or result of the argument of the sentence. Sentences like *This link is broken* or *The crops are damaged* are examples of adjectival passives in English.

Adjectival phrase: A syntactic phrase headed by an adjective, such as *green, very exciting, fond of ice cream*, etc.

Adjectival subordinate clause: see **relative clause**

Adverbial clause: A subordinate clause with an adverbial function that expresses manner, frequency, location, temporality, etc. In the sentence *[After Mary arrived], she made herself a cup of coffee*, the part *After Mary arrived* is a temporal adverbial clause introduced with the word *after*. In the sentence *Unless the weather improves, we will not go camping*, the part *Unless the weather* *improves* is a concessive or conditional adverbial clause.

Age effects: The observation in L2 acquisition that the older the learner is when exposure to the L2 begins, the less likely it is that the learner will acquire native-like levels of grammatical accuracy in the target language. In heritage language acquisition, the sooner the introduction of the L2 (majority language) occurs in childhood, the more likely the heritage language will not develop native-like levels of grammatical accuracy.

Agent: Semantic role of the doer of an action described in a sentence. In the example *A tornado leveled the new neighborhood, a tornado* is the agent. In general, agents are mapped to the subject position of an active sentence.

Agree operation: When two elements are brought together so that their features match.

Allomorph: An alternate form of a morpheme which is determined by the phonological context. For example, *a* and *an* are allomorphs in English: they correspond to the same morpheme (the indefinite article) and the choice of one vs. the other is determined by the first segment of the following word.

Alternating verbs: Verbs that have a transitive and an intransitive version, such a *break, melt, open*. For example, *I broke the vase/The vase broke*. In English, the same form of the verb appears in the transitive and intransitive configurations, but in many languages (Spanish, Turkish, Japanese) either the transitive, the intransitive, or both versions, have overt morphology.

Anticausative marker: The morphological expression on an intransitive verb denoting an action affecting the patient argument of the verb with no indication about the syntactic or semantic agent. In Spanish, the reflexive pronoun *se* in the sentence *El jarrón se rompió* 'The vase broke' is an anticausative marker.

Argument: In syntax, an argument is an obligatory participant in the event described by the verb. Subjects are external arguments; direct and indirect objects are internal arguments (internal and external to the verb phrase or predicate).

Argument structure: Verbs have meaning, and the meaning of the verbs determines how many participants must participate in the event. Intransitive verbs have an argument structure that includes only one participant, transitive verbs need two participants, and ditranstive and locative verbs subcategorize for three arguments or participants.
The argument structure also includes information about the semantic roles of the participants, which can be *agent, patient or theme, experiencer, goal*, or *beneficiary*, among others.

Articles: Functional elements that mark such semantic distinctions as (in)definiteness or specificity and are very challenging to learners. English has two articles, definite *the* and indefinite *a/an*.

Baseline knowledge: The linguistic knowledge that learners possess prior to the start of an intervention. Pretests measure baseline knowledge.

Beneficiary: Semantic role of argument in a sentence denoting an entity that benefits from the action described by the verb. In the sentence, the argument is preceded by the preposition *for*, as in *Joan designed a new kitchen for Martha*, where Martha is the beneficiary of the new kitchen design.

Bound morpheme: A morpheme that must attach to another morpheme, such as the *-s* suffix or the *in-* prefix.

Canonical word order: The underlying word order of a language (such as SVO in English and SOV in Korean). It is typically the most frequent word order and the one easiest to process.

Causative/inchoative alternation: This alternation is also known as the "anti-causative" or the "ergative" alternation (Levin, 1993). It refers to verbs with transitive and intransitive uses, where the transitive form can be paraphrased as roughly "cause to V-intransitive." The intransitive form has an inchoative or resultative meaning, which expresses the result of the action describe by the verb. For example, *Low room temperature flattened the bread dough/The bread dough flattened.*

Clitic pronouns (or clitics): Pronouns that are phonologically weak, have no prosodic prominence, and must attach to a verb host. The Spanish object pronouns *lo, la, les* and the pronoun *se* are examples of clitics. The subject pronouns *il, elle, on,* are clitics in French.

Clitic doubling: The co-occurrence of the object clitic and the noun phrase or prepositional phrase it refers to, as in *Juan le dio una rosa a su madre* 'Juan her gave a rose to her mother' or *Susana la llamó a María* 'Susana her called María'.

Clitic left dislocation constructions: Spanish has a left dislocation construction in which the fronted phrase, typically an object, is doubled by a clitic within the core sentence (object–subject–clitic–verb). These constructions are frequent in spoken language to emphasize or stress the fronted constituent.

Cognate object construction: Some intransitive (ergative) verbs can have an object only when the object is related to the meaning of the verb. For example, *dance a dance, smile a smile.*

Communicative language teaching: Language instruction that places the focus on communication, meaning, and fluency.

Comparison groups: In an intervention study, groups that receive different interventions, with the goal of determining of which intervention is most effective.

Confederate: In a research experiment, confederates are individuals who are part of the research team but play the role of participants. They interact with real participants in an experiment.

Confounding variable: A feature of the study that is not being manipulated by the researchers but that nevertheless influences the results and may cause the results to look right for the wrong reason.

Consciousness raising: Language instruction designed to raise learners' consciousness of grammatical forms through structured activities; typically combined with input flooding and/or input enhancement.

Constituent: A syntactic phrase consisting of one or more words which function as a unit in a sentence. All phrase types (noun phrases, verb phrases, etc.) are constituents.

Content-based language teaching (CBLT)/Content and language integrated learning (CLIL): Language instruction that occurs when learners in an immersion program are taught content subjects in the target language.

Control group: In an intervention study, the group that does not receive the intervention, and thus serves as a baseline comparison to the instructed group or groups.

Copula: Copulas or copular verbs are linking verbs that link a subject and a nominal or adjectival predicate. The copula in English is the verb *to be*, as in *The cat is very clean* or *He is a wizard*.

Corrective feedback: Reactions to learners' errors that potentially inform learners that they have made an error; this may include explicit correction, metalinguistic information, and/or recasts, among other forms.

Count nouns: Nouns which name entities that can be counted and individuated, and that can combine with singular articles, plural marking, and numerals in languages like English. An example of a count noun is *chair(s)*.

Critical period: The period of brain maturation in childhood when the child must be exposed to a language; in the absence of exposure during the critical period, a native language cannot be acquired fully. Early exposure is critical to language development.

Dative case: The indirect object of a sentence is typically marked with dative case, which can be a particle or suffix, as in Turkish, Korean, and Russian, or a preposition, as in English.

Dative alternation: Some ditransitive verbs show alternative ways of expressing the indirect object, as a noun phrase next to the verb (*John sent his friend a message*) or as a prepositional phrase after the direct object (*John sent a message to his friend*). This is also known as double object alternation.

Debriefing questionnaire: A questionnaire administered towards the end of the study, in which learners answer questions about what they learned, noticed, etc., during the study.

Default forms: Forms that are used by L2 learners as a default in place of the target forms; for example, in the verbal domain, the bare or infinitival form is often used as a default in place of the finite inflected form (as in, 'She play piano').

Definite article: An article that encodes the semantic concept of definiteness, e.g., *the* in English.

Definiteness: Semantic concept that is generally analyzed as involving hearer knowledge and/or uniqueness of the referent. Informally, a definite noun phrase denotes an entity which is part of the shared discourse, known to both speaker and hearer.

Dependent variable: The variable that is measured in the study and which depends on the experimental manipulations.

Derivational morpheme: A morpheme that attaches to a word in order to derive a new word, such as *-ness* in *sadness* or *in-* in *intangible*.

Differential Object Marking (DOM): Overt morphological marking of direct objects that are semantically or pragmatically prominent. See also **a-personal**.

Dictogloss practice (DG): A grammar activity in which learners listen to a short text read by the teacher at a normal speed while writing down important words related to the text. Then the students work together in small groups to reconstruct the text as closely as possible to the original text by using the target grammatical form.

Direct object: Obligatory argument of transitive verbs that receives or is affected by the action denoted by the verb. In *Louise saw ghosts in the castle*, *ghosts* is the direct object of the transitive verb *see*.

Discourse: The context in which linguistic forms are used. There are many different types of discourse contexts, such as conversations, narratives, interviews, and formal essays. This term is also used more narrowly to refer to the immediate context surrounding a particular linguistic form.

Ditransitive construction: See **double object construction**. See also **ditransitive sentences**.

Ditransitive sentences: Sentences with a ditransitive verb that subcategorizes for a direct object and an indirect object. *John gave a rose to his mother* is a ditransitive sentence.

Ditransitive verbs: Verbs that take two obligatory internal arguments that are the direct and an indirect object of the sentence. Verbs like *give, donate, send* are ditransitive verbs.

Dominant language transfer: In L2 acquisition and in heritage language acquisition, many errors and linguistic patterns observed in the L2 or in the heritage language result from structural influence of the other language: the native language (L1) in L2 acquisition and the dominant language in heritage language acquisition. For example, we see in Chapter 4 that many French-speaking learners of English misplace adverbs in English because they follow the order of French.

Double object alternation: See **dative alternation**.

Double object construction: Some ditransitive verbs in English take two objects, one after the other, such as *gave his mother a rose*: *his mother* and *a rose* are objects. The indirect object (*his mother*) is not preceded by a preposition in this construction.

Experimental design: An intervention study design in which participants are randomly assigned to different groups (typically in a lab or online setting).

Explicit knowledge: Knowledge *about* something that can be consciously retrieved and verbalized.

External argument: The participant in an event described by the verb that is mapped to the subject position in the syntax. The argument is external to the verb phrase or predicate.

Eye tracking: A psycholinguistic technique in which a camera tracks where the participant is looking while reading or listening to sentences. In SLA research, eye tracking is often used with reading; it is used to examine whether learners slow down for errors of ungrammaticality while reading. Another common use of eye tracking is eye tracking with a visual world paradigm, in which participants look at pictures or objects while listening to sentences.

Feature strength: Property of features that determine whether they involve overt movement operations.

Features: Abstract morphosyntactic properties of lexical items, part of the universal lexicon. Examples of features are [+/−past] features on verbs and [+/−plural] features of nouns.

Finite verb: Verbal form inflected for person, number (agreement), tense, etc. (e.g. *I was, they walked*).

First language acquisition: The acquisition of a language from birth. Also called native language or mother language acquisition.

Focus on form (FonF): Language instruction in which focus on grammatical forms is incorporated into communicative activities.

Focus on formS: Traditional language instruction which focuses on grammatical forms without a communicative context.

Foreign-language setting: The context that arises when participants are acquiring the target language in a formal setting, in a country where the target language is not the dominant language.

Free morpheme: A morpheme that can stand on its own, e.g., *cat* or *walk*.

Functional categories: Syntactic categories that represent grammatical morphology for agreement, tense, aspect, and mood in verbs, and for gender and number in nouns. Functional categories such as tense phrase (TP) or aspect phrase (AspP) are represented above the verb phrase (VP) in a syntactic tree.

Gender agreement: The process by which one element (such as a determiner or adjective) reflects the gender feature of another element (a noun). For example, determiners and adjectives in Spanish must reflect the gender of the noun that they modify.

Gender assignment: The process by which a noun in a language such as Spanish or Russian is assigned a particular gender or noun class (e.g., feminine vs. masculine).

Generative linguistic framework: The approach, originating in work by

Noam Chomsky, according to which all humans are born with knowledge of core grammatical rules (Universal Grammar) which generate the grammatical structures of all human languages.

Genericity: Semantic concept that refers to making general statements about the state of the world and/or about categories or species. For example, *Cats like milk* is a generic statement about cats.

Goal: Semantic role of a ditransitive verb of giving or transfer of possession, information, etc. In the sentence *Bella sent flowers to her grandmother, her grandmother* is the goal argument.

Grammaticality judgment task (GJT): An experimental task commonly used in research with second language learners; in a GJT, participants read or listen to a series of sentences and indicate whether each sentence is grammatical or ungrammatical (or, alternatively, rate the acceptability of each sentence on a scale). This task is also often known as an acceptability judgment task.

Hawthorne Effect: The effect of participants in a study changing their behavior as a result of being observed.

Heritage language acquisition: The acquisition the native language (L1) in a specific sociolinguistic context, where the native L1 (heritage) language is a sociopolitically minority language and its acquisition may be restricted to the home environment.

Heritage speakers: Bilingual individuals who speak a heritage (family) language in addition to the majority or dominant language of the society.

Immersive setting: The context that arises when participants are acquiring the target language while immersed in the language, in a country where the target language is the dominant language; examples would be contexts of immigration or study abroad.

Implicit knowledge: Knowledge of *how* to do something that cannot be verbalized.

Inchoative verbs: Verbs that have an inceptive meaning and denote a spontaneous event, such as the verbs *realize, fall, begin, disappear*, and the intransitive form of the verb *break, finish*, etc.

Incidental learning: Learning that arises through exposure to language input, without an explicit focus on grammar.

Indefinite article: An article that encodes the semantic concept of indefiniteness, e.g., *a* in English.

Indefiniteness: Semantic concept that corresponds to an absence of definiteness. Informally, indefinite noun phrases denote entities that are not part of the shared discourse.

Independent variable: An aspect of the study being manipulated by the researchers. An example is the assignment of learners to different instruction groups.

Indicative: A type of grammatical mood used to express facts, statements, opinions, or questions.

Indirect object: The goal or beneficiary of the action described by a ditransitive verb. In a sentence like

John sent a message to Clarissa, *Clarissa* is the indirect object.

Indirect passives: Passive sentences with ditransitive verbs with double objects that make the indirect objects the subject of the passive sentence. For example, in *John was given a message*, *John* is the subject of the indirect passive sentence.

Infinitival verb form: A type of a nonfinite verb form; in English, infinitival forms are preceded by *to* (as in *to go*), while in many other Germanic as well as Romance and Slavic languages, infinitival forms are marked by a dedicated morpheme.

Inflectional morpheme: A morpheme that attaches to a word in order to change some grammatical property, such as number (in the case of plural *-s*) or tense (in the case of past-tense *-ed*).

Inflectional morphology: Endings for grammatical information, such as tense and agreement in verbs, and plurality, gender, and number in nouns.

Initial state: A learner's state of linguistic knowledge at the very beginning of the language acquisition process. For an L2 learner, the initial state includes all or some aspects of the first language.

Input: Samples of language (written, spoken) that are the data to the language acquisition mechanisms.

Input enhancement/input enrichment: Language instruction in which the relevant grammatical construction(s) are typographically enhanced.

Input flooding: Language instruction which involves "flooding" learners with many exemplars of the relevant construction(s).

Input processing: The processing of linguistic input during language comprehension and production.

Input processing instruction (PI): Language instruction whose goal is for learners to move away from default strategies and to fully process the input.

Instructed (or instruction) group: In an intervention study, the group (or one of the groups) that receives the intervention. Also known as the experimental group or the intervention group.

Intact classes: Existing classes of learners, with each class assigned to a different condition of study (e.g., one class receives the intervention while another serves as the control group).

Interlanguage (also interlanguage grammar): Implicit abstract grammatical system that second language learners build as they acquire a second language (i.e., their mental representation for their version of the target language). The interlanguage system includes elements from the L1 and from the L2 and other universal properties of human languages and language development.

Internal argument: Arguments of the verb internal to the verb phrase, such as the direct object and the indirect object.

Intervention (in reference to language studies): A manipulation of the instruction and/or input that learners receive, intended to improve learners' performance in the target language.

Intervention studies: Studies in which some aspects of instruction, feedback, input, and/or output are manipulated by the researchers, and the effects of this manipulation on learners' performance are measured.

Intransitive verb: A verb that has only one argument, such as *leave, disappear, fall, breathe, shudder*, etc.

Inverse scope: The interpretation that occurs when two scope-bearing elements (such as quantifiers or negation) are interpreted in the order that is the inverse of their surface structural order. For example, on the inverse-scope interpretation of *A dog bit every postal carrier, every postal carrier* is interpreted before *a dog*, with the resulting meaning, 'For every postal carrier x, there is a (potentially different) dog that bit x'.

Kind predicates: Predicates that can apply only to kinds/species rather than to individuals, such as *be extinct* or *be invented*.

Kind reference: A type of genericity, which involves reference to entire kinds, categories or species rather than individual entities. For example, *The dodo bird is extinct* is a statement about the kind 'dodo bird' rather than about an individual dodo bird.

L1: First language acquired since birth or the mother tongue.

L1 acquisition: See **first language acquisition**.

L1 transfer: See **dominant language transfer**.

L2: Second language, acquired during childhood, adolescence or adulthood, after (most of) the first language is already in place.

L2 acquisition: The acquisition of another language after the structural foundations of the native language are in place, typically after three to four years of age.

Learning: The development of language through explicit information about the language and/or through language teaching. Depending on the theoretical position, naturalistic L1 acquisition is also language learning.

Lexical categories: Syntactic phrases representing the lexical types: noun, verb, adjective, adverb, and some prepositions.

Linguistic competence: On the generative approach to language, the underlying knowledge that all speakers of a language possess.

Locative: Argument of the verb that refers to a location. In the sentence *I put the book on the shelf, on the shelf* is the locative argument.

Main clause: A simple declarative sentence with only one conjugated verb, e.g., *The president boarded the plane*.

Mandative or directive predicates: Verbs and verb phrases that convey an order or direction, such as *order, tell, require, urge*, etc. In the sentence *Mary requested that everybody be on time for her wedding party*, the verb *request* is mandative.

Markedness: The concept that refers to the distribution of linguistic forms:

Less marked forms have wider distribution and are easier to acquire.

Mass nouns: Nouns which typically (but not always) name entities that cannot be counted or individuated. In languages like English, mass nouns do not combine with *a* or with numerals and cannot take plural marking. An example of a mass noun is *mustard*.

Merge operation: When two syntactic objects are combined to form a new syntactic unit (a set).

Metalanguage: Language about language.

Modality: Modality refers to the degree to which an observation is possible, probable, likely, certain, permitted, or prohibited. In English, these notions are commonly (though not exclusively) expressed by modal auxiliaries, such as *can, might, should*, and *will*.

Model: The target form as provided to a learner during an interaction.

Monitor model: According to Krashen (1982), there is a difference between *acquisition* and *learning*. Learned knowledge of a second language acts as a monitor, or editor. It comes into play to make changes in the form of an utterance produced by the acquired linguistic system.

Mood: Grammatical instantiation of modality on the verb. There are subjunctive and indicative moods.

Morpheme: The smallest linguistic unit that has meaning.

Morphology: The branch of linguistics which studies how words are formed.

Morphosyntax: The branch of linguistics that combines morphology and syntax, addressing both word and phrase formation.

Move operation: Syntactic operation that brings elements into a local relationship by displacing them from their base position.

Natural kinds: Kinds that are well-defined; for example, *brown bear* and *cell phone* refer to natural kinds of animals or objects in our world, whereas *angry bear* or *green phone* do not.

Negative evidence: Information about what is not possible in the language (in the form of explanation, correction or feedback).

No-interface position: The view that explicit knowledge cannot turn into implicit knowledge.

Nominal clauses: Subordinate clauses or sentential complements that are the subject or the object of a main clause. For example, in the sentence *It is important [that everybody arrives on time for the flight], that everybody arrives on time for the flight* is a sentential complement with a subject function. In the sentence *John hopes [that his parents do not get sick], that his parents do not get sick* is a nominal clause with the function of object of the verb *hope*.

Nominative case: The case of the subject of the sentence.

Nonabsolute adjective: An adjective that names a gradient property, such as adjectives which name size or height.

Noncanonical word order: A word order that departs from the underlying word order in a language. For example, many SVO and SOV languages also allow OSV word order, which is noncanonical. Such orders tend to be less frequent and more difficult to process and acquire.

Noncount nouns (see **mass nouns**)

Nonfinite verb: Verb form that is not inflected for tense; nonfinite forms include infinitives (*to go*), gerunds (*going*), and past participles (*gone*).

Noninterventionist studies (in the classroom): Studies in which learners' performance is examined, but without researchers manipulating any aspect of the instruction or input.

Nonkind predicates: Predicates that apply to individuals rather than kinds, such as *be expensive* or *live in Chicago*.

Normative grammar: See **prescriptive grammar**.

Noun phrase: A syntactic phrase headed by a noun, such as *this cat, an interesting book*, etc.

Noun phrase accessibility hierarchy: An implicational hierarchy that governs relativization, such that the presence of a more marked type of relative clause in a language implies the presence of a less marked relative clause. For example, subject relative clauses are less marked than object relative clauses, so the presence of the latter implies the presence of the former.

Object pronoun: Pronoun that stands for a direct or an indirect object in a sentence, such as *him, her, them* in English.

Object relative clause: A clause that modifies a noun, such that the noun has the role of object inside the relative clause. For example, in the sentence *I can see the man [who the police stopped]*, *who* stands for *the man*. *The man* is also the object of the verb *stopped* in the relative clause (*the police stopped the man*).

Object scrambling: The movement of an object from its underlying position in the sentence to a position closer to the front of the sentence. For example, in many languages, OSV order is derived from SVO or SOV order via object scrambling.

Observational studies (in the classroom): Studies in which researchers observe what happens in a classroom, without intervening or manipulating what happens.

Operationalization: The process by which an abstract concept (such as implicit knowledge) is turned into a measurable construct (such as a slowdown during reading).

Output-based instruction: Language instruction whose focus is the output produced by the learners.

Overpassivization: The extension of the passive voice rules to intransitive verbs that do not have a direct object. *The money was disappeared* is an example of an error of overgeneralizing the passive rule to verbs that do not participate in this rule.

Parameters: In the Principles and Parameters framework, parameters are the grammatical rules that constrain crosslinguistic variation, having different instantiations in different languages.

Parametric variation: Systematic crosslinguistic variation in syntactic structure, which is due to different settings of a specific parameter.

Passive voice: In the passive voice, the subject of the sentence undergoes the action described by the verb. An example is *A spell was cast by the old witch*. *A spell* is the subject of the sentence and *the old witch* is the agent but appears in a phrase headed by the preposition by (the *by-phrase* in English).

Passivization: Syntactic operation that transforms an active sentence with a transitive verb (*The wizard cast a spell*) into a passive sentence by moving the patient or theme to subject position and the agent to a prepositional phrase (*A spell was cast by the wizard*). The passive form of the verb takes the auxiliary *be* and the past participle of the verb (*cast*➔ *was cast*).

Pedagogical grammar: A simplified version of descriptive grammar that explains grammatical rules of a language to help students of a second language learn and understand the language.

Person/number agreement: The process by which one element in a sentence (such as a verb) reflects the person/number features of another element (such as the subject). For example, English verbs in the present tense bear an *-s* suffix to mark agreement with a third-person singular subject.

Possessor: Semantic role of an argument who owns an entity described. In the phrase *Harry's teacher*, *Harry* is the possessor and *teacher* is the possessum, or entity being possessed.

Positive evidence: Naturally occurring samples of language that inform the learner about what is possible in the language.

Posttest: A measure of learners' knowledge after an intervention has ended; an immediate posttest is administered immediately or shortly after the intervention is over, while delayed posttests can be administered days, weeks, months, or even years later.

Preemption: A process by which the acquisition of the target form in the L2 expunges (preempts) the corresponding nontarget forms.

Prepositional phrase: A syntactic phrase headed by a preposition; in English, prepositional phrases typically consist of a preposition + noun phrase, e.g., *in the room; under a bridge; of chocolate;* etc.

Presupposition: Information that is assumed to apply even though it is not asserted out right. For example, use of a definite noun phrase, such as *the book*, presupposes the existence of a unique book; a sentence such as *Joan no longer writes fiction* presupposes that Joan wrote fiction previously.

Prescriptive grammar: Prescriptive or normative grammar (from norms) is the type of grammar taught in school or in writing classes, which describes "good" (standard) and "inappropriate" (non-standard) ways to speak or write the language. For example, "You should not end a sentence in English with a preposition" is an example of prescriptive grammar.

Pretest: A measure of learners' baseline knowledge before an intervention begins.

Principles: In the Principles and Parameters framework, principles are the grammatical rules that are part of Universal Grammar and that are instantiated in all languages.

Processing instruction (PI): See **input processing instruction**.

Processability Theory: The theory of an implicationally ordered processability hierarchy that constrains language acquisition.

Pseudopassives: The pseudopassive is a passive structure where the subject is the object of a preposition, as in the *This hall was lectured in by many Nobel laureates* (active version: *Many Nobel laureates lectured in this hall*).

Purpose clauses: Adverbial subordinate clauses that express a purpose. These are subordinate clauses introduced by expressions such as *so that, in order to, to*, etc. in English: *In order to understand this textbook, some basic knowledge of linguistics is required.*

Quantifier scope: The portion of a linguistic expression to which a quantifier applies. For example, in the sentence *Every child left*, or *I saw every child* the quantifier *every* takes scope over the rest of the sentence (for every x, if x is a child, then x left; for every x, if x is a child, then I saw x).

Quantifier: A determiner which denotes a particular quantity (e.g., *every, some, none*).

Quasi-experimental design: An intervention study design in which the different groups correspond to intact classrooms, with no random assignment of participants.

Random assignment: In experimental research, this corresponds to randomly assigning each participant to one of experimental conditions (groups). This is more typical with studies that are placed in the lab as opposed to in the classroom.

Recasts: A form of implicit corrective feedback which involves the instructor repeating (recasting) the learners' erroneous utterance with the error corrected.

Recipient: The recipient is a semantic role that receives the action of the verb of transfer. In *Jerry sent a hidden message to Angela*, Angela is the recipient (also the goal).

Reflexive pronoun: Reflexive pronouns typically occur in object position and (in English) refer to the subject of the sentence. For example, in *Mary combed herself*, *herself* refers to *Mary*, the subject, but is also the object undergoing the action of combing.

Relative clause: A subordinate clause that modifies a noun phrase and has adjectival function, also known as the adjectival clause. For example, in the sentence *The lamp [that Ms. Henry brought] is very old*, *[that Ms. Henry brought]* is a relative clause or an adjectival clause introduced by the complementizer *that*. The adjectival clause says something about *the lamp*, the head noun phrase in the main or matrix clause.

Restrictive relative clauses: An adjectival embedded clause that gives information about a noun phrase and limits its possible meanings. For example, in the sentence *The dog [that barked yesterday] lives next door*, *[that barked yesterday]* is a restrictive relative clause because it singles out one specific dog (the one that barked yesterday) from the set of all dogs.

Resultative construction: The English resultative construction establishes a causal relationship between the verb phrase and an adjective or prepositional phrase that is the result of the action depicted by the verb. For example, the sentence *The river froze solid* means that the river is now solid as a result of its water freezing. Similarly, *John painted the barn red* means that the barn is now red as a result of John painting it.

Scope ambiguity: Ambiguity that occurs when a sentence has two (or more) scope-bearing elements that can be interpreted in different order (surface-scope vs. inverse-scope).

Second language acquisition (SLA): The learning of a second or additional language after the linguistic foundations of the first or native language are in place. Second language acquisition can happen in childhood or in adulthood, unlike first language acquisition that nearly always begins in infancy.

Self-paced reading: A psycholinguistic task in which participants read sentences one word or one region at a time, advancing at their own pace; a slowdown in a particular word or region indicates difficulty with parsing, which can be due to such factors as ungrammaticality, implausibility, or reanalysis. In SLA research, this task is commonly used to study whether learners exhibit online sensitivity to ungrammaticality.

Semantics: The branch of linguistics that studies what words and sentences mean.

Sentential complements: See **nominal clauses**.

Sequential bilingual: An individual who is exposed to the second language during childhood, after the foundations of the first language are already in place.

Simultaneous bilingual: An individual who is exposed to two languages from birth or very early childhood, thus growing up with two first languages.

Small clause: A small clause consists of a subject and its predicate but lacks an overt expression of tense. For example, in the sentence *Robert considers Ellen a wonderful friend*, *[Ellen a wonderful friend]* is a small clause consisting of a subject *[Ellen]* and a predicate *[a wonderful friend]* but no verb.

SOV language: A language whose basic structure is Subject–Direct Object–Verb, like Japanese, Turkish, and Korean.

Specificity: Semantic concept that is generally analyzed as involving some form of speaker knowledge but without hearer knowledge. While English articles encode (in)definiteness rather than specificity, L2 English learners have often been found to make specificity-based errors.

Strong-interface position: The view that explicit knowledge can become implicit.

Strong pronouns: Pronouns that are phonologically independent and stand as one word, such as subject pronouns *I, he, she, they*, and object pronouns, *me, you, them, her, his* in English. They appear in subject position, in object position or after prepositions.

Subject relative clause: A clause that modifies a noun, such that the noun has the role of subject inside the relative clause, as in *I saw the cat [that came into the room]*: the cat is the subject in *the cat came into the room*.

Subjunctive mood: Type of mood whose verb form expressed a hypothetical situation, a wish, a demand, an opinion or a suggestion.

Subordinate clause: Dependent embedded clause with nominal, adjectival, or adverbial function.

Surface scope: The interpretation that occurs when two scope-bearing elements (such as quantifiers or negation) are interpreted in their surface structural order. For example, on the surface-scope interpretation of *A dog bit every postal carrier*, *a dog* is interpreted before *every postal carrier*, with the resulting meaning, 'There is a specific dog which bit all the postal carriers'.

SVO language: A language whose basic structure is Subject–Verb–Direct Object, such as English, French, Spanish.

Syntactic or structural priming: When a speaker hears and tends to repeat a structure that was used by the interlocutor or somebody else.

Syntax: The branch of linguistics which studies how sentences are built out of smaller units.

Target language: The language that is being acquired or learned. Depending on the learning scenario, the target language may be a monolingual child's L1, a bilingual speaker's heritage language, or an adult's L2.

Task-based learning: Language instruction in which learners complete communicative tasks that involve some degree of focus on grammatical form.

Teachability Hypothesis: The hypothesis that learners learn best if the instruction focuses on the next stage in the learners' development.

Telic verbs: Verbs that denote actions which have an endpoint, such as *realize, jump, arrive*.

Telicity: Aspectual property of a verb phrase (or of the sentence as a whole) which indicates that an action or event has a clear endpoint. A verb phrase presented as having an endpoint is said to be telic: For example, in the sentence *Pat ran a mile in 5 minutes*, *ran a mile* is a telic predicate because the event has a natural endpoint.

Tense: An abstract grammatical category which corresponds to the tense of the sentence (such as past or present). In some languages (including English), finite verbs bear tense marking.

Theme (patient): The internal argument of a verb undergoing the action depicted by the verb is the theme or patient. For example, in the sentence *Beatrice owns a pet owl*, *a pet owl* is the theme of the sentence.

***To*-dative construction:** Ditransitive verbs with indirect objects preceded by the preposition *to*: In the sentence, *Peter gave a rose to his mother*, the indirect object *his mother* is preceded by the preposition *to*.

Transitive verb: A verb that requires a direct object, such as *buy, see, visit*.

Transitivity: A property of verbs that determines whether they can have objects and the number of objects they can have. There are transitive verbs (with one direct object), intransitive verbs (no direct object), and ditransitive verbs (with two objects). Some verbs alternate in transitivity.

Trials-to-criterion: A measure, used in some input processing studies, which examines the number of test items (trials) that it takes for a learner to reach a predetermined performance level (the criterion).

Truth-value judgment task: A comprehension task commonly used in L2 research, in which participants judge a sentence as true or false in the context of a preceding story or picture. Learners' answers can inform researchers about the meaning that the learners assign to the sentences.

Unaccusative verbs: Intransitive verbs whose sole argument (the subject) is the theme or patient. The verb *leave* and the verb *fall* are unaccusative verbs.

Unaccusative Hypothesis: The hypothesis that intransitive verbs are not a uniform class and that they can be classified into at least two classes, unaccusative and unergative verbs, based on their meaning and their syntactic behavior.

Unergative verbs: Intransitive verbs whose sole argument (the subject) is the agent. The verb *run* and the verb *talk* are unergative verbs.

Universal Grammar: In generative linguistic theory, an innate system of rules and principles common to all human languages.

Verb movement: Displacement of the lexical verb from the verb phrase to the inflectional phrase.

Verb phrase: A syntactic phrase headed by a verb, such as *run, read a book, send a gift to a friend*, etc.

Verb second (V2): In many Germanic languages, the verb appears in the second position of the sentence in main declarative sentences.

Verbal passives: Passive structures that denote an event and have an agent by-phrase. The sentence *The spell was cast by the wizard* is a verbal passive.

Weak-interface position: The view that explicit knowledge can become implicit only under certain conditions.

Wh-in-situ: In many languages (such as Japanese, Korean), wh-questions are formed with the interrogative pronoun (wh-) in its base syntactic position (in-situ). In these languages there is no movement or fronting of the wh-pronoun to the front of the sentence as in English and many other languages. The wh-word in Japanese and Korean remains in-situ, i.e., in its original place.

Wh-movement: In questions and relative clauses, a wh-word that stands for a constituent in the basic sentence structure appears in another place in the sentence.

Zero morphology: Morphemes that have meaning but no phonological expression. For example, in English, the sentence *I play tennis* has zero first-person morphology on the verb form, whereas *She plays tennis* has overt third-person morphology (*-s*).

References

Abbott, B. (2003). Definiteness and indefinitenes. In L. Horn & W. Ward (Eds.), *Handbook of pragmatics* (pp. 122–149). Oxford: Blackwell.

Agirre, A. I. (2015). The acquisition of dative alternation in English by Spanish learners. *Vigo International Journal of Applied Linguistics, 12*, 63-90.

Aissen, J. (2003). Differential object marking: Iconicity vs. economy. *Natural Language & Linguistic Theory, 21*, 435–483.

Akhtar, N., & Tomasello, M. (1997). Young children's productivity with word order and verb morphology. *Developmental Psychology, 33*, 952.

Alonso, E. R. (1999). *Modo y modalidad. El modo en las subordinadas sustantivas.* Paper presented at the the Gramática descriptiva de la lengua española.

Ammar, A., & Lightbown, P. M. (2005). Teaching marked linguistic structures: More about the acquisition of relative clauses by Arab learners of English. In A. Housen & M. Pierrard (Eds.), *Investigations in instructed second language acquisition* (pp. 167–198). Berlin: Mouton de Gruyter.

Ammar, A., & Spada, N. (2006). One size fits all? Recasts, prompts, and L2 learning. *Studies in Second Language Acquisition, 20*, 93–108.

Anderson, C. (2004). *The structure and real-time comprehension of quantifier scope ambiguity.* PhD dissertation, Northwestern University.

Andringa, S. (2020). The emergence of awareness in uninstructed L2 learning: A visual world eye tracking study. *Second Language Research, 36*, 335–357.

Andringa, S., de Glopper, K., & Hacquebord, H. (2011). Effect of explicit and implicit instruction on free written response task performance. *Language Learning, 61*, 868–903.

Aoun, J., & Li, Y.-h. A. (1989). Scope and constituency. *Linguistic Inquiry, 20*, 141–172.

Aoun, J., & Li, Y.-h. A. (1993). *The syntax of scope.* Cambridge, MA: MIT Press.

Arechabaleta Regulez, B. (2019). *The processing of differential object marking in Spanish by monolinguals and bilinguals.* PhD dissertation, University of Illinois at Urbana-Champaign.

Armon-Lotem, S., Haman, E., Jensen de López, K., et al. (2016). A large-scale cross-linguistic investigation of the acquisition of passive. *Language Acquisition, 23*, 27–56.

Armon-Lotem, S., Rose, K., & Altman, C. (2021). The development of English as a heritage language: The role of chronological age and age of onset of bilingualism. *First Language, 41*, 67–89.

Armstrong, A., Bulkes, N., & Tanner, D. (2018). Quantificational cues modulate the processing of English subject-verb agreement by native Chinese speakers: An ERP study. *Studies in Second Language Acquisition, 40*, 731–754.

Ayoun, D. (1999). Verb movement in French L2 acquisition. *Bilingualism: Language and Cognition, 2*, 103–125.

Ayoun, D. (2013). *The second language acquisition of French tense, aspect, mood and modality*. Amsterdam: John Benjamins.

Baek, S. (2012). *Processing of English relative clauses by adult L2 learners*. PhD dissertation, University of Illinois at Urbana-Champaign.

Baker, C. L. (1979). Syntactic theory and the projection problem. *Linguistic Inquiry, 10*, 533–581.

Baker, M. C. (2003). Verbal adjectives as adjectives without phi-features. In Y. Otsu (Ed.), *Proceedings of the Fourth Tokyo Conference on Psycholinguistics* (pp. 1–22). Tokyo: Keio University.

Balcom, P. (1997). Why is this happened? Passive morphology and unaccusativity. *Second Language Research, 13*, 1–9.

Bartning, I., Lundell, F. F., & Hancock, V. (2012). On the role of linguistic contextual factors for morphosyntactic stabilization in high-level L2 French. *Studies in Second Language Acquisition, 34*, 243–267.

Bayona, P. (2009). The acquisition of Spanish middle and impersonal passive constructions from SLA and TLA perspectives. In Y.-K. I. Leung (Ed.), *Third language acquisition and Universal Grammar* (pp. 1–29). Bristol, UK: Multilingual Matters.

Beck, M. L. (1998). L2 acquisition and obligatory head movement: English-speaking learners of German and the Local Impairment Hypothesis. *Studies in Second Language Acquisition, 20*, 311–348.

Benati, A. (2000). "Processing Instruction": Un tipo di grammatica comunicativa per la classe di lingua straniera. Il caso del futuro italiano. *Italica, 77*, 473–494.

Benati, A. (2001). A comparative study of the effects of processing instruction and output-based instruction on the acquisition of the Italian future tense. *Language Teaching Research, 5*, 95–127.

Benati, A. (2005). The effects of processing instruction, traditional instruction and meaning: Output instruction on the acquisition of the English past simple tense. *Language Teaching Research, 9*, 67–93.

Benati, A. (2015). The effects of re-exposure to instruction and the use of discourse-level interpretation tasks on processing instruction and the Japanese passive. *International*

Review of Applied Linguistics in Language Teaching, 53, 127–150.

Benati, A., & Angelovska, T. (2015). The effects of processing instruction on the acquisition of English simple past tense: Age and cognitive task demands. *International Review of Applied Linguistics in Language Teaching, 53*, 249–269.

Benmamoun, E., Montrul, S., & Polinsky, M. (2013). Heritage languages and their speakers: Opportunities and challenges for linguistics. *Theoretical Linguistics, 39*, 129–181.

Berman, R., & Slobin, D. (2016). *Relating events in narrative: A crosslinguistic developmental study*. New York: Psychology Press.

Bialystok, E. (1994). Representation and ways of knowing: Three issues in second language acquisition. In N. C. Ellis (Ed.), *Implicit and explicit learning of languages* (pp. 549–569). San Diego, CA: Academic Press.

Bickerton, D. (1981). *Roots of language*. Ann Arbor, MI: Karoma Press.

Birdsong, D. (1999). *Second language acquisition and the critical period hypothesis*. Mahwah, NJ: Lawrence Erlbaum Associates.

Blake, R. (1983). Mood selection among Spanish-speaking children, ages 4 to 12. *Bilingual Review/La Revista Bilingüe, 10*, 21–32.

Blake, R. (1985). From research to the classroom: Notes on the subjunctive. *Hispania, 68*, 166–173.

Bley-Vroman, R. (1989). What is the logical problem of foreign language learning? In S. Gass & J. Schachter (Eds.), *Linguistic perspectives on second language acquisition* (pp. 41–68). Cambridge, UK: Cambridge University Press.

Bley-Vroman, R. (1990). The logical problem of foreign language learning. *Linguistic Analysis, 20*, 3–49.

Bley-Vroman, R. (2009). The evolving context of the fundamental difference hypothesis. *Studies in Second Language Acquisition, 31*, 175–198.

Bley-Vroman, R., & Yoshinaga, N. (1992). Broad and narrow constraints on the English dative alternation: Some fundamental differences between native speakers and foreign language learners. *University of Hawai'i Working Papers in ESL, 11*, 157–199.

Bock, J. K. (1986). Syntactic persistence in language production. *Cognitive Psychology, 18*, 355–387.

Bohannon, J. N., & Stanowicz, L. B. (1988). The issue of negative evidence: Adult responses to children's language errors. *Developmental Psychology, 24*, 684.

Borer, H. (1984). *Parametric syntax: Case studies in Semitic and Romance languages*. Dordrecht: Foris.

Borer, H., & Grodzinsky, Y. (1986). Syntactic cliticization and lexical cliticization: The case of Hebrew dative clitics. In H. Borer (Ed.), *The syntax of pronominal clitics* (pp. 175–217). Leiden: Brill.

Borer, H., & Wexler, K. (1987). The maturation of syntax. In T. Roeper & E. Williams (Eds.), *Parameter setting* (pp. 123–172). Dordrecht: D. Reidel.

Borer, H., & Wexler, K. (1992). Bi-unique relations and the maturation of grammatical principles. *Natural Language and Linguistic Theory, 10*, 147–189.

Borgonovo, C., Bruhn de Garavito, J., & Prévost, P. (2015). Mood selection in relative clauses: Interfaces and variability. *Studies in Second Language Acquisition, 37*, 33–69.

Borgonovo, C., & Prévost, P. (2003). Knowledge of polarity subjunctive in L2 Spanish. In B. Beachley, A. Brown, & F. Conlin (Eds.), *Proceedings of the 27th annual Boston University Conference on Language Development* (pp. 150–161). Somerville, MA: Cascadilla Press.

Bowerman, M., & Croft, W. (2008). The acquisition of the English causative alternation. In M. Bowerman & P. Brown (Eds.), *Crosslinguistic perspectives on argument structure and structure: Implications for learnability* (pp. 279–307). Hillsdale, NJ: Erlbaum.

Bowles, M. (2011). Measuring implicit and explicit linguistic knowledge: What can heritage language learners contribute? *Studies in Second Language Acquisition, 33*, 247–271.

Bowles, M., & Montrul, S. (2009). Instructed L2 acquisition of differential object marking in Spanish. In R. P. Leow, H. Campos, & D. Lardiere (Eds.), *Little words: Their history, phonology, syntax, semantics, pragmatics and acquisition (Georgetown University Round Table on Languages and Linguistics (GURT) 2007)* (pp. 199–210). Washington, DC: Georgetown University Press.

Bowles, M., & Torres, J. (2021). Instructed heritage language acquisition. In S. Montrul & M. Polinsky (Eds.), *The Cambridge handbook of heritage languages and linguistics* (pp. 826–850). Cambridge, UK: Cambridge University Press.

Branigan, H. P., Pickering, M. J., & Cleland, A. A. (2000). Syntactic co-ordination in dialogue. *Cognition, 75*, B13–B25.

Bresnan, J. (2001). *Lexical-functional syntax*. Oxford: Blackwell.

Brown, R. (1973). *A first language: The early stages*. Cambridge, MA: Harvard University Press.

Bruhn de Garavito, J. (1997). Verb complementation, coreference and tense in the acquisition of Spanish as a second language. In W. R. Glass & A. T. Pérez-Leroux (Eds.), *Contemporary perspectives on the acquisition of Spanish* (pp. 167–188). Somerville, MA: Cascadilla Press.

Bruhn de Garavito, J. (1999). *The syntax of Spanish multifunctional clitics and near-native competence*. PhD dissertation, McGill University.

Bruhn de Garavito, J. (2003). The (dis)association between morphology and syntax: The case of L2 Spanish. In S. Montrul & F. Ordoñez (Eds.), *Linguistic theory and language development in Hispanic languages* (pp. 398–417). Somerville, MA: Cascadilla Press.

Bruhn de Garavito, J. (2006). Knowledge of clitic doubling in Spanish: Evidence against pattern learning. In

R. Slabakova, S. Montrul, & P. Prévost (Eds.), *Inquiries in linguistic development: In honor of Lydia White* (pp. 305–334). Amsterdam: John Benjamins.

Bruhn de Garavito, J. (2009). Eventive and stative passives: The role of transfer in the acquisition of *ser* and *estar* by German and English L1 speakers. In J. Collentine & e. al. (Eds.), *Selected proceedings of the 11th Hispanic Linguistics Symposium* (pp. 27–38). Somerville, MA: Cascadilla Proceedings Project.

Bruhn de Garavito, J., & Montrul, S. (1996). Verb movement and clitic placement in French and Spanish as a second language. In A. Stringfellow, D. Cahana-Amitay, E. Hughes, & A. Zukowski (Eds.), *Proceedings of the 20th annual Boston University Conference on Language Development.* Somerville, MA: Cascadilla Press.

Bruhn de Garavito, J., & Valenzuela, E. (2008). Eventive and stative passives in Spanish L2 acquisition: A matter of aspect. *Bilingualism: Language and Cognition, 11*, 323–336.

Bruhn de Garavito, J., & White, L. (2002). The L2 acquisition of Spanish DPs. The status of grammatical features. In A. T. Pérez-Leroux & J. Liceras (Eds.), *The acquisition of Spanish morphosyntax: The L1/L2 connection* (pp. 151–178). Dordrecht: Springer.

Brumfilt, C. J. (1984). *Communicative methodology in language teaching: The roles of accuracy and fluency.* Cambridge, UK: Cambridge University Press.

Butler, Y. G. (2002). Second language learners' theories on the use of English articles: An analysis of the metalinguistic knowledge used by Japanese students in acquiring the English article system. *Studies in Second Language Acquisition, 24*, 451–480.

Butler, Y. G. (2017). ISLA in East Asian contexts. In S. Loewen & M. Sato (Eds.), *The Routledge handbook of instructed second language acquisition* (pp. 321–338). New York: Routledge.

Cabrera, M., & Zubizarreta, M. L. (2003). On the acquisition of Spanish causative structures by L1 speakers of English. In J. Liceras, H. Zobl, & H. Goodluck (Eds.), *Proceedings of the 2002 Generative Approaches to Second Language Acquisition (GASLA-6): L2 Links* (pp. 24–33). Somerville, MA: Cascasdilla Press.

Cabrera, M., & Zubizarreta, M. L. (2005). Overgeneralization of causatives and transfer in L2 Spanish and L2 English. In D. Eddington (Ed.), *Selected proceedings of the 6th Conference on the Acquisition of Spanish and Portuguese as First and Second Languages* (pp. 15–30). Somerville, MA: Cascadilla Proceedings Project.

Cadierno, T. (1995). Formal instruction from a processing perspective: An investigation into the Spanish past tense. *The Modern Language Journal, 79*, 179–193.

Calafato, R. (2019). The non-native speaker teacher as proficient multilingual: A critical review of research from 2009-2018. *Lingua, 227,* 1-25.

Cameron, R. (2011). *Native and nonnative processing of modality and mood in Spanish.* PhD dissertation, Florida State University.

Carreira, M. (2012). Meeting the needs of heritage language learners: Approaches, strategies, and research. In S. M. Beaudrie & M. Fairclough (Eds.), *Spanish as a heritage language in the United States: The state of the field* (pp. 223-240). Washington, DC: Georgetown University Press.

Carrier, J., & Randall, J. H. (1992). The argument structure and syntactic structure of resultatives. *Linguistic Inquiry, 23,* 173-234.

Carroll, S., & Swain, M. (1993). Explicit and implicit negative feedback: An empirical study of the learning of linguistic generalizations. *Studies in Second Language Acquisition, 15,* 357-386.

Cawalho, A. M., & Da Silva, A. J. B. (2006). Cross-linguistic influence in third language acquisition: The case of Spanish-English bilinguals' acquisition of Portuguese. *Foreign Language Annals, 39,* 185-202.

Chang, C. (2021). Phonetics and phonology of heritage languages. In S. Montrul & M. Polinsky (Eds.), *The Cambridge handbook of heritage languages and linguistics* (pp. 581-612). Cambridge, UK: Cambridge University Press.

Chang, F., Dell, G. S., & Bock, K. (2006). Becoming syntactic. *Psychological Review, 113,* 234.

Chang, F., Dell, G. S., Bock, K., & Griffin, Z. M. (2000). Structural priming as implicit learning: A comparison of models of sentence production. *Journal of Psycholinguistic Research, 29,* 217-230.

Chang, L.-H. (2004). Discourse effects on EFL learners' production of dative constructions. *Journal of National Kaohsiung University of Applied Sciences, 33,* 145-170.

Chen, L., Shu, H. U. A., Liu, Y., Zhao, J., & Li, P. (2007). ERP signatures of subject-verb agreement in L2 learning. *Bilingualism: Language and Cognition, 10,* 161-174.

Cheng, A. C., & Diaz-Mojica, C. (2006). The effects of formal instruction and study abroad on improving proficiency: The case of the Spanish subjunctive. *Applied Language Learning, 16,* 17-36.

Chiuchiù, G., & Benati, A. (2020). A self-paced-reading study on the effects of structured input and textual enhancement on the acquisition of the Italian subjunctive of doubt. *Instructed Second Language Acquisition, 4,* 235-257.

Choi, S. H., & Ionin, T. (2021). Plural marking in the second language: Atomicity, definiteness, and transfer. *Applied Psycholinguistics, 42,* 549-578.

Choi, S. H., Ionin, T., & Zhu, Y. (2018). L1 Korean and L1 Mandarin L2 English learners' acquisition of the count/

mass distinction in English. *Second Language Research, 34,* 147–177.

Chomsky, N. (1965). *Aspects of the theory of syntax.* Cambridge, MA: MIT Press.

Chomsky, N. (1981). *Lectures on government and binding.* Dordrecht: Foris.

Chomsky, N. (1986). *Knowledge of language.* New York: Praeger.

Chomsky, N. (1993). A minimalist program for linguistic theory. In K. Hale & S. J. Keyser (Eds.), *The view from building 20: Essays in linguistics in honor of Sylvain Bromberger.* Cambridge, MA: MIT Press.

Chomsky, N. (1995). *The minimalist program.* Cambridge, MA: MIT Press.

Chrabaszcz, A., & Jiang, N. (2014). The role of native language in the use of the English nongeneric definite article by L2 learners: A cross-linguistic comparison. *Second Language Research, 30,* 351–379.

Cinque, G. (2010). *The syntax of adjectives: A comparative study.* Cambridge, MA: MIT Press.

Clahsen, H., & Muysken, P. (1986). The availability of universal grammar to adult and child learners: A study of the acquisition of German word order. *Second Language Research, 2,* 93–119.

Collentine, J. (1995). The development of complex syntax and mood-selection abilities by intermediate-level learners of Spanish. *Hispania, 78,* 122–135.

Collentine, J. (1998). Processing instruction and the subjunctive. *Hispania, 81,* 576–587.

Collentine, J. (2010). The acquisition and teaching of the Spanish subjunctive: An update on current findings. *Hispania, 93,* 39–51.

Collentine, J. (2013). Subjunctive in second language Spanish. In K. L. Geestlin (Ed.), *The handbook of Spanish second language acquisition* (pp. 270–286). Oxford: Wiley.

Comrie, B. S. (1976). *Aspect: An introduction to the study of verbal aspect and related problems.* Cambridge, UK: Cambridge University Press.

Conradie, S. (2005). *Verb movement parameters in Afrikaans: Investigating the full transfer full access hypothesis.* PhD dissertation, McGill University.

Conwell, E., & Demuth, C. (2007). Early syntactic productivity: Evidence from dative shift. *Cognition, 103,* 163–179.

Correa, M. (2011). Heritage language learners of Spanish: What role does metalinguistic knowledge play in their acquisition of the subjunctive. In L. A. Ortiz-López (Ed.), *Selected proceedings of the 13th Hispanic linguistics symposium* (pp. 128–138). Somerville, MA: Cascadilla Proceedings Project.

Coşkun Kunduz, A., & Montrul, S. (2022). Relative clauses in child heritage speakers of Turkish in the United States. *Linguistic Approaches to Bilingualism, online first.*

Crain, S. (1991). Language acquisition in the absence of experience. *Behavioral and Brain Sciences, 14,* 597–650.

Crain, S., & Thornton, R. (1998). *Investigations in universal grammar: A guide to experiments on the acquisition of syntax and semantics.* Cambridge, MA: MIT Press.

Crain, S., Thornton, R., & Murasugi, K. (2009). Capturing the evasive passive. *Language Acquisition, 16,* 123–133.

Crawford, W. (2009). The mandative subjunctive. In *One language, two grammars? Differences between British and American English* (pp. 257–276). Cambridge, UK: Cambridge University Press.

Cuervo, M. C. (2003). *Datives at large.* PhD dissertation, Massachusetts Institute of Technology.

Cuervo, M. C. (2007). Double objects in Spanish as a second language: Acquisition of morphosyntax and semantics. *Studies in Second Language Acquisition, 29,* 583–615.

Curtiss, S. (2014). *Genie: A psycholinguistic study of a modern-day wild child.* London: Academic Press.

Cuza, A., Guijarro-Fuentes, P., Pires, A., & Rothman, J. (2012). The syntax-semantics of bare and definite plural subjects in the L2 Spanish of English natives. *International Journal of Bilingualism, 17,* 634–652.

Daskalaki, E., Blom, E., Chondrogianni, V., & Paradis, J. (2020). Effects of parental input quality in child heritage language acquisition. *Journal of Child Language, 47,* 709–736.

Davidson, D. J., & Indefrey, P. (2009). An event-related potential study on changes of violation and error responses during morphosyntactic learning. *Journal of Cognitive Neuroscience, 21,* 433–446.

De Cuypere, L., De Coster, E., & Baten, K. (2014). The acquisition of the English dative alternation by Russian foreign language learners. *Phrasis, 2,* 187–212.

Deen, K. U. (2011). The acquisition of the passive. In J. de Villiers & T. Roeper (Eds.), *Handbook of generative approaches to language acquisition* (pp. 155–187). Dordrecht: Springer.

DeKeyser, R. (1995). Learning second language grammar rules: An experiment with a miniature linguistic system. *Studies in Second Language Acquisition, 17,* 379–410.

DeKeyser, R. (1998). Beyond focus on form: Cognitive perspectives on learning and practicing second language grammar. In C. Doughty & J. Williams (Eds.), *Focus on form in second language acquisition* (pp. 42–63). Cambridge, UK: Cambridge University Press.

DeKeyser, R. (2003). Implicit and explicit learning. In C. J. Doughty & M. Long (Eds.), *Handbook of second language learning* (pp. 313–348). Oxford: Blackwell.

Demonte, V. (1995). Dative alternation in Spanish. *Probus, 7,* 5–30.

Díaz, E. M. (2017). The order of explicit information in processing instruction. *Applied Language Learning, 27,* 41–72.

Doughty, C. (1991). Second language instruction does make a difference: Evidence from an empirical study of

SL relativization. *Studies in Second Language Acquisition, 13*, 431–469.

Doughty, C., & Varela, E. (1998). Communicative focus on form. In C. Doughty & J. N. Williams (Eds.), *Focus on form in classroom second language acquisition* (pp. 114–138). Cambridge, UK: Cambridge University Press.

Doughty, C., & Williams, J. N. (Eds.). (1998). *Focus on form in classroom second language acquisition*. Cambridge, UK: Cambridge University Press.

Dracos, M., Requena, P., & Miller, K. (2019). Acquisition of mood selection in Spanish-speaking children. *Language Acquisition, 26*, 106–118.

Dudley, A. (2020). *An investigation into the acquisition and processing of the subjunctive by English-speaking second language learners of French*. PhD dissertation, University of Southampton.

Eckman, F. (1977). Markedness and the contrastive analysis hypothesis. *Language Learning, 27*, 315–330.

Eckman, F., Bell, L., & Nelson, D. (1988). On the generalization of relative clause instruction in the acquisition of English as a second language. *Applied Linguistics, 9*, 1–20.

Egi, T. (2007). Interpreting recasts as linguistic evidence: The roles of linguistic target, length, and degree of change. *Studies in Second Language Acquisition, 29*, 511–537.

Ellis, N. C. (1994). Introduction: Implicit and explicit language learning: An overview. In N. C. Ellis (Ed.), *Implicit and explicit learning of languages* (pp. 1–31). San Diego, CA: Academic Press.

Ellis, N. C. (1996). Sequencing in SLA: Phonological memory, chunking, and points of order. *Studies in Second Language Acquisition, 18*, 91–126.

Ellis, N. C. (2008). Implicit and explicit knowledge about language. In N. H. Hornberger (Ed.), *Encyclopedia of language and education* (pp. 1901–1911). Boston: Springer.

Ellis, R. (1984). Can syntax be taught? A study of the effects of formal instruction on the acquisition of WH questions by children. *Applied Linguistics, 5*, 138–155.

Ellis, R. (1989). Are classroom and naturalistic acquisition the same? A study of the classroom acquisition of German word order rules. *Studies in Second Language Acquisition, 11*, 305–328.

Ellis, R. (1993). The structural syllabus and second language acquisition. *TESOL Quarterly, 27*, 91–113.

Ellis, R. (2005). Measuring implicit and explicit knowledge of a second language: A psychometric study. *Studies in Second Language Acquisition, 27*, 141–172.

Ellis, R. (2006). Current issues in the teaching of grammar: An SLA perspective. *TESOL Quarterly, 40*, 83–107.

Ellis, R. (2008). Implicit and explicit learning, knowledge and instruction. In R. Ellis, S. Loewen, C. Elder, R. Erlam, J. Philp, & H. Reinders (Eds.), *Implicit and explicit knowledge in second language learning, testing and teaching* (pp. 5–25). Bristol, UK: Multilingual Matters.

Ellis, R. (2016). Focus on form: A critical review. *Language Teaching Research, 20*, 405–428.

Ellis, R. (2017). Task-based language teaching. In S. Loewen & M. Sato (Eds.), *The Routledge handbook of instructed second language acquisition*. New York: Routledge.

Ellis, R., Loewen, S., Elder, C., Reinders, H., Erlam, R., & Philp, J. (Eds.) (2009). *Implicit and explicit knowledge in second language learning, testing and teaching*. Bristol, UK: Multilingual Matters.

Ellis, R., Loewen, S., & Erlam, R. (2006). Implicit and explicit corrective feedback and the acquisition of L2 grammar. *Studies in Second Language Acquisition, 28*, 339–368.

Ellis, R., & Roever, C. (2021). The measurement of implicit and explicit knowledge. *The Language Learning Journal, 49*, 160–175.

Emonds, J. (1978). The verbal complex V'-V in French. *Linguistic Inquiry, 9*, 151–175.

Erdocia, K., Zawiszewski, A., & Laka, I. (2014). Word order processing in a second language: From VO to OV. *Journal of Psycholinguistic Research, 43*, 815–837.

Erlam, R., Loewen, S., & Philp, J. (2009). The roles of output-based and input-based instruction in the acquisition of L2 implicit and explicit knowledge. In R. Ellis, S. Loewen, C. Elder, H. Reinders, R. Erlam, & J. Philp (Eds.), *Implicit and explicit knowledge in second language learning, testing and teaching* (pp. 241–261). Bristol: Multilingual Matters.

Farley, A. (2001a). Authentic processing instruction and the Spanish subjunctive. *Hispania, 84*, 289–299.

Farley, A. (2001b). The effects of processing instruction and meaning-based output instruction. *Spanish Applied Linguistics, 5*, 57–94.

Farley, A. (2004). Processing instruction and the Spanish subjunctive: Is explicit information needed? In B. VanPatten (Ed.), *Processing instruction: Theory, research, and commentary* (pp. 227–240). Mahwah, NJ: Erlbaum.

Farley, A., & McCollam, K. (2004). Learner readiness and L2 production in Spanish: Processability Theory on trial. *Estudios de Lingüística Aplicada, 22*, 47–69.

Farrar, M. J. (1992). Negative evidence and grammatical morpheme acquisition. *Developmental Psychology, 28*, 90.

Fernández-Alcalde, H. (2013). Datives, prepositions, and argument structure in Spanish. In S. Baauw, F. Drijkoningen, L. Meroni, & M. Pinto (Eds.), *Romance languages and linguistic theory 2011: Selected papers from "Going Romance" Utrecht 2011* (pp. 125–142). Amsterdam: John Benjamins.

Fernández, C. (2008). Reexamining the role of explicit information in processing instruction. *Studies in Second Language Acquisition, 30*, 277–305.

Fernández Cuenca, S. (2019). *The effects of language instruction on L2 learners'* input processing and learning outcomes. PhD dissertation, University of Illinois at Urbana-Champaign.

Fernandez Parera, A. (2021). A comparison of the effects of mindful conceptual engagement for the teaching of the subjunctive to heritage- and second-language learners of Spanish. *Languages, 6*, 23.

Flores, C., Santos, A. L., Almeida, L., Jesus, A., & Marques, R. (2019). Portuguese as a heritage language in contact with German and French: A comparative study on the acquisition of verbal mood. In I. Feldhausen, M. Elsig, I. Kuchenbrandt, & M. Neuhaus (Eds.), *Romance languages and linguistic theory 15: Selected papers from "Going Romance" 30, Frankfurt* (pp. 35–52). Amsterdam: John Benjamins.

Flores, C., Santos, A. L., Jesus, A., & Marques, R. (2017). Age and input effects in the acquisition of mood in Heritage Portuguese. *Journal of Child Language, 44*, 795–828.

Fotos, S. S. (1993). Consciousness raising and noticing through focus on form: Grammar task performance vs. formal instruction. *Applied Linguistics, 14*, 385–407.

Fox, D., & Grodzinsky, Y. (1998). Children's passive: a view from the *by*-phrase. *Linguistic Inquiry, 29*, 312–332.

Franco, J. (1993). *On object agreement in Spanish*. PhD dissertation, University of Southern California.

Freidin, R. (1992). *Foundations of generative syntax*. Cambridge, MA: MIT Press.

Fukuda, S. (2017). Split intransitivity in Japanese is syntactic: Evidence for the Unaccusative Hypothesis from sentence acceptability and truth value judgment experiments. *Glossa: A Journal of General Linguistics, 2*, 83.

García-Mayo, M. P., & Hawkins, R. (Eds.) (2009). *Second language acquisition of articles: Empirical findings and theoretical implications*. Amsterdam: John Benjamins.

García Mayo, M. P., & Lázaro Ibarrola, A. (2015). Do children negotiate for meaning in task-based interaction? Evidence from CLIL and EFL settings. *System, 54*, 40–54.

Gass, S. (1982). From theory to practice. In M. Hines & B. Rutherford (Eds.), *On TESOL '81*. Washington, DC: TESOL.

Giancaspro, D. (2019). Over, under and around: Spanish heritage speakers' production (and avoidance) of subjunctive mood. *Heritage Language Journal, 16*, 44–70.

Gil, K.-H., Marsden, H., & Whong, M. (2013). Quantifiers: Form and meaning in second language development. In M. Whong, K.-H. Gil, & H. Marsden (Eds.), *Universal Grammar and the second language classroom* (pp. 139–159). Dordrecht: Springer.

Gili Gaya, S. (1972). *Estudios de lenguaje infantil*. Barcelona: Bibliograf.

Giorgi, A., & Pianesi, F. (1997). *Tense and aspect: From semantics to *morphosyntax*. New York: Oxford University Press.

Goad, H., & White, L. (2006). Ultimate attainment in interlanguage grammars: A prosodic approach. *Second Language Research, 22*, 243-267.

Goad, H., & White, L. (2009). Prosodic transfer and the representation of determiners in Turkish-English interlanguage. In N. Snape, Y.-k. I. Leung, & M. Sharwood Smith (Eds.), *Representational deficits in SLA: Studies in honor of Roger Hawkins* (pp. 1-26). Amsterdam: John Benjamins.

Gobes, S. M., Jennings, R. B., & Maeda, R. K. (2019). The sensitive period for auditory-vocal learning in the zebra finch: Consequences of limited-model availability and multiple-tutor paradigms on song imitation. *Behavioural processes, 163*, 5-12.

Godfroid, A., Loewen, S., Jung, S., Park, J.-H., Gass, S., & Ellis, R. (2015). Timed and untimed grammaticality judgments measure distinct types of knowledge: Evidence from eye-movement patterns. *Studies in Second Language Acquisition, 37*, 269-297.

Gómez Soler, I. (2015). Acquisitional patterns of Spanish anticausative *se*: The end of the road. *Revista española de lingüística aplicada, 28*, 349-381.

Goo, J., Granena, G., Yilmaz, Y., & Novella, M. (2015). Implicit and explicit instruction in L2 learning: Norris & Ortega (2000) revisited and updated. In P. Rebuschat (Ed.), *Implicit and explicit learning of languages*. Amsterdam: John Benjamins.

Gordon, P. (1996). The truth-value judgment task. In D. McDaniel, C. McKee, & H. S. Cairns (Eds.), *Methods for assessing children's syntax* (pp. 125-145). Cambridge, MA: MIT Press.

Green, J. N. (1975). On the frequency of passive constructions in modern Spanish. *Bulletin of Hispanic Studies* (Liverpool), *52*, 345.

Gregg, K. R. (1989). Second language acquisition theory: The case for a generative perspective. In S. Gass & D. L. Schachter (Eds.), *Linguistic perspectives on second language acquisition* (pp. 15-40). Cambridge, UK: Cambridge University Press.

Gropen, J., Pinker, S., Hollander, M., Goldbert, R., & Wilson, R. (1989). The learnability and acquisition of the dative alternation in English. *Language, 65*, 203-257.

Grüter, T., Lew-Williams, C., & Fernald, A. (2012). Grammatical gender in L2: A production or a real-time processing problem? *Second Language Research, 28*, 191-215.

Guasti, M. T. (2017). *Language acquisition: The growth of grammar:* (2nd ed.). Cambridge, MA: MIT Press.

Guijarro-Fuentes, P. (2012). The acquisition of interpretable features in L2 Spanish: Personal *a*. *Bilingualism: Language and Cognition, 15*, 701-720.

Guijarro-Fuentes, P., & Larrañaga, M. P. (2011). Evidence of V to I raising in

L2 Spanish. *International Journal of Bilingualism, 15*, 486–520.

Guijarro-Fuentes, P., & Marinis, T. (2007). Acquiring phenomena at the syntax/semantics interface in L2 Spanish: The personal preposition *a*. In L. Roberts, A. Gürel, S. Tatar, & L. Marti (Eds.), *EUROSLA yearbook: Volume 7* (pp. 67–88). Amsterdam: John Benjamins.

Hamann, C. (2000). Parameters and (L2) acquisition: Verb-raising. In E. Haeberli & C. Laenzlinger (Eds.), *GG@G (Generative Grammar in Geneva)* (Vol. 1, pp. 275–291). Geneva: University of Geneva.

Han, Z. (2002). A study of the impact of recasts on tense consistency in L2 output. *TESOL Quarterly, 36*, 543–572.

Harley, B., Cummins, J., Swain, M., & Allen, P. (1990). The nature of language proficiency. In B. Harley, P. Allen, J. Cummins, & M. Swain (Eds.), *The development of second language proficiency* (pp. 7–25). Cambridge, UK: Cambridge University Press.

Haspelmath, M. (1993). More on the typology of inchoative/causative verb alternations. In B. Comrie & M. Polinsky (Eds.), *Causatives and transitivity* (pp. 87–121). Amsterdam: John Benjamins.

Haverkate, H. (2002). *The syntax, semantics and pragmatics of Spanish mood*. Amsterdam: John Benjamins.

Hawkins, J. (1978). *Definiteness and indefiniteness*. London: Croom Helm.

Hawkins, R. (1987). Markedness and the acquisition of the English dative alternation by L2 speakers. *Second Language Research, 3*, 20–55.

Hawkins, R. (2003). *"Representational deficit" theories of adult SLA: Evidence, counterevidence and implications*. Paper presented at the EuroSLA, Edinburgh, UK.

Hawkins, R., & Chan, Y.-H. (1997). The partial availability of Universal Grammar in second language acquisition: The "Failed Functional Features Hypothesis." *Second Language Research, 13*, 187–226.

Hawkins, R., & Liszka, S. A. (2003). Locating the source of defective past tense marking in advanced L2 English speakers. In R. van Hout, A. Hulk, F. Kuiken, & R. Towell (Eds.), *The lexicon-syntax interface in second language acquisition* (pp. 21–44). Amsterdam: John Benjamins.

Hawkins, R., Saleh Al-Eid, I., Almahboob, P., et al. (2006). Accounting for English article interpretation by L2 speakers. In S. Foster-Cohen, M. Medved Krajnovic, & J. Mihaljević Djigunović (Eds.), *EUROSLA yearbook 6* (pp. 7–25). Amsterdam: John Benjamins.

Hawkins, R., Towell, R., & Bazergui, N. (1993). Universal grammar and the acquisition of French verb movement by native speakers of English. *Second Language Research, 9*, 189–233.

Haznedar, B., & Schwartz, B. D. (1997). Are there optional infinitives in child L2 acquisition? In E. Hughes, M. Hughes, & A. Greenhill (Eds.), *Proceedings of the 21st annual*

Boston University Conference on Language Development (pp. 257–268). Somerville, MA: Cascadilla Press.

Henry, N. (2022). The offline and online effects of processing instruction. *Applied Psycholinguistics, 43*, 945–971.

Henry, N., Culman, H., & VanPatten, B. (2009). More on the effects of explicit information in processing instruction: A partial replication in response to Fernandez (2008). *Studies in Second Language Acquisition, 31*, 359–375.

Henshaw, F., & Hawkins, M. (2022). *Common ground: Second language acquisition theory goes to the classroom*. New York: Hackett Publishing Company.

Hernández Pina, F. (1984). *Teorías psicosociolingüísticas y su aplicación a la adquisición del español como lengua materna*. PhD dissertation, Universidad de Murcia.

Herschensohn, J. (2007). *Language development and age*. Cambridge, UK: Cambridge University Press.

Hertel, T. (2003). Lexical and discourse factors in the second language acquisition of Spanish word order. *Second Language Research, 14*, 273–304.

Hiki, M. (1991). *A study of learners' judgement of noun countability*. PhD dissertation, Indiana University.

Hirakawa, M. (1995). L2 acquisition of English unaccusative constructions. In D. MacLaughlin & S. McEwen (Eds.), *Proceedings of the 19th Boston University Conference on Language Development* (pp. 291–302). Somerville, MA: Cascadilla Press.

Hirakawa, M. (2013). Alternations and argument structure in second language English: Knowledge of two types of intransitive verbs. In M. Whong, K.-H. Gil, & H. Marsden (Eds.), *Universal Grammar and the second language classroom* (pp. 117–138). Dordrecht: Springer.

Hirakawa, M., Shibuya, M., & Endo, M. (2018). Explicit instruction, input flood or study abroad: Which helps Japanese learners of English acquire adjective ordering? *Language Teaching Research, 23*, 158–178.

Hopp, H. (2005). Constraining second language word order optionality: Scrambling in advanced English–German and Japanese–German interlanguage. *Second Language Research, 21*, 34–71.

Hopp, H. (2009). The syntax–discourse interface in near-native L2 acquisition: Off-line and on-line performance. *Bilingualism: Language and Cognition, 12*, 463–483.

Hopper, P. J., & Thompson, S. A. (1980). Transitivity in grammar and discourse. *Language, 56*, 251–299.

Housen, A., & Pierrard, M. (2005). Investigating instructed second language acquisition. In A. Housen & M. Pierrard (Eds.), *Investigations in instructed second language acquisition* (pp. 1–30). Berlin: Mouton de Gruyter.

Howard, M. (2008). Morphosyntactic development in the expression of modality: The subjunctive in French L2 acquisition. *Canadian Journal of Applied Linguistics, 11*, 171–192.

Howard, M. (2012). From tense and aspect to modality: The acquisition of future, conditional and subjunctive morphology in L2 French. A preliminary study. In E. Labeau & I. Saddour (Eds.), *Tense, aspect and mood in first and second language acquisition* (pp. 201–223). Leiden: Brill.

Hudson Kam, C. L., & Newport, E. L. (2005). Regularizing unpredictable variation: The roles of adult and child learners in language formation and change. *Language Learning and Development, 1*, 151–195.

Huebner, T. (1983). *A longitudinal analysis of the acquisition of English*. Ann Arbor, MI: Karoma Press.

Hulk, A. (1991). Parameter setting and the acquisition of word order in L2 French. *Second Language Research, 7*, 1–34.

Hulstijn, J. H. (2002). Towards a unified account of the representation, processing and acquisition of second language knowledge. *Second Language Research, 18*, 193–223.

Hulstijn, J. H. (2005). Theoretical and empirical issues in the study of implicit and explicit second-language learning: Introduction. *Studies in Second Language Acquisition, 27*, 129–140.

Hulstijn, J. H. (2015). Explaining phenomena of first and second language acquisition with the constructs of implicit and explicit learning: The virtues and pitfalls of a two-system view. In P. Rebuschat (Ed.), *Implicit and explicit learning of languages* (pp. 28–47). Amsterdam: John Benjamins.

Hurtado, I., & Montrul, S. (2021a). How do construction frequency effects modulate L2 priming? In D. Dionne & L.-A. V. Covas (Eds.), *Proceedings of the 45th annual Boston University Conference on Language Development* (pp. 346–359). Somerville, MA: Cascadilla Press.

Hurtado, I., & Montrul, S. (2021b). Priming dative clitics in spoken Spanish as a native, second and heritage language. *Studies in Second Language Acquisition, 43*, 729–752.

Huttenlocher, J., Vasilyeva, M., & Shimpi, P. (2004). Syntactic priming in young children. *Journal of Memory and Language, 50*, 182–195.

Hwang, J.-B. (1999). L2 acquisition of English unaccusative verbs under implicit and explicit learning conditions. *English Teaching, 54*, 145–176.

Inagaki, S. (1997). Japanese and Chinese learners' acquisition of the narrow-range rules for the dative alternation in English. *Language Learning, 47*, 637–669.

Inagaki, S. (2002). Japanese learners' acquisition of English manner-of-motion verbs with locational/directional PPs. *Second Language Research, 18*, 3–27.

Ionin, T. (2010). Specificity. In L. Cummings (Ed.), *The Routledge pragmatics encyclopedia*. New York: Routledge.

Ionin, T. (2012a). Formal theory-based methodologies. In A. Mackey & S. Gass (Eds.), *Research methods in second language acquisition: A practical guide* (pp. 30-52). Oxford, UK: Wiley-Blackwell.

Ionin, T. (2012b). Morphosyntax. In J. Herschensohn & M. Young-Scholten (Eds.), *The Cambridge handbook of second language acquisition* (pp. 75-103). Cambridge, UK: Cambridge University Press.

Ionin, T. (2021). Semantics of heritage languages. In S. Montrul & M. Polinsky (Eds.), *The Cambridge handbook of heritage languages and linguistics* (pp. 668-690). Cambridge, UK: Cambridge University Press.

Ionin, T., Choi, S. H., & Liu, Q. (2021). Knowledge of indefinite articles in L2-English: Online vs. offline performance. *Second Language Research, 37*, 121-160.

Ionin, T., Goldshtein, M., Luchkina, T., & Styrina, S. (2021). Who did what to whom, and what did we already know? Word order and information structure in heritage and L2 Russian. *Linguistic Approaches to Bilingualism*, online first.

Ionin, T., Ko, H., & Wexler, K. (2004). Article semantics in L2 acquisition: The role of specificity. *Language Acquisition, 12*, 3-69.

Ionin, T., & Montrul, S. (2010). The role of L1-transfer in the interpretation of articles with definite plurals in L2-English. *Language Learning, 60*, 877-925.

Ionin, T., Montrul, S., & Crivos, M. (2013). A bidirectional study on the acquisition of plural noun phrase interpretation in English and Spanish. *Applied Psycholinguistics, 34*, 483-518.

Ionin, T., Montrul, S., Kim, J., & Philippov, V. (2011). Genericity distinctions and the interpretation of determiners in second language acquisition. *Language Acquisition, 18*, 242-280.

Ionin, T., & Wexler, K. (2002). Why is "is" easier than "-s" ? Acquisition of tense/agreement morphology by child second language learners of English. *Second Language Research, 18*, 95-136.

Ionin, T., Zubizarreta, M. L., & Bautista Maldonado, S. (2008). Sources of linguistic knowledge in the second language acquisition of English articles. *Lingua, 118*, 554-576.

Isabelli, C. A. (2007). Development of the Spanish subjunctive by advanced learners: Study abroad followed by at-home instruction. *Foreign Language Annals, 40*, 330-341.

Issa, B. I., & Morgan-Short, K. (2019). Effects of external and internal attentional manipulations on second language grammar development: An eye-tracking study. *Studies in Second Language Acquisition, 41*, 389-417.

Iverson, M., Kempchinsky, P., & Rothman, J. (2008). Interface vulnerability and knowledge of the subjunctive/indicative distinction with negated epistemic predicates in L2 Spanish. In L. Roberts, F. Myles, &

A. David (Eds.), *EUROSLA yearbook: Volume 8* (pp. 135–163). Amsterdam: John Benjamins.

Izumi, S. (2002). Output, input enhancement and the noticing hypothesis: An experimental study of ESL relativization. *Studies in Second Language Acquisition, 24*, 541–577.

Izumi, S. (2007). Universals, methodology and instructional intervention on relative clauses. *Studies in Second Language Acquisition, 29*, 351–359.

Izumi, S., & Lakshmanan, U. (1998). Learnability, negative evidence and the L2 acquisition of the English passive. *Second Language Research, 14*, 62–101.

Izumi, Y., & Izumi, S. (2004). Investigating the effects of oral output on the learning of relative clauses in English: Issues in the psycholinguistic requirements for effective output tasks. *Canadian Modern Language Review/La revue canadienne des langues vivantes, 60*, 587–609.

Jackson, C. N., & Roberts, L. (2010). Animacy affects the processing of subject–object ambiguities in the second language: Evidence from self-paced reading with German second language learners of Dutch. *Applied Psycholinguistics, 31*, 671–691.

Jäschke, K., & Plag, I. (2016). The dative alternation in German–English interlanguage. *Studies in Second Language Acquisition, 38*, 485–521.

Jegerski, J. (2014). Self-paced reading. In J. Jegerski & B. van Pattern (Eds.), *Research methods in second language psycholinguistics* (pp. 20–49). New York: Routledge.

Jegerski, J. (2018). The processing of the object marker a by heritage Spanish speakers. *International Journal of Bilingualism, 22*, 585–602.

Jiang, N. (2004). Morphological insensitivity in second language processing. *Applied Psycholinguistics, 25*, 603–634.

Jiang, N. (2007). Selective integration of linguistic knowledge in adult second language learning. *Language Learning, 51*, 1–33.

Jiang, N., Novokshanova, E., Masuda, K., & Wang, X. (2011). Morphological congruency and the acquisition of L2 morphemes. *Language Learning, 61*, 940–967.

Jisa, H., Reilly, J., Verhoeven, L., Baruch, E., & Rosado, E. (2002). Passive voice constructions in written texts: A cross-linguistic developmental study. *Written Language & Literacy, 5*, 163–181.

Ju, M. K. (2000). Overpassivization errors by second language learners: The effect of conceptualizable agents in discourse. *Studies in Second Language Acquisition, 22*, 85–111.

Juffs, A. (1996a). *Learnability and the lexicon: Theories and second language acquisition research.* Amsterdam: John Benjamins.

Juffs, A. (1996b). Semantics-syntax correspondences in second language acquisition. *Second Language Research, 12*, 177–221.

Jung, J.-Y. (2019). *Effects of implicit and explicit focus on form on L2 acquisition of the English passive.* EdD dissertation, Columbia University.

Kaan, E., & Chun, E. (2018). Priming and adaptation in native speakers and second-language learners. *Bilingualism: Language and Cognition, 21,* 228–242.

Kanno, K. (2007). Factors affecting the processing of Japanese relative clauses by L2 learners. *Studies in Second Language Acquisition, 29,* 197–218.

Kayne, R. S. (1975). *French syntax: The transformational cycle.* Cambridge, MA: MIT Press.

Keenan, E., & Comrie, B. (1977). Noun phrase accessibility and Universal Grammar. *Linguistic Inquiry, 8,* 63–99.

Kempchinsky, P. (2009). What can the subjunctive disjoint reference effect tell us about the subjunctive? *Lingua, 119,* 1788–1810.

Kim, M. H. (2019). *Processing of canonical and scrambled word orders in native and non-native Korean.* PhD dissertation, University of Illinois at Urbana-Champaign.

Kim, Y. (2017). Cognitive-interactionist approaches to L2 instruction. In S. Loewen & M. Sato (Eds.), *The Routledge handbook of instructed second language acquisition* (pp. 126–145). New York: Routledge.

Krashen, S. (1981). *Second language acquisition and second language learning.* London: Pergamon Press.

Krashen, S. (1982). *Principles and practice in second language acquisition.* London: Pergamon Press.

Krifka, M., Pelletier, F., Carlson, G., ter Meulen, A., Link, G., & Chierchia, G. (1995). Genericity: An introduction In G. Carlson & F. Pelletier (Eds.), *The generic book* (pp. 1–125). Chicago, IL: University of Chicago Press.

Kuiken, F., & Vedder, I. (2002). The effect of interaction in acquiring the grammar of a second language. *Journal of Educational Research, 37,* 343–358.

Kupisch, T. (2012). Specific and generic subjects in the Italian of German-Italian simultaneous bilinguals and L2 learners. *Bilingualism: Language and Cognition, 15,* 736–756.

Laenzlinger, C. (2005). French adjective ordering: Perspectives on DP-internal movement types. *Lingua, 115,* 645–689.

Lantolf, J. P., & Poehner, M. E. (Eds.). (2008). *Sociocultural theory and the teaching of second languages.* London: Equinox.

Lardiere, D. (1998a). Case and tense in the "fossilized" steady state. *Second Language Research, 14,* 1–26.

Lardiere, D. (1998b). Dissociating syntax from morphology in a divergent end-state grammar. *Second Language Research, 14,* 359–375.

Lardiere, D. (2000). Mapping features to forms in second language acquisition. In J. Archibald (Ed.), *Second language acquisition and linguistic theory* (pp. 102–129). Malden, MA: Blackwell.

Lardiere, D. (2003). Second language knowledge of [+/−past] vs. [+/−finite]. In J. Liceras, H. Goodluck, & H. Zobl (Eds.), *Proceedings of the 6th Generative Approaches to Second Language Acquisition Conference (GASLA 2002)* (pp. 176–189). Somerville, MA: Cascadilla Proceedings Project.

Lardiere, D. (2009). Some thoughts on the contrastive analysis of features in second language acquisition. *Second Language Research, 25*, 173–227.

Larsen-Freeman, D., & Celce-Murcia, M. (2015). *The grammar book* (3rd ed.). Boston, MA: Cengage Learning.

Le Compagnon, B. L. (1984). Interference and overgeneralization in second language learning: The acquisition of English dative verbs by native speakers of French. *Language Learning, 34*, 39–57.

Leal, T., Destruel, E., & Hoot, B. (2018). The acquisition of focus in L2 Spanish. *Second Language Research, 35*, 449–477.

Leal, T., & Slabakova, R. (2019). The relationship between L2 instruction, exposure, and the L2 acquisition of a syntax–discourse property in L2 Spanish. *Language Teaching Research, 23*, 237–258.

Leal, T., Slabakova, R., & Farmer, T. A. (2017). The fine-tuning of linguistic expectations over the course of L2 learning. *Studies in Second Language Acquisition, 39*, 493–525.

Lee, J.-H. (2010). Overpassivization and overcausativization: Was it happened because someone happened it? *Anglistics, 10*, 389–410.

Lee, J. F. (1987). Comprehending the Spanish subjunctive: An information processing perspective. *The Modern Language Journal, 71*, 50–57.

Lee, J. F. (2015). Processing instruction on the Spanish passive with transfer-of-training effects to anaphoric and cataphoric reference contexts. *International Review of Applied Linguistics in Language Teaching, 53*, 203–223.

Lee, J. F. (2019). The second language processing of passives, object pronouns and null subjects. *Hispania, 102*, 91–100.

Lee, J. F., & Benati, A. (2007). Comparing modes of delivering processing instruction and meaning based output instruction on Italian and French subjunctive. In A. Benati & J. F. Lee (Eds.), *Delivering processing instruction in classrooms and in virtual contexts: Research and practice*. Sheffield, UK: Equinox Publishing.

Lee, J. F., Cadierno, T., Class, W., & VanPatten, B. (1997). The effects of lexical and grammatical cues on processing past temporal reference in second language input. *Applied Language Learning, 8*, 1–27.

Lee, J. F., & Doherty, S. (2019). Native and nonnative processing of active and passive sentences: The effects of processing instruction on the allocation of visual attention. *Studies in Second Language Acquisition, 41*, 853–879.

Leeman, J. (2003). Recasts and second language development: Beyond negative evidence. *Studies in Second Language Acquisition, 25,* 37–63.

Leeser, M. J. (2013). On psycholinguistic methods. In J. Jegerski & B. VanPatten (Eds.), *Research methods in second language psycholinguistics* (pp. 247–268). New York: Routledge.

Leeser, M. J. (2021). Why does processing instruction work? In M. J. Leeser, G. Ward, & W. Wong (Eds.), *Research on second language processing and processing instruction: Studies in honor of Bill VanPatten* (pp. 295–323). Amsterdam: John Benjamins.

Leeser, M. J., Brandl, A., & Weissglass, C. (2011). Task effects in second language sentence processing research. In P. Trofimovich & K. McDonough (Eds.), *Applying priming methods to L2 learning, teaching, and research: Insights from psycholinguistics* (pp. 179–198). Amsterdam: John Benjamins.

Leeser, M. J., & DeMil, A. (2013). Investigating the secondary effects of processing instruction in Spanish: From instruction on accusative clitics to transfer-of-training effects on dative clitics. *Hispania, 96,* 748–762.

Leow, R. P. (1995). Modality and intake in second language acquisition. *Studies in Second Language Acquisition, 17,* 79–89.

Leow, R. P., Egi, T., Nuevo, A. M., & Tsai, Y.-C. (2003). The roles of textual enhancement and type of linguistic item in adult L2 learners' comprehension and intake. *Applied Language Learning, 13,* 1–16.

Levin, B. (1993). *English verb classes and alternations: A preliminary investigation.* Chicago, IL: The University of Chicago Press.

Levin, B., & Rappaport Hovav, M. (1995). *Unaccusativity at the syntax semantics interface.* Cambridge, MA: MIT Press.

Liceras, J. M. (1985). The value of clitics in non-native Spanish. *Second Language Research, 1,* 151–168.

Lichtman, K. (2013). Developmental comparisons of implicit and explicit language learning. *Language Acquisition, 20,* 93–108.

Lichtman, K. (2016). Age and learning environment: Are children implicit second language learners? *Journal of Child Language, 43,* 707–730.

Lightbown, P. M. (1983). Exploring relationships between developmental and instructional sequences in L2 acquisition. In H. Seliger & M. H. Long (Eds.), *Classroom-oriented research in second language acquisition* (pp. 217–243). Rowley, MA: Newbury House.

Lipski, J. (1993). Creoloid phenomena in the Spanish of transitional bilinguals. In A. Roca & J. Lipski (Eds.), *Spanish in the United States* (pp. 155–173). Berlin: Mouton de Gruyter.

Liu, D., & Gleason, J. (2002). Acquisition of the article the by nonnative speakers of English: An analysis of four nongeneric uses. *Studies in*

Second Language Acquisition, 24, 1–26.

LoCoco, V. (1987). Learner comprehension of oral and written sentences in German and Spanish: The importance of word order. In B. VanPatten, T. Dvorak, & J. F. Lee (Eds.), *Foreign Language Learning: A Research Perspective* (pp. 119–129). Cambridge, MA: Newbury House.

Loewen, S. (2014). *Introduction to instructed second language acquisition*. New York: Routledge.

Loewen, S., Erlam, R., & Ellis, R. (2009). The incidental acquisition of third person -s as implicit and explicit knowledge. In R. Ellis, S. Loewen, C. Elder, H. Reinders, R. Erlam, & J. Philp (Eds.), *Implicit and explicit knowledge in second language learning, testing and teaching* (pp. 262–280): Multilingual Matters.

Loewen, S., & Philp, J. (2012). Instructed second language acquisition. In A. Mackey & S. M. Gass (Eds.), *Research methods in second language acquisition: A practical guide* (pp. 5–73). Oxford: Wiley-Blackwell.

Loewen, S., & Sato, M. (Eds.) (2017). *The Routledge handbook of instructed second language acquisition*. New York: Routledge.

Lohdal, T. (2021). Syntax of heritage languages. In S. Montrul & M. Polinsky (Eds.), *The Cambridge handbook of heritage languages and linguistics* (pp. 644–667). Cambridge, UK: Cambridge University Press.

Long, M. (1981). Input, interaction, and second language acquisition. In H. Winitz (Ed.), *Native language and foreign language acquisition* (pp. 250–278). New York: Annals of the New York Academy of Sciences.

Long, M. (1983). Does second language instruction make a difference? A review of research. *TESOL Quarterly, 17*, 359–382.

Long, M. (1988). Instructed interlanguage development. In L. Beebe (Ed.), *Issues in second language acquisition: Multiple perspectives* (pp. 115–141). Rowley, MA: Newbury House.

Long, M. (2017). *Problems in SLA*. E-book. New York: Routledge.

Long, M., & Crookes, G. (1992). Three approaches to task-based syllabus design. *TESOL Quarterly, 26*, 27–56.

Long, M., Inagaki, S., & Ortega, L. (1998). The role of implicit negative feedback in SLA: Models and recasts in Japanese and Spanish. *The Modern Language Journal, 82*, 357–371.

Lopez, E. (2019). Teaching the English article system: Definiteness and specificity in linguistically informed instruction. *Language Teaching Research, 23*, 200–217.

López Ornat, S., Fernández, A., Gallo, P., & Arjona, P. (1994). *La adquisición de la lengua española*. Lingüística y teoría literaria. Madrid: Siglo XXI de España Editores.

Lozano, C. (2006). Focus and split intransitivity: The acquisition of word order alternations in non-native Spanish. *Second Language Research, 22*, 145–187.

Lubbers Quesada, M. (1998). L2 acquisition of the Spanish

subjunctive mood and prototype schema development. *Spanish Applied Linguistics, 2*, 1–23.

Lustres, E., Cuza, A., & García-Tejada, A. (2020). The acquisition of obligatory and variable mood selection in epistemic predicates by L2 learners and heritage speakers of Spanish. In D. Pascual y Cabo & I. Elola (Eds.), *Current theoretical and applied perspectives on Hispanic and Lusophone linguistics* (pp. 319–342). Amsterdam: John Benjamins.

Lynch, A. (1999). *The subjunctive in Miami Cuban Spanish: Bilingualism, contact, and language variability.* PhD dissertation, University of Minnesota.

Lyster, R. (1998). The ambiguity of recasts and repetition in L2 classroom discourse. *Studies in Second Language Acquisition, 20*, 51–81.

Lyster, R. (2004a). Differential effects of prompts and recasts in form-focused instruction. *Studies in Second Language Acquisition, 26*, 399–432.

Lyster, R. (2004b). Research on form-focused instruction in immersion classrooms: implications for theory and practice. *Journal of French Language Studies, 14*, 321–341.

Lyster, R. (2007). *Learning and teaching languages through content: A counterbalanced approach.* Amsterdam: John Benjamins.

Lyster, R. (2015). Using form-focused tasks to integrate language across the immersion curriculum. *System, 54*, 4–13.

Lyster, R. (2017). Content-based language teaching. In S. Loewen & M. Sato (Eds.), *The Routledge handbook of instructed second language acquisition* (pp. 87–107). New York: Routledge.

Lyster, R., & Ranta, L. (1997). Corrective feedback and learner uptake: Negotiation of form in communicative classrooms. *Studies in Second Language Acquisition, 19*, 37–66.

Mackey, A. (1999). Input, interaction, and second language development: An empirical study of question formation in ESL. *Studies in Second Language Acquisition, 21*, 557–587.

Mackey, A. (2017). Classroom-based research. In S. Loewen & M. Sato (Eds.), *The Routledge handbook of instructed second language acquisition* (pp. 541–561). New York: Routledge.

Mackey, A., & Gass, S. (2022). *Second language research: Methodology and design* (3rd ed.). New York: Routledge.

MacWhinney, B. (1997). Second language acquisition and the Competition Model. In A. de Groot & J. Kroll (Eds.), *Tutorials in bilingualism: Psycholinguistic perspectives* (pp. 113–142). New York: Psychology Press.

Maie, R., & DeKeyser, R. M. (2020). Conflicting evidence of explicit and implicit knowledge from objective and subjective measures. *Studies in Second Language Acquisition, 42*, 359–382.

Malovrh, P., & Lee, J. F. (2014). *The developmental dimension in instructed second language learning: The L2 acquisition of object pronouns in Spanish*. London: Bloomsbury Publishing.

Mandell, P. (1996). *The verb movement parameter and adult L2 learners of Spanish*. PhD dissertation, University of Illinois at Urbana-Champaign.

Marcus, G. F. (1993). Negative evidence in language acquisition. *Cognition, 46*, 53–85.

Marefat, H. (2005). The impact of information structure as a discourse factor on the acquisition of dative alternation by L2 learners. *Studia Linguistica, 59*, 66–82.

Marinis, T. (2003). Psycholinguistic techniques in second language acquisition research. *Second Language Research, 19*, 144–161.

Marinis, T. (2010). Using on-line processing methods in language acquisition research. In E. Blom & S. Unsworth (Eds.), *Experimental methods in language acquisition research* (pp. 139–162). Amsterdam: John Benjamins.

Marsden, H. (2009). Distributive quantifier scope in English-Japanese and Korean-Japanese Interlanguage. *Language Acquisition, 16*, 135–177.

Master, P. (1987). *A cross-linguistic interlanguage analysis of the acquisition of the English article system*. PhD dissertation, University of California Los Angeles.

Master, P. (1990). Teaching the English articles as a binary system. *TESOL Quarterly, 24*, 461–478.

Master, P. (1994). The effect of systematic instruction on learning the English article system. In T. Odlin (Ed.), *Perspectives in pedagogical grammar* (pp. 229–252). Cambridge, UK: Cambridge University Press.

Master, P. (1997). The English article system: Acquisition, function, and pedagogy. *System, 23*, 215–232.

Master, P. (2002). Information structure and English article pedagogy. *System, 30*, 331–348.

Matsunaga, K. (2005). Overgeneralisation in second language acquisition of transitivity alternations. *Second Language, 4*, 75–110.

Mayberry, R. I. (2012). Early language acquisition and adult language ability: What sign language reveals about the critical period for language. In M. Marschark, P. Spencer, & R. I. Mayberry (Eds.), *The Oxford handbook of Deaf studies, language, and education* (Vol. 2, pp. 281–291). Oxford: Oxford University Press.

Mayberry, R. I., & Kluender, R. (2018). Rethinking the critical period for language: New insights into an old question from American Sign Language. *Bilingualism: Language and Cognition, 21*, 886–905.

Mazurkewich, I. (1984). The acquisition of the dative alternation by second language learners and linguistic theory. *Language Learning, 34*, 91–108.

McCarthy, C. (2008). Morphological variability in the comprehension of agreement: An argument for representation over computation. *Second Language Research, 24*, 459–486.

McDonough, K. (2005). Identifying the impact of negative feedback and learners' responses on ESL question development. *Studies in Second Language Acquisition, 27*, 79–103.

McDonough, K. (2006). Interaction and syntactic priming: English L2 speakers' production of dative constructions. *Studies in Second Language Acquisition, 28*, 179–207.

McDonough, K., & Mackey, A. (2006). Responses to recasts: Repetitions, primed production, and linguistic development. *Language Learning, 56*, 693–720.

McDonough, K., & Mackey, A. (2008). Syntactic priming and ESL question development. *Studies in Second Language Acquisition, 30*, 31–47.

McManus, K., & Mitchell, R. (2015). Subjunctive use and development in L2 French: A longitudinal study. *Language, Interaction and Acquisition, 6*, 42–73.

Merino, B. J. (1983). Language loss in bilingual Chicano children. *Journal of Applied Developmental Psychology, 4*, 227–294.

Meurers, D., De Kuthy, K., Nuxoll, F., Rudzewitz, B., & Ziai, R. (2019). Scaling up intervention studies to investigate real-life foreign language learning in school. *Annual Review of Applied Linguistics, 39*, 161–188.

Mikulski, A. M. (2010). Receptive volitional subjunctive abilities in heritage and traditional foreign language learners of Spanish. *The Modern Language Journal, 94*, 217–233.

Mitsugi, S., & MacWhinney, B. (2010). Second language processing in Japanese scrambled sentences. In B. VanPatten & J. Jegerski (Eds.), *Research in second language processing and parsing* (pp. 159–175). Amsterdam: John Benjamins.

Montrul, S. (1999a). Activating AgrIOP in second language acquisition. In E. Klein & G. Martohardjono (Eds.), *The development of second language grammars: A generative approach* (pp. 81–108). Amsterdam: John Benjamins.

Montrul, S. (1999b). Causative errors with unaccusative verbs in L2 Spanish. *Second Language Research, 15*, 191–219.

Montrul, S. (2000). Transitivity alternations in L2-acquisition: Toward a modular view of transfer. *Studies in Second Language Acquisition, 22*, 229–273.

Montrul, S. (2001a). The acquisition of causative/inchoative verbs in L2 Turkish. *Language Acquisition, 9*, 1–58.

Montrul, S. (2001b). Agentive verbs of manner of motion in Spanish and English as second languages. *Studies in Second Language Acquisition, 23*, 171–206.

Montrul, S. (2001c). First-language-constrained variability in the second-language acquisition of argument-structure-changing morphology with causative verbs.

Second Language Research, 17, 144–194.

Montrul, S. (2004a). *The acquisition of Spanish.* Amsterdam: John Benjamins.

Montrul, S. (2004b). Psycholinguistic evidence for split intransitivity in Spanish second language acquisition. *Applied Psycholinguistics, 25,* 239–267.

Montrul, S. (2004c). Subject and object expression in Spanish heritage speakers: A case of morpho-syntactic convergence. *Bilingualism: Language and Cognition, 7,* 1–18.

Montrul, S. (2006). On the bilingual competence of Spanish heritage speakers: Syntax, lexical-semantics and processing. *International Journal of Bilingualism, 10,* 37–69.

Montrul, S. (2007). Interpreting mood distinctions in Spanish as a heritage language. In K. Potowski & R. Cameron (Eds.), *Spanish in contact: Policy, social and linguistic inquiries* (pp. 23–40). Amsterdam: John Benjamins.

Montrul, S. (2008). *Incomplete acquisition in Bilingualism: Re-examining the age factor.* Amsterdam: John Benjamins.

Montrul, S. (2009). Knowledge of tense-aspect and mood in Spanish heritage speakers. *International Journal of Bilingualism, 13,* 239–369.

Montrul, S. (2010a). Dominant language transfer in adult second language learners and heritage speakers. *Second Language Research, 26,* 293–327.

Montrul, S. (2010b). How similar are adult second language learners and Spanish heritage speakers? Spanish clitics and word order. *Applied Psycholinguistics, 31,* 167–207.

Montrul, S. (2016a). *The acquisition of heritage languages.* Cambridge, UK: Cambridge University Press.

Montrul, S. (2016b). The causative/inchoative morphology in L2 Turkish under the Feature Reassembly Approach. In A. Gurel (Ed.), *Second language acquisition of Turkish* (pp. 107–133). Amsterdam: John Benjamins.

Montrul, S. (2019). The acquisition of differential object marking in Spanish by Romanian speakers. *Revista española de lingüística aplicada/Spanish Journal of Applied Linguistics, 32,* 185–219.

Montrul, S. (2022). Heritage language speakers inform the Critical Period Hypothesis for first and second language acquisition. In T. Leal, E. Shimanskaya, & C. Isabelli (Eds.), *Generative SLA in the age of minimalism: Features, interfaces, and beyond* (pp. 265–286). Amsterdam: John Benjamins.

Montrul, S., & Bowles, M. (2010). Is grammar instruction beneficial for heritage language learners? Dative case marking in Spanish. *Heritage Language Journal, 7,* 47–73.

Montrul, S., & Bowles, M. (2017). Instructed heritage language acquisition. In S. Loewen & M. Sato (Eds.), *The Routledge handbook of instructed second language acquisition* (pp. 488-502). New York: Routledge.

Montrul, S., Foote, R., & Perpiñán, S. (2008). Gender agreement in adult second language learners and Spanish heritage speakers: The effects of age and context of acquisition. *Language Learning, 58,* 503-553.

Montrul, S., & Gürel, A. (2015). The acquisition of differential object marking in Spanish by Turkish speakers. In T. Judy & S. Perpiñán (Eds.), *The acquisition of Spanish in understudied language pairings* (pp. 281-308). Amsterdam: John Benjamins.

Montrul, S., & Ionin, T. (2012). Dominant language transfer in Spanish heritage speakers and L2 learners in the interpretation of definite articles. *Modern Language Journal, 96,* 70-94.

Montrul, S., & Perpiñán, S. (2011). Assessing differences and similarities between instructed heritage language learners and L2 learners in their knowledge of Spanish tense-aspect and mood (TAM) morphology. *Heritage Language Journal, 8,* 90-133.

Montrul, S., & Polinsky, M. (Eds.). (2021). *The Cambridge handbook of heritage languages and linguistics.* Cambridge, UK: Cambridge University Press.

Montrul, S., & Sánchez-Walker, N. (2013). Differential object marking in child and adult Spanish heritage speakers. *Language Acquisition, 20,* 109-132.

Morgan-Short, K. (2007). *A neurolinguistic investigation of late-learned second language knowledge: The effects of implicit and explicit conditions.* PhD dissertation, Georgetown University.

Morgan-Short, K., Deng, Z., Brill-Schuetz, K. A., Faretta-Stutenberg, M., Wong, P. C. M., & Wong, F. C. K. (2015). A view of the neural representation of second language syntax through artificial language learning under implicit contexts of exposure. *Studies in Second Language Acquisition, 37,* 383-419.

Morgan-Short, K., Faretta-Stutenberg, M., Brill-Schuetz, K. A., Carpenter, H., & Wong, P. C. M. (2014). Declarative and procedural memory as individual differences in second language acquisition. *Bilingualism: Language and Cognition, 17,* 56-72.

Morgan-Short, K., Sanz, C., Steinhauer, K., & Ullman, M. T. (2010). Second language acquisition of gender agreement in explicit and implicit training conditions: An event-related potential study. *Language Learning, 60,* 154-193.

Nassaji, H. (2017). Grammar acquisition. In S. Loewen & M. Sato (Eds.), *The Routledge handbook of instructed second language acquisition* (pp. 205-223). New York: Routledge.

Negueruela-Azarola, E., & Lantolf, J. (2006). Concept-based instruction and the acquisition of L2 Spanish. In R. Salaberry & B. Lafford (Eds.), *The art of teaching Spanish: Second* language acquisition from research to praxis (pp. 79–102). Washington, DC: Georgetown University Press.

Newby, D. (2000). Pedagogical grammar. In M. Byram & A. Hu (Eds.), *Routledge Encyclopedia of Language Teaching and Learning*. New York: Routledge.

Nicholas, H., Lightbown, P. M., & Spada, N. (2001). Recasts as feedback to language learners. *Language Learning, 51*, 719–758.

Norris, J., & Ortega, L. (2000). Effectiveness of L2 instruction: A research synthesis and quantitative meta-analysis. *Language Learning, 50*, 417–528.

O'Grady, W. (1997). *Syntactic development*. Chicago, IL: University of Chicago Press.

O'Grady, W., Lee, M., & Choo, M. (2003). A subject-object asymmetry in the acquisition of relative clauses in Korean as a second language. *Studies in Second Language Acquisition, 25*, 433–448.

O'Grady, W., Kwak, H.-Y., Lee, O.-S., & Lee, M. (2011). An emergentist perspective on heritage language acquisition. *Studies in Second Language Acquisition, 33*, 223–245.

Oh, E. (2010). Recovery from first-language transfer: The second language acquisition of English double objects by Korean speakers. *Second Language Research, 26*, 407–439.

Omaki, A., & Ariji, K. (2005). Testing and attesting the use of structural information in L2 sentence processing. In L. Dekydtspotter, R. Sprouse, & A. Liljestrand (Eds.), *Proceedings of the 7th Generative Approaches to Second Language Acquisition Conference* (pp. 205–218). Somerville, MA: Cascadilla Proceedings Project.

Oshita, H. (2001). The Unaccusative Trap Hypothesis in second language acquisition. *Studies in Second Language Acquisition, 23*, 279–304.

Paradis, J. (2011). Individual differences in child English second language acquisition: Comparing child-internal and child-external factors. *Linguistic Approaches to Bilingualism, 1*, 213–237.

Paradis, J. (2019). English second language acquisition from early childhood to adulthood: The role of age, first language, cognitive, and input factors. In M. Brown & B. Dailey (Eds.), *Proceedings of the 43rd Boston University Conference on Language Development*, (pp. 11–26). Somerville, MA: Cascadilla Press.

Paradis, M. (1994). Neurolinguistic aspects of implicit and explicit memory: Implications for bilingualism and SLA. In N. C. Ellis (Ed.), *Implicit and explicit learning of languages* (pp. 393–419). San Diego, CA: Academic Press.

Paradis, M. (2009). *Declarative and procedural determinants of second languages*. Amsterdam: John Benjamins.

Pereira, I. (1996). *Markedness and instructed SLA: An experiment in teaching the Spanish subjunctive.* PhD dissertation, University of Illinois at Urbana-Champaign.

Perez-Cortes, S. (2022). Lexical frequency and morphological regularity as sources of heritage speaker variability in the acquisition of mood. *Second Language Research, 38*, 149-171.

Pérez-Leroux, A. T. (1998). The acquisition of mood selection in Spanish relative clauses. *Journal of Child Language, 25*, 585-604.

Perlmutter, D. (1978). Impersonal passives and the Unaccusative Hypothesis. In J. Jaeger (Ed.), *Proceedings of the fourth annual meeting of the Berkeley Linguistic Society* (pp. 157-189). Berkeley, CA: Berkeley Linguistic Society, University of California.

Perlmutter, D., & Postal, P. (1984). The 1-advancement exclusiveness law. In D. Perlmutter & C. Rosen (Eds.), *Studies in relational grammar 2* (pp. 81-126). Chicago: University of Chicago Press.

Perpiñán, S., & Montrul, S. (2006). On binding asymmetries in dative alternation construction in L2 Spanish. In C. Klee & T. Face (Eds.), *Selected proceedings of the 7th Conference on the Acquisition of Spanish and Portuguese as First and Second Languages* (pp. 135-148). Somerville, MA: Cascadilla Proceedings Project.

Pienemann, M. (1984). Psychological constraints on the teachability of languages. *Studies in Second Language Acquisition, 6*, 186-214.

Pienemann, M. (1989). Is language teachable? Psycholinguistic experiments and hypotheses. *Applied Linguistics, 10*, 52-79.

Pienemann, M. (1998). *Language processing and second language development: Processability Theory.* Amsterdam: John Benjamins.

Pienemann, M. (2005). *Cross-linguistic aspects of Processability Theory.* Amsterdam: John Benjamins.

Pierce, A. E. (1992). The acquisition of passives in Spanish and the question of A-chain maturation. *Language Acquisition, 2*, 55-81.

Pinker, S. (1989). *Learnability and cognition.* Cambridge, MA: MIT Press.

Pinker, S. (1994). *The language instinct.* New York: William Morrow.

Pinker, S., Lebeaux, D., & Frost, L. A. (1987). Productivity and constraints in the acquisition of the passive. *Cognition, 26*, 195-267.

Platzack, C. (1986). COMP, INFL, and Germanic word order. In L. Hellan & K. K. Christensen (Eds.), *Topics in Scandinavian syntax* (pp. 185-234). Boston: Springer.

Plonsky, L. (2013). Study quality in SLA An assessment of designs, analyses, and reporting practices in quantitative L2 research. *Studies in Second Language Acquisition, 35*, 655-687.

Polinsky, M. (2007). Incomplete acquisition: American Russian. *Journal of Slavic Linguistics, 14*, 191-262.

Polinsky, M. (2018). *Heritage languages and their speakers.* Cambridge, UK: Cambridge University Press.

Pollock, J.-Y. (1989). Verb movement, Universal Grammar and the structure of IP. *Linguistic Inquiry, 20*, 365–424.

Potowski, K., Jegerski, J., & Morgan-Short, K. (2009). The effects of instruction on linguistic development in Spanish heritage language speakers. *Language Learning, 59*, 537–579.

Presson, N., MacWhinney, B., & Tokowicz, N. (2014). Learning grammatical gender: The use of rules by novice learners. *Applied Psycholinguistics, 35*, 709–737.

Prévost, P., & White, L. (2000). Missing Surface Inflection or impairment in second language acquisition? Evidence from tense and agreement. *Second Language Research, 16*, 103–133.

Qin, J. (2008). The effect of processing instruction and dictogloss tasks on acquisition of the English passive voice. *Language Teaching Research, 12*, 61–82.

Quer, J. (2009). Twists of mood: The distribution and interpretation of indicative and subjunctive. *Lingua, 119*, 1779–1787.

Radwan, A. A. (2005). The effectiveness of explicit attention to form in language learning. *System, 33*, 69–87.

Rasinger, S. (2014). *Quantitative research in linguistics: An introduction*. London: Bloomsbury.

Rebuschat, P. (2013). Measuring implicit and explicit knowledge in second language research. *Language Learning, 63*, 595–626.

Rebuschat, P. (2015). *Implicit and explicit learning of languages*. Amsterdam: John Benjamins.

Rebuschat, P., & Williams, J. N. (2012a). Implicit and explicit knowledge in second language acquisition. *Applied Psycholinguistics, 33*, 829–856.

Rebuschat, P., & Williams, J. N. (2012b). *Statistical learning and language acquisition*. Berlin: De Gruyter Mouton.

Redmond, M. L. (2013). *Action research in the world language classroom*. Charlotte, NC: Information Age Publishing.

Reinders, H., & Ellis, R. (2009). The effects of two types of input on intake and the acquisition of implicit and explicit knowledge. In R. Ellis, S. Loewen, C. Elder, R. Erlam, J. Philp, & H. Reinders (Eds.), *Implicit and explicit knowledge in second language learning, testing and teaching* (pp. 281–303). Bristol: Multilingual Matters.

Richards, J. C., & Rodgers, T. S. (2001). *Approaches and methods in language teaching* (2nd ed.). Cambridge, UK: Cambridge University Press.

Roberts, M. (2000). *Implicational markedness and the acquisition of relativization by adult learners of Japanese as a foreign language*. PhD dissertation, University of Hawai'i at Manoa.

Robertson, D. (2000). Variability in the use of the English article system by Chinese learners of English. *Second Language Research, 16*, 135–172.

Robinson, P. (2011). *Second language task complexity: Researching the cognition hypothesis of language learning and performance.* Amsterdam: John Benjamins.

Roeper, T., & Williams, E. (1987). *Parameter setting.* New York: Springer Science.

Rothman, J. (2008). Aspect selection in adult L2 Spanish and the Competing Systems Hypothesis: When pedagogical and linguistic rules conflict. *Languages in Contrast, 8,* 74–106.

Rumelhart, D. E., & McClelland, J. J. (1986). On learning the past tense of English verbs. In D. E. Rumelhart & J. J. McClelland (Eds.), *Parallel distributed processing (Vol 2): Psychological and biological models* (pp. 216–271). Cambridge, MA: MIT Press.

Rutherford, W. (1987). *Second language grammar: Learning and teaching.* London: Longman.

Sadri Mirdamadi, F., & De Jong, N. H. (2015). The effect of syntactic complexity on fluency: Comparing actives and passives in L1 and L2 speech. *Second Language Research, 31,* 105–116.

Saldanya, M. P. (1999). *El modo en las subordinadas relativas y adverbiales.* Paper presented at the the Gramática descriptiva de la lengua española.

Sanchez-Naranjo, J. (2009). *L2 learners' difficulties in the interpretation of the Spanish subjunctive: L1 influence and misanalysis of the input.* PhD dissertation, University of Toronto.

Sánchez-Walker, N. (2019). *Comprehension of Spanish relative and passive clauses by early bilinguals and second language learners.* PhD dissertation, University of Illinois at Urbana-Champaign.

Sánchez, L., & Al-Kasey, T. (1999). L2 acquisition of Spanish direct objects. *Spanish Applied Linguistics, 3,* 1–32.

Savage, L., with Bitterlin, G., & Price, D. (2010). *Grammar matters: Teaching grammar in adult ESL programs.* Cambridge, UK: Cambridge University Press.

Schachter, D. L., & Tulving, E. (Eds.). (1994). *Memory systems.* Cambridge, MA: MIT Press.

Schmidt, R. (1990). The role of consciousness in second language learning. *Applied Linguistics, 11,* 129–158.

Schmidt, R. (1993). Consciousness, learning and interlanguage pragmatics. In G. Kasper & S. Blum-Kulka (Eds.), *Interlanguage pragmatics* (pp. 43–57). New York: Oxford University Press.

Schmidt, R. (1994). Deconstructing consciousness in search of useful definitions for applied linguistics. *AILA Review, 11,* 11–26.

Schwartz, B. D. (1986). The epistemological status of second language acquisition. *Second Language Research, 2,* 120–159.

Schwartz, B. D. (1993). On explicit and negative data effecting and affecting competence and linguistic behavior. *Studies in Second Language Acquisition, 15,* 147–163.

Schwartz, B. D., & Gubala-Ryzak, M. (1992). Learnability and grammar reorganization in L2A: Against negative evidence causing the unlearning of verb movement. *Second Language Research, 8,* 1–38.

Schwartz, B. D., & Sprouse, R. A. (1994). Word order and nominative case in non-native language acquisition: A longitudinal study of (L1 Turkish) German interlanguage. In T. Hoekstra & B. D. Schwartz (Eds.), *Language acquisition studies in generative grammar: Papers in honor of Kenneth Wexler from the 1991 GLOW workshops* (pp. 317–368). Amsterdam: John Benjamins.

Schwartz, B. D., & Sprouse, R. A. (1996). L2 cognitive states and the Full Transfer/Full Access Model. *Second Language Research, 12,* 40–72.

Schwartz, B. D., & Vikner, S. (1996). The verb always leaves IP in V2 clauses. In A. Belletti & L. Rizzi (Eds.), *Parameters and functional heads: Essays in comparative syntax* (pp. 11–62). Oxford: Oxford University Press.

Scontras, G., Fuchs, Z., & Polinsky, M. (2015). Heritage language and linguistic theory. *Frontiers in Psychology, 6,* 1545.

Scontras, G., Polinsky, M., Tsai, C.-Y. E., & Mai, K. (2017). Cross-linguistic scope ambiguity: When two systems meet. *Glossa, 2,* 1–28.

Selinker, L. (1972). Interlanguage. *International Review of Applied Linguistics in Language Teaching, 10,* 209–232.

Sharwood Smith, M. (1981). Consciousness-raising and the second language learner. *Applied Linguistics, 2,* 159–169.

Sharwood Smith, M. (1991). Speaking to many minds: On the relevance of different types of language information for the L2 learner. *Second Language Research, 7,* 118–132.

Sharwood Smith, M. (1993). Input enhancement in instructed SLA: Theoretical bases. *Studies in Second Language Acquisition, 15,* 165–179.

Sharwood Smith, M., & Truscott, J. (2014). *The multilingual mind: A modular processing perspective.* Cambridge, UK: Cambridge University Press.

Sheen, Y. (2007). The effect of focused written corrective feedback and language aptitude on ESL Learners' acquisition of articles. *TESOL Quarterly, 41,* 255–283.

Shintani, N., & Ellis, R. (2010). The incidental acquisition of English plural -s by Japanese children in comprehension-based and production-based lessons: A process-product study. *Studies in Second Language Acquisition, 32,* 607–637.

Silva-Corvalán, C. (1994). *Language contact and change: Spanish in Los Angeles.* Oxford: Oxford University Press.

Silva-Corvalán, C. (2003). Linguistic consequences of reduced input in bilingual first language acquisition. In S. Montrul & F. Ordóñez (Eds.), *Linguistic theory and language development in Hispanic languages* (pp. 375–397). Somerville, MA: Cascadilla Press.

Silva-Corvalán, C. (2014). *Bilingual language acquisition: Spanish and English in the first six years.* Cambridge, UK: Cambridge University Press.

Silva-Corvalán, C. (2018). Simultaneous bilingualism: Early developments, incomplete later outcomes? *International Journal of Bilingualism, 22,* 497–512.

Silva, G. V. (2008). Heritage language learning and the Portuguese subjunctive. *Portuguese Language Journal, 3,* 1–28.

Slabakova, R. (2008). *Meaning in the second language.* Berlin: Mouton de Gruyter.

Slabakova, R. (2016). *Second language acquisition.* Oxford: Oxford University Press.

Snape, N. (2008a). *The acquisition of the English determiner phrase by L2 learners: Japanese and Spanish.* Saarbrücken: VDM Verlag.

Snape, N. (2008b). Resetting the Nominal Mapping Parameter: Definite article use and the count-mass distinction. *Bilingualism: Language and Cognition, 11,* 63–79.

Snape, N., García Mayo, M. P., & Gürel, A. (2013). L1 transfer in article selection for generic reference by Spanish, Turkish and Japanese L2 learners. *International Journal of English Studies, 13,* 1–28.

Snape, N., & Yusa, N. (2013). Explicit article instruction in definiteness, specificity, genericity and perception. In M. Whong, K.-H. Gil, & H. Marsden (Eds.), *Universal Grammar and the second language classroom* (pp. 161–186). Dordrecht: Springer.

Sorace, A. (1995). Acquiring linking rules and argument structure in a second language. In L. Eubank, L. Selinker, & M. Sharwood Smith (Eds.), *The current state of interlanguage: Studies in honor of William E. Rutherford* (pp. 153–175). Amsterdam: John Benjamins.

Sorace, A. (2000). Gradients in auxiliary selection with intransitive verbs. *Language, 76,* 859–890.

Sorace, A., & Shomura, Y. (2001). Lexical constraints on the acquisition of split intransitivity: Evidence from L2 Japanese. *Studies in Second Language Acquisition, 23,* 247–278.

Spada, N. (1997). Form-focussed instruction and second language acquisition: A review of classroom and laboratory research. *Language Teaching, 30,* 73–87.

Spada, N. (2007). Communicative language teaching. In J. Cummins & C. Davison (Eds.), *International handbook of English language teaching* (pp. 271–288). Boston: Springer.

Spada, N., & Lightbown, P. M. (1993). Instruction and the development of questions in L2 classrooms. *Studies in Second Language Acquisition, 15,* 205–224.

Spada, N., & Lightbown, P. M. (1999). Instruction, first language influence, and developmental readiness in second language acquisition. *The Modern Language Journal, 83,* 1–22.

Spada, N., Shiu, J. L.-J., & Tomita, Y. (2015). Validating an elicited imitation task as a measure of implicit knowledge: Comparisons with other validation studies. *Language Learning, 65*, 723-751.

Spada, N., & Tomita, Y. (2010). Interactions between type of instruction and type of language feature: A meta-analysis. *Language Learning, 60*, 263-308.

Spinner, P. (2013). The second language acquisition of number and gender in Swahili: A Feature Reassembly approach. *Second Language Research, 29*, 455-479.

Sportiche, D. (1996). Clitic constructions. In J. Rooryck & L. Zaring (Eds.), *Phrase structure and the lexicon* (pp. 213-276). Dordrecht: Springer.

Sproat, R., & Shih, C. (1991). The cross-linguistic distribution of adjective ordering restriction. In C. Georgopoulos & R. Ishihara (Eds.), *Interdisciplinary approaches to language* (pp. 565-593). Dordrecht: Kluwer.

Squire, L. R., Knowlton, B., & Musen, G. (1993). The structure and organization of memory. *Annual Review of Psychology, 44*, 453-495.

Staub, A. (2010). Eye movements and processing difficulty in object relative clauses. *Cognition, 116*, 71-86.

Stringer, D. (2013). Modifying the teaching of modifiers: A lesson from Universal Grammar. In M. Whong, K.-H. Gil, & H. Marsden (Eds.), *Universal Grammar and the second language classroom* (pp. 77-100). Dordrecht: Springer.

Suarez Cepeda, S. (2000). *L2 acquisition of Spanish telic se constructions*. MA thesis, University of North Texas.

Suzuki, Y. (2017). Validity of new measures of implicit knowledge: Distinguishing implicit knowledge from automatized explicit knowledge. *Applied Psycholinguistics, 38*, 1229-1261.

Suzuki, Y., & DeKeyser, R. (2015). Comparing elicited imitation and word monitoring as measures of implicit knowledge. *Language Learning, 65*, 860-895.

Swain, M. (1985). Communicative competence: Some roles of comprehensible input and comprehensible output in its development. In S. Gass & C. Madden (Eds.), *Input in second language acquisition* (pp. 235-253). Rowley, MA: Newbury House.

Swain, M. (1993). The output hypothesis: Just speaking and writing aren't enough. *Canadian Modern Language Review, 50*, 158-164.

Tenny, C. L. (1987). *Grammaticalizing aspect and affectedness*. PhD thesis, Massachusetts Institute of Technology.

Terrell, T., Andrade, M., Egasse, J., & Muñoz, E. M. (1994). *Dos mundos*. New York: McGraw Hill.

Terrell, T., Baycroft, B., & Perrone, C. (1987). The subjunctive in Spanish interlanguage: Accuracy and comprehensibility. In B. VanPatten, T. Dvorak, & J. Lee (Eds.), *Foreign language learning: A research perspective* (pp. 19-32). Boston: Newbury.

Thomas, M. (1989). The acquisition of English articles by first- and second-language learners. *Applied Psycholinguistics, 10*, 335–355.

Tode, T. (2003). From unanalyzed chunks to rules: the learning of the English copula *be* by beginning Japanese learners of English. *International Review of Applied Linguistics in Language Teaching, 41*, 23–53.

Tode, T. (2007). Durability problems with explicit instruction in an EFL context: The learning of the English copula *be* before and after the introduction of the auxiliary *be*. *Language Teaching Research, 11*, 11–30.

Tolchinsky, L., & Rosado, E. (2005). The effect of literacy, text type, and modality on the use of grammatical means for agency alternation in Spanish. *Journal of Pragmatics, 37*, 209–237.

Torres, J. (2018). The effects of task complexity on heritage and L2 Spanish development. *Canadian Modern Language Review, 74*, 128–152.

Toth, P. D. (2006). Processing instruction and a role for output in second language acquisition. *Language Learning, 56*, 319–385.

Toth, P. D., & Guijarro-Fuentes, P. (2013). The impact of instruction on second-language implicit knowledge: Evidence against encapsulation. *Applied Psycholinguistics, 34*, 1163–1193.

Trahey, M. (1996). Positive evidence in second language acquisition: some long-term effects. *Second Language Research, 12*, 111–139.

Trahey, M., & White, L. (1993). Positive evidence and preemption in the second language classroom. *Studies in Second Language Acquisition, 15*, 181–204.

Tremblay, A. (2006). On the second language acquisition of Spanish reflexive passives and reflexive impersonals by French- and English-speaking adults. *Second Language Research, 22*, 30–63.

Trenkic, D. (2008). The representation of English articles in second language grammars: Determiners or adjectives? *Bilingualism: Language and Cognition, 11*, 1–18.

Trenkic, D. (2009). Accounting for patterns of article omissions and substitutions in second language production. In R. Hawkins & M. P. García Mayo (Eds.), *Second language acquisition of articles: Empirical findings and theoretical implications* (pp. 115–143). Amsterdam: John Benjamins.

Trenkic, D., Mirkovic, J., & Altmann, G. (2013). Real-time grammar processing by native and non-native speakers: Constructions unique to the second language. *Bilingualism: Language and Cognition, 16*, 1–21.

Trofimovich, P., & McDonough, K. (Eds.). (2011). *Applying priming methods to L2 learning, teaching and research: Insights from psycholinguistics*. Amsterdam: John Benjamins.

Truscott, J., & Sharwood Smith, M. (2011). Input, intake, and consciousness: The quest for a theoretical foundation. *Studies in Second Language Acquisition, 33*, 497–528.

Tryzna, M. (2009). Questioning the validity of the Article Choice Parameter and the Fluctuation Hypothesis: Evidence from L2 English article use by L1 Polish and L1 Mandarin Chinese speakers. In M. P. García-Mayo & R. Hawkins (Eds.), *Second language acquisition of articles: Empirical findings and theoretical implications* (pp. 67–86). Amsterdam: John Benjamins.

Tsimpli, I., & Mastropavlou, M. (2008). Feature interpretability in L2 acquisition and SLI: Greek clitics and determiners. In J. Liceras, H. Zobl, & H. Goodluck (Eds.), *The role of formal features in second language acquisition* (pp. 142–183). London: Lawrence Erlbaum.

Ullman, M. T. (2001). The neural basis of lexicon and grammar in first and second language: the declarative/procedural model. *Bilingualism: Language and Cognition, 4*, 105–122.

Uludag, O., & VanPatten, B. (2012). The comparative effects of processing instruction and dictogloss on the acquisition of the English passive by speakers of Turkish. *International Review of Applied Linguistics in Language Teaching, 50*, 189–212.

Umeda, M., Snape, N., Yusa, N., & Wiltshier, J. (2019). The long-term effect of explicit instruction on learners' knowledge on English articles. *Language Teaching Research, 23*, 179–199.

Unsworth, S. (2005). *Child L2, adult L2, child L1: Differences and similarities: A study on the acquisition of direct object scrambling in Dutch*. PhD dissertation, Utrecht University.

Unsworth, S. (2007). L1 and L2 acquisition between sentence and discourse: Comparing production and comprehension. *Lingua, 117*, 1930–1958.

Vafaee, P., Suzuki, Y., & Kachisnke, I. (2017). Validating grammaticality judgment tests: Evidence from two new psycholinguistic measures. *Studies in Second Language Acquisition, 39*, 59–95.

Vainikka, A., & Young-Scholten, M. (1996). The early stages in adult L2 syntax: Additional evidence from Romance speakers. *Second Language Research, 12*, 140–176.

Valenzuela, E. (2006). L2 end state grammars and incomplete acquisition of Spanish CLLD constructions. In R. Slabakova, S. Montrul, & P. Prévost (Eds.), *Inquiries in linguistic development: In honor of Lydia White* (pp. 283–304). Amsterdam: John Benjamins.

vanCompernolle, R. A., & Williams, L. (2013). Sociocultural theory and second language pedagogy. *Language Teaching Research, 17*, 277–281.

VanPatten, B. (1990). Attending to form and content in the input: An experiment in consciousness. *Studies in Second Language Acquisition, 12*, 287–301.

VanPatten, B. (1996). *Input processing and grammar instruction in second language acquisition*. Westport, CT: Greenwood Publishing Group.

VanPatten, B. (2002). Processing instruction: An update. *Language Learning, 52*, 755–803.

VanPatten, B. (Ed.) (2004). *Processing instruction: Theory, research, and commentary*. Mahwah, NJ: Erlbaum.

VanPatten, B., & Borst, S. (2012a). The roles of explicit information and grammatical sensitivity in processing instruction: Nominative-accusative case marking and word order in German L2. *Foreign Language Annals, 45*, 92–109.

VanPatten, B., & Borst, S. (2012b). The roles of explicit information and grammatical sensitivity in the processing of clitic direct object pronouns and word order in Spanish L2. *Hispania, 95*, 270–284.

VanPatten, B., & Cadierno, T. (1993). Explicit instruction and input processing. *Studies in Second Language Acquisition, 15*, 225–243.

VanPatten, B., Collopy, E., Price, J. E., Borst, S., & Qualin, A. (2013). Explicit information, grammatical sensitivity, and the first-noun principle: A cross-linguistic study in processing instruction. *The Modern Language Journal, 97*, 506–527.

VanPatten, B., Collopy, E., & Qualin, A. (2012). Explicit information and processing instruction with nominative and accusative case in Russian as a second language: Just how important is explanation? *The Slavic and East European Journal, 56*, 256–276.

VanPatten, B., & Price, J. (2012). What does explanation do for the language learner? An experiment in processing instruction with causative faire. *The French Review, 86*, 106–121.

Vasiljevic, Z. (2010). Dictogloss as an interactive method of teaching listening comprehension. *English Language Teaching, 3*, 41–52.

Vygotsky, L. S. (1978). Socio-cultural theory. *Mind in Society, 6*, 52–58.

Wakabayashi, S. (1998). Systematicity in the use of the definite article by Japanese learners of English. *Gunma Prefectural Women's University Bulletin, 19*, 91–107.

Weinert, R. (1987). Processes in classroom second language development: The acquisition of negation in German. In R. Ellis (Ed.), *Second language acquisition in context* (pp. 83–99). London: Prentice Hall.

White, J. (2015). Primary and secondary effects of processing instruction on Spanish clitic pronouns. *International Review of Applied Linguistics in Language Teaching, 53*, 151–179.

White, L. (1989a). The adjacency condition on case assignment: Do L2 learners observe the Subset Principle. In S. Gass & J. Schachter (Eds.), *Linguistic perspectives on second language acquisition* (pp. 134–158). Cambridge, UK: Cambridge University Press.

White, L. (1989b). *Universal Grammar and second language acquisition*. Amsterdam: John Benjamins.

White, L. (1990). The verb-movement parameter in second language acquisition. *Language Acquisition, 1,* 337–360.

White, L. (1991). Adverb placement in second language acquisition: Some effects of positive and negative evidence in the classroom. *Second Language Research, 7,* 133–161.

White, L. (2003a). Fossilization in steady-state L2 grammars: Persistent problems with inflectional morphology. *Bilingualism: Language and Cognition, 6,* 129–141.

White, L. (2003b). *Second language acquisition and Universal Grammar.* Cambridge, UK: Cambridge University Press.

White, L., Spada, N., Lightbown, P. M., & Ranta, L. (1991). Input enhancement and L2 question formation. *Applied linguistics, 12,* 416–432.

White, L., Valenzuela, E., Kozlowska-Macgregor, M., & Leung, Y.-K. I. (2004). Gender agreement in nonnative Spanish: Evidence against failed features. *Applied Psycholinguistics, 25,* 105–133.

Whong-Barr, M., & Schwartz, B. D. (2002). Morphological and syntactic transfer in child L2 acquisition of the English dative alternation. *Studies in Second Language Acquisition, 24,* 579–616.

Whong, M., Gil, K.-H., & Marsden, H. (Eds.). (2013). *Universal Grammar and the second language classroom.* Dordrecht: Springer.

Williams, J. N. (2005). Learning without awareness. *Studies in Second Language Acquisition, 27,* 269–304.

Williams, J. N. (2016). Implicit learning in second language acquisition. In T. K. Bhatia & W. C. Ritchie (Eds.), *The new handbook of second language acquisition* (pp. 319–353). Bingley: Emerald Group.

Woods, R. (2015). The acquisition of dative alternation by German–English bilingual and English monolingual children. *Linguistic Approaches to Bilingualism, 5,* 252–284.

Wu, M.-J., & Ionin, T. (2019). L1-Mandarin L2-English speakers' acquisition of English quantifier-negation scope. In M. Brown & B. Dailey (Eds.), *Proceedings of the 43rd Boston University Conference on Language Development* (pp. 716–729). Somerville, MA: Cascadilla Press.

Wu, M.-J., & Ionin, T. (2022a). Does explicit instruction affect L2 linguistic competence? An examination with L2 acquisition of English inverse scope. *Second Language Research, 38,* 607–637.

Wu, M.-J., & Ionin, T. (2022b). L1-Mandarin L2-English learners' acquisition of English double-quantifier scope. In T. Leal, E. Shimanskaya, & C. Isabelli, (Eds.), *Generative SLA in the age of minimalism: Features, interfaces, and beyond (Selected proceedings of the 15th Generative Approaches to Second Language Acquisition Conference)* (pp. 93–114). Amsterdam: John Benjamins.

Yabuki-Soh, N. (2007). Teaching relative clauses in Japanese: Exploring alternative types of instruction and the projection effect. *Studies in Second Language Acquisition, 29*, 219-252.

Yang, C. (2015). Negative knowledge from positive evidence. *Language, 91*, 938-953.

Yang, C. (2016). *The price of productivity: How children learn and break rules of language*. Cambridge, MA: MIT Press.

Yeon, J. (2015). Passives. In L. Brown & J. Yeon (Eds.), *The handbook of Korean linguistics*. Oxford: Wiley Blackwell.

Yip, V. (1994). Grammatical consciousness-raising and learnability. In T. Odlin (Ed.), *Perspectives on pedagogical grammar* (pp. 123-139). Cambridge, UK: Cambridge University Press.

Yip, V. (1995). *Interlanguage and learnability: From Chinese to English*. Amsterdam: John Benjamins.

Yuan, B. (2001). The status of thematic verbs in the second language acquisition of Chinese: Against inevitability of thematic-verb raising in second language acquisition. *Second Language Research, 17*, 248-272.

Zara, J. V., Oliveira, F. L. P. d., & Souza, R. A. d. (2013). Selective transfer in the acquisition of English double object constructions by Brazilian learners. *Alfa: Revista de linguística (São José do Rio Preto), 57*, 519-544.

Zhang, R. (2015). Measuring university-level L2 learners' implicit and explicit linguistic knowledge. *Studies in Second Language Acquisition, 37*, 457-486.

Zobl, H. (1989). Canonical typological structures and ergativity in English L2 acquisition. In J. Schachter & S. M. Gass (Eds.), *Linguistic perspectives on second language acquisition* (pp. 203-221). Cambridge, UK: Cambridge University Press.

Zobl, H. (1995). Converging evidence for the "acquisition-learning" distinction. *Applied Linguistics, 16*, 35-56.

Zyzik, E. (2006). Transitivity alternations and sequence learning: Insights from L2 Spanish production data. *Studies in Second Language Acquisition, 28*, 449-485.

Zyzik, E. (2008). Null objects in second language acquisition: Grammatical vs. performance models. *Second Language Research, 24*, 65-110.

Zyzik, E. (2016). Toward a prototype model of the heritage language learner. In M. Fairclough & S. M. Beaudrie (Eds.), *Innovative strategies for heritage language teaching: A practical guide for the classroom* (pp. 19-38). Washington, DC: Georgetown University Press.

Index

absolute adjectives, 282, 284
acquisition, 15, 97, 316
action research, 30
adjectival clauses, 188
adjectival passives, 198, 204–205
advanced learners, 166
adverb placement, 90, 102, 303, 305
adverbial clauses, 159, 161, 167, 176
age effects, 10
agreement, 120
agreement morphology, 138
animacy, 261, 265
animate, specific direct object, 260–261
a-personal, 260, 262
argument structure, 195
article errors, 62, 68
articles, 303, 308
aural input, 290
automatic explicit knowledge, 25
awareness, 26

baseline knowledge, 35

canonical word order, 273
case marking, 273
causative/inchoative alternation, 196, 216
clitic doubling, 249–250, 253, 266, 305
clitic left dislocation, 250, 253
clitic pronoun, 253
clitic *se*, 224–226
clitics, 233, 248, 279
clustering effect, 92
cognate object constructions, 203
commands, 157, 161
communicative instruction, 20
Communicative Language Teaching (CLT), 49
comparison group design, 37
confounding variables, 40
consciousness raising, 20, 51, 219

Content and Language Integrated Learning (CLIL), 47
Content-Based Language Teaching (CBLT), 47
control group, 37
copula *be*, 139, 303
copulas *ser* and *estar*, 205, 312
corrective feedback, 22, 107–108, 135, 148, 308
count nouns, 58–59
critical period, 9

dative alternation, 195, 234, 236–237, 242
dative constructions, 253, 263, 265
debriefing questionnaire, 36
Declarative/Procedural Model, 17
declarative sentences, 273
default forms, 122
definite article, 57
definiteness, 59–61
dependent variables, 39
developmental stages, 110
Differential Object Marking (DOM), 249, 252, 260, 303
direct object, 232, 248, 284
direct object pronoun, 259, 306
direct object relative clause, 285
direct passive, 213
ditransitive sentence, 250
ditransitive verbs, 195, 238
double object construction, 234–235, 237, 245, 252, 305
double objects, 245, 308

error correction, 68
errors, 123, 125, 147
explicit feedback, 138, 308
explicit information, 175, 278, 280, 295
explicit instruction, 78, 139–140, 284, 287, 294, 298, 303–304, 316, 320
explicit knowledge, 15–17, 47, 78, 138, 140, 298, 304, 316

explicit learning, 17, 98, 295
explicit rule presentation, 67
eye tracking, 41, 167, 177–178, 211, 321

feedback, 68, 243, 260
first language acquisition, 2
First Noun principle, 276
flexible word order, 273
focus on form, 20, 48
Focus on Form (FonF), 50
focus on formS, 20, 48–49
foreign language setting, 33–34
form-focused instruction (FFI), 21, 107–108, 143, 150
Full Transfer/Full Access Hypothesis/Model (FT/FA), 5, 237, 302, 309
functional categories, 84

gender agreement, 121, 147
generalization, 315
generative linguistic framework, 3
genericity, 62, 72–73
genitive relative clause, 285, 292
grammar, 2
grammar-translation method, 48
grammatical gender, 121, 124–125, 141–142, 148, 308
grammaticality judgment task (GJT), 23, 35, 90, 165

heritage language acquisition, 7
heritage language learner, 12
heritage speakers, 4, 6, 13, 184

immersive setting, 33
imperfect subjunctive, 165
impersonal *se* construction, 224
impersonal *se* passive, 224
implicit instruction, 139–140, 303, 305
implicit knowledge, 15–17, 47, 78, 138, 140, 304, 316, 320
implicit learning, 17

implicit negative evidence, 142, 148
incidental exposure, 138
incomplete acquisition, 8, 10, 183
indefinite article, 57
indefiniteness, 60
independent variables, 38, 175
indicative, 154
indirect object, 233, 248, 250, 284
indirect object pronoun, 259, 306
indirect object relative clause, 285, 292
indirect passives, 198, 213
inflectional morphemes, 84
inflectional morphology, 122, 149
input enhancement, 20, 48, 50, 107, 305
input flooding, 48, 50, 284, 305
input-based instruction, 67
instructed group, 38
intact classes, 39
interaction, 110
interlanguage, 125, 161, 204, 302
intermediate learners, 167
intervention research, 1
intervention study, 44, 46
intransitive verbs, 194–195, 201
inverse scope, 293, 295

kind reference, 64, 72–73

L1 influence, 13
lab-based experimental design, 39
learning, 15, 97, 316
lexical categories, 84
linguistic competence, 3, 18
linguistics, 2

main clauses, 157
markedness, 285–286
mass nouns, 58–59
meaning output instruction (MOI), 174–175
metalinguistic feedback, 71, 308
metalinguistic knowledge, 184
Missing Surface Inflection Hypothesis, 123
mobile device applications, 323
modality, 154
models, 101, 283
modified output, 113
Monitor model, 163

mood, 154
morpheme, 119
morphology, 3, 119

near-native speakers, 164
negation, 165
negative evidence, 10, 14, 98, 141, 194
negative feedback, 100, 110, 113, 238
no-interface position, 19
nominal clauses, 162
nonabsolute adjectives, 282, 284
noncanonical word order, 273–275, 279
noninterventionist studies, 30
normative grammar, 14
noun phrase accessibility hierarchy (NPAH), 285–288, 291, 316
novice learners, 148
number agreement, 120–121

object-of-comparative relative clause, 285–286
object-of-preposition relative clause, 285–286, 288–289, 291
object pronoun, 233, 246, 257, 279
object scrambling, 273
oblique relative clause, 292
observational studies, 30
output, 288, 290
output-based instruction, 67, 306
overgeneralization, 228, 234, 237
overgeneralization errors, 11, 13
overpassivization, 215–217

parameter, 123, 316
parameter resetting, 91–93, 102
passive, 194, 204, 266, 303
passivization, 197
past tense, 134
past tense -ed, 133
past-tense marking, 128
pedagogical grammar, 14, 312, 314
PI (input processing instruction), 211
positive evidence, 10–11, 97, 194
possessive determiners, 147
posttest, 35
postverbal subject, 257
preemption, 98

prescriptive grammar, 14
presupposition, 60, 158, 162
pretest, 35
Processability Theory, 105–106, 301, 313, 321
processing instruction (PI), 55, 150, 168
prompts, 143, 147
Prosodic Transfer Hypothesis, 124
pseudopassive construction, 203
psych verbs, 259
purpose clauses, 159

quantifier scope, 293
quantifiers, 293
question formation, 107, 110

random assignment, 39
recasts, 10, 14, 22, 100–101, 141–143, 147, 283, 308
relative clauses, 89, 162, 166, 173, 189, 281–282, 284
restrictive relative clauses, 158
resultative construction, 202

salience, 141–142, 148, 168
scope ambiguity, 293
self-paced reading task, 25, 177, 322
semantics, 3
sentential complements, 162
se-passive, 199
sequential bilinguals, 7
shape adjectives, 282
simultaneous bilingual acquisition, 8
simultaneous bilinguals, 7
size adjectives, 282
specificity, 61, 72
strong-interface position, 19
structural priming, 113, 243, 263
structured input, 307
study abroad, 176, 284
subject pronoun, 233
subject relative clause, 285–286, 288
subjunctive, 153–154, 303, 306
subjunctive development, 161
subjunctive morphology, 161
subordinate clauses, 157, 168
surface scope, 293
syntactic priming, 113, 243, 245, 305
syntax, 3, 269

Teachability Hypothesis, 106, 109
Teaching Proficiency through Reading and Storytelling (TPRS), 140, 303
technology, 321
temporal clauses, 159, 164, 176
tense marking, 306
tense morphology, 150
to-dative construction, 234, 236
to-datives, 245
topicalizations, 273
traditional instruction, 20, 257, 307
transfer, 13, 92, 226, 252, 275, 309, 311
transitive verbs, 194–195
trials-to-criterion, 176, 279
truth-value judgment task (TVJT), 63, 165

Unaccusative Hypothesis, 201, 216, 313
unaccusative verbs, 197, 201–202, 214, 303
unaccusativity, 202, 214, 220, 223
Unaccusativity Hierarchy, 218, 220, 314
unergative verbs, 196, 202, 214
Universal Grammar (UG), 3, 7, 62, 83, 123, 302, 316

verb movement, 100
verb movement parameter, 83, 86, 91, 96, 98
verb placement, 150
verb second (V2), 83, 87
verbal agreement, 125
verbal morphology, 135, 139
verbal passives, 198–199, 205, 212

weak-interface position, 19
wh-movement, 89
wh-questions, 89, 108
word order, 269
written corrective feedback, 68

yes/no questions, 108

Printed by Printforce, United Kingdom